THE EASTERN ZONE AND
SOVIET POLICY IN GERMANY
1945–50

THE EASTERN ZONE AND SOVIET POLICY IN GERMANY

1945–50

by

J. P. NETTL

GEOFFREY CUMBERLEGE
OXFORD UNIVERSITY PRESS
LONDON NEW YORK TORONTO
1951

Oxford University Press, Amen House, London E.C.4
GLASGOW NEW YORK TORONTO MELBOURNE WELLINGTON
BOMBAY CALCUTTA MADRAS CAPE TOWN
Geoffrey Cumberlege, Publisher to the University

PRINTED IN GREAT BRITAIN BY
THE BOWERING PRESS PLYMOUTH

To My Friend

ZELMAN COWEN

Professor of Public Law, Melbourne University, formerly Fellow of Oriel College, Oxford

PREFACE

WRITING about Russia, or countries under Russian influence, is like interpreting a foreign language. Words and phrases take on a meaning quite separate from that to which we are accustomed. This applies to political catchwords as much as to economic terminology, such as 'productive' or 'national income'.[1] Far greater, however, is the difficulty that no information is released by official agencies in these countries except for propaganda purposes, and consequently no accurate account of conditions could be given if it were based only on published official sources. Naturally there is a dearth of accurate and unbiased studies.

Only in Eastern Germany has the iron curtain on information partially failed to achieve the desired object. In addition to the accounts available from refugees—of which there are many concerning all Eastern Europe—there are a number of more or less reliable published works, and much 'loose' information which has to be garnered personally and on the spot. This is not the first time many of the facts given in this book have appeared in print, indeed I have drawn liberally on previous publications. But I have tried to present a coherent whole for these five years of direct occupation, to provide a source for reference to the available material on this subject, and above all to avoid making the materials presented here a mere tool for underpinning a ready-made thesis. No doubt a good deal of material has gone unnoticed all the same; this is inevitable when an author has to track his facts down like easily scared chamois. But it is hoped that this volume will at least partially fill the gap, by drawing together some of what is known and has been written, and supplementing it with the impressions of a detailed personal study.

The subject itself seems to me to need little apology. The development of the Soviet zone of Germany is a partial cross-section of two of our most vital problems at the moment, the Russian-Communist problem and the German problem. The Eastern zone is not the permanent focus of Soviet policy, nor at the time of writing was it the main arena for the ebullition of the German problem, but it was equally not a mere backwater. Eastern Germany partly reflected its Eastern neighbours; in many respects it was unique. The fascination of the subject is therefore twofold, the

[1] See, for instance, Seers, *Current Marxist definitions of national income*, Oxford Economic Papers, New Series, Vol. I, No. 2, June 1949, p. 260.

intrinsic interest of five eventful years in the history of an important part of Europe, and the illustration they furnish of the great political and social forces influencing the present and the future of the world. Finally I believe that the attempt of the Governments of Eastern Europe to shroud their every act in secrecy makes an unsensational analysis of conditions there doubly worth while, for secrecy breeds sensation and in turn thrives on it.

In examining critically events and policy in the Soviet zone, I have in no way attempted to rehabilitate the expensive tragedy of errors which constitutes the Anglo-American Occupation since 1945. Recent writing on Germany has almost always defended one Occupation against the other. This may be political wisdom but it is historical nonsense. There has been such divergence in policy between East and West that comparison by a given yardstick is well-nigh impossible, the epithets right or wrong have become meaningless. Perhaps I may one day have the opportunity to examine the Western zones during these same five years; I am almost sure now that I shall not find there the consolation for what has happened in the East. It is possible to treat the Soviet zone as a separate entity without taking it out of its context. Therefore I have not examined in detail the activities of and conflicts in the Control Council, the only organization of an allegedly interzonal character, for it means studying the German question *in vacuo*; it would be like tracing American or Soviet policy from the speeches of the United States and Russian delegations to the United Nations.

Finally, I have only touched on the subject of Soviet diplomacy with regard to Germany since Potsdam. This subject is intricately bound up with the Soviet foreign policy as a whole. Though much primary and secondary material has been published on it, far more may be expected—nearly every American diplomat and official, on retiring, promptly publishes his memoirs, while even British reticence in this connection is sooner or later overcome. Such is the inevitable raw material for future histories of the post-war period, and they will be all the better for being written later rather than sooner. But the material I have dealt with is, in my experience, either forgotten after a few years, or, unless held fast at the time, becomes distorted by the impression obtained from the diplomatic material. The two require an entirely different approach, and therefore I have tried to give one side of the picture without prejudicing the issue likely to be presented by a full study of what are commonly known as 'the documents'.

I would like to thank my friends in Germany who have helped to find and sift information, and who have given me the benefit of their expert advice. My special thanks are due to Mr. F. A. Burchardt, Director of the Institute of Statistics at Oxford University, who gave me valuable criticism on the economic chapters and thus saved me from many errors, to Mr. Max Beloff, who did the same for the historical and political parts, particularly as regards Soviet Russia, on which he is (to apply the dictum of a distinguished Moscow Correspondent) one of the least ignorant people; and to Mr. Leonard Woolf who gave me much valuable help of a literary and stylistic nature. I am also grateful to Miss Helen Liddell and Mrs. Jane Degras of Chatham House for making material available to me and for their comments on the book itself. In view of the contentious nature of the subject, however, I must say that the opinions expressed below are entirely my own.

J. P. N.

ST. JOHN'S COLLEGE, OXFORD
July 1950

CONTENTS

MAPS

SOURCES

For the chapters on German developments and allied policy prior to 1945 the sources are everywhere quoted in the text, and since so many different subjects are involved, a satisfactory bibliography, embracing all the relevant matter, is outside the scope of this book. There is an enormous literature on Germany, the Soviet Union, and on the allied policy during the war.

On the Soviet zone itself there are two books dealing with this subject generally. *Russian Zone,* by Gordon Schaffer (Allen & Unwin, London, 1947) has a limited amount of information. It is the record of a journalist's visit during 1946; his information is almost entirely official, and the bias of the book is towards unqualified admiration of the regime. *News from the Soviet Zone,* by Fritz Löwenthal (Gollancz, London, 1950), is the reminiscences of an ex-official of high rank. It contains much useful information, heavily studded with individual examples of injustice and personal comment, which detract from the value of the book as impeccable source-material. The author himself is sufficiently biased against the regime to become involved in a number of factual errors and rather more errors of interpretation. *The Allied Military Government,* by W. Friedmann (Stevens, London, 1947), is a reliable and careful study of four-power relations and the Control Council structure and policies from 1945 to 1947. But it is written from the all-German background of Potsdam, and its information on Soviet policy and the Soviet zone is very limited.[1]

Much of the material used in the political chapters is unpublished and unpublishable. It was obtained by observation, in conversation, and from private and public statements of officials and political figures in the Soviet zone and Berlin. Even where a source could be quoted, it would neither be illuminating nor beneficial to do so. In addition much information has been gleaned by a systematic perusal of the Berlin press and the German press generally. Such material is mostly useful for providing the background to this study; where a particular piece of otherwise uncorroborated information is quoted the source has been indicated in the text. The *Tagliche Rundschau,* the official Russian organ, and *Neues Deutschland,* the voice of the Unity party, have a certain amount of useful information. Of the Western-licensed press, the *Telegraf* and *Neue Zeitung* are probably the best informed, particularly on economic matters. The *Wirtschafts-Zeitung* of Stuttgart has a number of valuable studies in the economy of the Soviet zone, and it is generally reliable. Of the foreign press, the *Neue Züricher Zeitung* has some valuable and

[1] Some interesting, if incidental points are raised in Ruth Fischer, *Stalin and German Communism* (Harvard University Press, Cambridge, Massachusetts, 1950).

well-informed articles, and both the *Manchester Guardian* and *The Times* (London) have printed useful summaries of information. I have not been able to undertake a systematic study of the American press, though a number of individual articles, particularly on Berlin, have been useful. There have, finally, been a number of longer articles in various English and American periodicals of varying interest and veracity. The *Europa-Archiv,* published in Frankfurt/Main, has printed a number of detailed and valuable studies of political and economic developments in the Soviet zone, which are among the most useful for a general study of conditions.

There is an enormous amount of propagandist literature from the Eastern zone, which merely says the same thing again and again in much the same way. Thus Pieck and Grotewohl have expounded SED policy in *Reden und Aufsätze* (Dietz, Berlin, 1948) and *Im Kampf um Deutschland* (Dietz, Berlin, 1948) respectively. The official function of Trades Unions is expounded in *Neue Deutsche Gewerkschaftspolitik* by Jendretzky (Berlin, 1948).

A certain amount of information has been made available by official Anglo-American sources. The British *Control Commission Bulletin* contained until 1948 snippets of gossip about the Soviet zone, and some of its articles occasionally include useful references. American material is more substantial. In addition to references in the monthly *Report of the Military Governor* and its statistical annex, the Americans have published a number of factual surveys, the nature of whose information is uncertain, but which contain much that has been useful to me. The most important has been the *Statistical Handbook on Potsdam Germany,* published by OMGUS, Berlin, 1947, which contains a good many basic figures for the four zones.

On the economic side most of the information comes from German sources. The survey undertaken by a private group of individuals for a Bremen Senator in 1947–8, under the title *Reparationen, Sozialprodukt, Lebensstandard* (Bremen, 1948), contains some valuable lists and calculations, and clearly benefited from privileged access to otherwise unobtainable material. Its conclusions and estimates are less reliable since it has an obvious and ready-made axe to grind. This work also has a useful bibliography, of which relevant material has been used here, particularly *Werkstatt und Betrieb,* Vol. LXXX, No. 3 (Munich, 1947), article by Stelter; *Die Wirtschafts-Kapazität der Zonen,* Special No. 2 of *Der Wirtschaftspiegel* (Wiesbaden, 1947); *Arbeitslosigkeit und Zonengrenzen,* by G. Lenschow, an unpublished thesis dealing with interzonal trade and employment, of which I have been given a summary, and *Die Lebensverhältnisse in Deutschland,* published in Stuttgart, 1947, by the German Evangelical Church.

The German economic institute (Deutsches Institut für Wirtschafts- und Konjunkturforschung) has published two compendia: *Die Deutsche Wirtschaft zwei Jahre nach dem Zusammenbruch* (1947) and *Wirtschafts-*

probleme der Besatzungszonen (1948). The latter is more accurate and more useful than the former, but both contain specialist papers on individual topics. The first volume is more concerned with war damage and post-war prospects of Germany as a whole, the later volume with particular zones and their condition. Finally there are occasional statistics in the United Nations ECE publications, and a lengthy and accurate study of inter-regional dependence in Germany in the third quarter of 1949 (Vol. I, No. 3), though I have not used the production figures given there.

Apart from the Two Year Plan figures, the only official Soviet zone publication I have used is the compilation of Land reform statistics under the title *Die Bodenreform in Deutschland* (Berlin, 1947), which appears to give accurate figures. However, I have been able to use a number of reparation, transport and industrial as well as agricultural production statistics which have been made available to me privately and have been indicated as such in the text. I have incorporated only these which can reasonably be expected to be accurate. My own estimates have also been quoted as such.

ABBREVIATIONS

SMA = Soviet Military Administration at Berlin and in the five provinces.
SPD = Social Democratic Party of Germany.
KPD = Communist Party of Germany.
LDP = Liberal Democratic Party. (Free Democratic Party in the Western Zones.)
CDU = Christian Democratic Union. (Christian Social Union in Bavaria.)
SED = Socialist Unity Party of Germany.
SAG = Soviet Industrial Corporations or Trusts.

In order to avoid any confusion of terminology, I have used the following:

1 ton, unless otherwise stated, equals 1 metric ton which equals 2,204½ lb. or 1,000 kilograms.

1 milliard equals one U.S. billion or 1,000 million.

'Russian Communism' is used as a technical term and is intended to cover the Marxist theory and practice as defined and applied in its present form by the Soviet authorities.

'Marxism', except where specifically qualified, is generally applied only to the philosophical doctrine of Marx and Engels, and carries no meaning wider than that inherent in what these men actually wrote.

CHRONOLOGICAL TABLE OF EVENTS

1945

May 7. Armistice signed at Rheims.

June 9. Formation of Soviet Military Administration.

June 25. Communist Party officially registered in Eastern zone.

July 15. The four party anti-fascist bloc established in the Eastern zone.

October 14. Suspension of Control Council discussions on all-German Central Administrations owing to French objections.

December 16–26. Conference of Foreign Ministers in Moscow.

1946

February 27. Fusion between Communists and Social Democrats in the Eastern zone announced.

March 1. Social Democrats in Berlin protest against fusion.

March 6. Large banks in Soviet sector of Berlin occupied by Russians and closed.

April 2. The new Unity Party holds its first rallies in the Eastern zone.

April 22. Fusion formally takes place at conference of new Socialist Unity Party of Germany in Berlin.

May 26. Delivery of reparations to the U.S.S.R. from the U.S. zone stopped by order of General Clay.

June 15–July 12. Conference of Foreign Ministers in Paris.

September 6. Speech at Stuttgart by Byrnes, the U.S. Secretary of State.

September 18. Speech in Paris by Molotov, in answer to Byrnes, stating that the Polish-German frontier had been settled at Potsdam.

October 20. Provincial elections in the Eastern zone and in Berlin.

December 3. Announcement of fusion of U.S.-U.K. zones of occupation.

1947

February. Measures of industrial nationalization adopted by Diet of Land Saxony and enforced throughout the zone.

March 10–April 24. Conference of Foreign Ministers in Moscow.

June 6. Conference of Prime Ministers of all provinces throughout Germany at Munich. Eastern zone representatives withdraw on the first day.

June 15. Economic Commission established in Soviet zone.

August 17.	Relaxation of Denazification ordered by Sokolovsky for the Soviet zone.
November 21.	Statement by Sokolovsky to the Control Council containing an all-round denunication of the Western Powers.
November 25–December 15.	Conference of Foreign Ministers in London.
1948	
January 14.	Publication in a Berlin paper of alleged Communist plan (Protocol M) to disrupt West German economy and administration.
February 13.	Economic Commission broadened and given extensive powers by an order of Sokolovsky.
February 17.	East European Conference on Germany in Prague.
March 20.	Soviet delegation withdraws from Control Council.
June 7.	London Conference on Germany.
June 20.	Currency reform in Western Germany. Communications cut off by the Russians between their zone and Western Germany.
June 23.	Warsaw Conference on Germany.
June 24.	Soviet blockade of Berlin begins with the closing of rail, water, and road communications.
June 29.	Soviet zone Two-year Plan announced by SED party congress.
July 17.	Democratic Peasants Party founded in Soviet zone, followed by foundation of National Democratic Party.
July 25.	Soviet zone Currency Reform completed after issue of temporary currency since 22 June.
July 26.	Western economic counter-blockade of Soviet zone announced.
October 15.	Large-scale reorganization of police reported in Soviet zone. Reinstitution of armed mobile squads of police (*Kasernierte Polizei*).
October 22.	'German People's Congress' meets in Berlin to draft a constitution for a united Germany and to press for a 'just peace'. A 'People's Council' (*Volksrat*) is elected.
December 11.	Dissolution of work councils, and their replacement by Trades Union directorate entirely composed of Unity Party members, announced in Berlin.
1949	
March 19.	Peoples' congress reconvened to approve draft constitution.
March 29.	Chuikov replaces Sokolovsky as Soviet Military Governor.

May 5.	Agreement reached in Washington to lift blockade and counter blockade, and for a quadripartite conference of Foreign Ministers.
May 9–12.	Restrictions on traffic lifted in Berlin.
May 21.	Berlin railway workers strike against payment in East German marks.
May 23.	Conference of Foreign Ministers in Paris. West German constitution signed at Bonn.
May 30.	Constitution of Germany adopted by Peoples' congress in Berlin.
June 20.	End of conference of Foreign Ministers in Paris.
June 28.	Railway strike ends in Berlin.
July 26.	Ulbricht, deputy Chairman of the Unity Party, announces the activation of the National Front.
October 6.	Proclamation of Democratic German Republic in Berlin.
October 8.	Trade agreement between East and West Germany signed at Frankfurt.
October 10.	Chuikov announces the end of Soviet Military Government and the creation of a Soviet Control Commission with supervisory functions.
October 14.	Stalin's congratulatory message to Pieck and Grotewohl.
1950	
January 16.	Chuikov writes to Ulbricht announcing the closing of Russian internment camps in the Eastern zone.
February 3.	National Front formally inaugurated by election of National Council.
February 6.	Iron and steel deliveries from Western Germany stopped owing to the East German Government's failure to carry out the provisions of the Frankfurt trade agreement.
February 8.	Creation of East German Ministry of State Security.
May 16.	Stalin, in a letter to Grotewohl, announces reduction of reparation demands from $10,000 million to $6,342 million, of which $3,658 will have been paid by the end of 1951.
May 24–8.	Whitsun Youth rally under Communist sponsorship in Berlin.
June 7.	East German treaty with Poland announced at Warsaw.

1. *Political Map of Soviet Zone*

CHAPTER I

THE DISSOLUTION OF THE THIRD REICH

I

THE POLITICAL STRUCTURE

ALTHOUGH the armistice was signed at Rheims on 7 May 1945, thereby officially terminating active hostilities between Germany and the Allies, the disintegration of the German state had begun long before. At that time the Americans, the British, the Russians, and the French already occupied more than half of the area of the Germany of 1937, the area of Germany proper. The Government of the Reich was in chaos and dissolution. Hitler was believed to have died eight days previously, on 30 April 1945, in Berlin; Goebbels was known to have committed suicide the day before. The other members of the Government, the Reich Defence Council, the Ministers, the Combined Services Command, and the Police chiefs were either trapped in Berlin, shut up in Flensburg on the Danish Border, or were stranded in what was to have been the Alpine redoubt. Some of them were wandering in Central Germany, others were behind the Allied lines, still others were bolting for cover. Similarly, the armed services were almost completely broken up; not only had losses in prisoners been enormous in the last British and American encircling movements, but the organization of the remaining forces had broken down. In Hamburg and Bremen the fire-service had been armed and put into action, in Schleswig-Holstein the traffic-police were intended for a similar fate. The general impression of ruined cities in both West and East, heaps and trails of abandoned materials, and the ever-increasing number of complete units surrendering to the Allies, made disaster for Germany seem complete.

None who took part in the last stages of the campaign against the remnants of the German Army Group *Nord* in the North-West, who saw the skeleton 12th Army, which was to have saved Berlin, disintegrate before Marshal Zhukov's forces, could fail to be struck by the overwhelming evidence of complete disaster. Many observers were surprised that resistance had not collapsed much earlier, when the situation on the German home front became clear. Some towns, such as Jülich and Stadtlohn, had been completely wiped out; others, like Cologne and Frankfurt/Oder, had been without water and electricity supply up to ten days before they were captured. In Berlin, on 1 May, there was no water supply, electricity had been cut off in most areas, and the city's communications had broken down; even the Underground Railway was flooded on two-thirds of its length. But these were only the surface signs of destruction.

In one sense the German Government had prepared well against invasion. When the German eagles were still victorious during the invasion of Poland in 1939, of the Netherlands and France in 1940, and later in 1941, in the early stages of 'Operation Barbarossa', the invasion of Russia, the German Intelligence Services, both of the Army and of the police, had carefully noted the effects of armed invasion on the administration of the country concerned. The administrative systems of those countries were all more or less centralized. Local government, for example in France, possessed little liberty of decision and depended on orders from Paris. The system of German invasion, the large encircling movements by the advance units without stopping to mop up the resultant pockets, apart from their tactical importance, had broken the channels of communications between the capital and the provinces. This had caused administrative chaos and had palpably assisted the advance of the invader; for example, it had been largely responsible for those mass migrations of refugees on strategic roads which had so successfully prevented effective counter-measures during the campaign in France and Belgium.

When Allied invasion drew near, it became the task of the German High Command and Government to avoid similar chaos in Germany. This task was both a military and an administrative one. As long as the Germans had the forces, arms, and space necessary for a planned defence the military problem was relatively easy. It became difficult from the moment when the German Command began to lose control over the fighting, and the strategical and tactical initiative lay entirely with the Allies. It is for this reason that the German General Staff was pressing all the time for retreats to avoid encirclement and complete loss of strategic initiative.

From the point of view of civil administration the position was different. By Prussian tradition and in accordance with National-Socialist principles, Germany was governed centrally from Berlin. This meant that from the moment further military retreat became impossible, conditions would be very similar to those which had existed in France in 1940. Any part of Germany, once over-run or surrounded by the Allies, would be irretrievably lost to the control of the central government. The Russian method would be difficult to emulate in Germany. In the first place, geography favoured the invader of Germany far more than the invader of Russia, and the administrative centralization of Germany was far more effective than that of Russia, in fact if not in theory. However, although the military defeat of Germany was plain to most of the High Command and the staffs of the services by the end of February 1945, the German Government and the Party leaders were almost unanimous in favour of a fight to the bitter end.

The National-Socialist party ended as it began, as an extra-governmental party duplicating, or attempting to duplicate, the civil administration. In 1945, as in 1933, it became *de facto* a state within a state, a little Nazi empire apart from the rest of the world. This development was by no means intentional. Hitler believed till the last that Berlin would be saved.[1] Some half-hearted attempts were made for a stand in the Bavarian and Tyrolean Alps. Himmler hoped as late as 4 May to keep National Socialism in power under the aegis of the Western Powers, through negotiation. All this came to nothing, partly because the Allies were at this time already too far in Germany for serious resistance, partly because the German Army was not capable of further fighting. Also the Mayors of towns and the Presidents of administrative areas had not shown any desire to fight to the bitter end, nor indeed had the great majority of the civilian population. The general falling off from National Socialism was in full swing.

This finally became clear to those among Nazi leaders who were still capable of digesting factual evidence. The only hope for the Government of keeping control in isolated and captured German territory lay not in the normal administration but only in the local organizations of the Nazi Party and its affiliated organizations. These, it was hoped, would carry on a relentless war against both Western and Eastern aggressors. Much mystery surrounds the real organization and plans of the famous werewolves. It is generally believed that Bormann was the moving spirit behind their formation. There is a certain amount of evidence that they were receiving army weapons (a proceeding against which the organizational

[1] cf. the testimony of Wenck, the Commander, and Reichhelm, the Chief of Staff, of the illusory 12th Army. This evidence has been used in Trevor-Roper, *The Last Days of Hitler* (London 1947).

department of the German War Office protested, and which it tried to hinder). But the werewolf organization was such a failure that many people later doubted its very existence. Some of the relevant evidence has since come to light.[1] It may now fairly be said that the idea and some organizational plans did indeed exist, and that some of the post-war subversive movements had partial links with this organization. Why did the organization fail so miserably?

When the impartial history of National Socialism in Germany comes to be written it will be found to be the history of the relationship between the party on the one side, and the administration, the armed services, and the various forces which go towards making the civilized life of the twentieth century, on the other. Existing books on the Third Reich either deal mostly with the Party, or with particular aspects of contemporary life and thought in Germany. From 1933 onwards there is an ever-increasing tendency on the part of the Nazi Party to encroach further and further on the functions of government in its many aspects, as well as on the intellectual movements and social and economic trends of the time. It was by no means enough that Hitler should be Chancellor and that all the Ministers should be National-Socialists. The aim was the complete identification of the German state with the Nazi Party, leading to the ideal *Ständestaat*,[2] the National-Socialist state. The civil service laws of 1937 and 1939,[3] the reorganization of the Army Security Services in 1943,[4] are legislative and administrative landmarks in this process. Apart from these legislative and functional measures, much more was done by individual appointments, by semi-official pressure, by personal terrorization, and by constant propaganda. Allied propaganda, in trying to divorce National Socialism from German Nationalism, was grist to the mill of the Nazi leaders.[5] In many ways the development was similar to that in Soviet Russia; the attempt to identify Government and Party in one and the same

[1] *ibid.*, Introduction to the Second edition, 1950.

[2] The phrase, which means literally 'a state organized by estates, or professions', was frequently used by Rosenberg. It is partly intended to be a modern version of the medieval guild system, and implies a state built up on the functional organization of all the trades and professions, permeated by one all-embracing party.

[3] These laws made membership of the Nazi Party obligatory for civil servants, teachers, lawyers, and doctors.

[4] The Army Intelligence organization (Abwehr) was almost entirely taken over by the SS and Gestapo, while Adm. Canaris was replaced by SS Gruppenführer (General) Schellenberg.

[5] See *The Goebbels Diaries*, trans. and ed. by Louis P. Lochner (London 1948)

person. Until this process was complete the party organization was to be kept in being as a constant check on the administration at lower levels, on the armed forces, on the cultural and economic life of the nation.

The process of identification was, of course, never completed. The success of National Socialism in grafting itself indissolubly on the many spheres of life varied considerably. Politically, its effects seemed greater than it really was. The total membership of the party was about 9,000,000 in 1939. Active resistance was exterminated with vigour, and it is difficult afterwards to assess passive indifference. Nor can the influence of National Socialism be properly estimated from the membership figures; many ardent Nazis at lower levels were not Party members[1] and, on the other hand, membership did not necessarily imply more than acquiescence. In the same way the signs of resistance did not necessarily mean fundamental opposition to National Socialism. In some cases opposition came from inside the Party over questions of policy and personalities, in others, particularly during the war, from differences of opinion on strategy. Economic divisions are equally unsatisfactory. While National Socialism was undoubtedly on economic grounds a middle-class doctrine, much of the early opposition was recruited in the main from that class. At the same time many of the early leaders of the Party had been workers, while its funds had been liberally supplied by some wealthy industrialists and aristocratic Army officers. It will be remembered that the 1929 meeting of Hitler and Papen had been arranged by the wealthy banker, Schroeder. Finally, the failure of effective Nazi resistance to Allied occupation is no evidence of lack of popular support during the golden years of the Third Reich.

An accurate assessment of National-Socialist influence on German political life is therefore impossible. We can only judge from the visible results and must renounce any logical comparison between ideas and actions. We know to-day that active National Socialism does not seem to have survived the defeat of Germany on any large scale. The realization that most Germans would renounce National Socialism with defeat was implied by the action of the Government in the last two months in separating once more the party machine from the government of the country. Local government had shown itself unable or unwilling to continue

[1] The Transport Services are an example of an efficient machine serving the State in its preparations for war, while resisting the political encroachments of the party. Dorpmueller, the head of the railways, was apparently never a member of the Party.

fanatical resistance against the Allies. But it is known that Bormann was acting independently of the Chancellery in the last weeks of April, and was in touch with the outside world at a time when the Chancellery had already lost contact completely. The organization of the werewolves, as far as is known, was entirely in the hands of the Party Headquarters, its members were mostly SS or Hitler Youth. What evidence there is seems to point to the theory that active and passive resistance to the occupation was to be carried on by the cream of the Party, particularly those who had been nurtured on National-Socialist ideology.

Moreover, planned resistance was intended to be carried out against the Western powers only. This may have been partly due to the persistent hope that the pressure of underground resistance might make the British and Americans come to terms with Germany.[1] On the other hand the Nazis had very little hope of making terms with the Russians. They had felt very differently about the war in the East to that waged against the Western Powers. 'Operation Barbarossa' had been from the first an operation of extermination for the Germans, a war of total victory or utter defeat. As Goebbels said: 'If Germany loses this war, she deserves to be exterminated.'[2] It was only after much hesitation and with little hope of success that General Krebs set out for Russian Headquarters at midnight on 30 April to ask for terms and permission for the remaining officials in Hitler's air-raid shelter to be allowed to leave the city. The answer was a blunt negative. The escape routes of Major Freytag von Loringhofen and Colonel von Below, the bearers of Hitler's testament, lay towards the west and the south, towards the areas occupied by the British and the Americans. As far as any positive policy of limited resistance or negotiation may be said to have existed, it existed exclusively towards the West. In effect neither in the East or West was there any real, active resistance to the occupying powers which could be traced back to National-Socialist fanaticism.

The hold of National Socialism on the armed forces had always been precarious. It is impossible to trace in detail here the delicate and interesting relationship between the Party and the forces. In the Navy and the Air Force, National Socialism played a greater part than in the Army. The German Navy was particularly

[1] Even the post-war subversive movements which claimed to be anti-Nazi, such as 'Selection-board', hoped to force the hand of the Western powers against Russia.

[2] *Das Reich*, 12 August 1944.

susceptible to the idea of a new trial of strength with the British, since the memories of the first world war still rankled. Hitler had early made the Navy his special care and paid frequent visits to Kiel and Wilhelmshafen before the war. Both Raeder and Doenitz, particularly the latter, had been ardent National-Socialists and were on far closer terms with the party than their opposite numbers in the Army. As the German naval tradition was far shorter and less glorious than that of the Army, the Nazi idea came in, as it were, on the ground floor, growing out of that self-consciousness which so distinguished the atmosphere of the German wardrooms before the war. But this Nazi influence should not be exaggerated. The formation of the OKW[1] tended to shut out the influence of the Party. Many of the regular naval officers had no particular love for politicians and felt more attracted by the example of the proud and exclusive Army General Staff. There can be no doubt, however, that the German Navy was the most loyal of the services to the Nazi cause.

The Air Force was to a lesser extent influenced by National Socialism. Although Goering and Milch were both ardent Nazis, the Air Force had a General Staff tradition and close links with the Army. Many of the air aces of the first world war were not very friendly to the Nazis and some mystery surrounded the death of Udet, though he had been an early supporter of the Nazi Party. There was little of the retrospective defeatism so evident in the German Navy. The Party made sustained attempts to capture the imagination of German Youth interested in flying. The NSF,[2] although affiliated to the Air Force, was primarily National-Socialist, as were the gliding clubs of the Hitler Youth. But in spite of the preferential position given to the Air Force in matters of research, finance, and training, in spite of the enormous growth of the Air Force under the Nazi régime, National Socialism remained a second-best philosophy in the Air Force, while the unit and arm *esprit de corps* tended to come first.

The Army was the most difficult proposition of all for the Nazis. The co-operation between the Army General Staff and the Party dated from 1934, though they had found each other useful long before that. But the alliance between the Nazi Government and the Army Command was based on a similar view of certain ends to be achieved: the resuscitation of Germany as a military power,

[1] Combined Services Command, the interservice organization at the highest level, and directly responsible to Hitler.

[2] The National Socialist Flying Corps, a para-military organization run by the Party.

the destruction of the Versailles Treaty, the reintroduction of conscription, the future of Germany as the dominant economic and military power in Europe. In order to achieve these ends, and being incapable of achieving them alone, the Army hierarchy acquiesced in many things which it disliked. For the same reason the National-Socialists at first did not interfere with the Army. The 1934 party purge may perhaps be counted as a victory for the Army,[1] but certainly from the beginning of the war the Army was subjected to an intense campaign of Party indoctrination and penetration.

The NS *Führungstab,*[2] the Army propaganda organization, was formed in 1940 with an active Nazi general in command. Its staff operated as far down as battalion level. At the same time an elite Party Army was reformed under the name of 'Waffen' or armed SS. These troops were controlled by the Reich Security Office[3] and were only tactically under command of the Army. There was only one division of them in France in 1940;[4] by 22 June 1941 there were nine divisions in the field or in process of formation. It became the practice to attach SS officers with special duties to Army Headquarters and the exchange of Army and SS officers between divisions was encouraged. A number of SS officers participated in the General Staff course. This process culminated in 1943 with the appointment of Himmler to the command of the Home Army to ensure SS control over the troops stationed in Germany.

Resentment against this infiltration was strong in the higher circles of the Officer and General Staff Corps. The attempt on 20 July 1944 on Hitler's life, with the object of setting up a government in which the Army Command would have been a strong influence, brought the conflict once more into the open. Even though it failed, the extent of the plot and particularly the great number of officers who knew about it and failed to inform the Security Police clearly showed the Nazis that the Army could not be relied upon as a prop of the régime. The number of reliable Nazi generals was small, that of Nazi General Staff Officers even smaller. During the remaining period of the war changes in command were frequent, both in the field and at Supreme Head-

[1] In spite of the fact that the Nazis took the opportunity of eliminating General Schleicher, a very tortuous and unpopular political figure, who was, however, later rehabilitated as a result of Army pressure.

[2] NS Leadership staff, a Party creation to foster indoctrination in the Army. This staff controlled at War Office level the political officers of all formations.

[3] See above, pp. 2, 4.

[4] Under the name 'Special disposal troops'.

quarters. It was plain that quite apart from the military position, the majority of the Army would not fight for the Nazi Government once the military position had clearly become hopeless in the eyes of the commanders in the field.[1]

More important still, the soldiers who returned home at the end of the war and were not taken into captivity by the Allies did not help to keep alive the spirit of National Socialism. Although there were more confirmed Nazis among the men and the junior officers than among the senior officers, and relatively more in the Air Force and the Navy than in the Army, these forces in disbandment did not prove the hot-beds of National-Socialist fanaticism which they were expected to be. Many of the returning servicemen were still imbued with the glories of the military life, except those who had been in Russia for a number of winters. Most of them were still Nationalists, some of them with extreme views, and very few admitted Germany's guilt. But there were relatively few active and virulent Nazis, far fewer than had been feared. The disbanded German Army was more of a dangerous tool than a dangerous craftsman.

Thus the collapse of National Socialism came in two stages, just as its establishment had done. The first stage was the divorce of National Socialism from administration and from the many currents which make up the complex view of modern life and thought. Naturally this was not a uniform process which could be chronologically isolated and noted. The second stage, the collapse of National Socialism itself, came with the Allied occupation both before and after the armistice. But the physical presence of the Allies alone would not by itself have been sufficient to prevent the German administration at the lower levels from remaining Nazi strongholds if the split between Party and administration had not taken place. The same is true of many other aspects of life. The administration of law for instance was deeply imbued with National Socialism. Most of the legislation after 1933 had been inspired and carried out by Nazis. It was therefore natural and relatively easy for the Party to control the legal system. Non-Nazi lawyers were removed from office and Bench soon after 1933 and reliable Nazis took their place. The same is true of education. Here the Party produced an overall plan and carried it into effect, not only in the Party schools, but throughout the educational

[1] Although this picture referred only to officers, it is generally true of the men. There were generally more Nazis among the wartime volunteers and conscripts and fewer among the regulars. The most fanatical Nazis were usually the junior officers.

system of Germany. The teaching profession was strongly influenced by National Socialism and would have remained so to a large extent even after the end of the war.

The effect of the Party on art, music, science, and medicine was much smaller.[1] National Socialism had nothing positive to contribute in these fields. The effort to establish a pure National-Socialist art and music was a chimera, in spite of frequent assertions to the contrary. Pressure was therefore purely negative and confined to personalities. Many doctors and scientists were strong Nazis, and some of them may still be so to-day, but in their capacity as individual men only. As art and science exist apart from political theories and can easily exist without them, whereas self-respecting political systems cannot dispense with the support of the former, the professional classes, the scientists, and the artists were easily able to throw off National-Socialist control once effective coercion had disappeared. It was natural that these men should be the first to come to terms with the new régime, and significantly the artists were the first profession to make their peace with the Russians.

Thus the split between National Socialism and administrative and cultural life took place with varying effect and to a widely differing degree. There remained the Party itself, and those of its members politically pledged to its ideas. We have seen that it was in them that the Nazi leaders placed their hope of continued resistance.

Owing to lack of planning and arms, and to vigorous Allied measures, physical resistance was made impossible for them. But they remained, at the time of the armistice, a politically dangerous enemy to Allied occupation and to the plans for the re-education of Germany. It is impossible to estimate their numbers. Membership of the Party or its affiliated organization cannot alone be taken as a guide. Experience of Nazi methods makes it possible to classify them to a certain extent. Thus the members of the Civil and Military SS, the Gestapo, the Security Services, the leaders of the male and female youth movements, the hierarchy of the Party from the Community Controller[2] upwards, the special sabotage forces[3] and the Army Indoctrination Officers, as far as they were still at liberty, might be said to have formed the nucleus of continued, if passive, Nazi resistance.

[1] An exception must be made in the case of literature, where Nazi influence was rather strong, and control over output a very simple matter.

[2] *Ortsgruppenleiter*, the lowest rank in the 'officer' hierarchy of the Party.

[3] Such special divisions as 'Brandenburg' and 'Grossdeutschland'.

The majority of these men and women were at the time of the armistice in western and southern Germany, the parts to be occupied by the Western powers. This was due partly to accident, partly to design. The High Command, the remaining members of the Government and the higher General Staff had moved north from Berlin in the middle of April, and made their way towards Flensburg. A large group of high-ranking officers were located in Bavaria, where the armies of the Southern Rhine, of Austria, Czecho-Slovakia, and Northern Italy were to occupy the Alpine Redoubt. It was natural that the majority of the Party leaders should accompany one or other of these last groups of military resistance. But this movement was not entirely strategic. For reasons already mentioned, armed resistance behind the Russian lines and in their zone of occupation was never seriously contemplated by the German Government. Quite the opposite, the Government had shown anxiety to prevent Party leaders and prominent National-Socialists generally from falling into Russian hands. In the general *sauve qui peut* of April 1945 the majority of prominent Nazis in eastern Germany, Poland, and Czecho-Slovakia trekked to the West in the hope of escaping detection. Moreover, it was generally believed in Germany at that time that the denazification policy and the arrest and trial of war criminals, to which all three Powers had pledged themselves at Yalta, would not be rigidly enforced by the Anglo-Americans.

So far we have dealt only with the Nazi Party and its relation to German life at the end of the war. What was the general attitude of the majority of Germans who had shown their unwillingness to fight underground for National Socialism?[1] Militant National Socialism seemed dead. For most Germans its rights and wrongs were of no great importance; it had failed to achieve victory and was therefore to be abandoned and, if necessary, execrated. The Allies had concentrated their propaganda on the Party rather than the German nation, and it became every German's post-war duty to uphold and foster this ready-made distinction. Indeed, it was carried to such lengths that Allied officers were soon to remark that it was impossible to find a Nazi in Germany.[2] Under this smoke-screen the population adopted a waiting attitude, depending on

[1] My information is taken mainly from Public Opinion Research Bulletins and from my own impressions. Thus the conclusions are only tentative expressions of personal opinions.

[2] The supreme example in the author's experience of such 'guilt-shedding' was perhaps the case of an SS concentration-camp guard who wrote to a former inmate asking for a testimonial of his anti-Nazi attitude in order to obtain release from British internment. The camp in question was none other than Auschwitz.

Allied actions as a guide to their own future actions. There was no feeling of remorse or any admission of guilt. Concentration camps and atrocities against conquered populations were either shrugged off as fair usage or were treated as post-war revelations. Nor was the essential claim for Germany to be the dominant political and economic power of Europe in any way renounced; though temporary limitations were recognized as inevitable. In most quarters the armed forces were held in esteem while the Party was condemned. Allied recriminations were generally met by the slogan that patriotism was not a crime.

With the exception of a two years' interval between 1939 and 1941, the Germans had been taught to hate and fear the Russians. This hatred was twofold. The historical German contempt for the Slavs was exploited to the full by the Nazis. German history in the schools was represented as the victorious struggle of the Germanic peoples against the usurping Slavs, who had entered Western Europe while the Germans were 'otherwise engaged' in the south, against Rome. Until 1941 this feeling was directed more against the Poles and Czechs than against the Russians. The anti-Slav tradition was, in any case, well established before 1933.[1]

The special hatred of the Nazis was directed against Bolshevism. This had been the chief link between Hitler and Papen, between the Army and the Party. The camarilla of officers which had been responsible for the murder of Rosa Luxemburg and Karl Liebnecht[2] was in contact with the Nazi Party as early as 1927. The campaign against the Red terror increased once National Socialism had disposed of its own syndicalist influence.[3] Above all, Communism would be conveniently labelled as a Jewish creed, and was therefore doubly hateful. The fact that some of the ablest generals had been trained in Russia was conveniently forgotten, as was the fact that even after 1933 economic relations with the Soviet Union continued, and German machinery was sold to Russia and installed by German engineers.

After the interlude between 1939 and 1941 the propaganda campaign was intensified. The Germans were fed on stories of

[1] One example of German academic denigration of Slav culture may be given. German research on Jan Hus always tended to exaggerate the Wyclif tradition, and made the Bohemian Utraquists into mere Lollard parrots. The German scholars also made extreme Norman claims in the controversy over the Norman or Slav origin of the Russian state. Many other examples could be cited.

[2] Known as formation 'Konsul'.

[3] It will be remembered that one of the Nazi slogans before 1933 was the 'destruction of the monopolistic chain-stores'. Such men as the Strassers, Ernst, and Heines had a partly Socialist background.

Russian atrocities at least as vile as those which are known to have been committed by the Germans. Any relaxation in the all out military effort against Russia was answered with the threat that the Russians, if victorious, would raze Germany to the ground. This propaganda was never out of date in its appeal.[1]

As the German retreat started in earnest the prophecies of woe increased. The story of Von Paulus provides a good illustration of the German attitude to Russia. At first reports of his capture at Stalingrad were denied. When rumours of the existence of the 'Committee for German Liberation' in Moscow became known it was announced that he had been killed by the Russians and his signature of adherence forged. Later it was stated that he had been drugged and hypnotized into acceptance. The German attitude towards the Russians always mixed contempt and hatred with almost superstitious fear.[2] In the last stages of the war refugees brought terrifying news of wholesale murders in East Prussia and on the Oder. The citizens of Berlin prayed that the Anglo-American forces would get to the capital before the Russians. Within three years the Germans had reached the heights of arrogance and tasted the abject terror of defeat.

The breakdown of normal administration at the end of the war produced a spontaneous series of reactions from the Germans. There were no riots, no attempts at usurpation of local government by fanatical champions of resistance and almost none by enthusiastic supporters of collaboration with the occupying forces. Nor was there much of the stunned surprise at the speed of the calamity, such as was noticeable in France during July 1940. No plans were being laid behind locked doors for future resistance and sabotage. Both in the country and particularly in the towns, society temporarily returned to the primitive unit of the family. Absent sons and wives were hastily collected and brought home. It has been estimated that half of the occupants of the last train between Schwerin and Berlin were evacuees from the latter city returning home.[3] As the Russians occupied Berlin the shutters of the houses were drawn, except for the slit through which the family watched their approach. Behind their remaining walls the Germans watched the occupation of their towns and villages, unrepentant, uncertain, fundamentally unchanged. The collapse of their Government made them return to their own small family circle, unwilling to take an

[1] See *The Goebbels Diaries*, under 11 February 1942.

[2] One of Hitler's wartime speeches described the Russians as frogs living in marshes.

[3] From an eye-witness account.

active part in their own future unless ordered by the conqueror. It was up to him to take the next step.

However misguided man may be, he can discard, or at least pretend to discard, political opinions and systems, when self interest dictates this course. National Socialism was not dominant in Germany for a sufficiently long time to drive out feelings and memories alien to itself in even one generation of Germans. Its political institutions were not strong enough to endure beyond the existence of a powerful Nazi Government, and when the men who founded and controlled these institutions withdrew or disappeared, the institution collapsed forthwith. It is therefore perhaps a blessing that the principle of case law does not exist in Germany and that the Nazi interlude does not establish a precedent. The difficulty of replacing the Nazis in the manifold administrative offices which became vacant or practically inoperative at the end of the war came later. Even before the Allies came to grips with occupational problems in Germany, National Socialism, as a practical theory of government, was dead for the moment.

2

THE ECONOMIC STRUCTURE

In the sphere of economics the position was different. National Socialism, unlike Communism, cannot boast of a fundamental economic theory. While some of the Nazi ideas spring directly from the economic conditions of Germany after the first world war, the practical economic remedies proposed by the Nazis before 1933 constituted at best a half-digested reiteration of various trends of economic thought. The early speeches of Goebbels and Strasser in the Berlin of 1932 contain hostile references to cartels and chain-stores with unity prices. Hitler was always fond of phrases such as that used at a rally in 1937: 'The salvation of Germany is not a financial question, but [depends] on the harnessing of the resources and capabilities of our people.'[1] It is significant that among the prominent Nazis of the Party's fighting days there was not one able economist.

Nor was it possible to adapt a system based on the political

[1] Before his accession to power, Hitler seems, from the evidence of his speeches and writings, to have had a well-developed hatred of economics and economists. As Schacht's memoirs show, the feeling never entirely disappeared. See *Account Settled* (Weidenfeld and Nicholson, London, 1949).

ideas of National Socialism, which rejected so much of what was good in civilized German life on grounds of religion and race, to an economy such as that of Germany. The application of the spoils system[1] would soon have reduced the German economy to a chaotic condition. The only general principle which was indeed applied to every sphere of life was the recognition of the absolute supremacy of the State. But this, of course, was not a principle of Nazi origin, and had its roots firmly embedded in Prussian tradition. The practical establishment of the idea of an all-powerful central government was in effect a restoration rather than a revolution. There were thus relatively few basic innovations in the National-Socialist approach to the economic problems of the Third Reich. The power of the State was a Prussian tradition; its control of a capitalist economy by various direct and indirect means may to some extent be traced to Keynes; its tools were mostly of Weimar republican origin. All the Nazis provided was a thoroughgoing execution.

The financial and personal support of many industrialists for the Nazi Party prior to 1933 had by no means been altruistic. Unlike their English colleagues, these German entrepreneurs had been forced to keep a close eye on political events since the revolts in the Ruhr of 1921, and subsequently played a very important part in the backstairs politics of the Weimar republic.[2] They had developed a very good eye for political trends and were, in spite of some misgivings of a personal nature, among the first to make their peace with National Socialism. The alliance became open after 1929. No arrangement then made has come down to us in writing, nor has the evidence at the trials of some of these early supporters of National Socialism tended to show any clear evolution of terms between the two contracting parties. A common foreign policy formed the basis of co-operation on internal questions. After 1933 it became a slogan of Nazi policy that the entrepreneurial organization of industry would not be disturbed, and that the rights of private property would be respected.

It would, however, be entirely erroneous to assume that the pre-Nazi economic picture was allowed to remain unchanged. The State owned a far greater share of the vital services and undertakings in Germany before 1933 than in England or the United

[1] Not only would faithful party hacks have occupied economically important positions, but the guild state implied an almost medieval economy in its logical development.

[2] See the documents of the IMT Nuremberg and the indictment of the I.G. Farben Directors.

States. Railways, radio, telephones, airway services, and the majority of hospitals, to name only part of the total, were owned and operated by the State. But this was the general rule all over the Continent, and England and the U.S. were the exceptions. Compared to other continental countries, Germany enjoyed a relatively free economy. The orthodox market mechanism dominated economic life. Unlike the Banque de France, the Reichsbank was not directly controlled by the Government and could not invade the open financial market. Nor did the institution of fixed statutory reserve exist for commercial banks. Being on the Gold Standard until 1931, an independent internal credit policy was impossible for the German government even if the machinery for it had existed. The organization of industry through chambers of industry and commerce was entirely in the hands of the entrepreneurs themselves. At a time when anti-cartel legislation already existed in the U.S., cartels and similar organizations were flourishing in Germany, and the influence of the industrialists over the Weimar government up to 1931 ensured that governmental influence, as far as it existed at all, would be no serious obstacle to their plans. As cartels were the product of a free economy in which individuals had the right to associate as they pleased it was argued that governmental interference was improper. This attitude continued even under a Socialist government.[1]

In the last days of the Republic certain hesitant steps were taken in the opposite direction. This was largely due to the catastrophic effects of the world crisis of 1929. After the credit and banking crisis of 1931, a skeleton control system was established by the Government over banking, consisting of a control board for the banking system and a corresponding executive in the shape of a Reichs-Commissioner.[2] The abandonment of the Gold Standard for the mark *ipso facto* brought with it the beginning of what was later to become the very close State control over the expenditure of foreign exchange by means of government supervisory agencies. The divorce of the mark from the absolute value of gold also paved the way for the intricate system of differentiation between the mark and individual foreign currencies, brought to its highest level during the middle thirties. All this required increased government interference.

In the other instance mentioned, the general control of cartels, the first effective measures were taken in 1930 and 1931. The

[1] See the German High Court decision of 1897 regarding cartels. This legal decision was not reversed until 1945.

[2] *Kuratorium and Reichskommissar für das Bankgewerbe.*

statutes of these two years gave the Government direct power through the Ministry of Economy to act against cartels suspected of 'conspiracies against consumer prices'. This was an abandonment of the previous procedure in which the Government became merely one party in a civil case brought against the offending cartel in the independent cartel court. But in practice the act was used chiefly in the opposite direction; one new compulsory cartel was established and the other previously existing ones were reorganized. Thus the period just before 1933 may be said to show the beginnings of a machine for increasing governmental interference in industry and finance, but little evidence of its intended use. They seemed to be intended chiefly as a safety measure against possible reoccurrences of the crises of 1923 and 1930.

We have taken only those two examples to illustrate the general trend of governmental influence on economic organization between 1918 and 1933.

The trend of events after 1933 is worth examining in some detail, for the twelve years' period of Nazi rule left an unmistakable imprint on the organization of the German economy. Quite apart from the secondary results caused by the National-Socialist policy, and the havoc in which its final bankruptcy left German economy, the reaction to the effort needed to harness German life in all its aspects to the programme of self-sufficiency in vogue till 1937, and to the concept of war economy predominating from 1937 till 1945, are still very evident to-day. Even if much of the purely administrative superstructure collapsed in 1945, the headless trunk of lower-level structure remained until the Russians destroyed most of it. In the face of disaster the economic spirit of National-Socialist Germany, once the fire of patriotism and aggressive pride had fallen away, consisted of mere passive inactivity in the absence of clear and positive orders. It will be seen later how this tendency to immobility produced an almost masochistic spirit in some industrial and agricultural circles both in western and eastern Germany.

Although the Nazis had no economic theory ready to be put into operation on the assumption of power, they had a definite object in view. The supremacy of the State was the fundamental maxim of National Socialism expressed through the periodical approval of a kind of 'general will'. Coinciding with this principle, and wholly dependent on it, was the desire to reverse the provisions of the Versailles Treaty and to restore the German economy to a state in which a general switch-over to a total war effort would be a relatively quick and easy matter.[1] Here the Nazis were much aided by the co-operation of many industrial entrepreneurs. The process, although based on a preconceived idea, was one of the most empirical and practical ever to be carried out by the Nazis. A start was made within four weeks of Hitler's entry into the Chancellery.

In the organization of industry the first step was a tightening in the control over the existing, and almost autonomous, entrepreneurial organizations. These were both regional (the chambers of industry and commerce) and functional (the Reichs Union of German Industry, divided into groups and associations according to the branches of industry). These organizations were not destroyed and replaced, but were simply made to serve a new purpose. At the same time the dual organization was expanded and evened out over the whole of Germany. An increasingly tight central control was established by an increase in the powers of the Ministry of Economy, and by the institution of a central planning office (The Office of the Four Year Plan) directly under Goering's control. As war came nearer the whole organization became increasingly detailed; in addition to the normal regulatory bodies mentioned above, there were the regional armament offices of the Army General Staff and the special government supervisory bodies controlling production, prices, and distribution (*Reichstellen*). Finally, supreme economic control was vested on 27–30 August 1939 in the cabinet for Reich defence (*Ministerrat für die Reichsverteidigung*) a top-level planning council subordinate only to Hitler, and controlling its own special planning and directing staffs (*Führungsstäbe der Wirtschaft*) at regional levels to co-ordinate the efficient harmonization of the economy in their particular areas.[1] Planning was highly developed in Nazi Germany.

[1] Many writers on the economics of National-Socialist Germany took the view that the German economy was prepared exclusively for war from the day the Nazis obtained power. Thus, for instance, Dr. Otto Nathan in his invaluable book, *The Nazi Economic System* (Duke University Press, Durham, N.C., 1944). This point of view is open to two objections: (*a*) The secret and indirect rearmament between 1919 and 1933, which took place on a considerable scale. (*b*) The relatively small increase of armament production in relation to the general increase in German production between 1933 and 1936. For the opposite view of a Germany tending towards full employment before the rearmament programme made itself felt, see C. W. Guillebaud, *The Economic Recovery of Germany, 1933–1938* (London, 1939). This view is perhaps an under-estimation of the rearmament programme and of the increasingly bellicose psychology of the Germans as a factor making for the increase in overall production between 1933 and 1938.

[1] The name and system of the small *Führungsstäbe* or directing staffs is taken in theory from the leadership principle (*Führersystem*) and in practice from the small top-level combined services planning staff (*Wehrmachts Führungstab*). Thus by 1939 the terminology as well as the spirit in the economic hierarchy is wholly that of the Army and Party.

The National-Socialist government also built on existing foundations in the matter of cartels. The earliest legislation might perhaps be interpreted in two ways. The decrees of 1932 gave the German government the power to dissolve existing cartels in the way originally provided for by Section 4 of the Cartels Act of 1923, by granting a dispensation of release to individual members of an association from the restrictive agreement. But now the Cartel Court was dissolved, the Government having powers of direct action. At the same time the government's power to establish compulsory cartels was confirmed and almost immediately put into operation on a much greater scale than before. In themselves these powers might have meant no more than the desire of the Government to re-establish German industry after the slump of 1930, through a centralized system of raw material allocations, price control, and production planning. Obviously a compulsory cartel established by decree would not be used as a means of financial exploitation of the consumer by an elected government. The very fact of governmental control would satisfy the more social-minded of the Party members. On the other hand a compulsory cartel naturally benefited the large firm or combine in the particular branch of industry. Not only was it probable that its own organization, its cost and price calculations, and its qualitative standards in manufacturing would be taken as the guiding standard for the new government cartel, but existing cartels would in fact achieve the complete elimination of competition. Presumably the leading figures of industry would expect to have a powerful voice in the running of the new organization, for, unlike a nationalized industry, a compulsory cartel is *ipso facto* operated by its constituent members, even if the Government has the over-riding control.

It is reasonable to assume that this ambiguity was deliberate. It was further emphasized by the repeated insistence of Nazi writers on economic questions that the principle of private ownership and management would continue unimpaired, in spite of increasing governmental control over the economy. Cartels had shown themselves a valuable means of German industrial recovery. The industrialists concerned had shown themselves even more useful to the militarist element in the Weimar republic, and therefore made very useful Allies after 1933 for the Nazis, who had adopted and improved on their predecessors' policy.[1] The majority

[1] Thus the extraordinary offer, as early as 1921, alleged to have been made in all solemnity by I.G. Farben, proposing the exchange of the formula of Bayer's

of large industrialists who were in agreement with the objects of Nazi policy combined the dual rôle of entrepreneurs and *ex officio* civil servants. We frequently find the chairman of a combine directorate acting as head of the local Chamber of Industry, as representative of his trade group, and as director of the national or regional Supervisory Office for raw material allocation or for production of certain goods. Sometimes he was even director of the Regional Armaments Office of the General Staff (*Rüstungsstab/OKH*).

In industry the real element of governmental control was obtained partly by 'enabling decrees', partly by administrative centralization, but chiefly through the personal and political loyalty of the majority of industrial entrepreneurs. In case of personal difficulties or political desertion legal powers of control could always be used.[1] The basis of Nazi control of industry was the placing in key positions of loyal supporters of the régime. It was for this reason that early in 1933 the government arrogated to itself the right to appoint the chairman of economic groups and chambers, which were nominally independent entrepreneurial organizations.

This does not of necessity mean that all industrialists were even nominally Nazis, and this should be remembered when the expropriation policy of the Communists comes to be discussed. A number of anti-Nazis who found their continued activities in their own professions impossible, were often able to find a reasonable job in industry or agriculture, even during the war. Party pressure on individuals was perhaps less evident in the economic sphere than anywhere else. But there can be no doubt that the leading figures in German industry were solidly behind the Party, at any rate until 1944.

Alongside the closely controlled but privately owned industry, the Government founded a number of state-owned and operated combines. These consisted largely of armament works and affiliated industries, and became an important economic factor from 1936 onwards. In some cases national undertakings filled the gap in the chain of war production left by private industry, in others they formed a nucleus which gradually attracted into its control a

'Germanin' for the return of the German colonies. Apparently the offer was made on the initiative of the I.G. directorate. See also Borkin and Welsh, *Germany's Master Plan*, (New York, 1943).

[1] Not invariably successful, for example in the case of Thyssen. Such desertions were, however, rare, and affected only those industrialists who thought themselves powerful enough to be independent.

number of private firms. Naturally these tended to operate in those branches of industry where the initial capital investment required was considerable, although the German Government always showed a tendency to obtain at least the co-operation of private firms in new development schemes, partly as a means of absorbing capital away from inflationary activity. After the occupation of Austria and Czechoslovakia, such national combines as the *Hermann Goering Werke* acted as the main receiver of the armaments industries of the occupied countries, and operated these industries on behalf of the German Government. Here again, there was no question of excluding non-national undertakings on principle. Both I.G. Farben and Rheinmetall, to name only two, participated to a great extent in the exploitation of the industries of the occupied countries. The State-owned undertakings cannot in any way be said to have been privileged competitors of the private sector, but rather filled the gaps in the war effort left by the non-national industries and acted as a spur to them. Frequently it was only the refusal of a private industry to accept certain commitments alone that made the Government take over a production task. The effectiveness of all these measures cannot be doubted. The 1936 economic survey shows that most of the difficulties caused by the world depression had been resolved. In view of the requirements of the four-year plan and the overt as well as secret rearmament programme, the existing industrial capacity and output were only just keeping pace with the demands made on them. The reversal of the previous credit policy[1] followed by intense Government pressure to make the maximum direct credit available to industry were beginning to show results.

The restriction of dividends, and the qualitative and quantitive control of credit by the Reichsbank, ensured that industrial expansion was confined to industries of national value, as well as forcing entrepreneurs to reinvest a considerable amount of their profits in their undertakings, and leave the private credit market at the disposal of governmental planning. Hence an overall modernization of industrial plants and buildings took place between 1934 and 1939. Apart from direct war damage, the general rate of depreciation of German industry was much less than that of Great Britain during the war.

[1] The *volte-face* of Dr. Schacht in 1934 with regard to the stabilization policy of the Mark may be remembered. He himself claims a logical sequence in what seems a complete reversal of policy.

The fiscal and foreign exchange policy of the Government was aimed at achieving the greatest possible self-sufficiency for Germany, and encouraging trade which would not be interrupted by war. Its export programme was based on the procurement of credit in those countries which supplied essential raw materials, including food, to Germany. The German export programme was basically a process of dumping excess manufactured goods rather than a scientific adjustment of production to the ever-changing niceties of demand abroad. Bilateral clearing agreements were therefore a normal part of German economic policy, particularly as these agreements, in the case of South-Eastern Europe, implied a considerable degree of economic dependence on Germany for the countries concerned. The military conquests during the war naturally increased this tendency towards industrial self-sufficiency in Germany. The industries of conquered countries were immediately brought into line with the Reich industrial system and its programme, and were closely controlled from Germany. The military situation at the end of the war thus left Germany in a specially unfavourable position in competing in multilateral world trade, although the tremendous demand for manufactured goods since has counter-balanced this to some extent.

The effect of the war itself did not radically alter the position, structure, and organization of German industry, owing chiefly to the fact that the pre-war organization was based on the probability of a world war, and was therefore designed to meet it. The tendency towards central control and high-level planning was carried to its logical conclusion. Occasional administrative difficulties arose from the great variety of organizations and their overlapping functions, but these were less serious than might have been expected, as important individuals often held many posts in different organizations. Moreover, such a complicated and delicate machine, reduced by shortages during the later stage of the war to ingenious and uneconomical methods of saving raw materials, could not stand up to serious reverses and damage without dislocation. The breakdown of the transport system late in 1944 and the imminent invasion of the Allies seem to have done far more to destroy the smooth functioning of German industry than the actual destruction of industrial plant through air-raids. No plans had been made for the systematic destruction of industrial capacity by the retreating German armies and the last-minute order for general destruction given by Hitler was disobeyed by Speer and his executives. Nor were any transfers of factories planned and undertaken in the menaced areas of the Reich. It seems therefore that effective Government control over industry lapsed at much the same time as its control over the local administration, probably even earlier.

It is difficult to estimate accurately the productive capacity of German industry in 1945 without taking into account factors, such as the food situation, which arose later,[1] or which, like dismantling and restriction of capacity, were the result of Allied policy. In any case, no attempt to survey the German economy in 1945 has been published. A very general estimate would show that the total productive capacity of Potsdam Germany[2] in 1945, including agriculture, was about the same as that of the same area in 1936. This estimate naturally presupposes full utilization of existing capacity, itself an impossibility in 1945. From a zonal point of view the capacity of the Russian zone was slightly higher in 1945 than in 1936, that of the British zone slightly lower, and that of the U.S. zone about the same. Thus, very broadly speaking, the war damage to industrial and agricultural capacity was roughly equal to the increase in the period of war economy 1936–43, and if 1936 is accepted as the year when Germany achieved her maximum purely peace-time prosperity and full employment, the necessary capital equipment for economic balance and prosperity existed in post-war Germany A considerable loss in food production had, of course, been sustained by the alienation of the eastern areas. However, the secondary effects of the war on the economy were such as to make an estimate of capacity merely of academic interest. The reasons for this are sufficiently obvious not to need discussion here. It is enough to say that the discrepancy between theoretical and practically exploitable capacity was such that even the economic experts at Potsdam entirely failed to arrive at plans which bore any relation to achievable reality. This discrepancy was in no small part due to the over-centralization of the German economy under the Nazis.

Nor can any accurate picture be given of the immediate results of the breakdown of the Nazi industrial organization. Although highly centralized, in effect by far the greater part of German industry remained in the hands of private owners, or associations of such owners. In the Anglo-American zones, where little structural change has taken place outside the State industries and the

[1] Except for the Ruhr, where periodical food shortages were in evidence since January 1944.

[2] Excluding the areas ceded to Poland and, of course, all acquisitions after 1937.

large cartels, and such firms as were owned by men particularly committed to National Socialism, the hangover from the situation of 1945 can to some extent be gauged. The results of the long years of State direction, and its complete collapse, seem to show a loss in flexibility. Even taking into account the enormous difficulties, little effort was made on the part of the German manufacturers until the currency reform to keep their factories going at the cost of a complete change from the pre-war production process and in the quality of the goods produced. The considerable raw material stocks remaining at the end of the war were not utilized to the extent which the example of the Russian zone has shown to be possible. As one American official privately put it in 1947: 'The Germans take the attitude of working either to full capacity or not at all.' The nature and methods of the occupation may be the cause of this attitude, but it seems reasonable to say that the organization existing between 1933 and 1945 did not tend to make German industry resilient in the face of administrative and economic conditions bordering on chaos. Even the more enterprising plans for industrial recovery produced in the West between 1945 and 1948 were long-term plans, with no provision for the hand-to-mouth existence of the moment, and depended on a central planning agency as well as large measures of financial and material Allied help.

The methods and actions of the Nazi Government with regard to industry have been discussed at some length since the spirit behind them is typical of their treatment of most economic questions, including agriculture, finance, commerce, and labour. Agriculture was also organized on the lines of centralized control, exercised chiefly through purchase and sale directions, price formation, subsidies, and the power of expropriation in cases of inefficiency. Germany had been an importer of some agricultural commodities such as wheat, since the first world war, and her home industry was concentrated on certain staples, such as rye and dairy produce. The prospect of war naturally made the stringent control of production and distribution imperative. Once again the head of the control organization was the ministry concerned, itself under the aegis of the office of the four-year plan, while the National Food Estate (*Reichsnährstand*), whose membership embraced all farmers, provided the combination of private enterprise organized to make State control easier. It was through the Reich Food Estate that Party influence made itself felt.

The position of the agricultural interest in Germany had always been relatively strong. Politically the governing class until 1918 was almost invariably recruited from it, and even after the so-called democratic revolution its strength was sufficient to keep the Government 'agriculturally minded'.[1] Nor was the republic called upon to protect a mere economic passenger; German agriculture had a high reputation for efficiency. In some respects the situation in the Germany after 1933 was not unlike that of the England of 1846, containing a landed class politically powerful and socially supreme (tendencies frequently in an inverse ratio) in a country whose main source of wealth was industry and commerce. Although the Nazis were anxious to combat the political influence of the agricultural interest with its strong affiliation to the Army, they did not succeed to any great extent. Agriculture is the part of national economy least affected directly by modern war and it was therefore natural that the reintegration of society, as well as the last strongholds of Nazism, should form round the farmers after 1945. Hence the almost unchanged aspect of a western German farm to-day compared to 1939, and hence also the priority given to land reform by the Russians.

One of the main governmental leadstrings on the economy was in the control offices. In this respect the practice of the Nazis was almost revolutionary. Certain tentative beginnings were made in the last days of the Weimar republic[2] and the effects of these plans on industry have already been mentioned. When the Nazis came to power in 1933 prices and wages were still dominated by the depression of 1930–2. The task of the Government immediately preceding the Nazis, and of the latter for the first fourteen months of power, was to speed up the existing deflationary process by forcing prices and wages down still further, particularly the administered and regulated prices of cartel organizations.[3] At the same time the heavy contraction of the consumer market, due to the withdrawal of foreign loans as well as the run on the banks in 1931, had to be tackled.

By 1935 the situation was changing. The stability of the mark was now beginning to be threatened by the expansion of production, the shortage of foreign exchange for industrial raw

[1] cf. Guillebaud, *op. cit.*, for the special measures of the government with regard to agriculture after the fall of prices in 1932.

[2] cf. Nathan, *op. cit.*, pp. 214 *passim*. A Reichskommissar for price supervision was created in 1932.

[3] The alternative, currency devaluation, was not used, partly because the general tendency towards devaluation of foreign currencies, such as the pound sterling and the French franc, was considered favourable to Germany's import and borrowing programme.

materials, and the consequent rise in price. The policy of the Government was therefore directed at the rising tide of prices, and it is here that a new financial machinery was evolved. It was found that price supervision was insufficient, and the Commissioner entrusted with this task changed his title to that of Reich Commissioner for price formation on 29 October 1936. On 26 November 1936 came the price stop.

This general price stop was not designed to be of more than a short duration, as its long-term implementation would have been impossible, in spite of the draconian penalties which the price control authorities could inflict. But the stop gave these authorities the time to investigate each part of the economy and to 'build' prices based on the cost-plus system which would be in accordance with the Nazi ideas of economic justice and with Nazi production policy.

After the price stop of 1936 this policy took various forms. As the shortages, particularly in the consumer market, became more acute, it became more and more difficult to keep prices and wages down. Agricultural prices were at first limited by minima and maxima,[1] and many were later definitely fixed. In industry, prices were formed by a complicated system of price provisions, both rigid and flexible, including margins for imports and rebates. Special provisions were made for the activities of the Government as principal customer, since bulk orders of that nature were considered to help in reducing the cost, and therefore the price, of the goods concerned.

With the advent of war, every effort continued to be made to keep prices down. Unavoidable rises in prices of any one commodity were to be balanced by corresponding decreases in neighbouring fields of the production process. The increasing rationalization and the expansion of industrial plant helped to balance the rise in prices of manufactured goods, though the latter usually outweighed any decreases in prices through these methods. Stringent punishments,[2] and priorities and bonuses for entrepreneurs belonging to the lowest cost price group of the five groups established in 1941, could not prevent a general rise in prices towards the end of the war, nor could they altogether stamp out the methods of price evasion common in Germany during the war.[3] The extent

[1] The so-called 'guide-prices' (*Richtpreise*).

[2] Price evasions were usually tried in the notorious People's Courts, and were, or could be, capital offences. Freisler, the president of the Berlin People's Court, made a speciality of such anti-social offences.

[3] Such as joint or bundle sales, of recent unlamented popularity in the retailing of scarce goods in England.

of the black market during the war, and particularly towards the end, cannot accurately be estimated, but there is no doubt that it was not a post-war mushroom growth. The manufacturers, as well as the housewives, were well trained during the war.

In a free economy, prices 'to a large extent, hover about the intersection of demand and supply, and determine how much will be produced'.[1] In Nazi economy, however, prices were an instrument of production control, providing incentive to manufacturers, adding an allocated spice of profits to the regulated dish of overall production. Nevertheless, 'prices did continue to perform some of the functions . . . of any price system';[2] for the public as well as for the entrepreneur, they continued to be the scale by which relative values were measured, and of the channels through which the national income was distributed. In this respect prices fulfil a somewhat similar function in the Soviet Union to-day. There also they emerge as part of the planning process, and are usually a factor in the plan of production. But here differences in price between the manufacturer and the retail trades are almost wholly appropriated by the Government in the form of a turnover tax.[3] The German price commissioner, Wagner, openly stated that 'the "cost of production" principle . . . is open to serious objection from the point of view of our general price policy.' The institution of 'reasonable' profit margins was indeed attempted for a time through a cost-plus computation of prices, even on Government war orders, with a profit calculation based on turnover, capital and entrepreneurial activity.[4] But eventually the method of plain price fixing was restored, at the cost of not even minimum profits in some cases. This tended to force the cost of production down to the lowest possible minimum, and therefore helped to achieve a maximum rationalization; at the same time, however, discouraging the expensive and uneconomical *ersatz* processes necessary in times of war, when normal imported raw materials were unobtainable.[5] The long-term effects of this system, on one part of the German economy at any rate, will be seen later.

As the price level in an industrial community is dominated by, and itself dominates, the level of wages, it will be necessary to discuss the Nazi labour policy. The price stop of 1936 was preceded

[1] Nathan, *op. cit.*, p. 217. [2] *ibid.*, *loc. cit.*

[3] cf. M. H. Dobb: *Soviet Economic Development since 1917* (London, 1948), p. 360. This policy has altered since 1939.

[4] Singer, 'The German War Economy' *Economic Journal*, 1942.

[5] This meant that the government had itself to undertake many of these processes. See above, pp. 20–21.

by a freezing of wages on a 1933 basis. This level was disadvantageous for the wage earner, as wages at that time were still at the low level of depression. It was hoped that a lowering of prices would increase the standard of living for workers, which, up to the beginning of the war, it did. Although, for instance, the nominal national income per capita was 1,166 RM in 1938 compared to 1,187 RM in 1929, the real income in 1938 adjusted from the cost of living index to 1929 prices, was 1,422 RM. The figures for the total earnings of wage earners are 23,754 million RM (real income 28,968 RM)in 1938, and 23,339 million in 1929. The chief reason is, of course, the substitution of full employment in 1938 for only partial employment in 1929 (16.39 millions employed in 1938 as compared to 14.76 in 1929).[1] The relative standard of living of wage earners in comparison with salaried employees went down considerably, however. The object of Nazi policy was a reasonable absolute minimum standard of living for wage earners irrespective of the changes in the position of other classes, a standard which must not be lowered or increased at the expense of the war potential of the Reich. It implies recognition by the Nazis that security even without hope of improvement is the prime object of the labour policy of the State.

In 1933 the German labour movement seemed well organized and powerful, embracing 20 per cent of all non-independent workers in 159 unions. The disruption of the Social Democratic Party in 1916 and 1922, and the tendency of German trade unionism to break up into fragments of different political views, only feebly held together by the common interest of class community as workers, undoubtedly weakened the collective power of the labour movement. In spite of this the rapid disintegration of the trade unions under the Nazi labour laws of 1933 remains one of the great surprises in the history of National Socialism in Germany. It is, at the least, an unanswerable rebuff to those who maintain that class consciousness has everywhere overcome nationalism in our day.

The Nazi system for the control of labour was partly founded on pre-Nazi methods of organization. The employment exchanges became a central State monopoly, being controlled by the Ministry of Labour. Their non-profit as well as private profit-making competitors, functional and regional, were abolished by statute.[2] The Office of the Four Year Plan, as supreme authority over the economy, obtained the power to order compulsory transfer of

[1] Figures from Nathan, *op. cit.*

[2] *Reichsarbeitsgesetz* 1933.

labour from one place to another, as well as from industries of secondary importance into the rearmament programme. *Mutatis mutandis,* free migration of labour was strictly prohibited. As the economy reached and 'passed' the stage of full employment in 1938, and it became clear that manpower was likely to be the main bottleneck of complete war economy,[1] a vast programme of national conscription for labour was begun. The order limiting hours of work, although it remained on the 'statute book', was circumvented, with the active connivance of the Government. At the same time the Reich labour force,[2] organized on military lines, was made compulsory for all men and women prior to military service. The maximum employment of women, even young wives, was made compulsory, and training in skilled work was begun for many unskilled workers.[3] The agricultural labour supply was kept up by the compulsory direction of school children and university students of both sexes during vacation. To ensure maximum rationalization of employment the work registration book for each working individual (employers included) was instituted; this contained a work dossier complete with qualifications and history in the hands of the labour offices.[4] It was emphasized that there existed no difference between workers and soldiers, both serving the State without question. The situation was well summed up by Dr. Ley's phrase 'Soldiers of Work'. The phrase is not unknown to Soviet Russia.

There was no workers' organization for the purpose of collective bargaining. Wage disputes, contract interpretation, and the other matters which occupy labour courts were settled arbitrarily by the Government agencies known as Labour Trustees, who also fixed wage rates and made the necessary adjustments to them.[5] Within single industrial, and to a lesser extent agricultural, units an attempt was made to 'nationalize' class distinctions through the 'works communities'.[6] These consisted of employers, managers, clerks, and workers, and were to represent the German corporative

[1] cf. Himmler's circulars, as well as those of Sauckel, to the police chiefs and labour recruiting services in the occupied countries (Documents of the International Military Tribunal).

[2] *Reichsarbeitsdienst,* an organization created by the Weimar republic as a kind of *atelier national.* It had certain para-military tendencies from its earliest days.

[3] It was hoped to recruit unskilled, particularly agricultural, labour from the occupied countries. See Docs. of the IMT.

[4] A book similar to the British Army AB 64, Pt. I.

[5] The comparison with the function of Justices of the Peace in Tudor and early Stuart England is interesting.

[6] *Betriebsgemeinschaft.* For a very favourable view of these see Guillebaud, *op. cit.*

state in miniature, and to compete with other communities for better results, thereby setting a higher standard of work. It seems wrong to say that these organizations were dominated by the entrepreneur. Admittedly his *ex-officio* position made him important in the community and he was usually the chairman of it. But Party influence in these organizations was such that the best Nazi, capitalist or worker, had the most influence. Clashes between a relatively non-political entrepreneur and a Nazi-dominated community were not infrequent, and usually culminated in a report to the local Party headquarters and a visit from there to the entrepreneur concerned.

The national organization of workers was the German Labour Front. This was neither a workers' organization nor did it exist to represent the workers' view. It was the Party's chief means of instilling propaganda and of combating possible class reflexes in the decaying body of working-class solidarity. Control of the organization was entirely in the hands of the NSDAP and was not subordinate to the Ministry of Labour. Thus its influence was political rather than economic, and interference in labour policy was especially forbidden by a decree of the Reich Chancellor. By way of compensation, and to solidify the direct bond between the worker and the State, the German Labour Front ran the 'Beauty of Work' and 'Strength through Joy' movement for the workers and their families. Under its auspices 1st May was still celebrated as Labour Day to show the kinship of National Socialism and the worker. The essential difference, however, between Nazi Germany and the Weimar republic may be summed up as the metamorphosis of labour questions into questions of work.[1]

Closely connected with the question of prices and wages was the handling of national revenue and public credit. The position of the latter had been in a parlous state under the Weimar republic. The inflation of 1922–3 had given investors a shock which did not aid the borrowing experiments of later governments, and which is even to-day vividly remembered. With the cessation of foreign loans in 1930 the Republican Government found both long-term and short-term loans almost impossible to obtain. Banks

[1] Guillebaud, writing in 1938, states that the influence of the Labour Front as a limiting factor on entrepreneurial freedom was considerable, and that employers privately used strong language about the organization. Employers were, it is true, continually mulcted by demands for large financial contributions to the Labour Front. However, Party influence on the works community was usually personal in the shape of individual Nazis in the community rather than through the Labour Front. The latter method would have resuscitated class distinctions in production and thus defeated their own purpose.

were extremely illiquid and heavily in debt to the Reichsbank, while the general public was also heavily affected by the depression. Hence the issue under the Von Papen plan of 'work creation bills' and tax remission certificates, both designed to raise immediate cash for the Government on favourable time-and-interest terms for the purchaser. As mentioned earlier, the Reichsbank was given power for open-market activities in October 1933, as well as permission to discount these and other Government certificates and bills. After 1933 the Nazis continued the issue of these bills, sufficient having been issued to raise 1.47 million Rm in all by 1935. At the same time short-term loans at 6 per cent were issued, a few for public absorption, the majority for credit institutions. In support of this, savings banks were permitted to hold 50 per cent of their statutory reserves in Government securities.[1] Commercial banks were also favoured with short-term treasury bills rediscountable at the Reichsbank. Large-scale consolidation was begun in January 1935, and long-term paper was also on the market for savings and credit institutions by 1935. This consolidation, which continued until the outbreak of war, was not designed to consolidate the floating debt so much as to make available to the Government a possible further means of covering current expenditure.[2] Moreover, the Nazis knew the sensitivity of a public to Government paper and issued a few open loans only between 1935 and 1936.[3] After that date Government paper was confined to banking and credit organizations. The first four issues made after 1933, both public and restricted, were heavily oversubscribed, a good indication that the financial world stood as solidly behind Hitler as the French financial world had stood behind Napoleon I.

By 1938 the Government had not only re-established confidence but had wiped off the material effects of the depression. Conversion was accompanied by a reduction of interest from over 6 per cent to 4½ per cent on Treasury paper, and it is generally believed that had the Government so desired it could have reduced interest still further. But since borrowing came to be less public and as the Government relied more on large credit institutions, as well as actual Reichsbank subsidiaries such as the Reich Credit Offices in the occupied territories, the payment of large interest percentages may not have been as disadvantageous as if the public had been

[1] Later this restriction was abolished altogether (1939), and banks could legally hold all their reserves in this form.

[2] 'Money and Banking', 1937 (*League of Nations Publication I*), pp. 56–7.

[3] During the greatest period of economic expansion for two and a half years after the outbreak of war no public war loan was issued.

involved. The war period saw the perfecting of the art of 'silent' finance. The money of the public went to the Government by two stages, first into the hands of savings banks and thence quietly but effectively into the Treasury. The appearance of depending on public confidence was thus avoided; in case of reluctance it is possible to coerce a number of banks, but difficult to force a public to buy.

The centralization of taxation, the transfer of the necessary powers from the Länder and provinces to the Reich Government, had begun to take place in 1919[1] and was continued by the Nazis. The system thus evolved was taken over by the Nazis without radical alteration, and showed 'great flexibility . . . [increasing the revenues] concurrently with any rise in national income'.[2] Taxes were indeed widely distributed, and there were almost twice as many in 1933 as existed in Great Britain. In spite of the enormous increase in revenue from taxation between 1933 and 1943 (6.7 milliard RM in 1933, 17.7 milliard in 1939, and 35 milliard in 1943)[3] there was no intention of financing the rearmament programme in the coming war even mainly by taxation. As the years passed the ratio of expenditure actually covered by tax and customs decreased, from about 62 per cent in 1935 to 40 per cent in 1941. Taxation was, however, heavy, constituting 20 per cent of the national income in 1928 and 36 per cent in 1940.[4] The Germans are a tax-trained people to an even greater extent than the British, and since the war this quality has been exploited more than ever.

The Nazi economy evolved a third method of raising public revenue not usual in normal capitalist systems. The majority of charitable institutions were nationalized. With a tendency for thorough organization, the propaganda ministry took over the encouragement of the public towards contributing to such organizations as the Winter Relief, the 'Strength through Joy' movement, the various aid days for the affiliated bodies of the Party, the SA, SS, HJ, etc., and the Adolf Hitler collection. Even if the majority of the contributions collected were used for their ostensible purpose, the saving for the Treasury, which thus found some of its normal expenses taken over by public generosity, was considerable and provided more available cash for other purposes. In this connection the membership dues of the Reich Food Estate, of the chambers and groups of industry, and even the unemployment

[1] The Erzberger tax reforms. [2] Nathan, *op. cit.*, p. 303.
[3] *Statistik des Deutschen Reiches*, 1938, No. 528, p. 41.
[4] My own calculations from official figures.

insurance should be taken into consideration as further means of revenue. Many of the mushroom 'charitable' organizations which sprang up during the Nazi period seem to have had little purpose beyond filling the Treasury coffers. Thus the BDA[1] was cynically stated to have provided the money which went towards the necessary 'organization' for 'liberating' the oppressed Sudeten Germans.[2] It will be seen that this continual demand for pseudo-charitable contributions is still effective in Germany to-day, and is much used in the Soviet zone.

To sum up the effects of twelve years' Nazi rule, itself partly engendered by pre-Nazi events and trends, on the German economy is a formidable task. Added to the planned results of twelve years' domination are the effects of five and a half years of total war, a war lost by Germany on a hitherto unknown scale. The war economy was planned for an offensive and a victorious struggle, not for a defensive war of attrition. Hence plans and facts diverged more and more as the war changed its character for the Reich. A last-minute change-over from one type of war economy to another is impossible at short notice, especially when the initiative of strategy is in the hands of the enemy. As German conquests increased, she depended more and more on the support of the enchained economies of the occupied countries for the support of her own overburdened war economy. The reverse process did not take place; the retreat of German arms was not accompanied by a contraction and concentration of her widely expanded economy.[3] The area of the Third Reich in May 1945 contained no longer the close approximation to a balanced and self-sufficient war economy it had been in 1939, quite apart from the actual war damage in German territory.

Bearing in mind this and other changes directly due to the war and its outcome, it is yet worth noting that Germany did not fall as a long-beleagured fortress, in which starvation and general neurosis have upset government after government. The Nazi régime, thinly disguised as a Naval Commander-in-Chief, formally handed over control to Allied occupation. It is clear that the new rulers perforce took over much of the old system in pattern as well as in personnel. The breakdown of Nazi administration could not mean the instant disappearance of at least twelve years' political, social, and economic influences. Just as individual parts

[1] The 'Union of Germans Abroad'.

[2] Henlein's speech at a rally of the BDA in Dresden, 1939.

[3] Thus the re-equipment and retooling of industries in Bohemia with German capital was still going on as late as October 1944.

of a body do not decay for some time after death, and can actually be preserved for a long time by the passive means of preventing the access of destructive agents, so the components of the body politic can live on after the death of the central organism as long as active destruction by force or decay be prevented. Unfortunately, if a corpse is the result of violent death, onlookers, needing no persuasion to be convinced of the presence of death, forget the fact that individual parts are still capable of continued life.

In spite of everything, May 1945 was not Armageddon, and the destruction of Germany much less deep than was supposed. A superficial visit immediately after the war left an indelible and misleading picture of destroyed towns, of hungry men and women, of a stranded society. These are signs which anyone may recognize. Political and economic patterns are difficult to survey as a whole and to understand in their full significance; they are also impossible to destroy in detail at one blow. We have tried to give a brief outline of some of the important political and economic trends emerging from Nazi rule and from the conduct of the war, and to sketch, as far as possible, the general situation in 1945, in order to show their importance in the post-war picture.

CHAPTER II

THE ALLIED PLANS

THE first expression of war aims was made public in the Atlantic Charter, in the form of a statement of the basic values which the Allies pledged themselves to uphold throughout the post-war world. The future of Germany itself only became subject to serious discussion once the prospects of victory seemed assured to the Allies. In the U.S. and Great Britain there were a few fundamental policies on which there was general agreement. The punishment of major war criminals, the economic weakening of Germany, the destruction of her armed forces, and the victorious entry of the Allied armies into her capital, were accepted as essential concomitants of victory. There was a strong feeling that what were considered to be the failures of Versailles must be avoided this time. These were twofold; the unprofitable reparations policy,[1] and the lack of effective post-war co-operation among the victors.

There was, however, violent disagreement over the extent to which Germany should be weakened and punished. This dispute was based on the extent to which the Germans as a whole were guilty of the war and the excesses committed in its prosecution. On one side were ranged those, for whom Lord Vansittart spoke powerfully,[2] who refused to draw any fundamental distinction between the Nazis and the German nation as a whole, and who saw in the history of Prussia and Germany one long series of aggressions, broken only by periods of preparation. Against this it was contended that the Nazis were a tyrannical minority driving the Germans on an aggressive course against their will. This was the view of the two Germanies: the peaceful bourgeoise Germany of the Rhineland or Bavarian ale-house, and that of the deceived and hysterical masses, whipped up by wicked leaders to a *furor teutonicus*. During the war the latter point of view found little vociferous support in Britain or the U.S.A., but, as afterwards appeared, this was due more to the restraint of its supporters than to the paucity of their numbers.

The Russians, as far as we can judge, generally supported the

[1] The most comprehensive attempt to refute the Keynesian view of reparations after the first world war was being prepared at this time, viz. E. Mantoux: *The Carthaginian Peace* (London, 1945).

[2] *Lessons of my Life*, (London 1943).

extreme view of German guilt. It was part of the psychological technique of the Soviet Government to raise popular hatred of the German invaders as high as possible, and no doubt this played a large part in the desperate struggles put up by Russian forces from the beginning of the campaign for Moscow in October 1941.[1] This official attitude only fanned the flames of hate engendered by the German brutalities, which characterized the Russian campaign from beginning to end.[2] The official and the popular view of the war was that it would be fought to the death on both sides, that it was in fact a war for survival on the one hand and extermination on the other. 'Our task is to exterminate every single German who has set his invading heel on the earth of our Fatherland.'[3] Great play has been made by Russian propagandists since the war with the phrase: 'Hitlers come and go, but the German people and the German State remain. It would be ludicrous to identify Hitler's clique with the German people and the German State.'[4] Molotov quoted the phrase at the Foreign Ministers' Conference in London in November 1947, when he opened the Soviet campaign for a strong and united Germany against the Western 'dividers', as proof of Soviet moderation even during the war. But as Stalin's latest biographer has pointed out: 'His propagandists, as a rule, failed to make this distinction until the final phase of the war.' Moreover, the phrase was originally used as a means of countering German propaganda to the effect that the Red Army notoriously refused to spare the lives of prisoners.[5]

The Allied intentions for defeated Germany were governed by the decision first taken at an unknown date early in the war, to make the German surrender unconditional. This meant that, though the plans were to be worked out jointly beforehand, the Germans were to receive no information about them. Together with the Germans, the public in the Allied countries was kept quite in the dark until after the conclusion of hostilities. The intention was to emphasize the humiliation of the defeated enemy. One of the results of this laudable intention was that the plans for Germany were shaped entirely in the seclusion of conferences, and, shielded from outside criticism, they tended to reflect the views

[1] See J. Stalin, *Orders of the Day*, (London 1945). For the German evidence of sudden stiffening of Russian resistance see Liddell Hart, *The Other Side of the Hill* (London, 1948). Statement of General Blumentritt.

[2] See, for example, the evidence at Nüremberg against Ley, Goering, and the SS, the indictment of the General Staff, and the indictment and evidence at the trial of Von Manstein.

[3] Stalin, *op. cit.*, p. 18.

[4] *ibid.*, pp. 29–30.

[5] Deutscher, *Stalin: A Political Biography*, pp. 489–90.

of the victors, sometimes at the expense of existing facts. Though Mr. Roosevelt was the originator, it seems that Mr. Churchill was later the main prop of the policy of unconditional surrender.[1]

As a result of the Moscow Conference of Foreign Ministers in October 1943 the Tripartite European Advisory Commission was set up in London. Its purpose was to recommend terms of surrender and the means of enforcing Allied policy in Germany to the governments of the U.S., Great Britain, and Russia. Hence allied policy was outside its scope, it was to study and recommend methods of execution. The terms of reference were contained in a memorandum presented by Hull to Eden and Molotov at the conference, and this was based on the assumption of joint responsibility for policy in Germany and joint occupation.[2] This principle, which at bottom presupposes the continuance of a single united Germany, was thus accepted for the future almost casually, without critical examination or conscious realization of the fact that only very close allied accord could make it work. For the first eighteen months of its existence, however, the work of the European Advisory Commission seems to have been hampered more by disagreements between the American Chiefs of Staff and the State Department, and by British-American divergencies, than by difficulties with the Russians.

The area of the future Soviet zone of occupation was suggested by the British representative on 15 January 1944 and accepted by the Russians on 18 February. At the same time the joint occupation of Berlin was accepted, with the principle of free and independent access to their sectors for the two Western powers. The Russians accepted what was eventually agreed upon without bargaining and without delay, and the only opposition was put up by the American Civil Affairs Division of the War Department, apparently working on lines of military convenience and topographical symmetry rather than political possibilities. The later claim, asserted in the Soviet note of 14 July 1948,[3] that 'Berlin is part of that Soviet zone' is clearly refuted by the EAC Protocol on zones of occupation of 12 September 1944.

The legal independence of Western Berlin was actually enhanced by the fact, which emerged as a result of the later necessity to provide a French sector of occupation, that the Russians were not

[1] See J. F. Byrnes, *Speaking Frankly* (London 1947); E. R. Stettinius, *Roosevelt and the Russians* (London 1950).

[2] Philip E. Mosely, 'The Occupation of Germany', *Foreign Affairs*, Vol. 28, No. 4, p. 580, July 1950.

[3] *Dept. of State Publications 3556* (Washington, 1950), p. 208.

prepared to undertake the permanent provision of food and fuel for the sectors of Berlin outside their control. This was made clear by Zhukov on 7 July 1950.[1] As a result, the Western powers ceased their demand for a Russian contribution of territory towards the new French sector of Berlin, and created this out of their own sectors. In the long run, this dispute over the French sector of Berlin had far-reaching consequences. By placing the responsibility for West Berlin's economy on the Western powers, particularly Britain and America, the Russians caused them to abandon the attempt to reduce the area of Soviet occupation in Berlin for the benefit of the French, but at the same time gave the Western powers that stake in the control of the city which made possible their readiness to resist at any price the Soviet attempt to evict them by a blockade in 1948. The right to be there was effectually supplemented, thanks to Soviet obstinacy in July 1945, by the economic benefit and the means of remaining there. 'It was Soviet insistence . . . which established West Berlin as a separate economic area' tied to Western Germany's economy.[2]

The first conference of the 'Big Three', at which the future of Germany was to be planned at the highest level, took place at Yalta, from 4–11 February 1945.[3] Previous to that, the only indication of Allied intentions which had emerged was the so-called Morgenthau plan.[4] This envisaged a reduction of German industrial potential sufficient to make Germany a predominantly agricultural country in the future. At Yalta it became clear that, while the Western powers appeared to have advanced further than the Russians in their technical studies of the German situation,[5] the Russians had formulated a more precise policy with regard to reparation demands than either Great Britain or the U.S. Whereas Stalin appears mostly to have contributed the Russian point of view himself at the meetings of the three leaders, he called on Maisky to explain the Soviet reparations plan at the meeting on the second day.[6] The Russian proposal stated:[7]

[1] Lucius D. Clay, *Decision in Germany* (Doubleday, N.Y., 1950), p. 27.

[2] Mosely, *op. cit.*, p. 601. The whole case of the Communists against the splitters of Berlin' thus collapses. See below, p 107, *passim*.

[3] There had been an exchange of views on the subject at Teheran, but no resolutions had been agreed.

[4] First propounded to Roosevelt and Churchill by Secretary of the Treasury, Henry Morganthau, Jun., at Quebec in September 1944. It was at first accepted by both leaders but rejected after strong protests by Hull and Stimson on one hand and Eden on the other. Stettinius, *op. cit.*, pp. 45–6.

[5] *ibid.*, p. 114. The statement is Molotov's. It has been frequently reiterated by the Russians as part of their campaign to prove Soviet 'open-mindedness' with regard to Germany. See below, Chapter III.

[6] Stettinius, *op. cit.*, p. 123.

[7] See Byrnes, *op. cit.*, p. 26; Stettinius, *op. cit.*, p. 123, *passim*.

On the basis of our plan two kinds of reparations are envisaged:

(1) A part of German property is to be withdrawn (consisting of) territory, factories, machines, railways, and foreign assets.

(2) For the next ten years a certain quantity of goods must be delivered.

By withdrawal I mean to confiscate and carry away physically for reparation payment.

It was later proposed by Maisky that 80 per cent of the German industrial potential was to be handed over, chiefly from the iron and steel industries, the building industry, and the chemical industry. The production capacity for synthetic oil and petrol, aeroplanes, and all armaments works were to be dismantled and handed over completely.

On the basis of Soviet contributions to the war effort, and of the losses sustained in the process, Russia demanded at least 10 milliard dollars out of capital goods and current production reparations. Reparations from German labour were deliberately left out of the discussion.

The chief objection to the proposed total value of reparations came from Churchill, who doubted both the German ability to pay and the Allied benefit from reparations, in view of the experiences of the victors after the first world war. The President also counselled moderation. Maisky then made the very important point that the fiasco of the previous experience was due, not to quantity, but to the concentration of the victors on financial reparations. This pitfall would now be avoided, he said.

Here were all the later difficulties and disagreements over reparations in embryo. The Russian demands were considered, with more or less outspokenness, as exorbitant by the Western powers. The shape of reparations was tacitly settled; solid reparations, as opposed to financial exactions. The sharing of reparations was based on two considerations, but though Soviet sufferings were generally recognized to be far greater than those of any other of Germany's enemies, the consideration, in apportioning her share of the reparations, of her effort towards the prosecution of the war could and did lead to the exclusion of the demands of other countries, based on their needs. By skilfully balancing the scale of her war effort and her needs, Russia could make the demands of other countries fade into relative insignificance.

Indeed, before the conference was over, there was disagreement between Russia and Britain with regard to Germany's capacity to pay.[1] The immediate question was the American-Soviet proposal that the total of reparations should be provisionally fixed at 20 milliard dollars, and that the Soviet Union should receive its original minimum claim, 50 per cent of that sum. The British refused to accept this figure as a basis for discussion by the Reparations Commission to be set up in Moscow. The disagreement even registered itself in the official protocol, where the American-Soviet and the British points of view appear severally and distinctly.[2] But the issue was only ostensibly one arising out of differing estimates of Germany's capacity to pay. For the British, important as was the compensation aspect of reparations, their real purpose was the weakening of Germany. The level of exactions would therefore be determined by the amount of reparations which Germany was capable of paying without becoming dependent on Allied aid in order to keep her population alive. The Russians, on the other hand, were above all interested in the positive gain which reparations would bring to a planned and under-developed economy.[3] Their demands would be such that the problem of weakening Germany would automatically be taken care of. The minimum level of the German standard of living was inevitably flexible, and it would therefore be difficult to show that reparation payments were reducing this level beyond the minimum, particularly when compared to the standard of life in the destroyed parts of Russia. Hence it was in the Soviet interest to commit the Western powers to a high figure, while British policy demanded the absence of any commitments until Germany's capacity to pay had been worked out in detail.

A proposal had been made by Harriman and Morgenthau that, in view of the economic devastation of the Soviet Union, a large long-term loan on easy terms should be offered by the U.S. Government to the U.S.S.R.[4] This would cement U.S.-Soviet relations and might also help to take the acrimony out of the Russian attitude on reparations. Since this loan, partly owing to Russian lack of apparent enthusiasm, finally came to nothing,[5] it is an open

[1] *ibid.*, pp. 154, 227. Also Byrnes, *op. cit.*

[2] *Protocol of the Crimea Conference*, V, 4.

[3] For the effect of reparations on the victor nations after this war, see for instance F. A. Burchardt, 'Reparations and Reconstruction', *Bulletin of the Institute of Statistics*, Oxford, Vol. VII, No. 11, Sept. 1945, p. 199.

[4] Stettinius, *op. cit.*, pp. 115–16.

[5] In addition, the proposal was dogged by the sort of bad luck which occasionally stalks even the most efficient organizations—the Soviet request was lost in the U.S. State Department. According to a friend then working there, the Russians refused to believe the shamefaced American explanation, and the proposal was left to evaporate.

question whether the difficulties over reparations, which later became the chief wedge in American-Soviet relations in Germany, might have been avoided. If the Russian preoccupation with removals from Germany had been toned down by American rehabilitation loans it might have led to a more constructive political policy in the Soviet zone. But whether this would have led to closer co-operation with the Western powers, or to a more ruthless backing for the East German communists—a Soviet zone more like Western Germany, or more like the other Soviet satellites—is quite uncertain in view of more recent developments.

It is important to notice that the dismemberment of Germany played an important part in the discussions of the Allied leaders, and that all three were in principle agreed in enforcing it. Details were referred to a special committee, while some general suggestions were discussed at the conference. A special paragraph of the protocol was devoted to this question.[1] The intention was to destroy the unitary German State by creating a number of partially independent administrative units. As proposed at Yalta,[2] these differed both from the later zones of occupation and from the provinces or Länder established after Potsdam. It was implied that the zones of occupation were intended only for Allied convenience, and were not to play an important part in the administrative division of Germany. It is clear, therefore, that what the Big Three appeared to have in mind at Yalta was very different from a division by zones into a federal republic. In addition, the principle of dismemberment conflicted with the then still hazy notion of centralized quadripartite control.[3]

At the time, these difficulties, actual and potential, were not apparent to the public in the Allied countries. From the available evidence—and it is one-sided and incomplete—the conclusion seems to be that the Russians made important concessions over Germany at Yalta. Roosevelt seems to have thought so, and Stettinius summarizes them in a special chapter at the end of his account. Except for their reparation demands, the Russians apparently did not go to a conference with a firm and final programme; indeed, Molotov stated that the United States and Britain seemed to be further advanced in their studies on the German question.[4] Nor was final Russian policy evident in the first weeks after the conference. On the question of dismemberment

[1] *Protocol*, para. III (1 and 2).
[2] Stettinius, *op. cit.*, p. 117.
[3] *ibid.*, pp. 153, 157.
[4] Stettinius, *op. cit.*, p. 114; Philip E. Mosely, 'The Dismemberment of Germany', *Foreign Affairs*, Vol. 28, No. 3, April 1950, p. 491.

of Germany, mention of which in the surrender terms for Germany had been agreed at Yalta, the Russian delegate at the European Advisory Commission never stated his Government's policy, though he showed himself anxious that his colleagues should commit themselves to definite views.[1] When the procedural question of informing the French of this Yalta decision came up, the Russians failed to answer the Anglo-American request for consent, and dismemberment was left out of the final surrender instrument by default, and because SHAEF, in consultation with Churchill at the last moment, on 6 May 1945 substituted its own purely military surrender instrument for that agreed by the Commission. During these months, the Russians were officially neither for nor against, while their policy was being shaped in Moscow.

At Yalta the curtain over the Allied plans for Germany was lifted a little for the first time.[2] It was admittedly stated that 'our demands (with regard to unconditional surrender) will not be made public before the final collapse of Germany is complete.'[3] This, of course, was in accordance with the principle of demanding unconditional surrender. But the trend of ideas is clear. Without any details, the report goes on to state the general Allied plans:

> It is our irrevocable intention to destroy German militarism and National Socialism and to make certain that Germany will never again be able to disturb the peace of the world. We are firmly determined to effect the disarmament of all German armed forces and to dissolve them, to destroy for all times the German General Staff, which has repeatedly brought about the revival of German militarism, to remove or to destroy all German military installations, to liquidate or control the whole of German industry capable of being used for production of armaments, to bring to trial and condign punishment all war criminals and exact restitution in kind for all damage caused by the Germans, to remove the laws, organizations, and institutions of the Nazi Party, to cut out from the public service as well as from cultural and economic life every Nazi and militarist influence and to take such steps in harmony as may appear to be necessary for the future peace and security of the world. It is not our intention to destroy the German people, but there will only be a hope for a decent life and a place in the community of nations when Nazism and militarism are extinguished.
>
> We have considered the problem of the damage caused by Germany to the United Nations in this war and recognize it as just that Germany should be compelled to make restitution in kind for this damage to the

[1] *ibid.*, p. 494.

[2] Churchill advocated the exclusion of all controversial matter from the official report and protocol, but was sometimes over-ruled. Stettinius, *op. cit.*, pp. 118, 119, 131, 205, 209, etc.

[3] *Report of the Crimea Conference*, para. II.

greatest extent possible. A commission for the Compensation of Damage will be established. The commission will be instructed to consider the extent and the means by which the damage done to the Allied Countries by Germany is to be made good. . . .[1]

A few further specifications are contained in the protocol issued by the three foreign ministers. After stating that the U.S.A., Great Britain, and the U.S.S.R. 'shall have supreme authority with respect to Germany[2] . . . including [the steps of] complete disarmament, demilitarization, and the dismemberment of Germany', the protocol states on the subject of reparations:

(1) Germany must pay in kind for the losses caused by her to the Allied Nations in the course of the war. Reparations are to be received in the first instance by those countries which have borne the main burden of the war, have suffered the heaviest losses and have organized victory over the enemy.

(2) Reparation in kind is to be exacted from Germany in three following forms:

(*a*) Removals within two years from the surrender of Germany or the cessation of organized resistance from the national wealth of Germany located on the territory of Germany herself as well as outside her territory (equipment, machine-tools, ships, rolling-stock, German investments abroad, shares of industrial transport and other enterprises in Germany, etc.) these removals to be carried out chiefly for the purpose of destroying the war potential of Germany.

(*b*) Annual deliveries of goods from current production, for a period to be fixed.

(*c*) Use of German labour.

(3) For the working out on the above principles of a detailed plan for exaction of reparation from Germany, an Allied Reparation Commission will be set up in Moscow. It will consist of three representatives —one from the Union of Soviet Socialist Republics, one from the United Kingdom, and one from the United States of America.

(4) With regard to the fixing of the total sum of the reparation as well as the distribution of it among the countries which suffered from the German aggression the Soviet and American delegations agreed as follows:

The Moscow Reparation Commission should take in its initial studies as a basis for discussion the suggestion of the Soviet Government that the total sum of the reparation in accordance with the

[1] In the absence of an English text, I have translated as closely as possible from a Russian one. The translation, though correct, is therefore not authentic. *Report*, II (2), III.

[2] *Protocol of the Crimea Conference.*

points (*a*) and (*b*) of the paragraph (2) should be 20 billion dollars and that 50 per cent of it should go to the Union of Soviet Socialist Republics.

The British delegation was of the opinion that pending consideration of the reparation question by the Moscow Reparation Commission no figures of reparation should be mentioned.

The above Soviet-American proposal has been passed to the Moscow Reparation Commission as one of the proposals to be considered by the Commission.

It could be seen that a definite figure for reparations was here for the first time proposed, and agreed by the U.S. and the U.S.S.R. as a basis for discussion, with British reservations. It is not clear whether the figure of 20 billion (milliard) dollars is based on a percentage of German production or productive capacity, or on an estimate of war damage in Allied countries, or, indeed, on anything at all. Certain it is, both from the text of the protocol and the evidence of the discussion at the Conference, that the U.S. did not consider itself tied to this figure as a definite target. Later Soviet claims, that the figure was confirmed by the Americans, cannot be based on the text of the protocol.[1]

This broad outline envisaged a radical programme of destruction and supervision in both the political and the economic field. No detailed plans had yet been made. To control and destroy all industries which might serve a rearmament programme implied a huge economic staff investigating and controlling the greater part of all industrial production. To bring to trial and punishment all war criminals called for an enormous detective and legal organization to classify the various crimes lumped under war-crimes, find the war criminals, and try them. The very principle of quadripartite control necessitated a large and cumbrous organization. But it is clear that these difficulties and disagreements did not prevent a genuine belief in Allied co-operation in planning the future of Germany on the part of the peoples of the Allied countries. According to the statements of the American participants at the conference, this feeling was shared by the President and his advisors.[2]

On 7 May 1945 the German Government surrendered. The

[1] As this figure of 20 billion dollars does not include a breakdown into removals and reparations from current production, it is impossible to compare this proposal with the 45–50 per cent at Potsdam. Twenty billions are, of course, 20 thousand millions, or 20 German milliards.

[2] R. F. Sherwood, *The White House Papers of Harry L. Hopkins*, Vol. II (London, 1949); Stettinius, *op. cit.*; Byrnes, *op. cit.*

terms of surrender were a military improvization, with an enabling clause which reserved to the Allies the right to carry out those plans which were to have been indicated in the two drafts for an instrument of surrender prepared by the European Advisory Commission.[1] The Russians had still given no indication of their views on dismemberment and the important questions connected with it. But before the preparation of the joint declaration of the four commanders-in-chief on Germany, scheduled for 5 June, made a decision urgent, Stalin spoke. In his 'Proclamation to the People' on 8 May[2] he specifically repudiated the dismemberment of Germany and its destruction. Had it not been for the lengthy negotiations on this question, this statement might have been taken as a meaningless phrase of victorious generosity; as it was, the Russian Government had clearly come to a decision, and a unilateral one at that, as to what their policy in Germany would be. Accordingly, the commanders-in-chief's proclamation made no mention of dismemberment either. It was evident that at the Four-Power Conference shortly to take place, the Russians, having decided, would be less likely to concede points of importance than at Yalta.

We now come to the Berlin conference, which has gone down to history under the single name, 'Potsdam'. Unfortunately, we have no detailed account of the discussions at the conference. Nevertheless, here was the long-awaited peace policy. But though Potsdam was supposed to provide the implementation of the outlines drawn at Yalta, there must have been considerable changes in the Allied attitude to the German question. Certainly there had been a great deterioration in Allied unity, though not primarily connected with the German question. It was clear that the zones of occupation would represent more than the areas occupied by the troops of different countries. They might well mark the borders on either side of which divergent occupation policies were enforced.

The Berlin conference was certainly the expression of the unchanged feeling existing in most of the Allied countries regarding the nature of Germany's guilt and the proper methods of expiation. In the light of information then available to the public, the decisions taken at Potsdam were received everywhere with approval. Given that the basic premises of the Potsdam plan were correct, that the provisions themselves were stated clearly and unequivo-

[1] Mosely, *Foreign Affairs*, *loc. cit.*, April 1950, pp. 496–7.
[2] *Obrashchenie I.V. Stalina Kuaarodu*, *Pravda*, No. 111, 10 May 1945, p. 1.

cally and were faithfully carried out, it was believed that the knotty German problem would finally be solved. It must not be forgotten that the spectre of an excessively powerful and warlike Germany still loomed large in the minds of both the general public and the statesmen. The decisions would be harsh and burdensome for Germany.

What were the basic assumptions underlying the Potsdam plan? In the protocol they are divided into two categories, political and economic. This already implies the twofold nature of the German problem as then understood, the problem of the men and women, and that of the potential and actual economic power in their hands. The Allies implicitly accepted a broad view of German guilt. Political re-education was indeed essential, but the first line of defence against future German aggression was to be the economic weakness of Germany, together with such institutional changes as would make her revival practically impossible. The two policies are administratively separate. Thus:

Politically the purposes of the occupation of Germany are:[1]

(i) The complete disarmament and demilitarization of Germany and the elimination or control of all German industry that could be used for military production.
To these ends:

(ii) To convince the German people that they have suffered a total military defeat and that they cannot escape responsibility for what they have brought upon themselves, since their own ruthless warfare and the fanatical Nazi resistance have destroyed German economy and made chaos and suffering inevitable.

(iii) To destroy the National-Socialist Party and its affiliated and supervized organizations, to dissolve all Nazi institutions, to ensure that they are not revived in any form, and to prevent all Nazi and militarist activity or propaganda.

(iv) To prepare for the eventual reconstruction of German political life on a democratic basis and for eventual peaceful co-operation in international life by Germany.

In economic matters the protocol states:

11. In order to eliminate Germany's war potential, the production of arms, ammunition and implements of war as well as all types of aircraft and sea-going ships shall be prohibited and prevented. Production of metals, chemicals, machinery and other items that are directly necessary to a war economy shall be rigidly controlled and restricted to Germany's approved post-war peacetime needs to meet

[1] *Protocol of the Berlin Conference*, IIA, para. 3.

the objectives stated in paragraph 15. Productive capacity not needed for permitted production shall be removed in accordance with the Reparations Plan recommended by the Allied Commission on Reparations and approved by the Governments concerned, or if not removed, shall be destroyed.

12. At the earliest practicable date, the German economy shall be decentralized. . . .

It was recognized that the political evil of Germany was itself twofold, being made up of National Socialism and militarism. Both were therefore to be eliminated with equal determination. Thus:

3. All German land, naval and air forces, the SS, SA, SD, and Gestapo, with all their organizations, staffs, and institutions, including the General Staff, the Officers' Corps, Reserve Corps, military schools, war veterans' organizations and all other military and quasi-military organizations, together with all clubs and associations which serve to keep alive the military tradition in Germany, shall be completely abolished in such a manner as permanently to prevent the revival or reorganization of German militarism and Nazism.

4. All Nazi laws which provided the basis of the Hitler régime or established discrimination on grounds of race, creed, or political opinion, shall be abolished. No such discriminations, whether legal, administrative or otherwise, shall be tolerated.

6. All members of the Nazi Party who have been more than nominal participants in its activities and all other persons hostile to Allied purposes shall be removed from public and semi-public office, and from positions of responsibility in private undertakings. Such persons shall be replaced by persons who, by their political and moral qualities, are deemed capable of assisting in developing genuine democratic institutions in Germany.

7. German education shall be so controlled as completely to eliminate Nazi and militarist doctrines and to make possible the successful development of democratic ideas.

8. The judicial system will be reorganized in accordance with the principles of democracy, of justice under law, and of equal rights for all citizens without distinction of race, nationality or religion.

It will be noticed that the distinction between National Socialism and militarism is made as clear as possible.

The Allies assumed that the basic structural evil of German adminstration and politics was excessive centralization. Here again the purpose of introducing decentralization was partly to destroy the remaining threads of National Socialist and militaristic connection.

9. The administration in Germany should be directed towards the decentralization of the political structure and the development of local responsibility. To this end:

(i) Local self-government shall be restored throughout Germany on democratic principles and in particular through elective councils as rapidly as is consistent with military occupation;

(ii) All democratic political parties with rights of assembly and of public discussion shall be allowed and encouraged throughout Germany;

(iii) Representative and elective principles shall be introduced into regional, provincial and State (Land) administration as rapidly as may be justified by the successful application of these principles in local self-government;

(iv) For the time being, no central German Government shall be established. Notwithstanding this, however, certain essential central German administrative departments, headed by State Secretaries, shall be established, particularly in the fields of finance, transport, communications, foreign trade, and industry. Such departments will act under the direction of the Control Council.

The Potsdam agreement states that 'for the time being, no central German Government shall be established'. As Germany was to be treated as an economic whole, and as it was not intended that the provinces (Länder) should become entirely independent and sovereign political units for ever, the control council was presumably to carry out the functions of a central government. This in turn demanded four-power agreement. The military governors of the four zones, acting jointly as the control council, must speak, as any successful executive is bound to speak, with one voice. Clearly, the control structure envisaged by Potsdam could not function in the absence of close quadrapartite co-operation.

In spite of the opportunity since Yalta for further detailed study of the economic problems, the basic figures on which the Potsdam plan was based are open to challenge. The primary assumption here is that the level of production in basic industry of 1936 is almost twice as large as that required by Germany to subsist without external assistance, and to assure the maintenance in Germany of average living standards 'not exceeding the average of the standard of living of European countries, excepting Great Britain and the U.S.S.R.'[1]

This figure of about 55–60 per cent of 1936 production represents a rough average in total monetary value of the levels in different

[1] *Protocol*, IIB, 15 (b).

industries listed as restricted and controlled.[1] Presumably the comparison is based on a 1936 figure for an area corresponding to Potsdam Germany, minus the Polish areas. This proportion was to ensure to Germany a standard of living not lower than that of central Europe as a whole. This 'average' standard of life is somewhat vague, and difficult to measure. In principle, foreign (presumably Anglo-American) help was not to be forthcoming. If this figure of German minimum needs proved inadequate, the effects would be disastrous, as there was no quick means of measuring comparative standards of living, and thus no definite limit to the reduction of German industrial potential. This vagueness suited the Russians, whose reparation demands proved enormous, very well.

The treatment of Germany as an economic whole was an essential concomitant of four-power unity. Zonal boundaries were not so much to be relaxed in economic matters, they were to be non-existent. The same policy would have to be pursued in all four zones with regard to reparations, dismantling, imports, and exports. Transit for goods and persons from one zone to the other would have to be easy. Finally, a conception of purely zonal balances of trade must not be allowed to exist. These logical conclusions were indeed drawn at Potsdam. It was decided that 'common policies shall be established in regard to

(*a*) mining and industrial production and allocation;
(*b*) agriculture, forestry, and fishing;
(*c*) wages, prices, and rationing;
(*d*) import and export programmes for Germany as a whole;
(*e*) currency and banking, central taxation and customs;
(*f*) reparation and removal of industrial war potential;
(*g*) transportation and communications.

In applying these policies account shall be taken where appropriate, of varying local conditions.'[2] Further, as quoted above,[3] a number of central German administrative departments, headed by State Secretaries, were to be established, to deal with finance, transport, communications, foreign trade, and industry. This represents a

[1] *The Level of Industry*, British Secretariat, Control Council, Berlin, 27 March 1946. Together with a number of German economists, I cannot agree that this plan would reduce German industry to only 50–55 per cent of the much greater output of 1938. It seems that the value to the German economy of those particular industries in which the greatest reductions were to be made, and of the most modern plants which were particularly to be dismantled, has been underestimated in this plan.

[2] *Protocol*, IIB, 13.

[3] Page 48.

recognition of the fact that common policies call for similar organizations, and also that different systems of organization make the enforcement of the same policy very difficult.

An important part of the economic plans was concerned with the question of reparations. Here we come up first against a legal issue, an issue of definition. The Potsdam agreement states:[1] 'in accordance with the Crimea decision that Germany be compelled to compensate to the greatest possible extent for the loss and suffering that she has caused to the United Nations and for which the German people cannot escape responsibility, the following agreement on reparations was reached.' This defines the basis of reparations according to the literal meaning of the word, that of repairing damages. Even this, however, is not yet an exact definition.[2] Does it refer only to the damage done by direct German war action, such as the effects of bombs and shells and to the restitution of loot, or does it include the financial and economic losses borne by the United Nations in order to fight the total war against Germany? At Yalta the British had upheld the former view, the Russians apparently the latter.[3] As no new figure, definite or tentative, is mentioned, it is impossible to decide this by a numerical calculation. Nor is there any legal discussion in the plan concerning this aspect of reparations. It may be assumed, however, that only real damage was taken into account, as the bill for damages as well as war costs would have been too enormous to contemplate. The indirect loss to the Allies, such as the forced sale of overseas assets, would have had to be commuted into payment in those commodities with which Germany was actually able to pay, and the total would have increased even more in the process.[4]

Particularly in the field of reparations the spectre of 1918 was ever present. Its influence can be seen from the fact that financial reparations were now barred, and that, unlike the Yalta conference, the Allied leaders now approached the question more from the point of view 'What can Germany pay?' rather than 'What are we owed?' It would have been all too easy to fix a total figure with the intention of getting as near to it as was later seen to be possible. Instead of this it was decided that no figure should be

[1] *Protocol*, IV, Introductory paragraph.

[2] See the interesting discussion of the legal aspect in Appendix A to *Reparationen, Sozialprodukt, Lebenstandard* (Bremen, 1947). Below referred to as *R.S.L.*

[3] Stettinius, *op. cit.*, pp. 155, 226–7.

[4] It should be noted that the term 'United Nations' is used in the protocol. Reparation claims would therefore include the demands of such countries as Brazil, whose trade balance for the period 1939–45 is surely positive.

announced until the technical experts had declared the maximum Germany could pay without bleeding to death—and then to stick to this figure. Hence the delay of eight months between the Potsdam conference and the announcement of the future level of industry.

On the other hand the absence of any definite reparation figures may be evidence of the lack of Allied agreement in the Moscow Reparations Committee. The experiences of 1918 were peculiar to the Western powers, Russia being at that time a debtor rather than a creditor. The damage caused to Russia by the German aggression of 1941 was really far greater than that any of the other Allies had suffered, both relatively and actually. It was therefore natural that the Soviet Union should have considered the reparation question as suprememly important, and have been strict and exacting in its demands. Her primary interest was restitution of damage, and it was doubly to her advantage that the industrial demilitarization of Germany should therefore be extensive. If direct reparation deliveries of industrial plant were limited and unable by themselves to repair the damage done to Russia, then reparations out of current production, indirect reparations through exports, and invisible reparations through local exploitation were to be obtained. The later attitude of the Soviet Union seems to show that it had already then been decided to obtain the greatest possible amount from Germany. She was to pay for the damage as far as possible, and not necessarily with *de jure* reparations only.

As the reparation question proved so vital its hidden difficulties have been mentioned first. It may be that its very dangers were due to differing ideas with regard to its importance. The Potsdam agreement made no mention of reparations in their literal sense as a primary reason for the occupation,[1] but significantly the declaration of the Russian Foreign Minister on 9 July 1946[2] gave the three Soviet reasons why 'Allied and Soviet troops are present in Germany:

(1) To ensure and conclude the military and economic disarmament of Germany.

(2) To ensure that the regime in Germany will become democratic.

(3) To ensure reparation deliveries.'

Nothing could be clearer than this Soviet emphasis on reparations. There was no reason why the Soviet attitude should in fact have changed since July 1945, and there was equally no reason

[1] See above, pp. 46–7.

[2] Speech by M. Molotov at the Conference of Foreign Ministers, Paris.

why the Potsdam agreement should not be interpreted according to this Soviet view of the importance and volume of reparations, providing no numerical limit was fixed. It is further significant that no definite figure could be agreed upon by the statesmen at Yalta or Potsdam, and that the discussions were passed over into the hands of the lesser experts of the Control Council, with no more felicitous results.[1]

This was probably the most vital omission of the Potsdam agreement. The form of reparations had been fixed at Yalta under the three heads of plant removals, deliveries of goods from current production, and use of German labour. In the preamble to the protocol dealing with Germany in the Potsdam agreement it was stated that 'the purpose of this agreement is to carry out the Crimea declaration on Germany'. The Yalta definition of reparations was nowhere repudiated and this definition must therefore stand, even though neither reparations from current production nor the use of German labour were mentioned in the Potsdam agreement.

It was agreed that the U.S.S.R. must primarily satisfy its reparations claim from its own zone of occupation, and the amount of the Soviet share of reparations from the Western zones in 'usable and complete industrial capital equipment' was defined. Therefore if any reparations from current production were taken by Russia they would have to come from the Soviet zone only. Nor can the sentence which stated that 'the proceeds of exports from current production and of [existing material] stocks shall be available in the first place for payment of [vital] imports' be taken to qualify the right to take reparations from current production. It merely ensures that the foreign exchange obtained from exports shall be used primarily to pay for imports, and shall not be transferred to the foreign exchange account of the occupying power, or to cover occupation costs and any imports connected with them.

The immediate exaction by the Russians of extensive reparations from current production and stocks makes nonsense of the claim that the intention of confining reparations to capital equipment and the use of German prisoner and civilian labour was a basic assumption of Potsdam. The later Anglo-American attitude[2]

[1] cf. the American account of these negotiations in B. Ratchford and W. D. Ross, *Berlin Reparation Assignment* (North Carolina University Press, Chapel Hill, N.C., 1948).

[2] Byrnes' speech at Stuttgart, 6 September 1946. Also H.M.G. statement, 8 August 1946, on Potsdam. The claim is doubly unjustified in view of the fact that the detailed level of industry in accordance with the Potsdam agreement

with regard to reparations from current production cannot be reconciled with the foregoing evidence. The assertion that the original intentions with regard to reparations conflicted with the proposed German standard of living may well be true, but is only admissible if the error of assuming that such a standard of living could be achieved by a productive capacity of some 55–60 per cent of 1936 is admitted. The preamble to the revised plan for level of industry in the Bizone of August 1947[1] states that 'experience has shown the necessity for revision of the plan which was based on specific assumptions that have not been fulfilled'. This is perfectly true, but omits to mention that some of these 'specific assumptions' of Potsdam were at best mental reservations by one or more of the contracting parties.[2]

What conclusions can therefore be drawn from the Potsdam agreement? Mr. Byrnes has called Yalta 'the high tide of Big Three unity'. The whole policy of the darkest days of the war was based on the belief in victory and four-power agreement. It was therefore only natural that large divergences of view should be unconsciously minimized as mere differences over details, and that it should be considered more important to issue some sort of a joint protocol at Potsdam than to admit the failure of Allied co-operation for the sake of adherence to a particular policy about Germany.[3] It was hoped that matters on which the Big Three had been unable to agree might be settled in the dark recesses of technical committees of the Control Council and other subsidiary organizations. If all the Allies had been prepared to take no decisive step until every effort at compromise had been exhausted, four-power agreement might yet have been saved. But it is impossible to propose theoretical ways and means of solving a problem which is already being solved by the arbitrary and unilateral actions of any one of the parties to the discussions. In this respect Potsdam

was published in March 1946, though in the eight months since the conference reparations from current production and stock had all the time been taken to an ever-increasing extent from the Soviet zone. The Western powers must have been aware of this.

[1] cf. *The Revised Plan for the Level of Industry in U.K./U.S. Zones* (Berlin, August 1947).

[2] Another equivocal statement in the protocol is that regarding Russian payment for 15 per cent of the reparations from the Western zones. Was this to come from the Soviet Union, as the Western powers assumed, or from the Soviet zone, as claimed by the Russians?

[3] '. . . do not, I beg of you, my friend, underrate the divergences which are opening about matters which you may think are small, but which are symbolic . . .'—Churchill to Stalin, 29 April 1945; quoted by Churchill in the House of Commons, *Hansard*, 10 December 1948.

may well be labelled by Mr. Marshall's phrase in another connection: 'Agreement for agreement's sake.'

Secondly, Potsdam marked the end of the approach to the German problem which had governed Allied policy during the war. The first sense of reserve with regard to reparations from Germany, and certain provisions, however vague, regarding German rights and hopes, began to appear. But the basic assumption that Germany must be greatly weakened above and beyond her war losses still held sway. It took only a few months of Allied contact with German reality to show that if Germany was to survive at all the Allies must temporarily give blood transfusions—from their own bodies. The idea of a dual safeguard through strict personal as well as physical control began slowly to be transformed into a desire to let the Germans be responsible for their own political future to some extent, by handing over to them the trial of minor Nazis and militarists in the West, as well as by the intense reactivation of political life everywhere. The Potsdam agreement, which was to provide the guide to Allied treatment of Germany for a considerable time, was based on uncertain information accumulated during the past, and hardly took into account the conditions of Germany in August 1945.[1] Its assumptions, even when accurate, looked back rather than forward.

These then are the basic evils of Potsdam: the assumption of a non-existant state of unity among the Allies, and the acceptance of incorrect facts about Germany itself as a basis for future policy, governed by a method of approach which was soon to be discarded. All treaties and agreements can be changed by mutual consent. But there is always the risk that before any particular agreement can be changed the contracting parties will have fallen out among themselves. In that case an agreement which can operate only if the contracting parties agree to operate it, becomes void in practice once such accord no longer exists. But it would seem wrong to state that any particular party had 'broken' the Potsdam agreement, in the sense of acting contrary to its explicit provisions, as long as the situation created by Potsdam still existed on the surface. Yet in spite of this the world has seen two radically opposing policies operated in Germany by two so-called Allies,

[1] For an example of a detailed policy based on perfectly correct assumptions in 1945, but in complete opposition to the 'revised' policy of the Western powers in Germany in 1947, see 'Rough Justice in Germany' in *The Economist*, 23 Oct. 1948, which deals with Denazification policy. In this case the original premise and the policy based on it were correct, while the revised policy, however correct in the wider political sphere, was entirely unrelated to the facts of the situation when applied to Denazification.

each accusing the other of having broken the Potsdam agreement. The West claimed that Russia obstructed economic unity and took illegal and excessive reparations, while the Russians accused the West of encouraging separatist movements and thus destroying German unity, of failing to deliver Russia's share of reparations from the West, and of building a Western Germany deliberately hostile to the Soviet Union. Yet both sides, in an attempt to gain the support of world opinion, claimed for three years that they were the true upholders of Potsdam, and that, as the last authoritative expression of Allied agreement, its provisions were still considered binding.

CHAPTER III

THE SOVIET OCCUPATION

THE immediate purpose of the Allied occupation was to complete the defeat of Germany. As the Germans had shown by their policy in occupied countries, this task was not accomplished with the cessation of hostilities; instead, only the occupation of a defeated country could make its accomplisment possible. This was soldiers' work, and the first phase of Allied occupation was exclusively military.

The task of the Allied armies was complicated by the fact that the civil administration in Germany had broken down. This was particularly noticeable in the Soviet zone,[1] from which a large proportion of civil servants and industrialists had fled through fear of the Russians. Consequently, the Red Army had to undertake the quite unexpected task of organizing the most essential services in their zone. This they did with considerable success. Their methods were naturally arbitrary in the extreme. Individuals who commended themselves to local Soviet commanders were given positions of responsibility on the spot, irrespective of their record, provided they were not obviously National-Socialists. In this way a whole new cadre of mayors, *Landräte*, and police officials was appointed in the zone. Whatever the long-term effects of this may have been, it is indisputable that the immediate breakdown of administration was overcome.[2]

If one may judge by the experience of the Western powers, these tasks of reconstruction were not part of the planned occupation. Instead of destroying the remnants of an existing administration, a new one had to be rapidly created. It is therefore misleading to regard the actions of the Russians, as well as those of the Anglo-American troops, in the light of a preconceived plan. Judging from the Potsdam declaration, there certainly were such plans, but these activities were no part of them. Hence an individual discretion was exercised by local Russian commanders, which was

[1] See above, Chapter I, p. 11.

[2] I do not accept the interpretation in Löwenthal, *News from the Soviet Zone*. He only saw events one year later, but claims that the Russians deliberately put in even crooks in order to have amenable underlings. British officials in Germany were only too well aware that it is very difficult for a foreign authority to find honest and reliable Germans on the spot, particularly when the task is urgent.

all the more remarkable as it was unusual in Soviet administration. For the time being each commander ordered what he considered necessary in the area occupied by his troops, and made and unmade German officials as he thought best. It is clear, on the other hand, that the campaign against Nazis and Fascists was based on definite instructions from Moscow, as well as on the personal hatred which had been fostered in the troops by Soviet war propaganda. From the very first, ex-inmates of concentration camps enjoyed a privileged position with the Russians, and the distinction between criminal and political internment was not taken into consideration. There was no means of checking the record of most of the *soi-disant* anti-Nazis, and thus many of the new officials appointed by the Russians later turned out not to have been anti-Nazis at all.

The extempore nature of appointments was most noticeable in those parts of the Eastern zone occupied for some months after the armistice by the Americans. They, like the Russians, appointed hurriedly from candidates who presented themselves, but a different kind of candidate applied to the Americans than to the Russians. When the latter moved in according to the agreed withdrawal of the U.S. forces, many posts had been filled, and in order to obtain them it was necessary for ambitious Germans to denounce the incumbents appointed by the Americans. If the denunciations could obtain the support of accepted communists or delegations of workers, the Russians usually sacked the official concerned; it was in their blood. But the initiative rested with the Germans; the occupation authorities at this time were more concerned with the creation of an administration capable of functioning, than with the dictates of political orthodoxy.

Many of the qualities typical of Soviet administration soon manifested themselves in the occupation of Eastern Germany. Among these was the element of competition in reconstruction between one town and another. Each local commander seemed anxious to achieve prodigies of rubble-clearing, of reorganizing food supplies, of reopening hospitals and reviving transport services. This intense and unco-ordinated activity had some very beneficial results. The general German apathy was shaken, and very soon some of the active elements of the population began to come forward and to co-operate. It may be argued that the Russian shock-treatment in administration, the setting of impossible tasks in an impossibly short time, the refusal to recognize anything as impossible, was the only method capable of success in such chaotic circumstances. This spirit may have led to great hardships in the

Soviet Union itself, but it had shown itself to great effect in the reactivation of industry transplanted from the West to Central Russia during the war.[1] At this time many non-Communists, and even Germans opposed to Communism, offered their services to the occupation authorities, and found their offer eagerly accepted. As a result the Russians obtained the services of some of the most capable men in the zone, while in the West there was a tendency on the part of many such Germans to stay away from work under the occupation authorities. Those who blame the Russians for the large-scale desertion of German civil servants in the years 1947 and 1948 never stop to inquire how the Russians came to obtain the services of these men in the first place.[2]

This co-operation was only little affected by the outrages committed by the Soviet troops against the population. There can be no doubt that a great many were committed.[3] But somehow, in the immediate aftermath of a bitter struggle, these things are accepted as inevitable, and the Germans particularly seem—as a result of their own atrocities during the war, perhaps—fairly hardened to such happenings. It is certainly true that Soviet maltreatment of the population only began to play a rôle in politics as an outcome of the anti-Communist campaign in 1947. For instance, in September 1947 the first German publications appeared whose purpose was a systematic collection of evidence against Polish and Russian 'war-crimes' in Polish-occupied areas and in the Eastern zone. These publications began as pamphlets for private circulation only, and, as the political campaign became increasingly acrimonious, appeared in public as 'Documents from the German East'.[4]

This lack of co-ordination in the Soviet occupation during the summer of 1945 had its disadvantages also. There was no organized hunt for war-criminals, Nazis, and militarists appearing in official search lists, as in the West. Indeed, the activities of the Central Registry of War Criminals and Security Suspects (CROWCASS) did not extend to the Soviet zone, though the Russians had a

[1] See, for example, Deutscher: *Stalin*, Chap. XII. This is confirmed by most visitors to Russia during the war.

[2] See below, Chap. V, p. 117. This spirit is reflected by Schaffer, *Russian Zone*, written in 1946. It is surely impossible to believe, as Löwenthal suggests, that all these men were deceived by false promises. In fact the Germans were led to believe the worst of the Russians all during the war, and would not have changed their minds on the basis of mere promises for the distant future.

[3] See, for example, Löwenthal, *op. cit.* Schaffer admits their widespread prevalence. See also Friedman, *The Allied Military Government in Germany*, p. 41, for some general remarks.

[4] The author has seen a private document, from another source, dealing with Anglo-American 'war-crimes'.

number of names first on the lists issued in the West. Thus, quite contrary to expectations, the minor war criminals and Nazis, if not locally known, had an easier life in the East than in the West, though happily the majority did not realize it until it was too late. Moreover, the fact that Soviet efforts at reconstruction were at first local in scope, made the administration almost entirely dependent on the personality of the local Soviet commander, and thus gave the zonal administration a very patchy appearance. Indeed, it is not too much to say that for many weeks after the cessation of hostilities, Soviet military organization seems to have disappeared, and centralized control had lapsed. Only in this way can innumerable instances of orders and counter-orders, dismantlings and restitutions, appointments and dismissals, be explained. Trains disappeared in transit, food supplies for one unit were requisitioned by another. Public ordinances by high Soviet commanders were countermanded at lower levels or simply disobeyed. The impression is that the Soviet army disintegrated for a time into a number of almost independent commands. The Western powers found it impossible for a time to get agreed decisions implemented by the Russians, in spite of the fact that the latter seemed anxious to comply. The situation was very fluid.

On 9 June 1945, the SMA[1] was officially constituted by the confirmation of the appointment of the Supreme Commander and Military Governor, Marshal Zhukov, his deputy, General Sokolowski, and the chief of staff, Colonel-General Kurassov. The occasion also saw the first of the series of proclamations by the chief of the SMA, which were to become the main instrument of government in the Soviet zone. By 9 July the detailed plans for the provincial military administration had been completed and were put into effect with proclamation No. 5 of that date. This proclamation appointed five colonel-generals and their deputies as heads of the Soviet Military Government in the five provinces of the Soviet zone, Land Saxony, Province Saxony or Saxony-Anhalt, Thuringia, Brandenburg, and Mecklenburg-Pomerania. It also put into effect the Control Council decision to create a new German administrative organization consisting of nineteen provinces, of which five were in the Soviet zone. Thus, two months after the armistice, the administrative picture of the zone took shape.

[1] Soviet Military Administration, corresponding to British Military Government and Control Commission, and the American Office of Military Government, United States.

At the head of the Russian occupation authorities was the Commander-in-Chief of the Soviet Military Government and the Commander of the Soviet Army of Occupation in Germany. This post was originally occupied by Marshal Zhukov, followed in June 1946 by Marshal Sokolowski. In March 1949 Sokolowski was replaced by General Chuikov. As in the British, French, and American zones, both civilian and military functions were vested in one Supreme Governor, responsible only to his Government on the one hand, and to the Control Council, consisting of the four military governors in joint session, on the other. In the Soviet zone, however, the Military Governor retained his direct military functions in practice, whereas in the British zone the control of the Army of Occupation was in fact in the hands of a commanding General, who was only nominally under the command of the Military Governor. This emphasizes the fact that until 1949, the Soviet occupation had a more military character than the British or the American.[1] The almost simultaneous replacement of the victorious field commanders, General Eisenhower, Field Marshal Montgomery, and Marshal Zhukov, took place for different reasons. For the Western powers the change seems to have marked the end of the military and the beginning of the predominantly civilian occupation, coupled with promotion for the British Commander-in-Chief. It has been suggested that Zhukov was removed as part of the Politburo's campaign against the over-popular and powerful soldier.[2]

The third function of the Military Governor was his quarter share in the only central government agency in Germany, the Control Council.[3] This body consisted of the Council proper, made up of the four military governors, of a co-ordinating committee, and of the various specialized four-power committees dealing with the different functions of government. The relation of the Control Council to the individual military governors was never really that of a superior authority, as decisions had to be unanimous, and the veto of one member automatically nullified the corporate authority of the Council. Although the military governors were given considerable latitude to decide individual questions regarding the government of their zones, early disagreements, by destroying the

[1] Nevertheless, as will be seen below, the power of the Russian Military Governor was actually less than that of his British or American colleagues, for he had far less discretion, while some matters were altogether out of his control.

[2] Deutscher, *op. cit.*, p. 561.

[3] For a detailed discussion of the technical organization of the Control Council and the four military governments, see Friedmann, *op. cit*, Chap. IV.

unanimity of the Control Council, threw the real responsibility for legislation back on the governments in Washington, London, Paris, and Moscow, and on the joint decisions of the council of foreign ministers. It was, however, understood that the zonal occupation authorities were bound by the decisions of the Control Council.

The SMAs in the five provinces were smaller replicas of the SMA at Karlshorst. The provincial commanders were army generals, Colonel-General Fediuninsky in Mecklenburg, Marshal Bogdanov in Brandenburg, Colonel-General Kuznetzov in Saxony-Anhalt, Colonel-General Chuikov in Thuringia, and Colonel-General Katukov in Saxony. The huge distances on the Russian front during the war, the often uncertain communications, and the demands of Russian strategy had placed great responsibility on the individual Russian Army and army-group commanders. This had led to a certain spirit of independence on the part of the local commanders, which was increased rather than diminished in the early 'viceregal' days of occupation, before a proper chain of command was established in the Russian zone. Added to this was the fact that many of the immediate occupation tasks, such as the organization of reparations and the seizure and transport of war booty, were carried out by special missions controlled directly from Moscow. These had considerable powers, and were independent of the SMA. In some cases special orders even seem to have been sent from Moscow direct to certain provincial SMAs. Not only was the authority of the central SMA thus limited, but it was at first incapable of asserting itself over the provincial commanders.

It was natural that 'federalist' tendencies should exist at the beginning, both on the Russian and on the German side. It had been the Soviet principle from the beginning of their occupation to substitute responsible German executive organs for what had previously been elective, or pseudo-elective positions. Thus the various *Bürgermeister* (mayors), *Landräte* (administrative heads of rural areas), and *Regierungs-präsidenten* (administrative heads of larger areas) were either confirmed if they had been elected after the capitulation, or else nominated by the Russian area commandants. These functionaries were given a number of immediate tasks to do, chiefly concerned with the organization of the daily life of towns and villages, and certain powers to enable them to carry out these tasks. For a time administration functioned in small local units, and these were gradually absorbed into the provincial organization. With the formation of provincial SMAs the political and social life of the Soviet zone was once more based on the Land or Province. Land governments were instituted during the summer of 1945. Their task was to carry out the orders of the provincial SMA.

This development was in accordance with the four-power decision that the Land should be the biggest administrative unit in Germany, a principle particularly dear to the decentralizing mentality of the French. Nor did it yet conflict with the Russian practice of centralization, which in this case weakened rather than strengthened the power of the SMA in Berlin, since the emphasis was always on the one great centre in Moscow. Apart from the various Moscow-controlled missions operating in the Soviet zone, many orders from Moscow regarding occupation duties were sent direct to provincial SMA without going through the 'normal channels' of command. This was the case with reparations, dismantlings, technical and scientific investigations, and the founding and operation of Russian-owned concerns in Germany (SAG). Conflicts were not infrequent.[1] The Russian dismantling teams sometimes chose electricity or gas works which the SMA considered essential for the supply of the area, and orders were given, countermanded, and repeated. Similarly, the demands of the Red Army often conflicted with the programme of the SMA. Occasionally the protests of the local German authorities, backed by the SMA, prevailed, but usually reparation demands were fulfilled against any protests.[2]

The departmental staff of the central SMA had acted as the Russian delegation on the various technical Control Council committees, and at the same time had been responsible for the control of its particular activity in the Soviet zone. In July 1945 it was decided that this technical arm of the Soviet Government should have a German extension.[3] Such an arrangement would, it was held, give added efficiency to the execution of the decisions of the central SMA, as well as providing a better means of obtaining detailed information. These German bodies (*Zentralverwaltungen*) could be represented as the nucleus of the all-German Central Adminstrations mentioned at Potsdam,[4] and the other occupying powers might be persuaded to accept them as such. Hence the full

[1] Friedmann, *op. cit.*, p. 25.

[2] An actual case in point took place near Magdeburg in early 1947. In the end the power station concerned was left in a half-dismantled condition. See also Chap. VII.

[3] The metaphor was actually used by the Russians.

[4] See above, Chap. II, p. 48.

title of these new bodies: 'German Central Administrations for the Soviet Zone of Occupation'.

By the autumn of 1945, the central SMA had firmly established its own position *vis-à-vis* the regional SMA. Gradually the powers of the latter were circumvented, though not officially curtailed, by the direct chain of command going from the SMA at Karlshorst via the Central Administrations to the local authorities or officials. Direct orders from Moscow to provincial SMA headquarters became increasingly rare. But a considerable number of Russian organizations directly controlled by Moscow, and beyond the jurisdiction of Karlshorst, continued to operate in the Soviet zone. The chief of these were the Russian trading companies, the control organization of the SAGs, the technical and scientific bureaux and their various organizations, and the agency for current reparations. At the same time the provincial SMA retained an unexpected discretion in many matters which only disappeared gradually. As long as the Soviet zone remained officially a confederation of independent provinces, the provincial occupation authorities retained much of their independent authority, especially in the eyes of the Germans.[1]

On the whole, the combat officers, acting as administrators, made a good impression on the Germans. Their instructions had been general, to arrest the outstanding Nazis (who had disappeared overnight), to get the German population to work, and to do it all just a little quicker than the next man in the neighbouring town. Soon, however, these men were replaced by the technicians and the politicians. The first wave of personnel changes took place about July 1945. A considerable number of technical officials appeared in Germany, in some cases with detailed instructions, in others with the task of familiarizing themselves with the German peculiarities of their particular subject, be it politics, coal production, or statistics. Not all of these men were necessarily great experts, but they were specially picked for the job, in some cases long before the end of the war. This is true only for the higher levels; the soldiers acting as executive officials in the provinces and local areas after July 1945 were often a poor advertisement for an efficient military government, and their only incentive were the orders from above. It was not unusual for such orders to be misunderstood or even ignored. The difference between the evident

[1] Löwenthal tacitly admits this by making his book a comparison between the conditions of the different provinces. He repeatedly explains certain events by putting the character of the local Soviet commander in evidence.

abilities of the man at the centre and their frequent absence in the man on the ground gave rise to the widespread idea that if you want anything officially you must always go to the man at the top; if illegally, to the man at the bottom. Certainly details are dealt with at a much higher level by the Russians than by the British or Americans.[1]

The position of the SMA technicians in Germany is interesting. For the first time men brought up in the atmosphere of Stalinist Communism were faced with the task of administering a predominantly bourgeois economy. Most of them were young men, and many of them reliable Communists. Apparently one of the objects of the large-scale replacement of the Red Army officers with civilian technicians in uniform was to ensure that as large a proportion as possible of the Soviet technicians should be fully trained Communists. A few of them had visited Germany between 1939 and 1941,[2] but the great majority were ignorant of German economic methods. The fact that the economy was largely in private hands troubled the occupation authorities but little, as their orders were paramount in any case. Indeed, Soviet methods of control had developed a settled routine before the measures of expropriation and socialization were completed; only by the beginning of 1948 some 65 per cent of industrial capacity had been nationalized. But what the Russians missed from the very beginning was the clear-cut system of personal responsibility which is the epitome of Soviet economic life. There were at first almost no intermediate authorities between the occupation authorities and the primary producers. Therefore these had to be created. One of the main reasons for the rapid growth of German administrative organs in the Soviet zone was the Russian need for a clear-cut chain of responsibility. But theoretical exercises of administrative planning, as opposed to the creation of machinery to fulfil a definite administrative need, tend to obscure rather than simplify the administrative process. Hence, in the whole of Soviet controlled Eastern Europe, the increase of bureaucracy has not made for administrative efficiency. In spite of central administrations, provincial governments, and local authorities, the Soviet authorities

[1] There is perhaps a natural tendency in any official organization, military or civilian, to shelve responsibility. But whereas the Western powers encourage local officials in Germany to deal with local queries themselves, the Russians tend to do the opposite. It is to be noted that the Russian system is more congenial to the German instinct to apply pressure from above rather than below.

[2] The majority of those Soviet officials acquainted with German conditions were employed by the reparations agency and the Soviet Trading Companies, not by the SMA.

were still forced, as late as 1947, to press for direct action against individual farmers or industrial producers who had failed to fulfil the plans. Pressure on the immediate German authority responsible to the SMA proved insufficient.[1]

The SMA considered its task to be the supervision of the German authorities in the execution of the plans. Directions as to methods were frequently issued, and added incentives were provided by the frequent use of injunctions issued to particular individuals with regard to matters of relative detail. This administrative *mandamus* first recited the shortcomings of the addressee, and then went on to prescribe the detailed methods of putting them right.[2] In addition to these public censures, German officials were frequently summoned to Soviet headquarters at all levels and given detailed administrative instructions which ran counter to the normal procedure of the department concerned. In extreme cases attacks against German administrative organs appeared in the Soviet German-language paper or in the Communist press. This happened after the first currency reform in 1948, when the vice-president of the financial administration was publicly accused of incompetence and reactionary finance.[3] Thus German administrative discretion, though officially quite broad, was very uncertain. The responsibility was fixed; powers were variable.[4]

On the other hand, the SMA took a far more direct share in the production of plans. Until 1948, there was no single co-ordinated plan, but a Soviet plan, a central German plan, and the sum total of the provincial plans. These were independently drawn up, and the Soviet plan was paramount. Officially the plans were based on the information supplied by individual firms. In fact, however, the Soviet plan and the central German plan usually exceeded that of the provinces by a considerable amount, and a detailed study shows them to be based on maximum utilization of raw material

[1] Löwenthal quotes innumerable instances of prosecutions against individuals at the direct instigation of the SMA.

[2] For example, Order of 16 April 1946. An order was issued to ensure hygienic control of food processing factories. '. . . Special investigation has shown that a large number of undertakings are in an unsatisfactory state.' Some outstanding examples are named. Then follow a number of detailed instructions similar to those contained in a British Factory Act. Finally, certain individuals are named as responsible in case of non-compliance. Another example is given by Löwenthal, *op. cit.*, p. 149, dealing with Thuringia.

[3] Compare this with the occasional attacks on individual Russian ministers in *Pravda*; for instance, the attack on Benediktov, the Minister of Agriculture, in March 1950.

[4] The Germans normally use the 'line and staff' method of administration. The Russians divide responsibility into execution, which is along a line, and responsibility for failure, which is individual, and thus make it impossible to fit their system into any category normally used in Western administration.

figures rather than on a series of actual output figures per factory. The agricultural plans particularly were often sadly out of touch with real conditions, taking no notice of distributional difficulties. Since 1948 there have been long-term plans agreed between the Russians and the German political and administrative organs, on the scale of the Soviet five-year plans.[1]

These early plans were issued to German authorities as orders to be carried out. This difference between planning and executive authority greatly reduced the status and independence of the German administrative bodies. Somehow planning seems to require, in the eyes of the Russians, a superior quality to mere execution, and this preserve was more exclusively reserved to the occupation authorities. The plans themselves were largely drawn on the Russian model. In this way the Russians soon managed to avoid losing themselves in the intricacies of the unfamiliar German economy, and left the onus of reconciling the Soviet style plans with a non-Soviet economy on the German authorities. The direct intervention of Soviet officers, which had been a feature of the early months of occupation, soon gave way to the organized separation of planning and execution. This must be borne in mind when considering the relative success of the Russians in adapting themselves to the German situation.[2]

This did not apply to the same extent to the non-economic departments of the SMA. There the Soviet administrators were perhaps at their best. In matters of education the Soviet authorities showed themselves well-informed and active in extending German educational services.[3] On the legal side the chief obstacle was the fundamentally different outlook on law as between German and Soviet lawyers, but the Russians were anxious to create the full complement of courts and officials.[4] In the administration of public health the record of Soviet officials and doctors was impressive. On the whole the Soviet administrators were very hard-working and well informed on matters under their control, and Germans and Russians worked well together, particularly in the more

[1] The more difficult the economic situation, the more high-sounding the plans. Compare the discussion of the first Soviet five-year plan in Deutscher, *Stalin*, pp. 325–32.

[2] Compare the statement in 1947 of the then Saxon Economic Minister, Selbmann, quoted by Schaffer, *op. cit.*, p. 53: 'We don't only draw up a general plan. We ascertain the figures by basing them on the capacity of the individual enterprise, its man power, and the raw materials at its disposal. Then we find out the figures for the whole plan, co-ordinate them, and finally distribute the production quotas to the factories.'

[3] See Schaffer, *op. cit.*, Chap. 9, pp. 119–28.

[4] See below, Chap. V, pp. 118–19.

technical fields. The mutual respect of experts is always considerable. It is thus possible to say that, where no fundamental matters of controversy or difference have arisen, the Russian officials were on the whole successful in their experiment of administering a foreign country.[1]

While the technicians and administrators worked fairly closely with the Germans, the Soviet political officials confined their German contacts to proved and reliable Communists to whom they issue direct orders. The political work of the Russian Military Government was carried out by two main organizations: the political department of the SMA, and the MVD, successor to the NKVD and the GPU. The political department fulfilled the function of representing the Russians on the four-power political committee, and governed the political policy and actions of the SMA in the Russian zone under the supreme control of the Politburo. In its capacity as the Soviet delegation to the Control Council it co-operated with other delegations in preparing and executing quadripartite orders affecting the political life of Germany. It will cause no surprise that the activities of the political committee of the Control Council were now marked by a great degree of unanimity.

Its zonal functions were far more important. As Marxist theory and Russian practice demand that everything be viewed from a political standpoint, the rôle of a delphic oracle fell to Colonel Tulpanov, the head of the department, and his staff. Its task was manifold. It was responsible for liaison with, or control of, the German political parties in the Russian zone. The amalgamation of Socialists and Communists in April 1946 took place under its auspices. At the very least the planning of policy and actions by the central Secretariat of the Unity Party was carried out in consultation with this department of the SMA.

Equally important was the control of the department over the Russians themselves in Germany. The information available about internal Russian organization is very sketchy and unreliable. But whatever political supervision was exercised over the Russian officials was in the hands of the political department. Its officials were responsible for the political indoctrination lectures which the majority of Russians in Germany attended. They also supervised

[1] Those who met Stalin during and just after the war have expressed their impression to the author that while the Russian leader considered the Germans to be political cattle, they were at the same time the most efficient people in the world. The only way to impress them was to be super-efficient towards them. This policy has to some extent been followed in Germany.

the activities and attitude of officials on the ground. To what extent the department was responsible for changes in personnel within the SMA it is impossible to say. In the eyes of German political personalities in the Eastern zone, at any rate, the political department of the SMA was extremely powerful, and, in the case of non-Communists, dangerous.

The activities of the MVD were also something of an unknown quantity. Like the Gestapo under Hitler's régime, it has become legendary to the extent that almost everything is attributed to its machinations. Its personnel was large, almost every big or small Russian headquarters had an MVD unit attached to it. Thus it combined the police activities of the Gestapo with the para-military duties of the former General SS. It carried out the arrests and internment of Nazis and other persons whom the Russians considered undesirable, and the political interrogations of all Germans in the Russian zone. Frequently discussions on an economic or technical subject between Germans and Russians were attended by an officer of the MVD. During the blockade of Berlin, many of the talks between members of the Magistrat and Russian military government officials were blessed with the presence of a silent delegation of the MVD. At the same time its duties seemed to include the running of minor spies and agents into the Western sectors of Berlin and the Western zones. Reciprocally, many of the Allied personnel arrested by the Russians in their sector of Berlin (invariably under the suspicion of spying) were interviewed by an MVD official.[1]

One of its most important tasks was the supervision and training of the new East German police. When the special administration for internal affairs was founded in 1947 police matters were transferred to it from the control of the provincial governments. The new department was directly run by the MVD. Gradually the secrecy surrounding the reorganization was lifted, and as the People's Police took shape it became increasingly associated with the MVD. Apart from its normal police activities, the German force assisted the Russians in the guarding of concentration camps, the protection of special security areas such as the Saxon uranium mines, and the operations against undesirable political elements in the Soviet zone and Western Berlin.[2] At the higher levels the

[1] For the details of MVD control over German administrative bodies in the Russian zone, see below, Chap. V.

[2] Several members of the East German police were sentenced to imprisonment by an American Court for an attempt at kidnapping in Western Berlin on Soviet orders.

new police appeared by 1949 to be permeated with MVD officials, and it is probable that if the Russians withdraw from the zone, these officials will remain. The MVD also directly controlled the Ministry of State Security, created at the beginning of 1950.

The Russian method of administration was on the whole not uncongenial to the Germans. Instead of being advised or counselled, they were commanded. In the chaos that existed at the end of the war, this was probably the only way to achieve results. One example will serve to illustrate this point. According to a Control Council decision of June 1945, the wearing of a German uniform, except on the part of prisoners of war, was forbidden throughout Germany. Owing to the shortage of clothes, this order was generally disobeyed all over Germany. On 25 July 1945 the head of the SMA, Marshal Zhukov, issued the following order:[1]

Former members of the German Armed Services are still wearing military uniform. I command:

I. The wearing of military uniform by former military personnel of the German Armed Services is forbidden as from 26 July 1945. Further, the wearing of all other uniforms of military colour is prohibited.

II. The military Commandant of Berlin and the Commandants of towns and districts will exercise the strictest supervision over the execution of this order.

With a very few exceptions the practice, apart from Army caps without badges, ceased forthwith. In the British and American zones, where the Order was never vigorously enforced, the practice continued to a far greater extent.[2]

Matters of personnel were decided on the basis of two simple questions. Was a man useful, and had he been a Nazi? The materialist conception of a man's usefulness as a general basis of approach has been used for a long time in Russia, and though strongly embodied in Marxist ideas is by no means exclusive to that philosophy. In Germany it was much in vogue during the Nazi period, and remains as a relic of that heterogeneous philosophy. To-day it is a *leitmotif* of government in the Eastern zone. One's future is always reckoned in terms of usefulness; if a superior is rude the question of the potential decline of one's usefulness immediately becomes actual. This criterion brought about some strange results. There existed, for instance, a considerable class of German experts of one sort or another in the Eastern zone who

[1] *Proclamation* No. 12, 25 July 1945.
[2] Davidson, *Germany: What Now?* (London, 1950), p. 66.

lived well under direct Russian protection without doing anything at all, merely because the Russians felt they might one day be useful. This applied particularly to technical experts in Berlin who repeatedly received tempting offers from the SMA, coupled with a generous measure of quiet assistance, and who at the same time, by living in the Western sector, could not be coerced. One of them, a chemist of some distinction, lived comfortably on this basis for three years after the end of the war without the slightest intention of ever accepting any of the offers. There were cases of political opponents of the SED who, while being slandered almost daily in the Eastern zone press, received gifts from time to time from the SMA, coupled with offers of a good position in the SED itself.

This consideration of value often overrode the most elementary political logic. Even after repeated purges of non-Communists in the German administration, it was still possible to come across a personal dossier in the political department which read: 'Politically intolerable, but technically irreplaceable on Russian orders.'[1] We shall see later how sometimes the political and technical considerations were in direct opposition for almost three years, and how they almost caused differences between Russian and German Communists. As far as the Russians are concerned, technical usefulness was always a very strong consideration, but it was still the exception where political orthodoxy is the rule. The test of political orthodoxy may, of course, have gone no further than membership of the Unity Party.

It should not, of course, be imagined that this Machiavellian attitude completely governed the outlook of every Russian at all times to the exclusion of all personal feelings. It happened not infrequently that even Germans high in Russian favour suddenly found themselves assaulted both verbally and physically by Russian soldiers. Rumour has it that late in 1946 Wilhelm Pieck, whose picture now forms an integral part of street decoration in Eastern Germany, was held up and robbed by some Russian soldiers in spite of repeated asseverations of his status. Many Germans who thought that they had the confidence of the SMA, could not help feeling all the time that they never really knew where they were. This feeling of uncertainty was not confined to the Germans; Britons and Americans were frequent sufferers.

National Socialism was another criterion. It was made one of the main Russian instruments of policy and propaganda, and a terrifyingly successful weapon it has proved. As denazification

[1] Löwenthal, *op. cit.*, quotes similar examples.

pure and simple, it will be discussed elsewhere, but as part of the general Russian attitude it must be mentioned here. The Soviet Government was careful to claim authorship of the distinction between Germany and Hitlerite, Nazi or Fascist Germany.[1] Their attitude, the Russians hoped, would bear fruit at the later peace conferences. In spite of the fact that circumstances had greatly changed, and that the German response was obviously not going to be impressive, the Russians went ahead in 1947 with their intention of making themselves the champions of a united Germany, at a time when M. Thorez was blowing the traditional French trumpet of a weak Germany. They were still doing so in 1950.

When the Russians first arrived in Germany, National Socialism was made taboo for Germans. On the Russian side the politics of usefulness sometimes prevailed over those of anti-Fascism. Prominent Nazis were employed under direct Russian supervision, without the knowledge or assistance of local German administrative bodies. Some flagrant cases were suddenly and devastatingly cited by Mr. Bevin at Moscow in 1947 in answer to Mr. Molotov's routine accusations that denazification in the West was a farce. The list was headed by the German tank expert, Augustin, who was designing tanks for the Russians, and Ochel, the best railway locomotive engineer of the Third Reich, who had been a *Wehrwirtschaftsführer*.[2] There are other examples which have never yet seen the light of day, such as the various research engineers employed in the 'technical stations'[3] of the SMA, dealing with submarine motor and jet propeller research. Then there were the various scientists in Berlin doing research for the Russians on German rainfall, flood incidence, and drainage, some of whom held high positions under the Nazis. In a moment of cynicism, a Russian officer once remarked to one of his German assistants, 'As we are unlikely to be affected politically, we use the brains of the Nazis as much as possible. It is a different matter for you.'[4]

On the other side is the fact that no special treatment was meted out by the Russians to those Nazis under arrest as distinct from the various other 'enemies of democracy', such as unrepentant members of the German Social Democratic Party after the amalgamation, factory owners whose works were on the nationalization

[1] See above, Chap. II, p. 36.

[2] A semi-honorary title given to those Nazi industrialists or technicians who were made responsible in their local areas for assuring the maximum production and alignment of industry for the war.

[3] So-called *Technische Büros*. Usually a cover name for scientific research, frequently in fields banned by the Potsdam Agreement.

[4] See also Löwenthal for some minor, though flagrant, examples.

list, black-marketeers, and others. All these were lodged in the same camps as the Nazis. In fact, while a general amnesty and release from internment for minor Nazis and even criminals was declared in 1948 on the order of Marshal Sokolowski, no such general relief was ever afforded to non-Nazi internees.

The former concentration camps were used to intern Nazis by the Western powers[1] as well as by the Russians. But Nazis were not the only inmates of the Soviet-controlled camps. Once the term 'Fascist' replaced 'Nazi' as a cognomen for the enemies of the régime, it was possible to include all actual and potential opponents in this category. Indeed, the word Nazi became a relic of former days, and reactionaries, recalcitrant capitalists, supporters of the Social Democrats, and economic saboteurs were placed on the same footing, except that their crimes, being more recent, were considered more grave. This again was normal Soviet practice, which makes little distinction between one political crime and another. In addition to the camps taken over by the Russians, such as Sachsenhausen-Oranienburg, and Buchenwald, new camps were opened at Frankfort-Oder, Lieberose, Forst, Torgau (formerly a prisoner of war camp), Bitterfeld, Muehlberg, Bantzau, Altenhain, Stern-Buchholz, Beeskow, and one just north of the Berlin boundary.[2] The total number of inmates during 1947 was estimated at 25,000 in an official American survey. In 1949, however, it was reported that on the request of the Unity Party, all the camps but one were closed, and the inmates placed into German prisons. These camps distinguished prisoners held direct by the Soviet authorities, as opposed to those held by the Germans, even on Soviet instructions. They were administered by Soviet officials with the assistance, from the summer of 1947, of the German police. There is definite evidence from German railway logs that large numbers of prisoners were transferred to the Soviet Union from time to time.[3] Conditions are believed to have been bad.[4]

After the formation of the East German Government the occupation altered its form considerably. The large centre staff of the central and provincial SMA was reduced, though not to the same extent as the Anglo-American staffs. Much of the work of the new

[1] Thus Dachau was used by the Americans, Neuengamme by the British.

[2] There were at one time as many as fifteen, but some have been broken up. See Löwenthal, *op. cit.*, p. 254–5.

[3] This is confirmed by Löwenthal, *ibid.*

[4] Nevertheless, statements in the press of Western Germany and Western Berlin should be treated with some reserve. In 1949, a church mission reported publicly that conditions were no worse than in refugee camps in the Western zone. The report added, however, that not all the camps could be visited.

ministries was taken over from the departments of the SMA and some of the responsibility as well. From the Russian point of view, the constitutional position of the Soviet Control Commission was one of a supervisory and advisory body, while the German authorities, within the sphere allotted to them, possessed independence of action and decision. On paper, indeed, the Control Commission renounced direct control over spheres which the Western powers had not yet handed over to the Bonn Government. One of these was foreign affairs. Thus, while the West German republic was limited to the control of consular representatives abroad, the Eastern Government had its own foreign affairs organization, headed by a minister. But Soviet constitutional edifices are notoriously at variance with political realities, and Eastern Germany is no exception to this rule.[1]

The close connection between the Unity Party and the Soviet political authority, and between the German police and the MVD, which survived the creation of the East German republic, in effect nullified the seeming independence of the latter. But the control was disguised and unofficial; instead of being exercised through open and peremptory directives, it was wielded in secret, but still peremptory, instructions. Such was the Soviet order of January 1950, addressed to the Unity Party headquarters, calling for a reorganization of the German Security Service. One result of this was to enhance the importance of the purely political functionaries at the expense of the administration, as the former were now the main channel for Soviet orders. This development is in accordance with the principles applied in the U.S.S.R. and in the other peoples' republics of the East. The creation of the East German Government changed the function and structure of the Soviet occupation authority and brought it into line with those Soviet bodies of control, the so-called Embassies, in the other Eastern European countries. This development was by no means complete in June 1950, for an official control authority then still existed and functioned in Germany.

[1] For instance, the Soviet constitution of 1936 is the only federal constitution in existence which enables the member-republics of the Union to secede if they so desire (Article 35). Yet, as Professor Wheare drily points out, 'the U.S.S.R. is the one [country] where the exercise of the right [to secede] is least likely to be permitted.' *Federal Government* (London, 1947), p. 92.

CHAPTER IV

THE DEVELOPMENT OF POLITICS

I

FILLING THE POLITICAL VACUUM: MAY 1945–OCTOBER 1946

THE importance of politics in the Eastern zone sprang from the fact that the Russians deliberately made them so important. Apart from being the great Marxist driving force, the dominant political party in newly Communist-controlled countries occupied a quite special position. Instead of coming into power as a result of democratic elections, it tried to persuade the people of the superiority of its programme after it has gained control. It is a grave error to believe that Communism, like Hobbes' Leviathan, is prepared to govern for people's ultimate good in spite of their unwillingness to accept it, without making every effort to popularize itself among the people who have perforce to accept its domination. This rôle of making Communism acceptable after it has been forcibly imposed is one of the main tasks of Soviet Marxist politics after political victory. The counterforce to established Communism is the resistance to Communism on the part of all those elements who feel their existence threatened by it. In the case of Germany, these elements were very various, and not even united by the joint fear of destruction. They included former Nazis, a few nationalists who had failed to find refuge under another temporary flag, liberals in economics and politics, Marxists who disagreed with the Russian interpretation of the common prophet, and, finally, non-political human beings who simply did not want politics forced on them. Political life in the Eastern zone, then, was quite unlike political life in the West. Far from being a mere pretence, it was very real. A certain amount of lip service was paid from time to time to non-political reconstruction, particularly at the beginning of the occupation, and this found expression in the creation of a number of allegedly non-political organizations like the Trade Unions and the peasants' co-operative. There is no doubt, however, that the dominant party took its political work very seriously.[1]

[1] See, for instance, the Unity party's tactical instruction sheet, *Wille und Weg*, published monthly for Party officials in Berlin.

The first parties to appear out of the political vacuum of 1945 in the Russian zone were the Communists and the Social Democrats.[1] During the twelve years of Nazi rule the two parties, who had been bitter enemies, adopted different tactics.[2] The Social Democrats were in a way worse off because as a heterogenous party they had lost all cohesion under Nazi pressure. Their relations with organized labour were destroyed when the Trade Unions were broken up. A few of their members had earlier joined the Nazis and formed the left wing of the Nazi movement, such as Strasser, though most of these were in turn 'purged' by the Nazis. Other Social Democrats left politics altogether and retired into private life, like Noske. Some emigrated, like the former editor of *Vorwärts*, Stampfer; still others, mostly the men who had not been right at the top of the Movement, went underground, like Leuschner, who was later hanged after 20 July 1944. Finally, a few made common cause with the Communists. The resuscitated SPD of 1945 reflected the long period of disunity.

The SPD, more than any other party, paid the price for its failures and disunity between 1918 and 1933.[3]

The KPD reacted, or was forced to react, quite differently. Its membership, which was reputed to have totalled almost two million in Germany in 1933, disappeared to nothing overnight. Most of its party leaders were either arrested and killed, like Ernst Torgler, or managed to escape to Russia[4] or to the West. There remained at liberty in Germany only minute, well-camouflaged cells of a few individuals, who exerted almost no influence around them, and whose main object was simply to keep alive. Periodically signs of life appeared from them, such as scrawls of 'Hamburg remains Red' on bombed houses after a heavy raid during the war. Investigations since the war have shown that they were a minor, but nevertheless consistent, source of anxiety to the Gestapo. Only in one case was an espionage and resistance organization uncovered by the Nazis which was directed from and reporting to Moscow, but the great majority of its leaders were in no sense

[1] KPD (Communist Party of Germany); SPD (Social Democratic Party of Germany).

[2] For the pre-Nazi relations between the two parties, see Ruth Fischer, *Stalin and German Communism.* For Soviet policy see Deutscher, *op. cit.*; Beloff, *Foreign Policy of Soviet Russia,* Vol. I (London, 1947).

[3] For an interesting if slightly biassed account of German Social Democracy between the two wars, see Friedrich Stampfer, *Die vierzehn Jahre der ersten Deutschen Republik,* Verlagsanstalt Graphia, Karlovy Vary, 1936.

[4] Many of its prominent leaders, such as Neumann, Remmele and Max Hoelz, were purged in the great trials or murdered in the Soviet Union, 1935–7.

Communists, but rather upper-class business-men and officers.[1]

In another sphere the Communists were, however, extremely active. The concentration camps established by the Nazis provided a fertile ground for Communist propaganda. The Communist inmates were often the only ones who had been politically active and who were politically trained. At first, before the mass pogroms against the Jews got under way, the Communists were in a majority among the inmates. Finally they tended to be deliberately selected by the Nazis for posts in the camp hierarchy, which gave them a sort of authority among the inmates.[2] Since joint suffering establishes strong bonds of comradeship, it is not surprising that the organizations of ex-concentration camp inmates, victims of Fascism, etc., started as genuine associations for social purposes and as economic pressure groups in all liberated countries, but were from the first largely controlled by Communists. In Germany, as elsewhere, this proved a useful political weapon for them. There are two such organizations of importance, the 'Victims of Fascism'[3] and the 'Society of Victims of National Socialism'.[4] As the chaotic conditions in Germany, and the resentment of the German population, made a just restitution of the property of Jews and other Nazi victims almost impossible, these organizations, the only effective native mouthpiece for these unfortunates, played an important rôle. The Communists were thus able to influence a considerable section of public opinion not necessarily sympathetic to their political ideas. It took a long time, and much hesitation, before non-Communist members of the organization were prepared to dissociate themselves from their leaders, and they were promptly denounced as ungrateful.

At the end of the war began the ruthless exploitation for Communist purposes of the prevalent anti-Nazi feeling. Communists in all countries came out as the arch-enemies of the Fascist or National-Socialist idea, and claimed to have been the first to fight whole-heartedly against it. This claim was pressed in all the Allied

[1] For the story of the so-called 'Rote Kapelle' see the Berlin periodical, *Illustrierte*, of July, 1947.

[2] The German system of 'self-government' in concentration camps and the duplication of the German administration by an internee hierarchy assisted this development. The system was particularly highly developed in Terezin, Sachsenhausen, and Auschwitz. See Eugen Kogon, *The Theory and Practice of Hell* (London, 1950).

[3] ODF (*Opfer des Faschismus*). This organization was founded in 1945 to help all those who had suffered under the Nazis in Germany. It also operated in Western Germany.

[4] VVN (*Verband der Verfolgten des Nationalsozialismus*), an almost completely Communist organization founded in the Eastern zone in 1946.

countries, and its effects on Communist strength in France, Italy, and the Balkan countries are well known. Its effects on Germany will be examined in some detail.

It must first of all be admitted that the claim itself is by no means fictitious or entirely unjustified. We now know the circumstances of the Russo-German mutual defence pact of August 1939,[1] and whatever its immediate effects, it was on neither side considered at best more than a mutually advantageous *modus vivendi*, at worst a short-term respite. After this two-year period, Communism, from whatever motive, was an uncompromising enemy of National-Socialist Germany. The particularly effective Communist resistance movements in the occupied countries towards the end of the war increased their moral prestige enormously.[2]

The possibility which these circumstances offered to the Russians and the German Communists was twofold. In the first place German political opponents could be very effectively silenced by the accusation of National Socialism. Whether this accusation was true or not was of little actual importance. Very few people in the first two years of occupation would openly speak up in defence of anyone who was officially decried as a National-Socialist, particularly if the charge was endorsed by the occupying power. In England the Communist tactic of calling their opponents Fascists has become a matter of polite amusement. In Germany, where every destroyed building bears silent witness to the armed detestation of National Socialism by the civilized world, the charge of sympathizing with National Socialism was a very serious and crippling indictment—often enough by itself to do the work of a denazification court. This method of public appeal[3] was highly successful in the Soviet zone, where it became the official way of eliminating unwanted possessors of desirable property, or potentially dangerous political opponents.

The second method of exploiting anti-Nazi sentiment was the disguise of every kind of activity under the cloak of denazification and demilitarization. Actions which in other Eastern countries

[1] cf. the selection of German F.O. documents, *Nazi-Soviet Relations 1939–1941*, published in 1948 by the U.S. State Department, No. 3023. Also A. Rossi, *Deux ans d'alliance Germano-Soviétique* (Fayard, Paris, 1948).

[2] It is not suggested that the Russian contribution to the war was greater or more wholehearted than that of anybody else. Nevertheless, for those who, since 1933, made it their first task to combat Nazi Germany with all the means at their disposal, the prestige of the Soviet Union was, and to some extent still is, considerable. Nor are these people a mere handful. It is only necessary to cite as an example the International Brigade in Spain, of which not even the majority were Communists.

[3] In its old legal sense of accusation.

needed the full support of Russian Marxist theory could conveniently be carried out in Germany as part and parcel of a policy aimed at the very worthy object of eliminating National Socialism and the German *Junkertum*. The best examples of legislation disguised in this way were the land reform of 1945 and the continuous process of nationalizing industrial capacity.[1] But again there is some measure of truth in the anti-Nazi label. The land reform has in fact broken the powers of the Junkers, while the expropriated proportion of the total value of industrial capacity in the Soviet zone does contain the great majority of the holdings of Nazis and of the big cartels and trusts.

It would not be an exaggeration to say that the claim of destroying National Socialism in all its forms was used for almost every action taken by the German Communists until the beginning of 1948. Thus the amalgamation of KPD and SPD was to 'strengthen the working class movement in its fight against Fascism in Germany'.[2] Similarly the attacks of the Communists on the bourgeois parties in the East were always aimed at alleged National-Socialist tendencies within them.[3] Even more important than the consistent use of this disguise was the spirit accompanying the practice. Everything was discussed in relation to the problem of National Socialism. Everything was compared to the facts of ten years ago. Officially, at any rate, there were only two kinds of people in the Soviet zone, Nazis and anti-Nazis, until 1948. During the three years 1945–8, the Communist programme at face value seemed nothing but the negative policy of eradicating National Socialism. Like any martial faith, indeed like National Socialism itself, Russian Marxism in Germany thrived on having something to destroy, although it has always prided itself on its 'positive policy'.[4]

Denazification in its broadest sense was discussed everywhere all the time. Two years of constant and public reiteration of its importance made it come to be accepted as as much a matter of

[1] Known throughout Germany as 'Socializing'.

[2] cf. *Täglische Rundschau*, 30 Oct. 1946.

[3] See, for instance, Löwenthal, *op. cit.*, p. 101, for a Unity Party election poster which stated: '. . . Fascists of the worst sort are on the . . . list of the CDU.'

[4] For the relation of these facts to Communist theory see below, Chapter XI. The red-herring of anti-Nazism as the sole *raison d'être* for most legislation in the Soviet zone has been swallowed, not without factual indigestion, by Gordon Schaffer in his book, *The Russian Zone*. In every discussion, relevantly or not, someone's or something's connection with National Socialism appears. Important as it is, it can be overdone, particularly when it is only a camouflage. Even Löwenthal meticulously gives the political record after 1933 of most of the people whose cases he cites, both Communists and non-Communists.

course as the rising and setting of the sun, and although many in their heart of hearts remained unconvinced, they accepted the post-war phraseology of condemnation, and acted accordingly. It was almost impossible for a declared or thinly disguised Nazi to escape the activities of the so-called *Antifa* committees in the villages and towns of Eastern Germany. There was nothing legalistic about Eastern denazification; it was intended to be political. In one respect it was more effective than in the West, for it never attempted to deal judicially with a purely political evil.

One of the developments of the anti-Nazi crusade was the fact that it enabled the Communists in the East to obtain many positions of power without the machinery of democratic elections. As usual there was a certain amount to be said for the Communist case. Elections immediately after the end of the war were obviously out of the question. Denazification had been accepted by all the occupying powers as a matter of absolute right and necessity. As the Communists claimed, not unjustifiably, that they were the only German party capable or willing to carry out really thorough denazification, many of the German administrative posts in the Eastern zone were filled by Communists. This was quite logical if it was held that the Germans should, from the very beginning, be responsible for denazification. That was the declared Russian view.[1] The fact that by this means Communists could be quietly installed in important positions for other purposes, is of course another matter.

The political groups in the Russian zone immediately after the end of the war, as far as they can be separated, divide into three: the very active and numerically small group of Communists; the broader, slower and larger group of Social Democrats; and the politically inert mass of the majority of Germans. As the working class, even those members of it who had been supporters of National Socialism, did not hesitate for long before availing itself of the new opportunity of participating in the one favoured working-class movement in the Eastern zone, the remaining raw material of politics was mostly middle class. There was not much opportunity of independent political action for the middle class. The Communist policy which we have described made it very difficult to be anti-Nazi and anti-Communist at the same time. A few, whose anti-Nazi attitude was irrefutable, succeeded in obtaining administrative positions at first, but their political support was

[1] See Molotov's speeches, as reported in *Pravda*, during the Foreign Ministers' Conference in London, November 1947.

cut away from them until they were almost isolated.[1] It was difficult to found political parties of middle-class origin and with middle-class aims from inside the Soviet zone. However, any 'democratic' party founded in one zone of occupation could apply for permission to extend its activities across the zonal frontiers. By the autumn two large middle-class parties had been organized in the British and American zones and applied for Russian permission to organize in the Soviet zone. Since it was not yet the fashion to denounce as Fascist political parties which had the open approval of the Western Allies, the Russian permission was given. A refusal would have disrupted the anti-Nazi dustsheet covering politics in the Eastern zone.

The two parties were the Christian Democratic Union and the Democratic Liberal Party.[2] Of these the former was the larger and more important. It was, and is, a very heterogeneous party of broad middle-class origin, with the support of the Christian Trades Union and, at first, a certain following among the working class. It did not exist as a separate party before 1933, but has absorbed many of the supporters of the various centre and right parties who were not too heavily compromised by later Nazi activities.[3] It was designed to embrace all the non-Socialist elements in a party advocating democratic reconstruction on Christian principles. Its strength was its wide basis and consequent large numerical support, and the fact that it compromised between the self-flagellation of many German Communists and Socialists on the question of guilt, and an openly unrepentant attitude unacceptable to the Allies. Its main weakness was a somewhat loose programme and organization.

The LDP was an emasculated resurrection of the old Liberals, the German Democratic Party of Weimar days. Like its counterpart in England, it had become, by 1933, a party the eminence of whose members far outweighted its importance or strength. Some of them fell by the Nazi wayside, though these were relatively few. After the war the Party retained its former characteristics; containing non-Nazis rather than anti-Nazis, it became a party of distinguished and elderly men who were often

[1] Thus, for instance, Dr. Ferdinand Friedensburg, deputy mayor of Berlin, and Dr. Jacob Kaiser, the former head of the CDU in the East, and in 1950 Minister for all-German Affairs in the West German Federal Republic.

[2] CDU (*Christlich-Demokratische Union*, known as CSU in parts of the U.S. zone); LDP (*Liberale Demokratische Partei*).

[3] These parties were: *Zentrums Partei* (Centre Party), *Deutsch-Nationale Volkspartei* (German National Party) and the *Christliche Volkspartei* (Christian People's Party).

given positions of importance more by virtue of their personal status than through their party's strength.

By the end of 1945 the political field in the Eastern zone was occupied by four parties, all of which also existed in the Anglo-American area of occupation.[1] The Communists were obviously based on the Russian zone, the Socialists were at that time uncertain if they should commit themselves in any direction and were operating equally strongly in the West and in the East. The two 'bourgeois' parties[2] were committed chiefly to the West. The popular strength of all four parties was still small, as the system of party politics was something which existed only in distant memories and those not altogether happy. While the Communists were probably the best-organized party in the East as well as the West, they were smaller in numbers than either the CDU or the SPD in any of the three zones. In the East, the organization of the Socialists and Communists was quicker than in the West. This was due to the priority which politics enjoyed in the East. All political parties benefited to some extent from the Russians' desire to cultivate political activity ostensibly as a weapon against the remnants of National Socialism.

We have already mentioned the initial advantages of the Communists over the Social Democrats. Nevertheless the period May 1945 to October 1946 was really the period of ascendancy for the Social Democrats in the Eastern zone. In view of the now obvious Russian intention of installing an uncompromisingly Communist régime there, and the traditional weaknesses of German Social democracy, this seems a strange statement. Yet it is an undoubted fact.

By July 1945 the Russians were ready to form the Central German Administrations for the Russian zone. In these the Communists were in a distinct minority as compared to members of the Social Democrats, the bourgeois parties, and those belonging to no political party. The main demand at that time was for personal capability. As many distinguished administrators, technicians, and economists as were politically untainted were approached in Berlin and in the zone. No lengthy personal investigations were made, provided there was no outstanding evidence or suspicion. If somebody had been in prison or in a concentration camp under

[1] The French disapproved of any sign of interzonal political life and put many obstacles in the way of any German political development which did not accept its own views of loose federalism. Who shall say that this was not also a 'breach of Potsdam'?

[2] Their usual name in the Soviet zone.

the Nazis, and thus was a member of the ODF, he was automatically acceptable. In some cases even years of devoted service to the National-Socialist State were overlooked for the sake of a week in a concentration camp. One of the outstanding examples of this was Dr. Landwehr, who had negotiated many of Germany's economic agreements with the Balkans. His membership of the ODF was due to his arrest in August 1944 on suspicion of having harboured Dr. Goerdeler, of 20 July 1944 fame. Under the Russians he became head of the economic department of the Berlin German city government. This recruitment of personnel coincided with the beginning of party politics. Many of the new functionaries who were not Communists joined the SPD, as being progressive without being revolutionary, and because that party seemed to be enjoying the Russians' favour, or at least was not being openly hindered by them. At the same time it was in the interest of the SPD to obtain the support of as many people 'in office' as possible, thus linking the purely political organization of the Party and the German administration, in the same way as the Communists were doing. The principle of non-political civil servants had never developed in Germany and it was quite in order even for members of the police force to be politically active. As the Russians encouraged political activity among their German functionaries, membership of the SPD seemed for many the best compromise solution between Communism and what were regarded as non-progressive middle-class politics. By the end of 1945 many local officials and members of the new Central Administrations belonged to the Social Democratic Party.

Outside its important rôle in the local and central administrative agencies, the purely political organization of the SPD in the Soviet zone was growing apace. The party operated with the Communists in the anti-Nazi front, and if it did not approve of all that was done under that cover, there were as yet no open signs of discord. The plea of working-class solidarity gave the impression that the Russians would be glad to see a strong SPD in alliance with the Communists. The Russians did little openly to contradict this point of view at this time, and for some SPD leaders, who had had pre-1933 experience of Communist tactics, to voice possible doubts of the future involved the danger of being charged with anti-Russian propaganda and bad faith, offences categorized at that time as 'neo-fascist'.

The SPD party organization was particularly strong in Berlin and in Saxony. Both areas had a Socialist tradition, and their dense population made them the two most important focal points. Saxony's position was pre-eminent in the Soviet zone owing to its size of population, its industrial resources, and its historic rôle as an independent province. Out of the total 20½ million population of the Soviet zone including Berlin in 1946, almost 6½ million lived in Land Saxony.[1] The other four provinces of the Soviet zone were either new administrative creations altogether, like Saxony-Anhalt, or consisted of a mixture of old and new boundaries, such as Mecklenburg-Pomerania with its new Polish frontier; Brandenburg, an enlargement of the old Kurmark created out of the geographical ruin of Prussia; and Thuringia, newly created in 1919. Saxony, however, had been an independent, if diminishing, kingdom until 1918, and a province under the Federal Republic. Its strong local character stood out particularly in the immediate post-war chaos of 1945, and was fully acknowledged by the Russians, who treated Saxon opinion as representative of, and equivalent to, the public opinion of the whole zone.[2] After the Saxon people had said 'yes' to a referendum on the expropriation and socialization of factories owned by 'nationalist monopoly-capital and Hitlerite Fascists', the decision was enforced throughout the zone without further democratic ado. In the other provinces the approval of the elected parliaments was an *ex post facto* formality.

Berlin was under four-power control and partly a zone of its own, partly a zonal no-man's-land. The Russian sector was the largest, with eight administrative districts, the other three sectors between them containing twelve such districts. The city was also the geographical centre of the Soviet zone, as well as the focal point for postal and railway services. Both Russian and German zonal authorities were established there, the former in Karlshorst, the latter mainly in the old Air Ministry in the Leipzigerstrasse. Obviously for geographical reasons alone the city was important for the Russians.

Berlin at the end of the war also contained a considerable number of Germany's best scientists, technicians, and administrators, who had obtained a priority in the panicky exit of the Nazi hierarchy from Eastern Germany in April 1945. The majority of Germany's artists and men of letters and quite a few of its future *eminences politiques* were to be found there. Berlin also

[1] From the population analysis in *Die Neue Stadt*, Frankfurt/Main, January 1948, p. 37.

[2] This is confirmed by Löwenthal, *op. cit.*, Chap. IV.

possessed an important share of industry, and was in 1936 responsible for 9 per cent of total manufactured net value, 8½ per cent of total industrial exports, and 12 per cent of national income, while its population was only 6¼ per cent of the German total in 1937. With the industry went a politically tough-minded proletariat, which had given the Nazis their hardest nut to crack.[1] This working class contained a relatively high percentage of Communists before 1933 and a very high membership of the SPD. After the war the numerical strength of the Social Democrats was particularly great, partly because this party at once adopted the popular course of basing its organization on the city, and giving support to Berlin's strong local pride. The Social Democrats were fully aware, as indeed were the other parties and the Soviet authorities, that while the party which controlled Berlin largely controlled the Soviet zone, political control of the zone by no means carried with it control of the city, and that the absence of the latter could be a great hindrance even to successful control of the zone.

Another valuable political prize to be contended for was the control of the organized workers' movements, particularly important in a state of a Socialist or Communist character. The Free German Trades Union Association[2] was founded in the summer of 1945, and extended its activities over the Western zones as well, though it was based on Berlin and derived its main strength from the Russian zone. The Union at first assumed the character of a class instrument rather than that of a political party. This did not prevent members of the Trades Union Association also being members of a political party; though membership of the Trades Union Association was compulsory for all functionaries ('honorary proletarians') and workers, additional membership of a political party was greatly encouraged. Thus working-class strength would be increased and on paper it should in fact have doubled. In practice party issues were fought out within the Association, particularly when the paths of Communists and Social Democrats led in increasingly divergent and mutually exclusive directions. The Russians lavished much care and great sums of money on the Trades Union Movement,[3] and, having created it and nursed it through its political infancy, retained control over its policy. They

[1] See, for example, Josef Goebbels, *Kampf um Berlin* (Berlin, 1934).

[2] FDGB (*Freier Deutscher Gewerkschafts Bund*), successor to the pre-1933 ADGB.

[3] Financial contributions were made directly by the Russians, but more generally by provincial governments out of their budgets at Soviet instigation. See Löwenthal, *op. cit.*, p. 158.

were thus able to prevent the SPD from gaining too much power and numerical superiority in it, but it remained a powerful factor in the Trades Union Movement of the Soviet zone until 1947.

The other organization on somewhat similar lines and with the same purpose was the German Farmers' Co-operative.[1] It was an inevitable product of the land reform which had taken place in the Soviet zone, and was founded ostensibly to assist the many new, and often resourceless, farmers. Its other function was to provide, in accordance with the special position assigned to peasants in the Leninist development of Marxism, the same political means of class expression for peasants as the Trades Unions provided for the industrial proletariat. Membership of the Farmers' Co-operative, though it was partly a technical organization, did not preclude party politics. The potential Communist vote might therefore be further increased. The Farmers' Co-operative, like its industrial counterpart, obtained a direct influence on political affairs, both in the elected diets of the provinces, and later as the chief means of bringing 'public opinion' to bear on politically doubtful focal points, such as Berlin.

The Farmers' Co-operative and its supporters were essentially tied more than any other political party or class organization to the continuation of the *status quo* of land distribution after the reform. Since the land reform is directly responsible for the politics of the organization, it is necessary to examine the political results of this important measure.

The land reform in the Soviet zone is perhaps the most important post-war measure carried out in Eastern Germany. Its obvious purpose was to destroy the dominant agricultural interest in Eastern Germany, the big farmers and Junkers. The details of the reform had been planned during the war, and represented the highest point of Russian post-war planning for Germany. In July 1945 one of the chief planners, Hörnle, a German Communist of long standing, was flown to Berlin with instructions to carry out the scheme.[2]

The destruction of the large Eastern German estates was, however, only part of the scheme. The land was to be redistributed among the existing smaller farmers, and was to provide a new basis for the German refugees who were being expelled from Eastern Europe. A new class was to be created, whose existence

[1] VDGB, literally United German Farmers' Mutual Aid (*Vereinigung der Deutschen Bauernhilfe*). Compare, for example, with the Peasant Party of the Red Republic in Bavaria in April 1919.

[2] For the economic details of the land reform see Chapter VI.

and prosperity would replace the previous pattern of agricultural life. Clearly the existence of this new class was closely tied up with that of the régime in Eastern Germany. Irrespective of Party politics the new agricultural proprietors as a body would support whatever Government protected them against the possibility of a return of the old owners.

Though radical, the land reform cannot be described as Communist. Distribution of holdings was not by any means equal, since many old-established farmers, officially labelled as 'under-enfeoffed'[1] (to borrow a term normally applied to the Middle Ages) increased their acreage, while the allotment of land to new farmers[2] was relatively small. Only 51 per cent of the total redistributed area was given to those not previously farmers.[3] Some of the available land was to be used for allotments only, and thus became the property of only part-time farmers. Secondly, the measure established a tentatively co-operative system. Land was definitely private property, and the sharing of implements and cattle was represented as a measure of expediency in times of shortage rather than as a result of political or economic theory. In the early days of the land reform the idea of nationalization of land was as undesirable as the possibility of returning the land to its previous owners. It was, moreover, a measure of which the Social Democrats approved as wholeheartedly as the Communists, while even the two middle-class parties did not protest against the obvious necessity of destroying the power of the Junkers, but only at the absence of compensation. Whatever the further intentions of the Communists might be, the land reform could be successfully represented as a measure essentially aimed at destroying the roots from which an aggressive militarist tree had grown.[4]

[1] The official term is *land-arm*, literally 'poor in land'. Since the pre-1945 land system is treated as basically feudal by the Communists (without any real justification), the use of this medieval term is probably the best translation.

[2] The word 'new farmers' is a translation of the technical German term *Neubauern* and refers to those beneficiaries under the land reform who had not previously owned land in Eastern Germany, or to farmers who had previously worked in non-German countries from which they had since been expelled as members of the German minority.

I use the word 'farmer' in preference to the 'peasant' usually employed by the Press and by the translater of Löwenthal. The word 'peasant' is bound up with a social system of a more feudal kind, as pre-war Hungary or Poland. The German organization of agriculture was predominantly freehold, in spite of the Junkers.

[3] From *Die Bodenreform in Deutschland* issued under Russian auspices by the Bauernverlag, Berlin, 1947, p. 20. These figures are generally reliable.

[4] There is a curiously individualistic tradition in the German labour movement regarding Land reform. Although the largest as well as the most orthodox Marxist party in the world, the German Social Democratic Party before 1914 never fully accepted, even in theory, collectivization of the Land. After 1918, the SPD and

The political influence of the farmers was distinct from that of any other class or political party in the Eastern zone. While nationalization of factories made little essential difference to the direct share of the workers in the production, planning, or profit distribution of industry, the land reform turned labourers into owners on a considerable scale. Thus a new possessing class was created which owed its allegiance not to the Communists but to the administration of the zone, of whatever political colour it might be. Its enemies were the advocates of the *ancien régime* and the supporters of collectivization. But its greatest fear was to offend the Russians. Collectivization might be a future prospect, but the danger of expropriation as a result of acting contrary to the declared wish of the occupying power was very real.

The big question as to whether the Russians would carry their policy of comparative political impartiality to its logical conclusion, at least in public, remained to be settled. Under present circumstances it was possible to vote for the SPD and still carry out wholeheartedly the policy as laid down by the occupying power. If Russian aims were indeed what they were declared to be, the present trends of genuine co-operation in party politics would be confirmed and continued. If, however, the Russians had hoped that their policy would benefit the Communists at the expense of the other parties something further had to be done. The Social Democrats on the one hand enjoyed the predominant popular support, while the beginnings of resistance to Socialism of any kind was making its appearance in the programme of the Christian Democrats and the Liberals. The Communists were indeed strong in their occupation of important positions. But it was certain that the forthcoming election for the full governmental machinery of the Soviet zone would not show a Communist victory. The Potsdam Agreement[1] had stipulated that elective and representative government should be introduced into regional and provincial administration as soon as the stability of the local authorities would permit it. The Russian policy for local government was, as we have seen, relatively successful, and the provisions of the Potsdam Agreement were now to be carried out as far as the Länder were concerned. Elections for the land diet or parlia-

the Trades Unions (ADGB), in so far as they supported Land reform in practice, advocated the parcelling-up of big estates to provide a living and a home for the unemployed. See for instance Striemer, *Volkswirtschaftliche Vorträge*, (ADGB, Berlin, 1922) for the official Trade Union view, also Damaschke, *Marxismus und Bodenreform* (Jena, 1922). The conflict with Soviet theory is obvious.

[1] Section 3 (a), para. 9 (1).

ment on a proportional basis of representation would take place and be followed by the appointment by the occupying power of a Government from leaders of the majority party or parties. The first task of the new parliaments would be the drafting of a constitution for the Land, and its ratification. This had to be followed by the confirmation of legislation which had been administratively imposed, such as the land reform and the socialization of Nazi-owned factories. In fact the people of the zone were to express their opinion of the Soviet measures, and show in which of the parties they had the most confidence for the future. In view of the comprehensive policy of legislative action adopted by the Russians, their own measures, and therefore they themselves, were on trial. For the occupation authorities it was not only a question as to whether their ideological supporters did well at the polls, but whether the German people accepted the underlying principles of Soviet occupation.

A vote for the middle-class parties or for the Social Democrats, in spite of the official all-party agreement on the anti-Nazi campaign and all that it covered, would be taken by the occupying power as to some extent directed against itself.

2

THE TURNING POINT IN POLITICS: OCTOBER 1946–DECEMBER 1947

During the early spring of 1946, the political department of the SMA showed signs of unusually intense activity. German political leaders of the KPD and of the SPD could be seen going in and out of the buildings of the SMA in Karlshorst. One of the most frequent visitors was Otto Grotewohl, the leader of the SPD in Berlin and joint chairman of the Party with Dr. Kurt Schumacher of Hanover. Finally, on 22 April, came the announcement of the formation of a new Socialist Unity Party,[1] which 'in the interests of working-class solidarity' was to combine Social Democrats and Communists in one irresistible proletarian movement. In most political circles in Germany this caused great surprise. The first suggestions from the Russians and the Communists to the SPD, made some weeks before, had been flatly turned down by the great majority of the Social Democratic leaders. The official list of

[1] SED (*Sozialistische Einheitspartei Deutschlands*).

adherents to the new Party nevertheless contained the names of some prominent Berlin social democrats, among them Otto Grotewohl himself. It was known that he had spoken against fusion only four days previously at an SPD conference, and had told the Russians, in the words of Luther at Worms: 'Here I stand, I can go no further.' Now he and a number of his followers signed the statement from Communist Headquarters that the new Party would fight on a joint programme and with joint candidates in the forthcoming election. The liquidation of both Social Democrats and Communists as separate parties was announced.

We may never know the means by which the new party was formed behind the scenes. The motives of those SPD leaders who promised their support and adhesion seem to have been various. The left wing of social democracy may have doubted the ability of a heterogeneous party like the SPD to follow a truly Marxist line. Others realized that with a Labour Government in London, the driving force of the German Social Democratic Party would in future come from the West rather than the East, and so would the possibilities of promotion and power, making the Berlin SPD an isolated detachment. A considerable number saw in this combination of Social Democrats and Communists a first step in the direction of a united Marxist movement everywhere. They believed that the new Party would have a Socialist rather than a Communist bias if a sufficient number of Social Democrats could be persuaded to join it. Unofficial promises to that effect were made by the Communists.[1] For whatever reason, a considerable number of SPD functionaries in Berlin, and a smaller number from the West, gave their support to the new Party. But the main body of the Social Democrats in the West, and the greater section in the Berlin city group of the SPD refused to accept the fusion and continued to follow an independent party line. In Berlin there would still be four major parties with the prospect of a particularly fierce contest between the SPD and the Unity Party.

The amalgamation completely changed the political picture in the Soviet zone. In the absence of the Social Democratic Party, its previous members either voted for the SED or abstained altogether. Even if the official poll figures are exaggerated, there seems no doubt that the majority chose the former course. The propaganda of the SED pointed out that nothing was changed and that the previous co-operation of Social Democrats and

[1] This is evident from the statement of those who later changed their minds and returned to the Social Democratic Party.

Communists in a policy of reconstruction would simply continue by means of an identical programme instead of a similar one. Those who realized the final implication of the fusion and saw the need for immediate action had no choice but to vote for the bourgeois parties. These now changed their attitude in the Eastern zone. Influenced perhaps by a number of supporters formerly Social Democrat, they took over a more progressive line, but were from that time onwards the direct opponents of the SED, without any intermediate party of moderates. The peculiar difficulties of bourgeois politics in a Communist-controlled State gave these parties a character very different from that of their branches in the West, operating in the middle-class background of Anglo-American occupation.

These were some of the immediate effects of the fusion. The reinstitution of party politics in the Soviet zone was still too recent to have any immediate effect on the political attitude of the voting population—especially as the amalgamation had taken place before the election. The choice of new political allegiances could thus be made before commitment at the polls. Nor were the party issues sufficiently defined to make clear any obvious difference between the probable future policy of the SED and the previous 'bloc' policy of the Communists and the Social Democrats.

The results of the election were announced on 21 October 1946. They were as follows:

TABLE I

Results of Election to Provincial Diets, 21 October 1946

LAND SAXONY	*Votes*	*Percentage*
SED	1,595,723	49.6
CDU	756,740	23.3
LDP	806,163	24.8
Farmers' Co-operative	57,229	1.6
Women's Organization in conjunction with Farmers' Co-operative	35,960	0.7
	3,251,815	
Total population	5,543,345	58.66 voted

The total votes polled represent roughly 90 per cent of those entitled to vote, i.e. men and women over 21 not suffering from insanity and without more than nominal Nazi Party record.

PROVINCE SAXONY-ANHALT	*Votes*	*Percentage*
SED	1,030,889	45.8
CDU	507,397	21.9
LDP	695,685	29.9
Farmers' Co-operative	56,630	2.4
	2,290,601	
Total population	4,162,090	55.03 voted

Once again about 90 per cent of those eligible to vote polled their votes.

LAND THURINGIA	*Votes*	*Percentage*
SED	816,864	49.3
CDU	313,824	18.9
LDP	471,415	28.4
Farmers' Co-operative	55,093	3.3
	1,657,196	
Total Population	2,943,251	56.30 voted

About 86 per cent of those eligible to vote polled their votes.

LAND PROVINCE BRANDENBURG	*Votes*	*Percentage*
SED	634,786	44.5
CDU	442,206	30.8
LDP	298,311	20.6
Farmers' Co-operative	70,728	4.8
	1,446,031	
Total population	2,516,369	57.47 voted

About 85 per cent of those eligible to vote polled their votes.

LAND MECKLENBURG POMERANIA	*Votes*	*Percentage*
SED	547,663	50.0
CDU	377,868	34.0
LDP	138,572	12.0
Farmers' Co-operative	43,260	4.0
	1,107,363	
Total population	2,148,526	51.54 voted

About 70 per cent of those e igible to vote polled their votes.

This made the total number of votes cast in the Soviet zone 9,753,006 out of a total population of 17,313,581 and a voting population of 11,368,340 (excluding Berlin) and the percentage of possible votes 85.8 per cent.[1] Out of this total the SED obtained

[1] The outstanding difference between the percentage of votes polled as against those eligible to vote on the one hand, and the total population on the other is due to the widely varying number of refugees still coming in to the Soviet zone at this time. Thus the population of Mecklenburg was 45 per cent higher in 1946 than in 1939, Brandenburg plus 4 per cent, Saxony-Anhalt plus 21 per cent, Saxony plus 1 per cent, Thuringia plus 20 per cent. These statistics are taken from official population figures published under the zonal population count of 1947 and from the table quoted in *Die Neue Stadt* of January 1948.

4,625,925, the CDU 2,398,035, the LDP 2,410,146, and the VDGB 282,940.

The distribution of seats in the five provinces of the Soviet zone was as follows:

TABLE II

Distribution of Seats in Provincial Diets

LAND SAXONY

Party	Seats
SED	59 seats
CDU	28 ,,
LDP	30 ,,
Farmers' Co-operative plus Women's Organizations	3 ,,
	120

PROVINCE SAXONY-ANHALT

Party	Seats
SED	51 seats
CDU	22 ,,
LDP	24 ,,
Farmers' Co-operative	2 ,,
	99

LAND THURINGIA

Party	Seats
SED (in combination with VDGB on identical list)	47 seats
CDU	19 ,,
LDP	28 ,,
	94

LAND BRANDENBURG

Party	Seats
SED	44 seats
CDU	31 ,,
LDP	20 ,,
Farmers' Co-operative	5 ,,
	100

LAND MECKLENBURG POMERANIA

Party	Seats
SED (in combination with VDGB on identical list)	48 seats
CDU	31 ,,
LDP	11 ,,
	90

Ministerial appointments according to this representation were as follows. The selection of personalities was made by the SMA, officially with the consent of the parties concerned:

TABLE III

Distribution of Provincial Ministries

Ministry	Minister
LAND SAXONY	
Minister President	Herr Seydewitz (SED/SPD)[1]
Minister of the Interior	Dr. Kurt Fischer (SED/KPD)
Minister and Vice-President of Finance	Gerhard Rohner (CDU)
Minister of Agriculture and Forestry	Dr. Uhle (LDP)
Minister of Justice	Prof. Dr. Kästner (LDP)
Minister of Social Affairs	Walter Gähler (SED)
Minister of Economics and Labour	Fritz Selbmann (SED/KPD)
Minister of Education	Erwin Hartsch (SED)
Minister of Trade and Supply	Dr. Georg Knabe (CDU)
LAND PROVINCE SAXONY-ANHALT	
Minister President and Minister of Justice	Dr. Hubner (LDP)
Vice-President and Minister of Interior	Robert Sievert (SED/KPD)
Minister of Finance	Werner Bruschke (SED)
Minister of Agriculture, Trade and Supply	Dr. Erich Damerow (LDP)
Minister ofArt and Science	Ernst Thape (SED)
Minister of Labour and Social Affairs	Dr. Leo Herwegen (CDU)
LAND THURINGIA	
Minister President	Dr. Paul (SED/SPD)
Minister of the Interior	Werner Eggerath (SED/KPD)
Minister of Finance	Leonhard Moog (LDP)
Minister of Justice	Dr. Helmut Külz (LDP)
Minister of Administration	Ernst Busse (SED/KPD)
Minister of Cultural Affairs	Dr. Wolff (SED)
Minister of Economic Planning	Dr. Georg Appelt (SED)
Minister of Supply	Georg Grosse (CDU)
Minister of Education	Margarete Thorhorst (SED)
LAND PROVINCE BRANDENBURG	
Minister President	Dr. Karl Steinhoff (SED)
Minister of the Interior and Administration	Dr. Walter Kurse (LDP)
Minister of Justice	Dr. Ernst Stargardt (CDU)
Minister of Labour and Social Affairs	Fritz Schwob (CDU)
Minister of Education	Dr. Fritz Rucker (SED)
Minister of Economic Planning	Heinrich Rau (SED/KPD)
LAND MECKLENBURG POMERANIA	
Minister President	Wilhelm Höcker (SED)
Minister of Finance	Dr. Strasse (LDP)
Minister of Trade and Supply	Alfred Starossen (SED)
Minister of Agriculture and Forestry	Otto Möller (Farmer's Co-op.)
Minister of Administration	Hans Warnke (SED/KPD)
Minister of Cultural Affairs and Education	Gottfried Grünberg (SED/KPD)
Minister of Economic Affairs	Dr. Friedrich Witte (CDU)
Minister of Labour and Social Affairs	Fritz Burmeister (CDU)

It will be seen that the allotment of Ministries to any particular party was roughly in proportion to the percentage of seats held by the parties. Not only were the formation and number of

[1] In the case of members of the SED this shows the political origin from either the SPD or KPD. For the importance of this distinction, see below.

Ministries different in each Land but the allotment of Ministries to particular parties also varied. In no case was the same Ministry in each Land occupied by the same party throughout the zone. The nearest approach to such a position was the SED control of four out of five Ministries of the Interior, the Ministry of Administration in Mecklenburg being responsible for internal affairs. On the surface, therefore, the fact that the SED nowhere received a large absolute majority was reflected in the staffing of Ministries.

The election results showed primarily that the SPD and the KPD, had they contested the election separately, would have obtained a majority, and might well have obtained an absolute majority in each Land, if the SPD votes transferred as a result of the fusion to the CDU and LDP are taken into account. On the evidence available, it is probable that the SPD would have been the main beneficiary of what was now the joint vote. As far as the two middle-class parties were concerned the elections showed that in the industrial areas the Liberal Party was more successful than the Christian Democrats, while in the agricultural district the opposite held true. These parties together could out-vote, or at least checkmate, the SED in the diets of all provinces, more easily in Brandenburg and in Saxony-Anhalt, than in Land Saxony, Thuringia, and Mecklenburg.

In Berlin the situation was very different. The fact that the city was under four-power administration had enabled the Social Democrats, now recognized only by the English and Americans, to fight the election of the 21 October 1946 throughout the city, while the SED was reciprocally able to operate in the Western sectors. The results had been a decisive victory for the Social Democrats and a pointer to what might have happened in the Eastern zone. The results had been:

TABLE IV

Results of Election of 21 *October* 1946 *in Berlin*

SPD	..	999,170	votes and	63	seats in the city assembly
CDU	..	454,202	,, ,,	29	,, ,, ,, ,, ,,
SED	..	405,992	,, ,,	26	,, ,, ,, ,, ,,
LDP	..	192,527	,, ,,	12	,, ,, ,, ,, ,,

The percentage of possible votes given was 87.3 per cent. The SPD were thus in unquestionable control of the Berlin Magistrat or city government, whose powers were increased by the growing ineffectiveness of the four-power *kommandatura* responsible for the city owing to the differences between the constituent delegations.[1]

The situation in Berlin brought some strange anomalies in its train. Those German bodies, such as the new Central Administration, who were located in Berlin, but responsible for the zone, could not be effectively controlled by Russian standards. These administrations, although the highest administrative bodies for the Soviet zone, contained official members of the Social Democratic Party as late as January 1948. Socialist counter-propaganda to the political claims of the SED could be obtained by officials working in Berlin at any bookstall, even in the Russian sector. Meetings with political leaders from the West could without difficulty be arranged. Consequently a noticeably stiffer attitude towards the encroachment of the Unity Party was apparent among the non-Communist functionaries in Berlin—at just those high levels at which complete subservience to Russian ideas was most necessary. Two things could be attempted by the Russians to deal with this situation. Either the SED in the city must become numerically so powerful and its policy so popular that it could successfully ignore its opponents and internal deviators, or Berlin must be brought sufficiently into the orbit of the Russian zone to apply the full strength of Russian pressure on the opponents of the SED. The second method implied the ejection of the 'Western' elements from Berlin, both of the 'West Germans' and possibly even of the Western powers. At the time the second method appeared incomparably more difficult to employ.

The elections had far-reaching effects on the administrative as well as political pattern of the zone. The powers of the new provincial Ministries were far smaller than in countries whose constitution is based on an elected House of Parliament, from which Ministries are constructed on the basis of seats held by any one or number of parties. The decisive power in all things lay with the Russian occupation authorities. The powers of the Länder in relation to a future central German Government, although not closely defined, were not as great as the absence of a central government at this time might lead one to think. All the constitutions afterwards voted by the land diets affirmed that these pro-

[1] The recent assumption that, during the blockade and the disruption of the Allied *kommandatura*, the Magistrat was correspondingly weakened is a superficial and erroneous view. In fact the Magistrat, the only 'intersectorial' organ of administration, gained greatly in power and responsibility, at any rate for a time. Its own internal difficulties came later. The constitutional maxim that the weaker the power of the central government, the stronger that of the provinces, is fully applicable here.

vinces were part of a democratic German republic,[1] a fact which in itself limited the supremacy of the provincial governments. The powers of these governments were thus threefold. Their own indigenous and presumably permanent power, their powers as agents of the SMA which would last only as long as the occupation and the vague powers temporarily shared between the Land Government and the Russian SMA as custodians for a central German Government, which would return to such a government once it was reconstituted.

On the surface, the constitutions of the five Länder in the Soviet zone provided for the means of democratic and responsible representative government. They were almost identical, and may be briefly summarized. Legislative power was vested in a single-chamber diet, elected by universal suffrage and secret ballot, according to the system of proportional representation. In certain specified cases provision was made for popular referenda. The administrative and the judiciary were under ultimate legislative control. There was no collective ministerial responsibility, but ministers were individually responsible to the diet. The judiciary was subject only to the law, but could not question the constitutionality of properly enacted legislation. This task was left in all five provinces to a committee consisting of the chairmen's committee of the diet (Präsidium), members of the Supreme State Courts and the Law Faculties of the Universities. The Constitutions enumerated certain basic rights of the individual. Taking the Saxon constitution as a model in accordance with the general practice in the Eastern zone until 1948, the equality before the law, the unassailable freedom of the person, the right to be brought before a magistrate within forty-eight hours were guaranteed.[2] Further, freedom of movement, of speech, writing, and democratic assembly, freedom of conscience, the right to work, to pay, and to holidays, and to agitate for their increase were all provided for.[3] In fact, the constitutions are models of successful combination of paternal government and individual rights. Finally, as in the 1923 constitution of the U.S.S.R., the dominant political party was nowhere mentioned at all. In fact, under conditions where several parties competed for political power the Soviet zone constitutions would have provided the basis for thoroughly democratic single-

[1] For example, Article I (1) of the Thuringian Constitution, 20 December 1946, of the Saxony-Anhalt Constitution, 10 January 1947, Brandenburg, 6 February 1947, Saxony, 28th February 1947.

[2] Articles 8 (1), 9 (1) and (2).

[3] Articles 10, 11 (1), 12 (1), 15 (2), 16, 17 (1), 18 (1), 19 (1).

chamber government under popular control.[1] These essays in continental constitutional idealism were the sum of the hopes and beliefs of the Germans in the Soviet zone during 1945 and 1946. It is ironical that their publication should have taken place soon after the definite abandonment of the liberal Russian policy.[2]

Moreover, the constitutions were partly inoperative owing to the fact that provincial ministers of all parties felt their primary allegiance to the occupying power as such. The relative immunity of dishonest officials was due partly to the absence of a trained administration, to the fright of the people in a period of considerable official expropriation, and only in small part to conscious Russian tolerance of such men. Official depredations were another matter. The relation of the political parties to the provincial governments was thus quite different to the relationship existing in England or France. In 1946, a minister chosen by the SMA was officially under no obligation and owed no responsibility to the party of which he happened to be a member, even though he may have been appointed on the strength of his party's representation in the provincial Diet. The Ministers were not chosen as party leaders but as individuals beloning to the Party concerned. Their task was primarily to carry out the reconstruction of economic and administrative life in the Eastern zone according to the directions of the Russians. Party control over the activities of ministers at this time was quite unthinkable and impracticable.

Nevertheless the provincial governments, according to the new constitution, could not be considered impotent. Their power, such as it was, was delegated and not intrinsic. But Russian control over the provincial governments was democratically disguised. The activities of the provincial governments and aims of Russian policy were combined into one uniform stream of political, social, and economic activity. The instrument for this was to be the SED. In order to understand the purpose of the SED in Russian eyes and the instrument which they made of it, the organization of this party is worth investigation.

The tradition of political organization exists among the Germans as a nation and the Communists as a party. The SED embodied

[1] Preface to the Constitutions of the German Länder in the Soviet Zone of Occupation, *Constitutions of the German Länder* (OMGUS, Berlin, 1947), p. 99.

[2] Löwenthal, *op. cit.*, p. 152, states that the Thuringian constitution was incapable of being 'a bar to tyranny' as it fails to provide for complete separation of powers, and for judicial review of properly enacted legislation. As a lawyer, he should know that there is no constitutional separation of powers in England, and that the Swiss constitution also expressly forbids judicial review of federal legislation.

both traditions. Like the Nazi Party it was controlled by a central secretariat at the top, working through the provincial organizations, local area (*Kreis*) groups and town groups to the small cells in factories, streets and houses.[1] With this carefully graded administrative hierarchy went an almost military spirit of obedience to higher orders and superior functionaries. The pattern of the SED was borrowed partly from National-Socialist precedent, in so far as the relationship between party and civil administration was concerned, and from the highly developed cell organization of the Communist Party, with its particular attention to the almost microscopic groups at the bottom. Much of the basic structure was taken over ready made by the SED from the Communist and Social Democratic parties.

The organization of the Central Secretariat is reflected in the provincial and, to some extent, in the local organizations. Nominally the Party was headed by two men, Wilhelm Pieck,[2] formerly of the KPD, and Otto Grotewohl, of the SPD. Directly under them were a number of functional departments, whose head was in each case a member of the Central Secretariat. These departments deal with organization; personnel administration; propaganda (including press, radio, films); information; recruiting; social affairs; party indoctrination and economic affairs. The supreme legislative body of the Party in theory was the periodical session of Party leaders elected by the regional groups to which the Central Secretariat makes its reports. The resemblance to the theoretical subordination of the Russian politburo to the Central Committee and through it to the Party Congress is obvious.

The original Soviet proposal had been to allot an equal number of positions in the Central Secretariat to members of the SPD and the KPD. As late as the end of 1947 there was actually one more former Social Democrat than there were Communists. The principle was to be applied at lower levels. However, from the earliest days certain positions were invariably given to Communists, among them that of the chief of the regional or local information service,

[1] For instances of the rôle of the *concierge* as an instrument of political supervision over the tenants in an apartment house, see Löwenthal, *op. cit.*, p. 274, *passim*.

[2] Pieck, a founding father of the *Spartakusbund* and the German Communist party, was the Senior German Communist in 1945. He seems to have been present at all important moments in the history of the KPD before 1933, to have been friendly with all its great personages, from Rosa Luxemburg to Ernst Torgler, to have supported them in power and vilified them in disgrace, like Paul Levi, and to have survived the zig-zag of both German and Russian Communist tactics. This feat is almost unique among communists; like Fouché, Pieck was an expert in the art of mere survival.

a job increasingly akin to political espionage. It was commonly accepted in the Eastern zone that after 1947 the most important personage in the SED was Walter Ulbricht,[1] the member of the Central Secretariat in charge of the Information Services. It was he who significantly launched the Two-Year Plan in 1948. The organization which he controlled was responsible for the supervision of Party members and for the infiltration of the other political parties. This was done by the employment of spies disguised as members of the other parties, or as non-party technicians. Each SED office at all levels up to the provincial organization had its own network, and reports were carefully forwarded through the normal channels of responsibility. The task of the Information Services, known as IFO, ended with the collection and transmission of information; the action on it was taken by the police, by the Russians, or by the disciplinary committees of the Party. Officially the IFO was concerned with public opinion surveys, as its terms of reference stated;[2] it was but a small step from these to omnipresent espionage.

The other departments closely resembled ministries. Indeed, many SED functionaries held the equivalent post in Ministry and Party secretariat. Just as all ministerial figures were secret to outsiders and were never published, so the SED had unqualified access to information obtained by official bodies. In spite of this very close liaison, however, the position in June 1950 was analogous to that existing in the U.S.S.R.; the party kept its own detailed organization as a check on and a duplicate of the official administrative organs.

The two primary tasks facing the SED immediately after its foundation were first to increase its membership by every possible means, and secondly to annihilate the internal distinction between the Social Democrats and Communists. Recruitment became increasingly successful once it became evident that membership of the SED carried with it considerable personal privileges. As in Russia, the political mind was wooed through the stomach, an easy matter in a country where necessities were almost unobtain-

[1] Ulbricht was the Stalin of the German party, his background that of a local party organizer—in his case Thuringia. He was known before 1933 for his ruthlessness and violence in organizing the network of party cells, and for his touchiness with regard to his work in Thuringia. He was partly responsible for the Comintern decision to go ahead with the revolution in Saxony and Thuringia in October 1923. During the war he was effective head of the German Liberation Committee in Moscow.

[2] Circular from SED central secretariat to all provincial IFO departments, July 1947. See also Löwenthal, *op. cit.*, p. 275.

able. The privileges consisted of personal assistance in matters of food, clothing, and fuel for higher functionaries as well as general privileges extending to all members of the Party.

As an example, the special rations issued daily in the headquarters of the SED in Berlin,[1] under the Russian title *Pajok*, may be mentioned.

TABLE V[2]

Distribution of Extra Rations to SED Functionaries

	Butter grammes	*Meat grammes*	*Cereals, etc. grammes*	*Vegetables grammes*	*Fruit grammes*	*Cigarettes*
On Tuesdays ordinary workers, charwomen and chauffeurs received:	100	150	500	1000 to 1500	1750	48
On Thursdays functionaries in the departments:	180	250	1000	2500	1750	72
On Saturdays Department heads:	300	600	1500	4000	1750	120
The sixteen members of the Central Secretariat received weekly *Generals' pajoks*:	1750	4000	2000	4000	2000	As required

Issues of sugar were made at fixed intervals, and at Christmas there were special allocations for everyone.

It is hardly necessary to point out what difference in the Eastern zone these additions made to the ordinary rations, or how important they were in persuading possible doubters of the truth of Russian Marxist theory.[3] On top of all this there were the numerous schemes of paid holidays in those country seats formerly belonging to the landed aristocracy, which had now become national property and had been assigned for the use of the party executive.

Special travel facilities on the railways, a considerable pool of motor-cars available to members of zonal, regional, and local party organizations, and priorities in the allocation of houses or flats, fuel, etc., were available to all SED functionaries.

Coupled with its recruiting efforts, the party had to rid itself of a vast number of opportunists who had joined early on in the hope of feathering their own nests. In the days of relative Russian non-interference, these people had flourished in their machinations not as Communists, but as anti-Fascists.[4] The early period of

[1] Known as the 'Glass Palace' on account of the repeated installation of new window panes, which were unobtainable for the ordinary consumer.

[2] Based on a reliable private report.

[3] For example, the butter ration issued to members of the Central Secretariat equaled three months' rations on heavy workers' allocation.

[4] It is not true, as Löwenthal suggests, that providing a member of the SED followed the Party line he could commit almost any criminal activities.

'liberty' was also a period of licence, the Russians only interfering spasmodically. It was then that the great number of abuses of official positions for private ends took place. At the end of 1947, a party control commission was instituted and investigated all cases of personal dishonesty. According to its statistics, some 1,700 members were expelled between October 1947 and May 1949 for material dishonesty.

Every effort was made by the Russians to assist the Party in its political task of recruitment. One example of this is particularly telling. Paper, one of the rarest commodities in the Eastern zone, was allocated to political parties on the following basis:[1]

TABLE VI

Distribution of Newsprint to Political Parties, 1947–8

1947	*Total Issue*	*SED*	*CDU*	*LDP*
1st quarter	900 tons	845 tons	17 tons	38 tons
2nd ,, ...	700 ,,	653 ,,	23 ,,	24 ,,
3rd ,, ...	700 ,,	653 ,,	23 ,,	24 ,,
4th ,, ...	700 ,,	646 ,,	30 ,,	24 ,,
1948				
1st quarter	585 ,,	548 ,,	20 ,,	17 ,,

The average issue of newspapers daily in 1947 was roughly 27.4 million sheets controlled by the SED, 1 million by the CDU, and 85 thousand by the LDP.[2]

Other examples could be cited. The SED rallies were usually better provided with food and drink than those of other parties, and members were usually able to arrive and depart in Government owned lorries. Work in factories ceased while an SED meeting was in progress in the vicinity. All this made for greater comfort and therefore for greater numbers. No secret was made of the official and unofficial privileges of the SED and the other parties accepted them as inevitable. At the same time the other two parties were increasingly hampered in their activities by the Russians. Under the guise of a continued anti-Nazi 'bloc' policy the two middle-class parties were loosely joined with the SED in the so-called 'Democratic bloc'. 'Bloc' committees sat in small towns and rural districts to supervise the activities of the local administration and to work against the possible recrudescence of National Socialism. Some committees dealt with denazification, others with expropriation of factories. It was usually the SED representative who

[1] *Der Tag*, 22 April 1948. The same figures have been quoted by the SPD in their Eastern Propaganda Sheet, and appear to be based on official material.

[2] *Telegraf*, 15 January 1948. This article also quotes the same figures for paper allocation given above.

proposed action, and opposition to his proposals was represented as a negative, reactionary attitude at best, or even as support for Nazis or war criminals. In this way a good deal of outright theft was committed in the name of all the parties and under the guise of destroying the remnants of National Socialism.[1]

The change in the function of the anti-Fascist bloc well illustrates the political development in the Soviet zone. It had been one of the earliest political institutions in the zone, and still existed in June 1950. Originally it represented a sort of supra-party unity on questions of fundamental importance, such as denazification, socialization of industry, and land reform. Through its cohesive influence political differences were kept out of reconstruction as a general rule. During 1947 it gradually developed into a means of compromising the bourgeois parties by associating them with almost all major public actions of the SED, and thus ensuring that they could not take up an independent political attitude. The bloc committees acted in the name of anti-Fascism, and this helped, at any rate locally, to continue the chosen cloak for Communist activities. Finally, they ensured unanimity and majorities in support of SED policies. After the formation of the East German State in 1949 the bloc lost its purpose and its composition, for individual functionaries of the SED did not hesitate to usurp its authority for their unilateral actions. However, the phrase and the fiction of anti-Fascist blocs continued to be used.

The two bourgeois parties were thus in a very difficult position. Unlike their counterparts in the people's democracies, they were suffered to exist, in fact they were forbidden to dissolve.[2] Open opposition to the SED was impossible, and leaders such as Jacob Kaiser and Kastner who attempted it, were forced out. The middle-class parties were thus forced to take up an almost non-political attitude; to co-operate in those measures with which they could agree and to remain silent about the others. Contact with the branches in the West became more and more spasmodic, and almost impossible after the beginning of 1948. Members of the bourgeois parties in the administration could not afford to take

[1] The same strategy has been used by the Communists with success in Czechoslovakia and the Balkans, though in those countries 'monopoly capitalists' replaced 'Nazi' as a term of abuse. Some particularly outstanding examples of the misuse of this weapon in Germany will be given later.

[2] The evidence is oblique, but leads to this conclusion. After Kaiser's dismissal, an attempt was made to proclaim the forcible dissolution of his party. The Russians appeared to forbid this categorically, and imposed a new chairman on the party. There was a movement in the SED in August 1948 to agitate for the suppression of the CDU. This was abandoned on the orders of the SMA's political department. Instead, many disguised Communist sympathizers joined the CDU.

any active part in politics. The SED encouraged this unpolitical attitude as much as possible.

Within the SED the enemy was fought as ruthlessly as without. In spite of great efforts by party headquarters the distinction between Social Democrats and Communists continued to be made by the public and within the Party. In private conversation about members of the SED a person's previous political record is even now mentioned as a matter of course. The difference between ex-Communists and ex-Social Democrats would be very real. The first desertions from the SED took place in spring 1947, at a time when it was still possible to return to the SPD in Berlin and in the Western zones without loss of too much face. The possibility of recrossing the Styx was made easier by the political situation at that time existing in Berlin.

The first voluntary desertions of disappointed members of the SED were followed by forced resignations, which began in the summer of 1947. At first only those holding administrative positions in the Central Administrations were under attack, but SED functionaries were affected. Open dismissals from the Party were obviously undesirable and quiet persuasion was used instead. The weapon of arrest, except for alleged Nazis, had up to this time been confined, as a rule, to those who openly spoke against the fusion. Now members of the SED began to be arrested as 'Social Democrat agitators'. Even former Social Democrats who had retired from politics altogether at the time of the fusion were in danger of arrest for their very passivity. The fear of losing personal freedom became a formidable factor in the political life of the Eastern zone. Formerly only those who had been a danger to the democratic idea (National-Socialists) or to the Soviet Union's attempt to found a peaceful Germany after the war (monopoly capitalists, unrepenting nationalists, etc.) were affected. Now those whose future actions or whose mere presence might conceivably harm future Soviet intentions in Germany had cause to be afraid. A violent attack by the Communist Press on any public figure in the Eastern zone was usually enough to reduce the person concerned to obedience, or at least silence. Public denunciations sufficed to cow the 'bourgeois' leaders who followed in the footsteps of eliminated or muzzled predecessors.

Like mushrooms, a series of 'democratic' organizations sprang up beside the already existing Trades Union organization and the Farmers' Co-operative, though with less technical functions to support their claims. They were similar to the workers' and peasants' organizations in having a functional basis to disguise their political purpose. The 'Cultural Union' was to embrace all artists, musicians, film personnel, writers, and dramatic actors. Its president was the poet Johannes Becher, who had been in Moscow for a considerable time during the war. The union was favoured by receiving a particularly liberal entertainment allowance in food and accommodation. It was used among other things for making the life under Soviet rule attractive to men of culture in the West. During 1946 its propaganda, directed at distinguished individuals, succeeded in bringing about the migration or return of a number of professors and writers to the Eastern Universities, particularly Leipzig and Halle. It must also be acknowledged that it seems to have made a genuine and successful effort to foster cultural activities in the Eastern zone, and provides some evidence of a genuine Russian interest in this sphere. In Berlin, up to the middle of 1947, the most active cultural life took place under Soviet auspices. The women's organization, Democratic Women's Union[1] took up the housewives' cudgels in the Marxist cause. The organizations of victims, already mentioned,[2] contained a useful means of contact abroad. The youth organization, the Free German Youth, provided an extra-institutional means of educating youth to the Communist ideal.

A special word must be said about the Free German Youth. The possibilities of influencing the next generation gave it a quite outstanding importance in the Eastern zone. The special facilities for recreation and holidays which its members enjoyed, and the lavish financial support it received, made it already in 1947 an attractive organization to a generation which had relished the combination of military training and nationalistic youth activities provided by the Hitler Youth. The Catholic Youth movements, permanently short of money and out of favour with the Russians and the SED, could provide no serious competition.[3] By the end of 1947 the numbers of the Free German Youth had risen to nearly 800,000, and, once failure to be a member had become a definite social and economic stigma, this figure was doubled by the beginning of 1949.[4] From this time onwards the Free German Youth began to play the rôle of an unofficial army for the SED by providing indignant and spontaneous demonstrators wherever required.

[1] *Demokratischer Frauenbund.*

[2] See above, p. 76.

[3] Löwenthal, *op. cit.*, p. 26.

[4] From *Die Jugendwelt*, the official FDJ organ. The accuracy of the figures cannot be vouched for. See Löwenthal, p. 25.

These were the main organizations which were closely allied to and controlled by the SED, but prided themselves on their primary concern with functional interests. Membership of all these bodies increased rapidly during 1947, partly from genuine interest, partly on account of the privileges available, above all because membership of the appropriate organization was often made an essential condition of employment or advancement. These organizations received lavish financial aid from both Russian and German authorities, and members therefore obtained definite economic advantages.

One further organization deserves mention. The 'People's Welfare'[1] was an organization primarily designed to give help to the old and disabled and to provide certain essential cultural and recreational facilities where these are non-existent. It did not play a very important rôle in Eastern zonal affairs outside its own sphere, and though it was not Communist-dominated as early as the other organizations, it nevertheless followed the general Party line faithfully.

3

COMMUNISM OF OPPORTUNITY: JANUARY 1948–MARCH 1950

By the beginning of 1948 one Party dominated the political life of the Soviet zone to an extent quite out of proportion to its size and strength. In the nine months following the fusion the power of the SED had grown so enormously that its very qualified success at the last elections, and consequent small representation in the provincial diets, seemed an anomaly. The SED controlled by far the greater part of the zonal Press. Members of the Party occupied the great majority of positions in the central administration, and the most important posts in the provincial governments. In contrast to October 1946, the members of the SED occupied in January 1948 the position of Prime Minister in all the provinces except Saxony-Anhalt, and had the exclusive control of all Ministries of the Interior and of Education. The Party received the unqualified support of a number of powerful functional groups, which

[1] *Volkswohlfahrt*, a social organization existing in Germany before 1933, but suppressed by the Nazis. It also existed as a co-operative organization in some Western European countries.

covered every sphere of economic or social activity. Finally, the Party could count on the full backing of the Russians.

There were important differences at this time between the position and tasks of the SED as compared to those of the Communist parties in the other Eastern European countries. The German Unity Party did not possess even the vestiges of independence enjoyed by the latter. Its relations with the Soviet Union were conducted through the more or less open control of the Soviet occupation authorities instead of being disguised by a seemingly co-operative organization like the Cominform. Its powers of direct action were limited by the fact that all important decisions were taken by the Russians, and frequently had to be implemented by them. Thus prosecutions for alleged sabotage, for non-fulfilment of the production quotas, all arrests of subversive elements, frequently took place on Soviet orders and by Soviet police. The SED had little or no voice in zonal economic planning until the summer of 1948. It was clear that whatever powers the Unity Party possessed were only delegated by the SMA to its political arm, and not the revolutionary achievement of a national Communist Party as in Czechoslovakia.

The duties of the SED were as onerous as its independence was slight. Instead of furthering the rapid advent of a bolshevist state, it was forced to make palatable Soviet measures intended to benefit only the Soviet Union, without the power to complete the destruction of a society still largely bourgeois in structure. Reparations had to be defended without any real insight into the amount actually removed, the permanence of the new Polish-German frontier had to be driven home to the Germans while the Polish press still seethed with anti-German propaganda. As we shall see, the period summer 1946 to summer 1948 witnessed the height of Soviet economic exploitation. It was the task of the SED to take the attention of the population away from the facts to the realms of political fancy. This it did by the continued anti-Nazi campaign, by the promises of Russo-German co-operation, by a smokescreen of anti-Western propaganda, and by an increasing wave of chicanery against all opponents. Apart from the continuation of the previously inaugurated campaign of expropriation and nationalization of industry, no important social changes took place during 1947 and 1948. The SED was the vanguard for Soviet exploitation, not the advance guard of the communist society in Germany.

It was therefore not surprising that the SED made no headway in its bid for popular support, but that instead it lost ground.[1] Its utter dependence on Soviet bayonets became more than ever noticeable during the Berlin blockade, when great efforts had to be made to furnish sufficient demonstrators against the Socialist City Council. The SPD headquarters in Berlin were visited by a considerable number of Unity Party members from the Soviet zone, who made it clear that even within the Party there was considerable latent opposition to the Russians. Among the leaders no open discord was possible, for the direct control by the Soviet authorities made even such internal differences as appeared in the Communist parties of Eastern Europe impossible.[2] In spite of its powerful position in the Soviet zone, the Unity Party inevitably reached its nadir of popular support during the time of the blockade. It was even rumoured that the Russians would abandon it in favour of an openly Communist Party. This proved erroneous, and indeed unnecessary, for the important ex-Social Democrats in the SED had either been eliminated, or had fled, while those who remained, like Grotewohl or Fechner, were utterly committed to the policy of the Party and could be relied upon to avoid any divergence from Soviet wishes. By the end of 1948 the SED may be said to have been a party from which almost all really unreliable elements had been removed from the higher levels.[3]

The Berlin blockade brought out clearly the compact isolation of the Unity party against a popular background of apathy and discontent. It is difficult to say why the Russians chose this moment to bring the Berlin question to a crisis. The background for it had existed ever since 21 October 1946, when the political structure of Berlin had taken on a form violently and inherently inimical to that imposed on the Soviet zone by Russian action. The city had become the administrative capital of the Soviet zone by reason of its geographical situation and the structure of its communications. At the same time it had provided the bigger of the two loopholes in the European iron curtain and the Western powers had made good

[1] No elections took place until the formation of the 'People's Council' in summer 1948. But for the first time open protests against the SED took place in the summer of 1948, for instance at Leipzig University, in the Trades Union groups of several large factories, including a number controlled by the Russians, and in cinemas and theatres.

[2] The disgrace of individual Communists, such as Gomulka in Poland, Kostov in Bulgaria, and Clementis in Czecho-Slovakia, has not had its equivalent in Germany, for SED leaders never reach the stage of disagreement.

[3] The work of cleansing the party was given to the SED Control Commission, established early in 1948. It immediately conducted a large-scale investigation into the political attitude of members. For its supervision of the material honesty of members, see above, p. 101.

use of their opportunity. Almost everything which happened in the Soviet zone was known in Berlin within twenty-four hours. The number of daily neswpapers appearing in Berlin almost equalled the sum of the different dailies of London and Paris. At the meetings of the Foreign Ministers, both the American and British representatives had presented statements of Soviet reparation demands which astounded the Russians by their accuracy, considering that all reparation matters are treated as top secret by the Russians.[1]

It was therefore frequently held that the Berlin blockade was an attempt to bring this state of affairs to an end, and to ensure that Soviet political and economic measures could be carried out in relative secrecy. At the same time the influence of the Western political parties, particularly the Socialists,[2] could be eliminated from the Soviet zone, and the contact between East and West broken. This would bring to an end the SED's lack of political success, and the perennial German failure to fulfil the economic plans, both of which were allegedly due to Western sabotage. More recent developments indicate, however, that the Berlin blockade was more in the nature of a prologue than an epilogue. In spite of the difficulties created by the loophole in the iron curtain, Soviet economic exploitation had not been hampered, or modified, by one jot. Though the lack of popular support for the SED was patent, open Soviet support had nevertheless clamped the Unity Party on the administrative and political life of the zone But if Soviet policy was to undergo a significant change, and, not content with the complete subservience and exploitation of the Eastern zone, was to take the offensive against Western Germany with the object of bringing the whole of Germany under Soviet domination, it might be necessary to build a physical striking force for this task, to mobilize Youth into shock troops, even to rebuild a German army. Western unpreparedness could only be ensured by their removal from the Berlin vantage point. Most observers at the time connected L. Berya's visit to Berlin in June 1948 with the blockade. It seems that this was already decided earlier, and

[1] Immediately after the London Conference in November 1947, strict orders were issued to all German administrations regarding the secrecy of all production figures. At the same time a thorough purge of German technicians in Soviet companies and factories was carried out.

[2] The SPD in Berlin was specially organized to deal with the clandestine propaganda in the Eastern zone. Some of the party's ablest members worked in Berlin, and the peculiar task of the party in its entrenched position, surrounded by enemy territory, gave the Berlin SPD a militant spirit and efficiency quite out of proportion to that of its Western headquarters, which was more concerned with normal political work.

that the head of the Soviet police came to arrange for the creation of the new German police army, after the removal of the Western Allies from Berlin.[1]

The Russians expected the blockade to succeed within a few weeks, and their plans for the creation of an East German Republic were ready. The economic plan, the first one to be publicly issued, was announced during the blockade.[2] Provisional appointments seem to have been made to ministerial posts, and the unofficial People's Council, called to give expression to the Russian policy for German unification and a just peace treaty, was quietly told to expect to undertake the rôle of an East German legislature. Rumours were afoot that the bourgeois parties as well as the provincial parliaments were to be eliminated. The failure to remove the Western powers prevented the execution of the Russian plans for the moment. Instead, the *status quo ante* continued for another twelve months, and the new policy for a united Germany had to be carried on in a roundabout way. The new police had to be created and trained more surreptitiously, that is, more slowly.

The united Germany policy replaced the old anti-Nazi campaign completely. A political amnesty for ex-Nazis was closely followed by the creation of a new party, the National Democratic Party, specifically designed to embrace minor Nazis and nationalists. This party was dominated by Communists who had not previously appeared in the public eye. Its lower functionaries were mainly ex-Nazi opportunists who had lived on the edge of political outlawry since the war; journalists, lawyers, politicians. Its new journal spoke in a tone which outdid the SED papers in scurrility. In the Eastern zone one of the new party's main tasks was to attract CDU and LDP votes for a programme which the Russians considered far more congenial to the lower middle-classes. A special party was also founded for the peasants, the Peasants' Party. Its leadership was largely in the hands of Farmers' Co-operative officials, and its purpose was to mobilize the peasants' vote for the cause of United Germany and generally for Russian policy. The peasants had been unexpectedly difficult to detach from their support of the bourgeois parties. But the obvious Communist control, and the moment chosen for their foundation, made the

[1] Strangely enough, the English and American papers rarely went beyond the statement that the blockade was designed to bring about the evacuation of the Western troops, while the SED press, probably unconsciously, hinted at the ultimate purpose. cf. *Neues Deutschland* quoting some of Grotewohl's speeches of July 1948: 'Our party, with the help of the Soviet Union, will unite Germany.'

[2] See below, p. 247 *passim*.

new parties an object of ridicule in the East. Membership, after a preliminary jump, remained admittedly small, and reached little over ½ million for both by the end of 1948.[1] This did not greatly worry the Russians, for the main purpose of the National Democratic Party was in the West, not in the East.[2]

At the same time the SED began a vociferous propaganda campaign. This was directed at the worst, not the best, aspirations for German unity. No suggestion of compromise with the West was made; instead, unity, strength, and power under Russian control was promised. Soviet economic depredations were played down, and great play was made of the lingering remains of British dismantling policy and German resistance to it. The SED, with Russian approaval, put notices on the bombed buildings of Dresden as a warning of the beastliness of Anglo-American imperialist warfare.[3] On 13 February 1950 Seydewitz, the Minister-President of Saxony, went so far as to refer to the raid on Dresden as 'unnecessary vandalism'. Anti-British films made by Goebbels were shown in the Soviet-licensed cinemas, such as the film *Titanic.* The high rate of unemployment in the West eighteen months after the currency reform was exploited to the full, and the SED economic experts, Fred Oelssner and Jürgen Kuczinski[4] gazed into the Marxist crystal and predicted the economic collapse of Western Germany. The effects of all this in Eastern Germany are difficult to estimate correctly. No doubt this campaign gave the policy of the Russians and of the SED an attraction for many which it had not previously possessed. But it is doubtful whether a body of genuine public opinion was therefore enrolled behind the SED, and whether many of those who remained politically silent, or merely paid lip service to the SED, came to support the party wholeheartedly. No public expression of opinion, such as elections, took place between 1946 and the summer of 1950. Probably the political situation in 1950 was much the same as in 1948, the SED was in control, backed by armed force, and no opposition was possible. Equally there was little genuine political support for the Unity Party.

The position of the bourgeois parties had also reached a *status quo.* Their political activity had been extinguished beyond the

[1] Based on a reliable private report.
[2] See below, Chap. VIII, p. 264.
[3] This was confirmed by the English press, for instance, the *Daily Express.*
[4] Oelssner edited a new edition of Marxist German classics, such as Hilferding's *Finance Capital.* Kuczinski was the head of the Economic Faculty of Berlin University. He returned to Germany after failing to obtain a permanent post at Oxford during the war.

routine of keeping their organization alive. Their members in official positions kept well away from all political activity, except for those who were Communists in disguise.[1] Relations with their Western headquarters were practically non-existent. Yet officially their strength in the provincial parliament had remained unabated since 1946, apart from the death, arrest, and flight of members. The three parties were still associated with the SED in the anti-Fascist bloc.[2] The bloc committees had by now done their work, the preparation for the expropriations, denunciations and the land reform, and remained as an ornamental façade of all-party association. The two new parties never became an important part of the zone's political life and were quietly left to their own devices by the Russians.

The creation of an East German Government was tactically deferred until it could be made to appear as the spontaneous answer to the formation of the West German Government at Bonn. Since the preliminaries to this had been a series of long-drawn-out discussions and conferences, openly reported, the Russians had full knowledge of the proposed step, and could make their preparations accordingly. Within weeks of the final evolution of the Western Occupation Statute, the East German Government was formed, seemingly out of a hat. The People's Council had remained in permanent session awaiting the big day, ever since its convocation to give expression to the 'spontaneous people's agitation',[3] against the splitting of Germany. This referendum, the declaration of whose verdict was 'delegated' to some four hundred representatives, had been designed to bring pressure in June 1948 on the three-power conference on Germany in London. In this respect the referendum and People's Council had been a failure, but on the basis of the alleged delegation elections to the new legislature were avoided. In fact, since the agitation had been almost entirely sponsored by the SED under cover of the bloc, the new chamber was unrepresentative of the provincial parliaments, and far more so of the people.

[1] For instance, Steidle, an ex-vice-President of the Central Administration for Agriculture and Forestry, and a Minister in the East German government, had been a former Colonel of the Wehrmacht. In Soviet captivity he joined the Free German officers' organization, and became an alleged Communist. After his return to Germany he joined the CDU.

[2] It is not quite clear if the two new parties sat on the bloc committees, but in the absence of any positive information, it seems unlikely.

[3] It is interesting to note that this agitation went under the name *Volksbegehren*, a term which was used for the popular demonstrations financed by Hugenberg and other nationalistic industrialists to agitate against the Versailles Treaty in 1931. This fact was even mentioned by one of the SED papers.

On 10 October 1949 the SMA handed over its administrative functions to the provisonal governments, and turned itself into a Soviet Control Commission of roughly similar construction but with greatly reduced numbers. The new Government consisted of a Prime Minister, Herr Grotewohl; three deputy Prime Ministers, Herren Ulbricht (SED) and Nuschke (CDU), and Prof. Kastner (LDP); Herr Dertinger (CDU) as Foreign Minister; Herr Steinhoff (SED) as Minister of the Interior; Herren Rau (SED) and Selbmann (SED) as Ministers for Planning and Industry respectively; Herr Loch (LDP) as Minister of Finance, Herr Steidle (CDU) as Minister of Labour and Health, Herr Wandel (SED) as Minister of Culture, and Herr Fechner (SED) as Minister of Justice. With one exception, all the non-SED Ministers proved staunch supporters of the régime.

Behind the Government stood the Peoples' Council, transformed willy-nilly into a Lower House (*Volkskammer*) whose executive committee was constitutionally responsible for the formation of the new government. An Upper House (*Länderkammer*) was elected by the diets of the five provinces, and its thirty-four deputies represented the political complexion of these diets. East Berlin sent seven observers to this body, after election by the three-party *bloc*.

The whole was legalized in advance by the constitution previously voted for all Germany by the People's Congress. Like those of the provinces passed in 1947, it mentioned all that was lacking in human rights in the Soviet zone, while omitting the real factors governing political life. Less play was made, it is true, with individual liberties than had been made in 1947, but the federal nature of the Republic was emphasized. Like that of the individual republics of the U.S.S.R., however, the liberty and independence of the German provinces remained ephemeral.[1] The importance of the constitution can be judged from the fact that within nine months of its enactment changes in the force of its provisions were made by *ex post facto* legislation, without any attempt at constitutional amendment.[2]

Indeed, unlike the effects of the institutions created at Bonn, those which followed the establishment of the Pieck republic (as it is called) were negligible. The political situation remained as

[1] For the structure of the new government see also below, Chap. V, Part 3.

[2] The constitutional ideas of the SED changed but little. The 1949 all-German constitution is based on the SED proposal for an all-German constitution issued on 19 Nov. 1946, though greater lip-service was paid to decentralization in the zonal constitution than was considered necessary in the propaganda *ballon d'essai* of 1946. See Friedmann, *op. cit.*, p. 76.

before, in spite of the impressive nomenclature of the new government. The only change may have been in the increasing delegation of powers by the Soviet authorities to the new government. Contact between Moscow and Berlin now ostensibly took place to some extent through the establishment of embassies in the two capitals. Stalin saw fit for the first time to address an official message to a German politician when the new President was inaugurated. The enhanced position of the East German Government over the Bonn Republic was ostensibly emphasized by the creation of a ministry of Foreign Affairs, prohibited by the Western Occupation Statute. But though all this gives a superficial impression of independence, the Soviet control remained as much a reality as ever, though the channels of command may have been disguised and changed. The campaign for German unity, the partial curtailment of reparation demands, the return of some measure of prosperity as a result of this and of increasing trade with East and West may have raised the popular prestige of the SED and of Russia, closely identified in the view of the population, to some extent. Nevertheless it was in 1950 still as doubtful as ever whether free elections would give the SED an overall majority in the provincial or republican legislatures. For this reason the elections, due after four years in October 1949, were provisionally postponed for one year for 'economic reasons'.[1] It was promised, however, that they would almost certainly be held in October 1950. Until then the spurious representation of the People's Council was to continue.

[1] *Tägliche Rundschau, Neues Deutschland,* 27 October 1949.

CHAPTER V

THE DEVELOPMENT OF ADMINISTRATION AND GOVERNMENT

I

JULY 1945–OCTOBER 1946

BETWEEN July and October 1945 twelve central administrations were founded to help the SMA to co-ordinate the work of the provinces. Their official title was 'German Central Administration for the Soviet Zone'.[1] They can best be divided into two main groups; those dealing with economic affairs and the remainder.

ECONOMIC GROUP

Central Administration for Industry was responsible for planning and supervising the production of industry in the Soviet zone until the moment that the finished goods left the factory. It included all industry with the exception at first of agricultural production and food processing, pharmaceutical industries, and production of fuel, though these branches, except the last, were finally transferred to it as well. Functionally it was divided into three departments:

1. *Basic Industries.* Metal production, including steel (crude and refined), Stones and Earths, Chemical Industry.
2. *Heavy Industry.* Electrical Industry, machinery, Precision and Optical Industry, Vehicles.
3. *Light Industry.* Textiles, Paper, Leather, Rubber, and Wood processing.

This grouping was apparently based on the Russian model, and corresponded to the organization of industry in the U.S.S.R. and the Eastern European countries.[2]

Central Administration for Fuel and Power controlled the production of all solid and liquid fuels as well as their distribution. It was also responsible for the upkeep and construction of gas works and power stations and for the distribution of electricity and gas.

[1] *Deutsche Zentralverwaltungen für die Sowjetische Besatzungszone* (DZV)

[2] The departments of this Central Administration early resembled the so-called Head-Administrations (GLAVKI) of the Soviet ministries, both Union and Republic, responsible for branches of industry in Russia.

Central Administration for Trade and Supply organized the distribution on the market of all consumer products, including the retail of solid and liquid fuels, though not the allocation of raw materials and semi-processed goods to and between industries. It was also responsible for the distribution of food, agricultural processing, and clothes rationing. The suppression of the Black Market was administratively its concern.

Central Administration for Agriculture and Forestry controlled agriculture and forestry. Originally it had responsibility for food processing industries, but these were transferred in January 1947 to the Administration for Industry. Its prime concern was the execution of the land reform. It was also responsible for fisheries and had under its control a special department for dealing with irrigation, canals, and reservoirs.

Central Administration for Transport provided the joint top level co-ordination for three departments:

1. German State Railways.[1]
2. Road Traffic.
3. Water Traffic, Inland and Seaborne.

Central Administration for Finance was responsible for price control and price structure, financial Black Market supervision, credit policy, taxes, and official budgets.

Central Administration for Statistics was the post-war successor of the old central statistical department[2] responsible for all statistics undertaken on behalf of the zonal authorities or the SMA. Its task was partly the compilation of original statistics and partly the co-ordination of statistics produced by the specific departments of the individual Central Administrations.

Central Administration for Labour and Social Affairs directed Labour allocation and the control of Labour offices in close conjunction with the Trades Unions. Its task included the drafting and implementation of a zonal scheme for Social Insurance and Benefits.

Central Administration for Posts and Telegraphs, the post-war successor of the German State Post (*Deutsche Reichspost*). Although not strictly economic in its functions it is nevertheless to be included in this group.

NON-ECONOMIC GROUP

Central Administration for Education was responsible for all schools and universities, adult education, cultural affairs, religious

[1] *Deutsche Reichsbahn* (DR). [2] *Statistisches Reichsamt.*

affairs; also all State propaganda, and the licensing and supervision of Press, radio, and theatre.

Central Administration for Justice. Its chief task was the preparation of the new legal system in accordance with the Control Council Directive abolishing all those laws passed after 1933 conducive to racial and political intolerance. It organized the large-scale recruitment of all non-Nazi lawyers and controlled the administration of justice in the Soviet zone.

Central Administration for Health was responsible for the double task of drafting and putting into effect the new health scheme, very similar to that enacted in Britain by the Labour Government since the war, as well as the control of hospitals, clinics, and medical services generally throughout the zone. At the beginning the Administration also controlled the pharmaceutical industry.[1]

Central Administration for Refugees. This Administration was small and soon became a mere appendage to the Administration for Labour and Social Affairs. Its immediate responsibility was the welfare of the two million odd refugees, or, as they were euphemistically called, 're-settlers'.

The original purpose of these organizations was twofold. They were first intended to assist the SMA, of whose organization they were an exact copy, in its task. The SMA would prepare legislative or administrative ordinances and would pass these on to the DZVs for action under Russian supervision. It was intended that the Russians should obtain the benefit of German experience in the details of administration in all its spheres and yet keep the general control of policy as well as administrative supervision in their own hands. This might be called the efficiency motive.

The second purpose was the institution under Russian control of a series of functional German organizations in accordance with the Potsdam Agreement.[2] If these administrations proved themselves efficient they might, by virtue of their unique experience, become the backbone of whatever administrations were finally agreed upon for the whole of Germany. It was clear that no intention seemed as yet to exist in the West to found similar organizations,[3] and therefore the Russian-sponsored administra-

[1] It is not quite clear why the experiment was made at first of giving the Administration for Health and Food the control of the industries connected with their fields. Soon, however, the Soviet system of concentrating all control of industry in the three 'Industrial' ministries was adopted.

[2] See above, Chap. II.

[3] In the British zone, the Zonal Advisory Council, consisting of delegates from the provincial ministries and party leaders, had no executive function at all. In the US. zone there were no executive organizations above provincial levels either.

tions, being the first in the field, stood a good chance of obtaining jurisdiction over the whole of Germany. This was the political motive.

In accordance with these two aims an effort was made to obtain the services of all capable anti-Nazis irrespective of their political views. The appointment of presidents and vice-presidents was by decree of the Supreme Soviet Commander in favour of named individuals. Of the twelve presidents of the new Central Administration, five were members of the SPD, one of the CDU, three of the KPD, one of the LDP, and two Non-Party. Of the seventeen vice-presidents, three were Social Democrats, three were CDU, ten were Communists, one Non-Party. The Communists among the presidents were in a distinct minority, and their majority among the vice-presidents, though absolute, was not overwhelming. Since the post of vice-president, or first vice-president where there were several, carried with it control over internal administration and staff questions, the Communists from the very beginning occupied the majority of vice-presidencies.[1] Their control over internal questions was thus considerable at a time when they still had little say in technical policy. Among the presidents, Edwin Hörnle,[2] the head of the Administration for Agriculture, Paul Wandel of the Administration for Education, and Henry Meyer of Finance were the only Communists. Every central administration, with the exception of three, had one Communist vice-president, the exceptions being the Administration for Statistics, where the lack of Communist statisticians made itself felt, and the Administrations for Agriculture and Finance, where the President supplied the necessary Communist element himself. Among the remaining presidents was one industrialist who had been active in anti-Nazi Resistance Movements, a business man with Socialist tendencies, a former Minister for Justice under the German Imperial Régime prior to 1914, and an expert on coal production with distinctly right-wing tendencies. The class bias in the selection of officials was not strikingly obvious.

The appointment of departmental heads had to be sanctioned by the Russians, but that of lesser officials was left to the discretion of the president, vice-president, and personnel department of each

[1] See also Löwenthal, *op. cit.*, p. 124.

[2] Hörnle's connection with agriculture dates back to 1921, when he was put in charge of a department at KPD headquarters concerned with agitation and organization in rural areas. This was the time when the German central committee was becoming conscious of the need to have a mass party behind it. The department was a failure.

Central Administration. The majority of the officials selected were Social Democrats or members of the middle-class parties, the Communists being a distinct minority. The success of the recruitment was cumulative; as the Germans became aware of the seemingly unbiased method of selection they came forward to join these organizations in increasing numbers. Between July and October 1945 a complete administrative organization of considerable efficiency came into being.

The detailed work of the economic administrations will be discussed in the next chapter. The work of the others between July 1945 and the beginning of 1947 is a good illustration of the general Soviet policy at the time. In the fields of Justice, Education, and Medical Services their first task was destructive. The remains of the Nazi system, and the remaining Nazi personnel had to be eliminated. A new legal system had to be drafted which embodied as much of the old German law as possible, and yet excluded all specifically Nazi legislation. The existing rank and file of practising lawyers and justices had to be examined individually for their previous political record, and to a large extent removed. This left an enormous gap in trained personnel which the few non-Nazi lawyers still in practice, and those who had been in emigration and were now willing to return, could not fill. Yet at the very time of these administrative upheavals, the work of the courts was particularly heavy; not only had a record number of cases of current crime to be tried, but there was also awaiting trial a large backlog of crimes against humanity and other atrocities committed under the Nazis.

A scheme for the replacement of trained lawyers was therefore worked out, which was to provide in the shortest possible time a number of partly-trained judges working under the supervision of the existing local and provincial court judges.[1] A school was established in each Land for men locally prominent and capable in their professions, recommended to the provincial Minister of Justice by either a committee of the four existing political parties or by other local organizations such as the Trades Unions. Those selected were to undergo a course given by trained teachers in the essentials of jurisprudence. The accent was naturally on Criminal Law rather than Civil Law in view of the disproportionate number

[1] The German system of law administration is copied from the normal administrative organization. The Court of a *Kreis* deals with roughly the area of that administrative unit, while the Provincial Court deals with the area of a former German province. Since the new German provinces were generally larger than those of the Federal Republic the exact administrative boundaries of civil government and justice did not always correspond.

of cases outstanding of the former category, but also in accordance with the Russian emphasis on Justice as a weapon of the State. Candidates were given a chance as far as possible to show their talents in group discussions instead of having to confine themselves solely to bookwork and lectures. At the end of the course those successful in passing the final examinations were to be 'apprenticed' to a working judge for a period of six months, and if considered suitable were then to sit on their own. This system was obviously not perfect, but a number of reputable lawyers had given their name to it, and in view of the acute shortage of trained personnel it might have provided a reasonable substitute to the normal administration of justice such as had existed in Germany before the Nazis.[1]

A similar scheme was evolved in the field of education. The need for trained teachers was possibly even more urgent, since the destruction of the National-Socialist system of education and the consequent shortage of suitable staff coincided with a number of ambitious adult and part-time education schemes, introduced soon after the beginning of the Russian occupation. In the circumstances then existing in Germany there was perhaps less excuse for lowering the standard in the training of teachers than of lawyers, since the institution of new educational schemes did not seem as essential as the trial of already existing court cases. However, in the interests of educational rebuilding and the destruction of Nazi influence on youth, the principle of training more teachers in less time might nevertheless have had successful results. The shortage of staff also made itself felt in the universities and technical colleges. The Nazis had already replaced a number of prominent professors on account of their political views and religion. The remaining university professors of reputation were almost compelled to receive honour and even rank within the Nazi party, quite apart from those eager to accept them. The economists, political theorists, philosophers, and sociologists, whose views had not coincided with those of the Nazis, had been sacked, and those whose views had been acceptable under Hitler were now unsuitable to remain in their positions.

Scientists particularly were pressed into the service of the Nazi

[1] Löwenthal, himself an ex-official of the Central Administration for Justice describes the system at length (Chap. II). His scathing verdict takes little account of the problems and he does not mention the fact that even non-communist lawyers saw good prospects of success in the scheme when it was first proposed by the Russians. The fact that it degenerated later was not an inherent fault of the system, and cannot be blamed on the scheme itself.

State, and had consequently to be relieved of their positions in the Soviet zone, if they had not already fled to the West. The shortage of staff was emphasized by the desire of the Russians to open university education to everyone, and this promise was embodied in the 1947 Constitutions of the five provinces. It was the declared aim of the Central Administration for Education that within five years 'the majority of University Students should be from the working classes'.[1] Either the middle classes must be barred from the universities, or many more wage earners would have to be admitted.[2]

Similar conditions existed in the medical services in Eastern Germany. All doctors who were physically fit had been called up into the German armed forces, and many of the remaining civilians had fled to the west at the approach of the Russians. At the end of the war the distribution of doctors was roughly one to seven thousand of population in the east.[3] The political colour of medical practitioners was not as important a bar to future employment as in the case of lawyers and teachers, and the Communist influence in the Central Administration was weak.

Plans existed for the institution of a National Health Scheme very similar in detail to that created in post-war Great Britain, but were not put into operation as rapidly as in the case of the new educational system, since the importance of immediate medical services for the underfed population, and the often destitute refugees, was considered a priority which made any large-scale rearrangement of the basis of social medicine a momentary impossibility. As an emergency measure, abortions were legalized in certain cases for the time being, thus reducing the demand for drugs in short supply, and for hospital accommodation.[4] The danger of epidemics had also to be combated, and for this purpose the doctors with a Nazi record were made to expiate their political past by service in potential danger areas. The early decrees of the SMA gave the German Central Administration and the Medical Departments of the Provincial Governments power for

[1] Statement by the President of the Central Administration.

[2] As has been pointed out, the statements by Schaffer, *op. cit.*, Chap. IX, are on the whole accurate. Above, p. 66, n. 2..

[3] Official count, published by Central Health Administration, May 1947.

[4] Löwenthal, *op. cit.*, p. 240, states that the order permitting abortions was due to the numerous cases of rape committed by the Red Army. The order was not published until the beginning of 1946, when the worst wave was over. The official German statement gives as reasons the lack of medical facilities for childbirth and the bad condition of health of the refugee population from the separated territories.

compulsory direction of doctors. There can be no doubt that in the field of medical services the SMA and the Central Administration for Health achieved an immediate success.

The Central Administration for Labour and Social Welfare was responsible for the institution and supervision of the new insurance plan. Here again the Nazi system, which had clamped a state contributions scheme on a chain of large private insurance companies, made the Russian plan easy to carry out. The insurance companies were expropriated, and their funds vested in provincial trusts administered by the five ministries of Labour. Rates of payments and benefits were prescribed uniformly for the whole zone, and the execution of the scheme was closely controlled by the Central Administration. The scheme provided for benefits at a high rate against relatively low contributions, and had, therefore to be heavily subsidized. Established in January 1947, it spent 1½ milliard marks during that year, against contributions totalling 800,000,000 marks.[1] In form the scheme resembles that existing in France and Great Britain since 1947. A number of workers' rest centres and sanatoria are controlled directly by the Central Administration, and special arrangements have been made with the Transport and Health Authorities for cheap services.

The other important task of the Central Administration was the liaison with the Trades Union Association (FDGB). During this period, before the formation of the SED, the FDGB was partly controlled by the Social Democrats. The relationship therefore resembled that normally existing between organized labour and government in the Western countries; a permanent attempt to solve difficulties by consultation and agreements. Since the FDGB was only slowly becoming organized, and the Central Administration was under direct Russian orders, labour had little or no opportunity of challenging official decisions. Before 1948 the importance of the Trades Union Association lay in the influence of its works' organization in individual factories. There the frequent changes of management gave the workers a large amount of control in policy, organization and production.

The curious position of the peasants in the U.S.S.R. was reflected in Eastern Germany from the start. Having an organization of their own, farmers were not represented in the Trades Unions, and, as far as can be seen, were not subject to the jurisdiction of the Central Administration for Labour in their normal capacity. Only

[1] *Tägliche Rundschau*, 27 April 1948.

in cases where peasants were directed to other work do they come under its control. Normally they were controlled by the Administration for Agriculture.

Finally the Labour Administration was used as a means of mobilizing labour for the Russians. Apart from spasmodic kidnapping of a few individuals, usually for rush jobs, the recruitment of labour for the Russians, either in the U.S.S.R or in the zone, was carried out by the labour exchanges, who received their instructions from the Central Administration, though under the administrative control of the provinces. According to the size of the labour mobilization required for German or Russian purposes, the Soviet authorities either acted through the Administration, or descended directly on specific labour offices. Recruitment and direction of labour was greatly facilitated by the thorough system of registration established in 1945 by Order No. 42, dated 27 August 1945, and by administrative SMA instruction dated 30 September 1945. This instruction, which foreshadowed later labour directions on a vast scale, is quite contrary to the spirit and the letter of the provisions of the provincial constitutions dealing with the right of labour to emigrate and change employment.[1] The labour exchanges thus became important instruments of control long before the political dictatorship of the SED was established. Punishment in cases of disobedience was starvation as a result of the withdrawal of ration cards.

A special problem was created by the influx of nearly three million propertyless Germans from the separated territories and from Eastern Europe during 1945 and 1946. They were first housed in camps and then distributed to those parts of the zone most capable of receiving them. In this respect the task of the East German authorities was similar to, and was solved in the same way as, that in the West. The work was the responsibility of the Central Administration for Re-settlers. The record of the Administration, and indeed of all the German authorities, was impressive in this respect. The authority of the Russians, and the propaganda of the political parties, strongly combatted local feelings of resistance to the new drain on the small zonal resources, and collections of necessities were rigorously carried through. The SED, after its formation, carried on in this spirit, and it must be admitted that Eastern methods of coercion were here more effective than Western appeals to the sympathy of the German population. There was a tendency, however, from the earliest days,

[1] See above, p. 96.

for the 'resettlement' camps to be looked upon as the special preserve for Soviet labour demands.

The official *raison d'être* of the Central Administrations as 'the prolonged executive arm' of the SMA had sufficed to define their position in relation to the provincial governments. Since the Administrations could not issue any orders or give directives on their own account without express command of the relevant departments of the SMA, orders to the provincial governments were treated as given in the name of the Soviet Commander-in-Chief. All the directives issued by the Russians through the Central Administrations went to the provincial government under the signature of the President of the Administration concerned 'by command of the SMA'. Alternatively, matters of importance were made public as direct proclamations by the Soviet Military Governor, and the German authorities were either specifically instructed to carry them out, or were left to do this automatically.[1] The Central Administrations dealt with the requisite ministries in the provinces, but could not deal directly with the local governmental bodies. Since they had no property or local executive staff[2] they had perforce to rely on the machinery of the provincial governments in almost everything.

Matters not dealt with specifically by the Central Administrations were left to the initiative of the provincial governments. The selection of factories to be sequestrated and taken over within a province, their operation and administration, the methods of collecting and distributing food, etc., were all at first the responsibility of the provincial ministries concerned, unless specific orders on any of these subjects had been given by the Russians through the central administrations. As long as the position remained thus, there could be no question of the Central Administration encroaching on the power of the provincial governments. Certainly the provincial governments considered themselves as the supreme German authorities of the zone under the orders only of the SMA.

The system of local government need only be dealt with briefly, as the traditional German system was continued without significant alteration. It is based on elected mayors in rural and urban communities. As in France, these officials, though popularly

[1] In the majority of cases, such as orders for spring-sowing, for harvest-gathering, and for special ration issues, the proclamation specifically instructed the Administration concerned in its task and responsibility.

[2] Except the Railways and the Post Office, who took over the property of their predecessors, and the Administration for statistics, which had its own investigators.

elected, are the agents of higher authority more than the representatives of the local population. Above them are the *Landräte* or area sub-prefects (to continue the analogy with France) who are responsible for a rural *Kreis,* an area approximating to that of a county in the U.S. or a rural district in Britain, and rather smaller than a French department. These officials are appointed by the provincial government, officially on the basis of the municipal elections. In larger towns a mayor for the town *Kreis,* an elected official, replaces the *Landräte* as the superior authority of the mayors of the town's constituent communities. We have seen how all these officials were first appointed hurriedly by the Russians; by the end of 1945 appointments were in the hands of the provincial governments, and mayors were elected at the beginning of 1946, naturally subject to the approval of the SMA. After April 1946 the SED played an important part in sponsoring candidates for these offices and in getting them elected. By the end of 1947 all but a very few of the large numbers of non-Communist mayors and *Landräte* originally appointed had been dismissed or otherwise removed and were replaced by candidates of the SED.

Only two changes of significance took place in local government structure after the war. In the East the intermediary level between *Kreis* and province, the administrative department, or *Regierungsbezirk,* was abolished for administrative purposes.[1] In the West it has remained. The area of a *Regierungsbezirk* corresponds roughly to a French department, and the position of the *Regierungspräsident,* its chief official, to that of a French prefect. The reason given in the SMA order abolishing these departments was that administration would thus be simplified. Since these units had been greatly strengthened in authority by the Nazis, as a means of increasing centralized control,[2] it was only natural that the proposed federal structure of post-war Germany should transfer much of the authority of the administrative departments to the elected provincial governments.[3]

The other important change was the status in local government of the new bloc committees, controlling the preparation of such

[1] It remained, for instance, in legal administration, and in railway and postal organization.

[2] The police administration, particularly the Gestapo, was increasingly based on the department instead of being divided, as previously under the Weimar republic, between *Kreis* and province.

[3] It is strange that in the U.S. zone, where relatively extreme forms of federalism were much in vogue for a time, the abolition of *Regierungsbezirke* was never officially proposed.

measures as the nationalization of factories and the land reform. Although officially local authorities were in no way subordinate to such bodies, the political nature of these schemes and the important place assigned to political matters and groups by the Russians from the very first made these committees very powerful indeed. In practice few mayors or *Landräte* openly dared to disagree with their recommendations. Once the SED had occupied the great majority of local government posts, its control over both committees and officials made any public disagreement impossible. The system of local government established during 1945 and 1946 continued unchanged, irrespective of the political and administrative changes in the zonal superstructure. In this field more than any other the old German system survived relatively unscathed into the era of Communist control.

2

OCTOBER 1946–JANUARY 1948

The political changes which followed on the formation of the SED were reflected by increasing control and supervision of the individuals in the administration of the Soviet zone. The independents, who had created the Central Administrations, resigned in rapid succession, and were replaced by members of the SED. The pressure was greatest at the levels of local government in the zone, and relatively less in the Central Administrations, where odd members of even the Social Democratic Party managed to keep their posts until the end of 1947.[1] It was the increasing political influence in the work of the Administrations, which were supposed to be non-political, that drove such men as Dr. Buschmann, President of the Administration for Trade and Supply, to resign. On the other hand, the demand for uniformity of political opinion accounted for the departure of many minor functionaries. It was this latter influence which showed itself less strongly at first in the Central Administrations. Nevertheless, after 1946 political motives played an increasing part in their work, as regards both policy and personnel.

About the beginning of 1947 there were two new additions to the thirteen existing Administrations. An Administration for

[1] In the August 1947 elections to the Trades Union Office Council of the Administrations, the majority of seats actually went to open Social Democrats. This was one of the results of having the offices of the Administrations in Berlin.

Internal Affairs, in whose title the customary words 'German' and 'Central' were dropped, was formed with great secrecy in the office block of a former shoe factory in Berlin-Pankow. Press inquiries as to its purpose were answered evasively, usually to the effect that it was still in a formative stage and was not yet operating. Even the other Central Administrations were not informed of the work of the new department, whose representatives did not attend the monthly general meetings of all Central Administrations. The composition of its headquarters staff, and a variety of other circumstances, soon gave an indication as to what its task was likely to be. It was headed by a post-war Police President of Thuringia and former army colonel. His chief assistants were police officers from the Soviet zone, of whom some had had their first contact with police in a very different capacity. One was believed to have been implicated in an unsolved murder of certain black marketeers in Saxony-Anhalt in 1946, another in the shooting of two German police officers, Aufbau and Lenk, in 1931, followed by a prison sentence in 1932, for espionage on behalf of a foreign power. A few officials were regular policemen, including one from the police administration of the city of Berlin. In view of these facts, and of the 300-strong armed police guard which was stationed in the garages attached to the offices, it was commonly accepted that this new administration was concerned with police affairs. Further evidence showed that its task was in fact the reconstruction of the police force in the Eastern zone, at first in co-operation with the provincial ministries of Internal Affairs, whose responsibility police matters had been until this time. In 1945, in accordance with four-power decisions, it had been decided to reconstruct the German police on the basis of local government control, similar to the system existing in the U.S.A. In the Soviet zone this tendency was already being reversed in favour of provincial control as early as October 1946. Soon this new Administration seems to have obtained the power to issue orders to the ministries on its own account and to direct the reorganization of the police force as well as to standardize training and pay.[1] The suspicion that this new administration was under the direct control of the Soviet secret police was confirmed by the fact that a number of Germans who had been working for the MVD in Russia were stationed in the Administration's Headquarters. Staffing of guards in some of the

[1] For details of Soviet zone police organization see Collins, *Die Ostzonenpolizei*, Polizeizeitung 1949, No. 1; Warrner, *Aufgaben und Aufban der Ostzonenpolizei*, Die Polizei, 1949, No. 1, p. 3; Piech, *Organization der Polizei*, Deutsche Verwaltung, Vol. II, 1949, No. 10, p. 258.

internment camps in the Eastern zone was also partially taken over by the new police force (July 1947) under the control of the Administration in Berlin. These secret preparations presumably bore fruit when the announcement of a 'People's Police' for the Eastern zone was finally made in December 1947, establishing a 'democratic means of crushing secret reactionary elements'.[1]

The other addition to the ranks of the Central Administrations was the so-called Commission for Sequestration and Requisitioning. This Commission, headed by an official of no obvious party allegiance, was to co-ordinate and control the work of the local Sequestration Commissions formed from committees of the three-party bloc.[2] The ostensible reason was to provide a zonal board of review for all cases and to prevent injustice and local bias. It is worth noting that the Soviet industrial undertakings in Germany were being reorganized and extended at this time, and a central agency investigating works for disposal would assist the operation. The Commission was invested with the power of collating and reviewing all cases of proposed seizure and presenting them, with its recommendations, to the SMA for final decision.

These decisions show that while much of the early sequestration had been carried out to deprive Nazis and Nazi sympathizers, the powerful weapon of sitting in judgement on their neighbours was being increasingly used by those in favour of Socialization for furthering the ends of the State.[3] By 1947 the form of anti-Nazi procedure remained to disguise a policy aimed not primarily at depriving the guilty but at benefiting the State. Even non-Nazis and *emigrés* were expropriated, and rarely succeeded in reversing the original decision by appeal to the Central Commission, if their industrial property was of any value. Even municipal property was nationalized in certain cases. Some of the best industrial plums were taken over by the Russians as trustees, though some of those works were later given back to the German provincial governments.

The expropriated industry was vested in the provincial government, in Saxony by referendum, in the other provinces by administrative decree. The SMA stated, in its administrative instruction on the subject, that 'the democratic expression of

[1] *Berliner Zeitung*, 8 February 1948.
[2] See above, Chap. IV.
[3] For this and the following paragraphs, see a detailed article in *Wirtschafts Archiv*, Vol. II, No. 6, Dec. 1947, p. 1026 *passim*, and June–July 1948, p. 1421 (*Europa-Archiv*). Though it tends to exaggerate the extent and speed of organizational achievement in the Soviet zone, this article is extremely well-informed and valuable.

opinion by the people of Saxony gave a sure indication of the feelings of the people in the Eastern zone', which apparently made further samplings unnecessary.[1] At first the precedent of the U.S.S.R. was not followed, for the industry concerned was administered direct by the provincial Ministries of Industry. For the purposes of allocating supplies and distribution of finished products as between one factory and another, a special board was first set up in Saxony at the beginning of 1947, under the name of Saxon Industrial Board.[2] Soon the other provinces followed suit with similar organizations. By the time of the Autumn 1947 Leipzig Fair the administration of national industries had been broken down into groups according to product, but the management of individual groups, who each had a headquarters in the appropriate industrial centre of the province, was still in the hands of the provincial ministry for industry.[3] These group organizations resembled the various industrial federations in the U.S. and Britain, though they were generally less powerful. Where in the latter case the power of the federations depends upon the delegation of independence which individual members are prepared to make, in the case of these Soviet zone groups the group organizations were merely a means to make provincial control more effective. Chambers of Commerce and Industry, already much vitiated by the Nazis, were now suffered to exist only in exceptional cases, where a local effort had to be organized, such as the Leipzig Fair. Within the provincial ministries a special department was created to administer the nationalized industries. In Saxony it was called 'Land Administration for Saxon State Industries'.[4]

The early organization of East German nationalized industry is thus different to that of any other country, in that it represents more direct ministerial control than exists anywhere else except, in a somewhat different way and in a more limited sphere, in France. For instance, the Soviet zone is probably the only country in the world where the railways are directly administered by the equivalent of a ministry, through the incorporation of the State Railway Organization into the Central Administration for Trans-

[1] Instruction dated February 1947. See also Löwenthal, *op. cit.*, p. 112.

[2] *Sächsischer Industrie Kontor* (SIK).

[3] In order to avoid misunderstanding it should be mentioned that the administration of the provincial works was specially controlled by a board consisting of the economic minister of the Land, civil servants, and a few representatives of the Trades Unions. Though registered as a corporation, this board was in fact a ministerial department only, even in Saxony.

[4] Löwenthal, *op. cit.*, p. 113. It is safe to take Saxony as a model province in this respect. See above, p. 83.

port at the beginning of 1946.[1] There is little genuine provision for workers' representation at the top of the hierarchy,[2] and, of course, none for consumers. In this respect alone, recent Soviet practice has been followed, based on the principle that the Communist manager of a factory *ipso facto* represents the party and therefore to some extent the workers.

The next step was to increase the powers of the Central Administration at the expense of the provinces. Orders now began to be issued under the signature of the Presidents of the Administrations without the usual preamble. The Central Administrations began to call the provincial governments to account, and, under the plea of zonal co-ordination, to counteract measures already taken by those governments. The Administration for Finance, for instance, co-ordinated the budgets of the various provinces after these budgets had been passed by the provincial SMAs and submitted its recommendations for their acceptance or refusal to the SMA at Karlshorst; a fact which alone gave the Administration enhanced constitutional status in relation to the provincial governments as well as to the provincial SMA. The fact that certain Central Administrations, such as that for Transport, controlled organizations which had previously been at *Reich* level and were outside the jurisdiction of the provincial governments, also enhanced the status of the former. The State Railways directorate controlled the local railway directorates (*Reichsbahndirektionen*), the Central Administration for Post and Telegraphs controlled its higher postal directorates (*Oberpostdirektionen*). This exclusive control placed the provincial governments at a disadvantage in any constitutional struggle.

There was no evidence at first of the beginnings of any official resistance on the part of the provinces to the increasing powers of the Central Administrations. Any protest would indeed have been futile, as it would have been a protest against the SMA itself. However, the elements of conflict existed. We have mentioned that the provincial governments recognized the eventual return of a centralized government and had admitted in their constitutions the purely temporary nature of some of their powers.[3] The administrative structure of each province was basically identical, their

[1] Direct ministerial administration of postal services exists in England and France, as well as in the Soviet zone.

[2] It is now held by many in Great Britain, following Professor G. D. H. Cole, that the presence of a senior Trades Unionist on the board of a nationalized industry is not automatically synonymous with workers' representation. If this is true of England, it is far more true in a Communist country.

[3] See above, p. 96.

legislation also. There were a very few signs of individualism; Brandenburg created an organization of 'Peoples Solidarity' peculiar to itself (*Märkische Volkssolidarität*), and Saxony on the 23rd March 1948 enacted a law to safeguard the cultural rights of its Sorb or Slav minority. In the absence of a zonal constitution no clear division between the powers of central government and of provincial governments was possible, and in the constitutions of the provinces no definition had been attempted. Now the actions of the Central Administrations seemed not only to be based on the powers of a mythical central government but began to encroach upon the powers specifically allocated to the provinces under their constitutions. This can clearly be seen from the method of production planning. Three plans for the zone were made each year, divided into four quarters: the plan of the SMA, the plan of the Central Administrations, and the sum total of the plans of the five provincial governments. It was the task of the DZV for Industry, Fuel and Power, and Agriculture to ensure that the plans were carried out on a zonal basis, and if one province fell behind in its share of the total plan it could be, and was, called to account. Any failure on the part of a Land to fulfil part of its plan, automatically gave the Central Administrations the right to take the necessary remedial measures themselves until the emergency was over. This involved direct interference in local production. Such central interference became frequent during and after the hard winter of 1946–7. In July 1947 the Central Administrations were given long-term emergency powers by decree of the SMA to control production even in individual factories, without having to go through provincial ministries at all. This brought the latent conflict out into the open.

The internal situation varied from province to province. Saxony was the most unified Land and contained by far the biggest share of the zone's industrial capacity and nearly a third of its population. Its Minister for Economic Affairs was a Communist of long standing who had been trained in Russia and had returned to Germany with the task of making Saxony a model Communist state. Socialization and State control of industries had gone much further in Saxony by December 1946 than in any other part of the zone. The Government controlled not only industrial production but competed with the Central Administration for the control of Saxon trade by establishing its own home trade and import-export agency for this purpose. The measures of the Saxon Government had been a success, and Saxony had contributed more than its planned share to the economic recovery of the Soviet zone during

1946. It was therefore natural that the Saxon Government should protest particularly strongly against the interference of the Central Administrations, on the grounds that it had been outstandingly successful in carrying out Russian wishes, while the dislocation due to winter was *force majeure* and unavoidable. The Saxon case was strengthened by the fact that the organization of industry and economy in Saxony was so closely in the hands of the Saxon Government and its subordinate institutions that it could effectively prevent the interference of the Central Authorities, which could never rival local ties and sympathy with mere centralized efficiency. The conflict had its political as well as constitutional aspects. Since both parties in the dispute were leading members of the SED, the issues tended to be fought out within the Party. The emergence of such a conflict would be a mockery to the very word 'unity' which figured so prominently in the name and programme of that party. It was difficult to side with the Central Administrations against such a prominent political figure as Selbmann, the Saxon Minister for Economic Affairs; on the other hand, to side against the Central Administrations meant a decision against an organization directly under Russian control. The situation was similar in the other provinces. In Saxony-Anhalt and Thuringia the organization of industry and economy by the provincial government had not gone as far, but the rudiments of an organization, based on the Saxon model, existed. In Brandenburg and Mecklenburg, where industry played a relatively small part in provincial life, the Central Administration had less difficulty in asserting itself, since neither of these provinces could attempt to carry out an independent policy without facing economic ruin. The predominantly peasant population of these areas did not desire any policy which would provoke conflict and thus endanger their new holdings.

By the summer of 1947 the position had become acute. Reports indicated that the meetings between the provincial ministers and the presidents and vice-presidents of the Administrations were increasingly stormy, and signs of disagreement became noticeable in public—which in a Communist State meant that a very serious conflict was going on.[1] It became essential for the Russians to decide the issue. Their decision would be in effect a statement of future policy. The choice was not simply between Central Administrations and provincial governments but went far deeper.

[1] Statements of Selbmann, Seydewitz and others in the Saxon Press, reports in the *Telegraf* and *Neue Zeitung* in Berlin, July 1947.

Politically, it meant a verdict on the continued existence of provincial autonomy. Economically, it involved a decision between a rigidly centralized economy and the continuation of the present system of 'mixed' economy which enabled the Russians to continue the pursuit of their own special interests in greater obscurity. The crisis was as acute, if not as spectacular, as that facing the Russians before the change-over to NEP.

In the spring of 1947 the heads of the economic Central Administrations, together with the Chairman of the Trades Union Association and the Farmers' Co-operative, and certain of the more prominent ministers of the provinces, had begun, on Russian instructions, to meet on a semi-official basis at regular intervals in order to co-ordinate planning throughout the zone. This unofficial committee, which was known as the Economic Commission, was now used as a means to resolve the conflict. It was first made official and became the overall co-ordinating agency for economic planning. Its membership was defined and increased, it was allocated a secretariat and a considerable executive staff. Its powers were superior to that of the Central Administrations as well as to those of the provincial governments. At first glance it seemed that the problem had been settled by giving the decisive authority to neither of the two parties, but by creating a third.

However, the Economic Commission, far from being an independent body, was in fact a synthesis of the most influential men in the Central Administration, the most important representatives from the political headquarters of the SED, and the most prominent provincial ministers. The presidents of the economic group of Central Administrations were *ex officio* members, as well as the head of the Economic Department of the party headquarters responsible for personnel administration, and the Economic Ministers of Brandenburg and Saxony. In order to placate the powerful Saxon minister he was given the most important post in the new Economic Commission, that of Vice-President, applying once more the well-known Soviet *Eminence Grise* principle. The presidency was given to the Minister of Economic Affairs for Brandenburg, Heinrich Rau, an old and reliable Communist. Not that the creation of the Economic Commission was intended to placate the wounded feelings of the provincial governments as a whole; only certain powerful individuals had to be satisfied Provincial pride counted for nothing.

The Commission itself consisted of a Plenum, a Secretariat, 17 general departments and a sub-commission for the Safety of the

National Property, later in 1948 merged into the new Central Control Commission.[1] The Plenum consisted of 101 members; 48 representatives from the provinces, 15 from the political parties or 3 from each, including the Farmers' Party and the National Democratic Party, 3 representatives of the Trades Unions, 2 of the Farmers' Co-operative, 2 of the industrial Consumers' Co-operative, one each from the Democratic Youth, the Democratic Women's organization and the Cultural Union. The remaining members of the Plenum represented the Economic Commission itself. This body, officially the governing organ, was in fact the audience to which decisions were submitted for automatic approval by the Secretariat, which consisted of the Commission's chairman, vice-chairman, three deputy-chairmen and a representative of the Trades Unions and the Farmers' Co-operative. This was the real policy-making body. The 17 general departments were a more detailed reproduction of the Central Administrations, as follows:

- Economic Planning
- Statistic
- Coal
- Fuel
- Metallurgy
- Machines and Electrical industry
- Chemicals
- Light industry
- Material control and allocation
- Trade and Supply
- Inter-zonal and Foreign Trade
- Transport
- Agriculture and Forestry
- Labour and Social Welfare
- Post and Communications
- Finance
- Health

What had been a mere shadow of centralization at the time of the Central Administrations now became a powerful reality. The SED gained by obtaining a direct voice in civil administration through its representatives on the Commission, among whom were Leuschner, their economic expert, and the son of Wilhelm Pieck. This arrangement, by increasing direct party control, effectively prevented any recurrence of internal conflicts; its direct voice in the Economic Commission enabled the affairs of that body to be openly discussed at party meetings, and differences of opinion to be eliminated. The real position of the SED *vis-à-vis* the Economic Commission was clearly shown in July 1948 over the handling of the Two Year Plan. This was first presented as the plan of the Party at the annual congress of the SED, and was launched by Ulbricht

[1] Lassig, 'Die Entwicklung des öffentlichen Rechts in der SBZ im Jahre 1948', *Deutsche Verwaltung*, 2nd year, No. 18, 15 Sept. 1949, p. 492; No. 19, 1 Oct. 1949, p. 519.

and Grotewohl. It was adopted by the Economic Commission as a working basis without further ado, and there was no hesitation in admitting afterwards that the experts of the Economic Commission had in fact assisted in the preparation of the plan. The Party's plan could not but be that of the Economic Commission. It is therefore no exaggeration to say that the policies of the Economic Commission, in so far as they were not dictated directly by the SMA, were controlled by SED headquarters—with Russian approval.

3

JANUARY 1948–MARCH 1950

One of the first results of the change was the creation of a new and powerful group of zonal industries, or 'People's Undertakings', as they were called, as an invidious distinction from the provincially-owned works. The transfer of power from the provincial governments to the Economic Commission was thus completed by a transfer of property. The biggest and most important nationalized factories were concerned in the transfer, so that two-thirds of the capacity of nationalized industry was vested in the Economic Commission, and one-third remained under the control of the provincial governments. The zonal industry was administered by the departments for industry and fuel and power of the Economic Commission, which had special sections dealing with the 'people's works', divided into groups according to product. In spite of the centralization of vesting and control, the peculiar system of direct ministerial administration remained. Not even the provincial system of group combinations in any one industry were at first established. Just before the establishment of the East German Government, some intermediary system of at least partially independent trusts was in the process of emergence.[1]

The provincial governments continued unchanged in form, though in a much-reduced sphere of activity, and increasingly as the executive agents of the central authority. They lost in their new rôle what little responsibility they had to the elected parliaments of their Land, while the latter were now impotent and played an entirely fictitious and decorative rôle. The Commission,

[1] According to the article in the *Wirtschafts Archiv* for June 1948, noted above, the formation of these trusts was under consideration as early as May 1948 (p. 1425).

in spite of its name, embraced not only the economic administrations but all Central Administrations, except Education, Justice, and Police, which now all became departments.[1] The former presidents were reduced to departmental directors.

It was natural that such enhanced responsibility should bring in its train another purge of politically unreliable members. However, political reliability was often in inverse proportion to administrative efficiency, since no amount of political faith could make, to take the Eastern zone's most notable instance, a statistician out of an untrained party man, however keen.[2] This decrease in the standard of work contributed to the deterioration of the economic situation in the East. There were in 1949 a number of men in important positions in the Economic Commission whose main guide to economic affairs seemed to be the figures of the innumerable planning departments of party and administration. In matters of economic administration in which the Russians were genuinely and immediately interested it was, as will be seen, always possible to provide their own economic experts. But the system demanded that the hunt for saboteurs should be cumulative and perpetual.[3] The more saboteurs were found the more remained to be discovered. Even co-operative members of the SED were not immune; persistent attacks in the SED press caused the resignation of the Deputy Director of the Department for Finance (formerly Vice-President of the Central Administration). Other members of the SED were marked for dismissal as soon as a suitable replacement could be found. A Control Commission for the administration, on top of the party's own commission, was set up on 15 June 1948, to supervise the activities of individual members and to co-ordinate the work of the extensive internal espionage organization controlled by the personnel section of each department of the Economic Commission under the Vice-President. This Commission was directly supervised by the Russian police, which had from the earliest days established liaison offices in the building of the

[1] Thus the identity of terminology with the Soviet Union became complete when the East German Republic was formally created in October 1949, the former Central Administrations becoming head departments or *Glavki* of ministries. See note 2 on p. 114.

[2] One of the outstanding examples of statistical carelessness was the figure for penicillin production for the year 1948 in the final Economic Commission production plan 1947. In the overall as well as the detailed plans the figure was given as 300,000 tons instead of a quantity to the value of 300,000 Marks—a simple mistake which should have been removed at the first mathematical check, of which there are supposed to be six before the plan is finally approved.

[3] For details of the sabotage craze among the Russians, see Löwenthal, *op. cit.*, pp. 66, 209–35.

Central Administrations. The work of the Control Commission was not confined to the headquarters of the Economic Commission, but extended to the provincial governments, to the *Kreise*, and to individual factories. It was their task to produce individuals as scapegoats for the general denunciations of saboteurs which, after January 1948, became more and more frequent to explain non-fulfilment of production plans.

The schemes put into operation by the Central Administrations in 1945 and 1946 also took on a new aspect. The Education plan had long overstepped the narrow boundary between post-war necessity and deliberate political intention. The teachers' courses became open forcing-grounds for Communists, with an increasing emphasis on Marxist indoctrination and political 'progressiveness'. Thus, teachers attended not only professional courses but also Party lectures and seminars to an increasing extent. The system of Hitler Youth *Ordernburgen* or Party schools seemed to have come to life again in the organization of SED leadership schools in the provinces, with its academy for higher educational officials at Machnow, near Berlin. Similarly, candidates for universities were now required to submit to a political examination, and those who had reactionary tendencies were refused admission. The University of Berlin, under the energetic direction of the chemist, Professor Rompe, who at the beginning of 1948 was Rector as well as the head of the sub-department for University Education in the Central Administration was particularly notorious for its political bias.[1]

The 'people's' justice followed suit. While the training course itself did not radically change, the selection of candidates came almost entirely into the hands of the SED, and the control of the scheme passed to the legal Administrations. Since political offenders until October 1949 were either interned without trial or tried by the Russians themselves behind closed doors, no flagrant examples of judicial injustice or major political trials were reported. The legal procedure was, however, very slow, litigation almost an impossibility, and criminal trials, particularly those connected with anti-social activities, almost invariably ended in conviction.[2] The chief characteristic of Eastern German legal practice became the fact that the safeguards of personal liberty, where they existed at all, were not under the jurisdiction of the Courts, but based on

[1] For the fate of the faculties of Philosophy in the Eastern zone, see *Der Monat*, Berlin, Vol. II, No 21, June 1950, p. 250.

[2] From the figures in the official Soviet Zone Law publications *Die Justiz*, Berlin. See also Löwenthal, *op. cit.*, for many instances of alleged injustice.

political privilege, and it was possible to be arrested and interned without trial.[1]

The organization of the police force in the Soviet zone since the summer of 1947 proceeded in the direction of centralized control and resembled the development during the period 1925–33. The institution of a police in lieu of an army, with a large percentage of motorized forces equipped with automatic weapons such as tommy guns and pistols, in order to suppress internal disturbances in the absence of a suitable armed force, was then known as *Kasernierte Polizei* (literally 'Police in barracks'). After the official institution of the 'People's Police' in December 1947, this process was repeated. The Police Department was taken over about this time by that notorious Communist, Dr. Kurt Fischer, formerly Minister for Internal Affairs in Saxony. Pictures of him taking marches-past in an S.S.-like uniform have been published in the Press. A considerable number of indoctrinated former Wehrmacht officers reappeared in Germany as police officials, the most notable case being that of Markgraf, the Russian-sponsored police chief of Berlin until 1949, and former army colonel, and Reschke, first president of the Central Police Administration. An effort was made to contact released army officers in the West with a view to obtaining their services in a similar capacity. Markgraf was alleged to have been placed in charge of this work after his retirement as Berlin's Chief of Police. These appointments, as well as the type and amount of equipment being issued to the police, gave a strong indication of its para-military qualities.[2] In May 1949 the Department for Internal Affairs was divided into the following sections:

1. Personnel.
2. Local Government affairs.
3. Administrative police. Since October 1948 economic matters have been taken from this section to be dealt with by a separate section.
4. Economic affairs.
5. Criminal police, including group K5 dealing with political subversion.
6. Railway police.
7. Protection police.[3]
8. Frontier police.
9. Police troops.

[1] For instance, the discretionary powers of courts such as bail, *prima facie* jurisdiction, the interpretation of the rules of evidence, and other limitations on arbitrary conviction are severely limited in the lower courts, and almost at the discretion of the legal department of the Economic Commission in the higher courts. For many individual instances, see Löwenthal, *op. cit.*

[2] See the report in the *Manchester Guardian*, 30 Sept. 1948.

[3] This section (*Schutzpolizei*) deals with the routine of traffic direction, accidents and all matters appertaining to 'the beat'.

The system of police organization in the East was fundamentally the same as before 1945, and as different as ever from the British and American systems. Thus the Prussian police law of 1 June 1936 and the corresponding laws of the other Länder remained in force, though in the Western zones they were repealed soon after the war. The chief features in the East were the highly centralized direction, the organizational division according to purpose, and, since 1949, the special expansion of sections 5, 8 and 9. In 1948 the fire brigade was removed from the control of the police once more, and restored to that of the municipalities.

The purpose of all this, beyond the quelling of disturbances, was less immediately evident. It may be well, however, to recall that the famous Hermann Goering Regiment was formed chiefly from policemen and that SS Division No. 3 rejoiced in the name of *Polizei* division. By the beginning of 1950 the force had swelled to some 50,000 men,[1] quite apart from the policemen on normal duties, and was scheduled to reach 70,000 by the end of 1950. It was organized like an army, into *Bereitschaften* or companies, and regiments, though police nomenclature was retained. Pay was good; a captain's real salary, including rationing allowances, corresponded to that of a very high civil servant, such as the head of a ministerial department. The individuals who appeared on parade had none of the pallor usual among the habitually under-nourished population of Eastern Germany. There was no direct evidence before March 1950 that anything heavier than machine guns were issued as weapons, but the number of the latter was high, and they were partly of German, partly of Czech and Hungarian manufacture. The composition of the men of this police force was curious. Workers formed a very small proportion of its numbers, but ex-bourgeoisie affected by the land reform and the measures of industrial expropriation seemed to have joined in large numbers. A solid backbone of former regular officers and N.C.Os was also recruited, partly from among German prisoners of war in Russian hands, but after the campaign for German unity began, mostly demobilized ex-soldiers joined, or were persuaded to join, through motives of economic advantage and national aspiration. Up to May 1950 there were no signs that ex-soldiers in the West had been persuaded to migrate and enlist in any number. Nevertheless, the policy of secrecy was abandoned at the beginning of 1950, and this Eastern Army could

[1] This figure was repeatedly mentioned in the English press during March 1950. According to official British sources in Germany, the numbers were as high as 100,000. Even the extreme figure of 400,000 has been mentioned in England.

be seen on parade at most week-ends with the avowed object of swelling its ranks still further.

There was, of course, a civilian counterpart in the shape of the various political and administrative control organizations, which became unified as a result of the formation of the Ministry of State Security early in 1950. Its personnel consisted of the members of the various control commissions, the *Bereitschaften* of the 'People's Police', and the anti-sabotage squads of the criminal police. Though there appeared to be no single organization corresponding to the ubiquitous officials of the MVD in the Soviet Union, all these bodies came under a ministry of much the same title, and had a headquarters organization supplied by the Russians with all the technical paraphernalia, ranging from listening devices to sound-proof torture cells, which goes to make the modern police state. The organization, since 1947, employed a considerable number of part-time agents and spies, in addition to those employed direct by the MVD.[1]

The work of the former Central Administration for Labour had partly been that of a Labour supply-and-demand agency for the needs of a normal economy. We have seen[2] that at first it co-operated with the Trades Union Association, and as long as the latter was still a relatively genuine Trades Union movement officially unattached to any party (what the Russians contemptuously call 'syndicalist') the co-operation had not always been harmonious. Before October 1946 protests were made by local organizations against SED encroachments on their jurisdiction and against the severity of the 1944 price-stop, which hit the workers especially hard. The last of such official protests seems to have been made in August 1947 in the headquarters of the Central Administration, where a predominantly CDU and LDP, and even partly SPD 'office council'[3] of the Trades Union Association protested against SED 'terrorism'. The Association was one of the last organizations to submit without question to SED control. As a result, Control Council Order No. 22, requiring notification to the Trades Unions in cases of dismissal in official organizations, was ignored by the Russians.[4] But since the complete alignment of both the Trades Unions and of the Labour Department of the Economic Commission with SED party policy, such unhealthy

[1] This information is based on recent reports from a fairly reliable private source.
[2] Above, pp. 115, 121–122.
[3] The Civil Service equivalent of industrial works' councils.
[4] *Neue Zeitung*, 3 April 1948.

signs of reaction have disappeared. On 29 April 1948 the official Soviet newspaper in Berlin, the *Tägliche Rundschau,* was proud to report that membership of the Trades Unions had risen from 3¼ million at the end of 1947 to 4 million.

From the beginning of 1946 the Administration for Labour had been a special instrument in Russian labour policy. Labour for the Soviet Trusts in Germany was supplied as a priority. The enormous demands of the uranium mining scheme operated by the Russians since the beginning of 1946 in the mountains on the Saxon-Czech border, estimated at their peak in August 1947 at over 100,000 workers, were also supplied by the organization of the Labour Administration. This was done partly by voluntary recruitment, through speakers and posters glamorizing the work into a patriotic duty. To supplement the ever-decreasing trickle obtained by this method, wholesale conscription was resorted to during 1947, particularly in Saxony. All those not considered gainfully or wholly employed were registered and transported to Aue or Winterberg. Finally, illegal border-crossers, minor and major black-marketeers, political internees, and even convicted criminals were pressed into service. It was possible during 1947 to estimate the relative strength of each new recruiting drive from the size of the refugee movements from East to West. Working conditions were bad and the rate of accidents high, as some of the shafts were either of a very temporary nature or had fallen into disuse since silver-mining virtually ceased thirty years earlier.[1] The Russians tended to make up by excessive numbers what they lacked in machinery and organization, and reduced the work to an uneconomical mass scramble. The number of arrivals often exceeded the arrangements for accommodation and feeding, and disease broke out. During the first part of 1948 the total number of workers employed at one time is estimated at about 90,000, the reduction being due partly to better organization, and partly to the disappointingly small yield of uranium from the ore. Since then the number has further decreased somewhat, as the accent seems to have been shifted gradually to the workings on the Czech side near Jachymov. This change may have been partly due to the better security facilities on the Czech side, as well as the richer deposits there.

One of the most important tasks of the Administration for Labour, and its junior partner, the Administration for Re-settlers or Refugees, was the provision of skilled and unskilled labour for

[1] For greater detail about conditions, etc , see Löwenthal, *op. cit.*, pp. 186–200.

transfer to Russia. In addition to the considerable number of German prisoners working in Russia in 1947,[1] a series of recruiting drives and removals of a more or less compulsory nature increased this figure by about 305,000. The Russians were chiefly interested in scientists, technicians, and certain classes of highly skilled workers, such as optical specialists and workers from Zeiss, machine-tool operators and electrical engineers from Siemens, and, above all, turbine, jet motor, and aircraft engine specialists and workers. Political internees were conscripted for labour in the Soviet Union,[2] and the official daily load detail of the railway directorate at Frankfurt/Oder frequently lists 'political prisoners' or 'labour' as freight carried to Russia together with reparation goods. Usually, pressure in the form of house arrest and threats or tempting offers was applied to those who were unwilling to sign a voluntary contract. Specialists were usually offered good terms and often the chance to take their families. In any case, the removal of a plant to Russia often left little desire on their part to remain unemployed in Germany when they could continue their work in Russia. Duration of contract varied between three and fifteen years.

This Eastward movement of labour, compensated only by the return of sick or incapable prisoners to Germany,[3] culminated in the biggest mass transfer to date, the removal of over 100,000 at one fell swoop in May-June 1947, under the code name 'Operation *Ossawakim*'. Like its predecessors, it was organized under Russian supervision by the Administrations for Labour and Re-settlers, and coupled with a propaganda campaign of considerable dimensions. After that the flow was reduced very considerably, but the Department for Labour of the Economic Commission continued as a potentially efficient instrument for particular and pressing Soviet labour demands.

The field of commerce was the last to be reorganized. Just before the 1947 Autumn Leipzig Fair, the finishing touch was put on the new programme of centralization by the institution of a Central Administration for Foreign and Inter-zonal Trade, which was to replace the provincial export-import organizations with the means

1 No accurate figures are available. A survey undertaken by a German authority and based on German figures of January 1945, and on the units known to be in Russia or Poland and their strength just before the collapse, put the figure at a minimum of 1,100,000 in July 1946.

2 This is confirmed by Löwenthal, *op. cit.*, pp. 88, 201, etc. He cites numerous instances of Russian labour recruitment and its methods.

3 The physical state of prisoners returning from Russia contributed largely to popular resentment against Russia, in Italy and Austria as well as in Germany.

of centralized control. Between the end of 1948 and the summer of 1949 the process of organizing commerce was completed on Russian lines, and two monopoly organizations, the German Import-Export Corporation and, shortly after, the Commerce Organization (*Handels Organization*), were founded. The former was to handle all foreign contracts on behalf of the department for Foreign and Inter-zonal Trade, and to co-ordinate the various provincial import-export firms and the Saxon and Thuringian export-import corporations, the latter to give the commerce department a monopoly of certain internal trade. The Department also controlled the Foreign Trade Account Conversion Office, which handled the German mark accounts of import and export transactions. The machinery for centralized control of all the branches of administration was therefore complete, needing only the Economic Commission itself to give it a head. The personnel was now politically reliable, all heads of departments, except one, and all sub-department heads, except two, being members of the SED.

Since the field of commerce was reorganized at the beginning of 1949, over a year later than industry, the Russian model was copied much more closely from the very beginning. This was to some extent due to the fact that the provinces, particularly Saxony, had established their own disguised import-export firms.[1] and these could be most easily absorbed by zonal corporations. The functions of the *Import-Export Gesellschaft* and the *Handels Organization*, established by decree, were somewhat different. The former only acted on behalf of the Foreign Trade department of the Economic Commission in handling the bulk shipments of national or provincial works, or in cases of regulated bilateral trade arising out of specific agreements. In cases of individual orders from abroad private firms had to obtain the corporation's permit before shipment, and it authorized specific imports on behalf of the department. The *Handels Organization*, on the other hand, acted as a direct national competitor to the private sector of commerce. It owned its own chain of stores and retail shops, its own restaurants and hotels. This fixed capital was mostly property previously expropriated from 'Nazis' and vested in the corporation, or acquired by it through its own more or less normal commercial methods. Thus a serious competitor even to the private shopkeeper and to the co-operatives had arisen, and though no general move towards

[1] They masqueraded as private organizations, chiefly for the benefit of foreign business men, under such names as Füting, and Kegel, of Leipzig. See also Löwenthal, *op. cit.*, p. 117, though he is mistaken in labelling them as covers for Russian exports.

nationalizing commerce was made, the means of State monopoly in this field existed.

The final evolution of the process of building up an administration satisfactory to Russian purposes was achieved by the summer of 1949. As has been said in dealing with the political picture, the establishment of the East German republic made little difference to the administrative reality in the Soviet zone beyond a change in nomenclature. The economic commission became a government, its departments became ministries, the legislature a permanent chorus of approval, who saw little of the activities of government and perforce approved of the little they saw. The formation of the government and its ministries did not need the long preliminaries which heralded the establishment of the West German republic, for its organization and personnel were ready made. Only two new administrative bodies subsequently made their appearance. The Ministry of Foreign Affairs, whose diplomatic and domestic staff was limited by the fact that only a few countries accepted its representation in addition to the U.S.S.R. and Russian satellites, fulfilled few valuable functions beyond establishing tentative liaison with Eastern Europe and receiving Soviet orders in a new form. The Ministry of State Security merely completed the control of the official and secret police, and stepped up their activity. Its creation was justi fied to the public by the alleged need to counter increased Western sabotage, and coincided with some trials for economic offences.

The acceptance of a highly centralized economic system in the Soviet zone meant that a considerable number of Germans at the top were able to obtain a clear insight into the real economic position of Eastern Germany, and the exact extent of Russian interests there. This was a relatively late development; as late as the summer of 1947 there was not one German in Germany who knew the full extent of Russian-owned capacity and property, or the real value of reparations. Few Russians, even, had any access to more than pieces of this information. Now, a simple sum of subtraction gave the necessary information to those who controlled the economic policy of the Commission. We may be certain that they were, for the moment at any rate, considered reliable. This may seem an extraordinary deduction to make from their mere possession of information, but an examination of the economic position will show the real importance of possessing a clear guide to the extent of Russian holdings. For with this knowledge it was possible to make a good guess at Russia's real wishes and intentions in Germany.

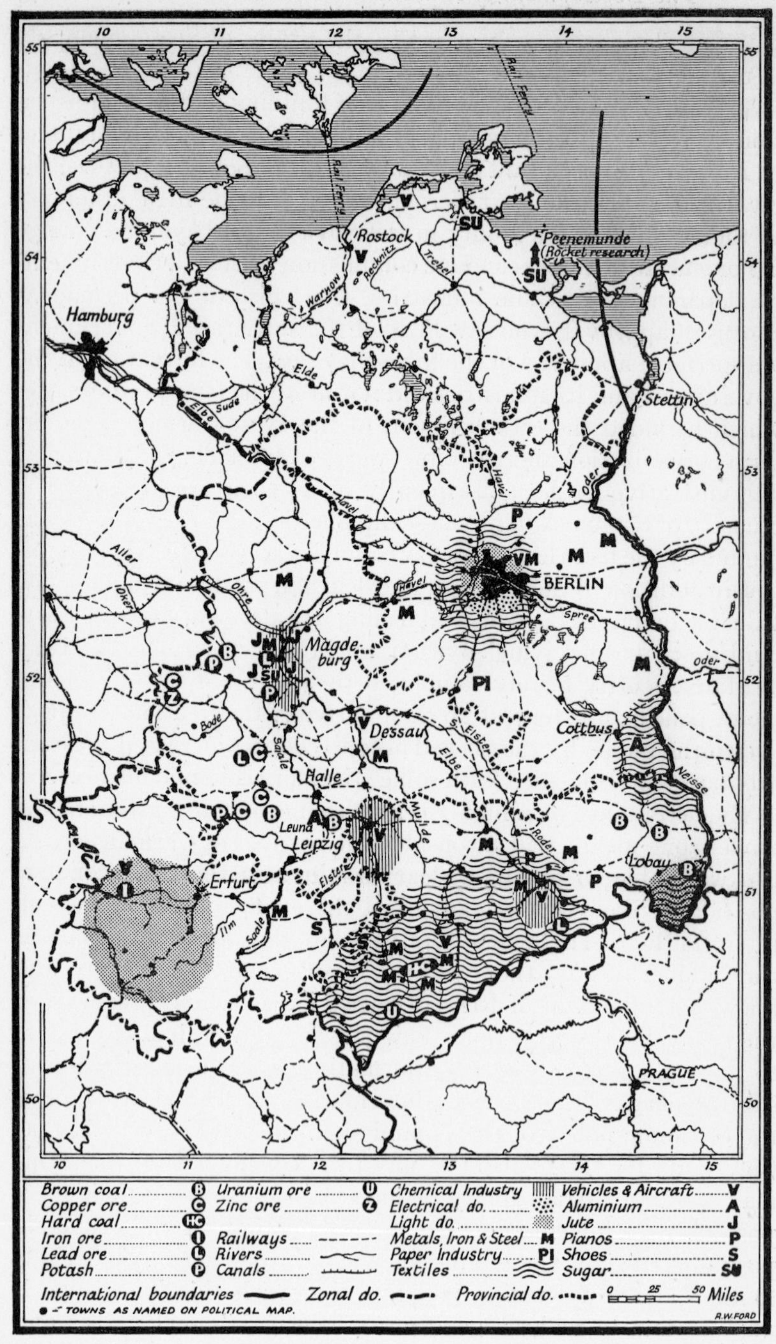

2. *Economic Map of Soviet Zone*

CHAPTER VI

THE ECONOMIC REVIVAL 1945–6

THE breakdown of administration, which began in the winter of 1944–5 and culminated in the chaos of summer 1945, greatly affected the German economy. Any system of full employment must involve a considerable measure of governmental control over investment and finance. In the German experiment two special reservations were present. 'Full employment in Germany was associated with a large increase in the compulsory powers of the State, in particular, the free organizations of labour had been destroyed at the outset of the Nazi régime. . . . Secondly, full employment was only a short transitional stage in a development which in peacetime already transformed the under-employed German economy into an over-employed war economy; and in any case, full employment was not achieved for its own sake (or for the sake of social welfare) but was a mere by-product of re-armament.'[1] Both these special pillars of full employment, the unlimited economic sovereignty of the State and the production devoted exclusively to the prosecution of the war, disappeared in 1945, and thus sharpened the inevitable effects of administrative collapse.

With the disappearance of the elaborate economic structure described earlier, a considerable recession was to be expected. But even more serious were the effects of the breakdown in distribution. Germany at the end of the war was divided into several areas of occupation according to the fortunes of war of the various allied armies. Her transport system, the main target of allied tactical and strategic bombing, had suffered greater damage than any other economic sector. Where movement of goods was physically still possible, the risk of transport into the unknown of another zone deterred any attempts at distribution. As in the field of politics, the economic organisation of Germany disintegrated into innumerable, almost independent, cells. These were based on the towns, and depended for existence on their success in establishing a barter relationship with the surrounding agricultural hinterland.

The situation, which was common to all four zones, was dominated by the food shortage. We have seen since the war, even in

[1] *The Economics of Full Employment.* Oxford Institute of Statistics (Oxford 1945). Part VI, p. 181.

countries enjoying relatively stable administrations, how difficult it can be to coax farmers into exchanging their produce for a currency in which they feel little confidence.[1] In Germany they succeeded in dictating their own terms, and all goods took on a new value in relation to the farmers' propensity to consume them. Durable consumer goods were in demand, and workers in consumer-goods factories who succeeded in being paid in kind achived an expendable income far greater than that of a salaried employee having to convert his money into food in various stages. The shortage of consumer goods was such that farmers' demand for them exceeded the demand for articles of potential investment, such as jewellery, or the 'classical' grand piano.

The effects of this system made regional and local prosperity altogether arbitrary. Densely populated industrial areas, the Ruhr or Saxony, were in a worse position than the partly industrial country towns in which Germany abounds. Moreover, productivity decreased considerably since the problem of barter could take up as much as a third of the normal working week. Figures of employment distribution for 1945 would show an exodus from the towns into the country, from productive employment to distributive employment, from heavy industries into consumer-goods industries This decrease in productivity was disguised by the figures of employment for 1946 and 1947, which in all zones showed a surprisingly high level compared to 1936. It can best be gauged by the sudden decrease in the level of employment after the currency reform in the West in June 1948.

A general lack of confidence in the currency made for inflation. The failure of the Nazi government to keep wholesale prices pegged to the level of 1936 was not reflected by a corresponding rise in wages, and the suppressed inflation of the war years gave way to open and runaway inflation at the end of the war. The volume of currency at first remained unaffected by the drop in production, and no measures were taken against this until July 1945. The impending disintegration of the banking system caused a run on the banks during the spring of 1945, and many banks suspended payment at this time. At the very moment that production reached its lowest point in 1945, the inflationary pressure of a volume of currency designed for an extended war economy, in the hands of consumers scurrying towards illiquidity, was at its greatest.

[1] The Russians developed a particular technique for dealing with recalcitrant farmers in 1929–30, and have used many of the methods then employed in Eastern Germany.

The effect of these economic phenomena far exceeded that of the physical destruction as a result of the war; for the whole of Potsdam Germany, excluding the now separated areas, the effects of the war are generally considered to have reduced industrial capacity to the 1936 level, thus cancelling out the added investment between 1936 and 1944. For the British zone, the war damage works out as proportionately more than the all-German average, for the U.S. zone slightly less. For the Soviet zone a reduction to 1936 level of industrial capacity is estimated to be correct.[1] In agriculture the capacity of land under cultivation was rather greater in 1945 than in 1936. It can thus be appreciated that industrial and agricultural levels of production in 1945 could be raised considerably without any extension of capacity through new investment, in the case of industry the output being capable of as much as 50 per cent increase. The measures required for this, the essential means of economic revival, can be summarized briefly, and apply throughout Germany:

1. The reorganization of distribution and transport on a national or at least provincial basis.
2. The re-establishment of contact with the outside world, particularly with a view to obtaining those imports made doubly necessary by the restriction of production in Germany, and especially food.
3. Immediate action to deal with the galloping inflation and the volume of unstable currency.
4. A full mobilization of existing industrial materials and consumer-goods stocks to tide over the coming years of shortage as equitably as possible.

TABLE VII[2]

Basic Economic Data on Potsdam Germany in 1936

Area	*(Million hectares)*	%	*Arable land*	%	*Population*	%	*Capacity for manu. prod. Milliard RM*	
Soviet Zone ..	10.9	30.5	5.1	36.7	18.9[3]	32.7[3]	11.2[4]	34.9[4]
Potsdam Germany ..	35.8	100	13.9	100	58.8	100	32.0	100

[1] Official Eastern Zone statistics are based on the rough equivalence of the zone's industrial potential in 1936 and 1945.

[2] *Statistical Handbook on Potsdam Germany* (OMGUS, Berlin 1947), p. 9.

[3] Including 4 million for Berlin. Population figures corrected from 1939 to 1936.

[4] Including 3 milliards (9.3 per cent) for Berlin.

Before the war the national income of the Soviet zone had been 21 milliard Rm. compared to a total for Potsdam Germany of 58 milliard Rm. (1936), a percentage of 36.2. Of this, 7 milliard Rm. (12.1 per cent) originated in Berlin. Out of a total German employment figure of 30.1 million in 1939, 10 million had been employed in the Soviet zone and Berlin.[1] Thus the Soviet zone represented slightly less than a third of the total area and population of Potsdam Germany, and slightly more than a third of the total arable land, manufacturing capacity, and source of pre-war national income. It was the most balanced of the four zones in 1945, containing a higher relative agricultural capacity than any other zone except the French zone, and a substantial industrial capacity second only to that of the British zone.

The Russian zone was the main producer of brown coal, optics, and precision instruments, pulp and paper, non-ferrous metals and goods, textile machinery and textiles, particularly stockings, and it predominated in weaving and dyeing processes. Its dependence on the rest of Germany for hard coal, steel, and machinery will be discussed in another connection.[2] Further, the zone predominated in potato and rye production, accounting in 1936 for about 38 per cent of the total production in these commodities in Potsdam Germany. It contained 48 per cent of the total sheep population and about 23 per cent of dairy cattle.[3] Thus not only had it a strong agricultural sector which relieved the vicious circle of food shortages reacting on industrial output, but its manufacturing industries were in a favourable position with regard to future exports, since its industries produced many of the pre-war export staples. In 1936 the Soviet zone and Berlin accounted for exports worth 1,453 million Rm. out of a German (Potsdam area) total of 4,477 mill. Rm., or 32 per cent.[4] The zone's chief problem was the shortage of certain basic raw materials. Clearly the position of the Soviet zone was far more favourable on both long- and short-term bases than that of the British or U.S. zones.

The importance of all-round self-sufficiency as an ideal can be seen from a glance at the industrial geography of Europe after the war. Given the collapse of foreign trade, an industrial country like Germany would immediately be faced with the prospect of food

[1] *Statistical Handbook*, p. 9.
[2] See Chap. VIII, Part 1.
[3] *Handbook*, p. 10. Figures slightly amended against a private calculation, based on *Reichsnährstand* data for 1939.
[4] *Handbook*, p. 9. Figures slightly amended for Soviet zone against the figures of the Economic Survey of 1936, published by the *Statistisches Reichsamt*.

shortage. The time required to restore industrial production to the level of competitive export, even with all available incentives from the occupying powers, would exceed the immediate reserves of food available and would throw the entire national food consumption on to local agricultural production, which could not cover more than about 70 per cent of the requirements of the population. The natural preponderance of agriculture in one zone would therefore give that zone a strong bargaining power in relation to the others. On the other hand, the physical and legal restrictions in industrial production made any readjustment in this lop-sided balance impossible for the moment. The relationship was therefore static, and, as long as West German industrial production lagged behind the demands of the Eastern zone, unrestricted economic intercourse between East and West could only result in further inflationary movements of prices, without necessarily satisfying the needs of the Soviet zone. Limited barter or compensation trade between East and West was thus the only satisfactory arrangement to satisfy some of the needs of the Soviet zone in iron, hard coal, fuels, lubricants, and steel. Not that the latter produced an exportable surplus of all agricultural goods or was even self-sufficient in all such commodities. The so-called surpluses of the Soviet zone for inter-zonal export were often the result of arbitrary rationing or requisitioning by the occupying power to make available as much as possible of the hardest commodity currency in existence in Germany.

The considerable exodus from the Soviet zone at the end of the war enabled some of the mushroom committees of socialists and communists to gain a voice in the control of some partially deserted factories. In this way a continuity of production was provided for some firms, particularly the large national combines such as the Hermann Goering Werke and Siemens. From these committees later sprang the Trades Union Association, the Co-operatives, and the local anti-fascist committees. But later Communist panegyrics on the action of the workers in spontaneously taking over the means of production deserted by their defeated capitalist masters is an exaggeration to fit in with orthodox Marxist theory.[1] The real battle was to be between the owner-managers of small undertakings and the provincial governments, and came much later.

[1] Shaffer, *op. cit.*, makes a great deal of this action to keep the factories working. The story of individual works makes it clear that in reality such 'enlightened Marxism' was the exception rather than the rule, and that most managers remained in their factories, and were only prised out by later nationalization.

The Russians encouraged a rapid restarting of industrial production wherever possible. We have unfortunately no definite figures for 1945. From the available material I would hazard a figure of about 1,200,000,000 Rm. for the second half of 1945,[1] which would be about 21 per cent of the corresponding period in 1936 and rather more in relation to 1950 capacity, as reparation from capital goods was by then getting under way. Prevailing conditions naturally contributed much to this low level of output.

TABLE VIII[2]

Index of Industrial Production, Soviet Zone, 1945

	1936	*1945 (Average on fig. for second half)*
Index of Total industrial production	100	21
Index of primary production (solid fuels and ore mining only)	100	44
General index of value added by manufacture (in consumer goods industries only)	100	13

This proportion was usual throughout Germany, but the discrepancy was particularly noticeable in the Soviet zone after the effort in the autumn of 1945 to increase primary production. The figure of 44 per cent of 1936 for the second half of 1945 divides into 38 per cent and 50 per cent respectively for the 3rd and the 4th quarter of 1945.[3] The increase is mainly due to *ad hoc* efforts by the Russian authorities in co-operation with German individuals and a few local bodies. By the autumn of 1945 a new organization began to take shape and soon co-ordinated the isolated efforts of the summer. Since many of the economic tendencies in the zone during the next two years were the result of this economic organization, it is necessary to explain its form before discussing the effects of its activities on the economic situation. Therefore we must leave this short discussion of the condition of economic affairs in the summer of 1945 and turn for the moment to the question of organization.

The chief unit of the new organization was the Land Government, one of whose first tasks was the administration of the works 'liberated' by the Denazification Commissions, or their successor, the Commission for Sequestration. Some of these firms were taken

[1] This figure is based on the scrappy production figures which were officially available for coal, and on the declared stocks at the beginning of 1946. In this return a column was included for manufactured quantity in 1945.

[2] These figures represent a mean of various private estimates. See *Handbook*, p. 19, *passim*.

[3] Private estimate.

over by the Russians themselves, but at a conservative estimate the Land governments controlled a total of 4,400 undertakings in the summer of 1946,[1] according to Shaffer. I would put the figure at about 7,000 (including 'mixed' firms in which a controlling voice was held by the government), and these the largest firms in the zone. The provincial governments consisted of functional ministries, though these were differently arranged in each province. Below them was a mixture of old and new administrative organizations. The Saxon arrangement, which formed the model for the zone, was on the lines of the diagram below:

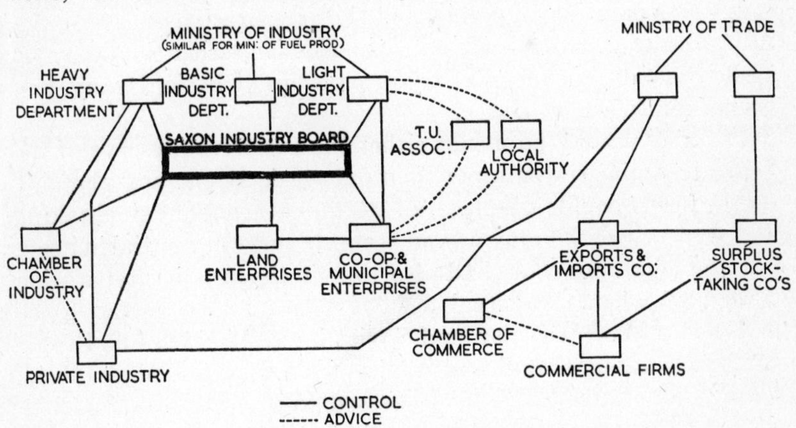

Fig I *Organization of Industry and Trade in Saxony, 1946*

The power of the provincial ministries can be appreciated from this diagram. The ministries themselves were, of course, under the close control of the SMA. At the same time the tendency towards multifarious advisory bodies is noticeable. The word 'advisory' could, however, mean the voice of the political organizations, and therefore, as far as the individual enterprise was concerned, it acted more as another authority than as a source of advice.

Long before even this structure had taken shape the existence of the Central Administrations had made itself felt. What we have

[1] The figures are from Shaffer, *Russian Zone*, p. 48. Although they seem dubious, I quote them since even the low figures given show that from the beginning the control of the provincial governments in industry was not inconsiderable. The doubt arises from the fact that in Saxony, where State control was strongest from the start, 4,000 enterprises are alleged to have been examined by the commission, while for Saxony-Anhalt 25,000 is given. Shaffer states that of this total: 'just over 10 per cent were finally appropriated'. 'The provincial government received 691, . . . local councils 54, co-operatives 284, and 706 went to private owners.' This makes a total of 1,735 enterprises, or about 7 per cent of 25,000, not 10 per cent. Finally, what is meant when a sequestrated firm 'goes to' a private owner? Surely not a normal capitalist transfer of property!

already seen of their structure enables us also to understand their economic function. They were primarily the technical extensions of SMA administration. Their complete dependence on the SMA for orders made them non-controversial; the inevitable squalls accompanying any political and economic policy-making were missing for the moment. In spite of exceptions and anomalies the Central Administrations were clearly intended as the central German planning authority, for the moment in an advisory capacity, but with the prospect of taking over increasing responsibilities from the SMA if they proved capable of doing so effectively. It is worth pointing out again that the organization of the Central Administrations tended to follow the Russian rather than German model. The division of industry into groups of Basic, Heavy, and Light is a Russian practice.

Planning was by no means either the exclusive preserve of the Central Administrations, nor their only task. Before any planning for the future could take place, an attempt at economic stocktaking had to be made. Not only was an accurate survey essential in itself, but the resultant plans had also to suit the Russian reparation demands;[1] when the actual task of reconstruction began to be undertaken, both German and Soviet interests always had to be taken into account, and reconciled as far as possible. Since official four-power government still professed to advocate economic restrictions, a programme of open industrial expansion in basic industries, even if it were possible, could not be undertaken. The reconciliation of conflicting interests made the intrinsically difficult task of the Central Administrations almost insuperable.

Before examining the measures taken to deal with the various economic problems of the Eastern zone, it is vital that the mutual relations of the various elements of economic organization should be understood. One would like to define the sphere of activity of the SMA, the Central Administrations and the provincial ministries more neatly, but a diagrammatic exposition would not conform to the facts. Although the Russians frequently issued definitions of competence to German organizations it was impossible to avoid altogether that delicate variation of influence which predominates in England and the U.S., and which is governed by such factors

[1] I have deliberately avoided reference to the requirements of the Control Council's level of industry in March 1946. The only provisions even partially carried out were those relating to the destruction of war material and certain primarily warlike industries. A discussion of this plan would bring in unnecessary complications, since the principles were abandoned before the detailed plan was published.

as the ability and political power of individuals, or the prestige accruing from a particularly successful action by one department. It frequently happened at this time that a plan or idea proposed by a provincial ministry found more favour with the Russians than one originating from the Central Administration, and thus their relationship was subtly altered for a time. Sometimes one of the latter obtained far greater control over the provincial ministries associated with it than other central administrations, the Administration for Finance being a case in point. Saxon ministries occupied a peculiar position *vis-à-vis* both the Central Administrations and the SMA. In the Administration for Labour, and the provincial labour ministries, a special situation was created by the powers of the Trades Unions. All these factors operated in a system which was supposed to present a uniform picture of planned authority, and though the smooth façade could not prevent the effect of personal and functional influences, it made their detection difficult for the outsider.

I would not hesitate to select industrial production as the focal point of the economic situation in the Soviet zone, as indeed in any target economy. The reasons are obvious. In the first place the whole economic structure of the zone had been gradually built up in relation to a certain industrial capacity and output, and since the war the one had been greatly reduced by circumstances which left the other related factors, currency, labour, and agriculture, relatively untouched. Either production had to be raised to the level of employing both the available labour and the existing capital, or the latter had to be reduced to conform to the available production potential, governed by capacity or availability of raw materials, whichever set the lower limit in any particular industry. The control of the planning authorities over its choice of methods was limited, as it had to take into account certain internal constants, such as labour supply[1] and reparation demands, over which it had no control, as well as all aspects of foreign trade, normally within the competence of the central economic authority, but in this case regulated by superior allied authorities. This left only the possibility of an adjustment of the volume of currency to the

[1] Orthodox economic theory does not treat the labour force as a constant factor. It was, however, a fundamental principle of the SMA that there must be no unemployment, frictional or permanent, in the zone. Therefore the labour force had to be reckoned as a constant, if necessary at the expense of productivity or marginal utility. The object of this policy was partially welfare, partially to make labour available for Soviet demands in the zone and in the Soviet Union. It must be borne in mind that workers might prefer unemployment to work in the uranium mines of Saxony, at least for a time.

existing level of industrial output, or to that level likely to be attained in the near future, by means of currency reform.

Reform of the currency can mean one of two things, or a combination of both. It can concentrate primarily on the volume of spending power available to consumers by attacking their liquid and semi-liquid savings. This normally leads to a reduction in wages and prices, but may not greatly affect the quantity or circulation-velocity of the currency. Its chief effect is the full mobilization of all economic resources. Alternatively or simultaneously currency reform can tackle the actual volume of currency in circulation by reducing the nominal quantity of money held by individuals and increasing the purchasing value of the currency unit. Theoretically it is possible to carry out either measure independently; in practice the former has been taken alone, while the latter is always carried out in conjunction with the former. The latter measure increases the deflationary tendency of the former, but attacks the velocity of circulation as well and usually leads to a propensity towards holding money—towards liquidity. It is designed above all as a means of restoring confidence in a tainted currency.

The division between the two measures is often difficult to distinguish in practice, but in Germany circumstances made the distinction clear. The blocking of bank accounts, and the cancellation of interest-bearing State securities, could be carried out in any one of the four zones without universal repercussions throughout Germany. On the other hand a reform of the currency proper, if carried out unilaterally, might establish a foreign-exchange situation between one zone and the others, and destroy with one blow the attempt to achieve the economic unity of Germany as stipulated at Potsdam. We shall therefore find the one action taken by the Russians as early as July 1945, while the other, the reform of the Reichsmark, was discussed at quadripartite level for over a year, and when joint action proved impossible, the consequences of two unilateral measures in the West and in the East were such as to split Germany in two.[1] By that time, even the original effects of deflation in the Soviet zone had been cancelled by the inflationary demands of reparations finance.

Let us now examine the individual sectors of the economy and the measures taken to deal with them.

[1] The Americans proposed a currency reform scheme as early as 1946, but were obstructed by the British. See Friedmann, *op. cit.*, for details of the early proposals. British immobility was partly due to the fact that financial policy was in the hands of an accountancy expert instead of an economist.

(A) *Currency and Credit*

Possibly the most important step taken by the SMA in 1945 was the blocking of bank accounts in July. This immediately counteracted the tendency to migrate from the towns into the country, and provided the necessary stimulus for the direct measures to increase industrial production. The middle classes were the most affected by the virtual cancellation of their savings, and were thus often anxious to do work which otherwise they would not have undertaken, particularly in co-operation with the Russians and the new socialist or communist local authorities. The blocking of bank accounts was thus a measure of great social as well as financial importance.[1]

On the other hand the liquidation of the big banks and national credit institutions made it impossible at first to redirect credit into the basic industries where increased production was most necessary. The destruction of financial savings was coupled with an almost complete breakdown of the banking system. The branches of the big banks became independent local banks with greatly restricted assets, and until the new provincial banking organization took shape in 1946 the only function of these local offices was that of safe deposits for the small volume of savings which gradually began to trickle back from the personal incomes of the population.

Much of the funds of the big banks and of the former Reich government were transferred to the SMA and to the provincial governments. The details of the liquidation and transfer in the zone are very obscure, while in Berlin the city financial department, through the only remaining major bank, the *Berliner Stadtkontor*, took over most of the assets of the Berlin banks. The latter appointed a trustee organization to watch over their interests with the allied *kommandatura*. It is certain that the foundation capital of the Russian *Garantie und Kredit-Bank* and of the Soviet corporations[2] came out of the general liquidation, while the provincial credit organizations and the funds for the subsidies to the 'democratic organizations' and co-operatives were also created from this source.

During 1946 the new zonal banking organization came into existence. It was based on a central bank in each province, the *Land Emissions- und Giro Banken*. These banks were responsible

[1] Precisely because the middle classes were the greatest sufferers, the same measure was only half-heartedly carried out in the West.

[2] For which see below, Chap VII, p. 230.

for note issues, the legal reserves of other banks, and rates of interest, but they were anyhow closely controlled from the first by the Central Administration for Finance. The absence of a security market worth speaking of destroyed discount policy and open market operations as a means of financial control. It is not clear how far these central issue banks also engaged in normal banking activities, but if they did so engage, which is doubtful, they were confined to handling the accounts of provincial ministries and other official bodies.

In addition there existed five *Landes Kreditbanken* or Land credit banks. These were designed to fulfil the rôle of the big commercial banks which had always been a particularly powerful factor in the German credit market. Their primary task was to finance the new national undertakings which occupied an increasingly important place in industry. Their means of accommodation, and rates of interest, for both short- and long-term loans to private and provincial industry were strictly limited by the orders of the Central Administration for Finance and of the provincial finance ministries. It was through these Land credit banks that the greater part of industrial production came to be financed. The continuous deficits of the nationalized undertakings were covered by these banks against their considerable reserves and against special subsidy allocations to them by the provincial governments. The Land credit banks at first also handled time deposits for individuals.

Finally, there remained the personal credit institutions of prewar vintage, the Post Office Savings Banks, the Post Office banking accounts (*Postcheckkonten*), the few remaining commercial banks, private savings banks, and the agricultural credit co-operatives.[1] Just after the creation of this new banking system, a new national insurance system was set up with a considerable capital, believed to have been largely put up by the provincial governments through their central banks. We know very little of the capital structure of this banking organization. The figure of 100 million Rm. each has been quoted for the foundation capital of the central provincial banks just after the heaviest credit restriction at the end of 1945, and a roughly similar figure for the provincial credit banks, though there is no check on the accuracy of these figures.[2]

[1] A new creation arising out of the land reform.

[2] These figures were quoted by the Administration for Finance at a July 1946 press conference. Although official Eastern zone financial institutions, like those of the U.S.S.R., work with seemingly low foundation capitals, these figures are obviously still on the low side.

After the deflationary effect of the freezing of bank accounts, the year 1946 witnessed a gradual expansion of savings and increasing speed of currency circulation, due to the gradual increase in production in 1946, much of which escaped from the official channels of distribution into the black market, and to the increasingly inflationary effects of reparations finance. The greater the quantity of reparations to be extracted from the German economy the greater the need of the Russians to have 'cheap money' available to finance this extraction. For this purpose a great deal of new money was printed. It was about the autumn of 1946 that the Russians turned their back on effective deflationary measures in favour of full-scale reparation finance and all its inflationary consequences. At the same time the increasing extension of the black market counteracted the remaining shreds of the financial control apparatus, the system of price control and price administration.

(B) *Wages and Prices*

The policy of the SMA with regard to wages and prices was simple. The price and wage stop of the war period was continued without legislative interruption, though the break in its effective operation during the spring of 1945 accelerated the wartime tendency of loosening the restrictions. In the upward spiral, wages had remained well below prices, and now the disproportion increased even more. Any severe enforcement of prices in the German economy tended to make price-controlled goods unobtainable. Wages on the other hand could be effectively limited in the absence of organized opposition. Price limits were variously based on 1936, 1938, and 1944, and the permitted increase rose with the labour value required in the production of the goods concerned. Thus coal prices were fixed at the 1938 level, and shoes and stockings could be sold at 1944 levels plus 40 per cent. Price revisions were carried out spasmodically by the DZV for finance, which had a department not only for price supervision but also for price formation. The decision rested with the Central Administration, subject to SMA approval, though the final level might be reached after consultation with the Trades Unions or the Land ministers. Compared to the other Central Administrations, that for finance enjoyed power earlier in time and greater in extent.

Continuing the policy before 1945, wages were also controlled very strictly. They were generally calculated on a 1944 basis, and certain increases were announced early in 1946. Demands for wage increases were strongly discouraged, and agitation for such an end was forbidden by SMA decree, as were strikes. Instead, official quarters predicted economic recovery for wage earners more often in terms of increased real wages than through increases in money wages, a good capitalist panacea.[1]

Thus the partial lapse of money as currency was made inevitable. Any comparison between official money wages and official prices between 1946 and, say, 1936 is of purely theoretical interest as a guide to the cost of living. Labour in receipt of 'official' earnings only was probably in a minority except for industries under direct Russian control. Manufacturing costs were always twofold: cost of allocated material and services, and private purchases of materials and incidental overheads at unofficial prices.[2] Hardly any German factories, even those on reparation tasks, could work exclusively on a basis of official costs.[3] Since real costs did not determine the price of the product, part of the output in consumer-goods industries went into the open market to pay for the extra cost of unofficial materials and for the payment of the workers in kind. The greater the marginal demand for a product, the greater the value of wages in kind paid by the manufacturer. In basic industries, where payment in kind to operatives was impossible, this was frequently compensated for by a four-day working week at full wages, leaving the remaining working hours for private economic activity. Finally, in industries such as provincially-owned undertakings or those working on reparation orders, where either expedient was difficult or impossible to use, the provincial government ensured real-wage bonuses for the workers in the shape of favourable ration scales or consumer priorities.

Thus real wages in the Soviet zone, as indeed in all Germany, between the years 1945 and 1948 must be reckoned, not primarily in terms of money wages, but in terms of money wages plus wages in kind against goods and services which fell into two main categories, controlled prices for rationed and allocated goods, and free prices for black market goods. Means of increasing one's real wage did not primarily depend on an increase in money income, but on obtaining an increasing quantity of exchangeable consumer goods as payment in kind, or on enlarging one's ration of goods purchase-

[1] The point was made again in the introduction to the *Two Year Plan*, official edition (Berlin, 1948), p. 18.

[2] The term 'black market', although used by the authorities, is really unsatisfactory. This market was black only in so far as it was forbidden officially, but its extent was beyond such stigmatization.

[3] The Russians made no allowance for this, either as an excuse for non-fulfilment of contracts or for increased costs. See Löwenthal, *op. cit.*, p. 169.

able at controlled prices. A worker with a small money income might obtain a higher proportion of his total purchases at 1936 prices than a business man with a larger money income on the same ration. A slight increase in the worker's availability of rationed goods might give him the same real wage as someone with a much larger money income and only the standard allocation of controlled-price goods. It must be remembered that prices of black market goods were up to ten times as high as 1935; food about sixteen times as high; rents twelve times as high; household goods eight times as high.[1] Since political influence often meant favourable allocation of rationed goods, this system also had its political effect by avoiding the painful necessity of paying politicians enormous money salaries. At the same time, unlike most economies suffering from runaway inflation, it did not bear particularly heavily on the worker as opposed to the other classes. The same cannot always be said of the 'resoundingly successful'[2] West German currency reform.[3]

Unfortunately, no estimates of family budgets and income in the Soviet zone exist. Owing to the devious nature of supplementing official wages, the official wage scale helps little in estimating real wages. Since the unofficial sources of income vary greatly from one individual to another, though they may have the same money wage, any standard real wage is almost impossible to calculate. There is, however, little doubt that the difference between money and real wages compared to 1936, and between official money wages and money plus goods wages, is considerable.

Taxation formed an important method from the first of skimming off the excess currency in circulation in the inflationary consumer market and directing it into capital-intensive industries. The level of taxation, which had become very high during the war, continued at the same level, and during 1946 increased still further. Direct tax evasion became more and more common owing to the

[1] Private estimate. This subject is outlawed in official calculations.

[2] Some astonishing claims for the beneficial effects of the Western Currency Reform on the working classes may be found in F. A. Lutz's article 'The German Currency Reform', in the May 1949 issue of *Economica*, Vol. XVI, No. 62, p. 122.

[3] In terms of a formula, real wages can be shown as $(M-t) + G = G^1 + \frac{G^2}{y}$ in terms of 1936, where the 1936 real wage was $M-t^1 = G^3$; with M as the money wage, t the 1946 taxation, t^1 the 1936 taxation, G, G^1, G^2, G^3, value of goods paid in kind, of goods bought on the ration, of goods bought in the black market and of the total goods bought in 1936 respectively, while y is the number of times prices have increased in 1946 over 1936. The same 'rationed goods sector of expenditure' calculation of real wages has been used in post-war surveys of cost of living, for instance by the French Trades Unions.

small proportion of money income to total income, and so the greater part of taxation had to be raised from indirect taxation on such articles of consumption as spirits and tobacco. No attempts were made to change the tax system in the direction of that existing in the U.S.S.R. As Soviet reparation finance largely arose out of demands on the current receipts of the provinces, the burden was passed directly on to the taxpayer. We shall examine taxation in more detail later on.

The price and wage scale for 1945–6 must take these facts into account. The post-war planners inherited a divergence between wages and prices which originated during the war, and aggravated rapidly. The relationship between wages and prices was thus correspondingly thrown much further out of balance. The Nazi system of price control and price administration had depended on the enormous powers of the government for its successful operation. Even in the heyday of its powers, the Nazi government had not succeeded altogether in stamping out price-control evasion or the pressure of inflation on the official price ceilings. The Russians, in spite of their unlimited authority, were not sufficiently in touch with local German conditions to prevent a much larger measure of price-control evasion, and the black market soon enjoyed a quasi-legal existence. Once inflationary reparation finance dominated Soviet policy, control of the black market became almost impossible, and the Russians openly availed themselves of its facilities to their own advantage.

(C) *Industrial Production*

This field was the planners' natural paradise, and, as we have stated, was the most important issue facing the economy of the Soviet zone. From the very beginning investment by choice played no part in industrial production. Out of industrial production the all-important reparations had to come. Thus production by planning, or, more correctly, production by command, took the place of all other productive stimulants.

The situation between the end of the fighting and the first results of Russian measures has been noted. In some ways the Russian plan in Germany followed that adopted in the Soviet Union just before and during NEP and that of the new communist states of Eastern Europe after the late war. Priority was given to basic industries and the production of industrial raw materials: coal, steel and other metals, timber production, potash, chemicals. This scheme sometimes cut across the developed German industrial pattern. For example, timber had never been a German staple product, except for pit props. Though considerable quantities of all these supplies were destined for reparations, the programme was also beneficial to the zone as relatively the heaviest incidence of reparations fell in the secondary and tertiary stages of manufacture, both in plant removal and in the exploitation of current production. Priority in industrial re-expansion was given to industries destined for absorption by the Russian trusts in Germany or for heavy reparation deliveries out of current production. But an expansion of these basic industries was essential also for the general economic revival of the zone. So far German and Russian needs called for the same stimulation of production.

Leaving aside for the moment further details of reparation policy, the effect of the Russian plans at first looked like a revival on a considerable scale. The size of the problem called for desperate measures executed by the might of an all-powerful occupation force. The destruction of savings, strict prevention of hoarding, and a system of vigorous checks and investigations into material assets acted to some extent as a substitute for those normal economic processes which make for an extension of productive activity. A comparison between Western and Eastern Germany illustrates the relative success of the Russians. The hoarded stocks of consumer goods in Western Germany, which only appeared after the 1948 currency reform, were forced into the market much earlier in the Soviet zone, though not necessarily the official market. Detailed production plans coupled with the threat of personal punishment and sequestration for failing to fulfil them did affect the spirit of those responsible for managing factories. The general attitude in Eastern Germany in the early part of 1946 was one of economic activity and hope, and it remains to be shown that a situation of this sort can be more effectively solved by a system of *laissez faire*.

A short survey of different industries will illustrate the extent of the revival. The figures given below cover total production, both for the home market and for direct and indirect reparations. It must be borne in mind that the full impact of Russian reparation demands from current production was neither known nor appreciated, and that it was generally hoped that by far the greater part of industrial production in the zone would soon accrue to the benefit of the Germans.

TABLE IX[1]

Total Industrial Production (excluding mining, building industries and food processing)

	Million Rm (1944 prices)	Per cent of 1936
4th Quarter 1945	635	25
1st Quarter 1946	1100	44
2nd ,, 1946	1200	48
3rd ,, 1946	1515	60
4th ,, 1946	1680	67
TOTAL	6130	49

Production of selected items

	Hard coal (1,000 m.t.)	% 1938	Brown coal (1,000 m.t.)	% 1938
4th Quarter 1945 ..	561	64 (80—1936)	24.069	72 (87—1936)
1st Quarter 1946 ..	600	—	26.703	—
2nd ,, 1946 ..	612	—	26.481	—
3rd ,, 1946 ..	645	—	27.942	—
4th ,, 1946 ..	660	—	27.498	—
TOTAL 1946 ..	2517	72 (90—1936)	108.624	81 (98—1936)

	Steel ingots (m.t.) Production	% 1936	Aluminium (m.t.) Production	%1936
4th Quarter 1945 ..	14.800	5	2020	34
1st Quarter 1946 ..	19.400	8	3490	48
2nd ,, 1946 ..	42.500	18	2620	36
3rd ,, 1946 ..	52.400	22	5210	72
4th ,, 1946 ..	54.600	23	6140	85
TOTAL 1946 ..	168.900	18	17.500	60

	Textile yarns (Cotton, woollen, worsted) (m.t.) Production	% 1936	Footwear (million pairs) Production	% 1936
4th Quarter 1945 ..	6200	30	—[2]	18
1st Quarter 1946 ..	8100	37	—	26
2nd ,, 1946 ..	9500	38	—	45
3rd ,, 1946 ..	19700	80	—	60
4th ,, 1946 ..	21900	88	—	62
TOTAL 1946 ..	59200	60	16.98	48.25

[1] Constructed partly from the American *Statistical Handbook* and the statistical appendices to the monthly report of the U.S. Military Governor. The figures in *Reparationen, Sozialproduct, Lebenstandard* have also been used. There is finally the data given in an article in the *Wirtschafts-Archiv* of Dec. 1947. p. 1027, but this appears to be based on American figures also. A few of the detailed figures are my own, particularly in the column on textiles.

[2] The average quarterly figures are not available, and the quarterly average percentages are the estimate of officials in the trade, which should be treated with some reserve.

In the diagram below these figures are illustrated graphically on the basis of an index figure of 100 for 1936 in the various products illustrated.

These curves show some interesting results:

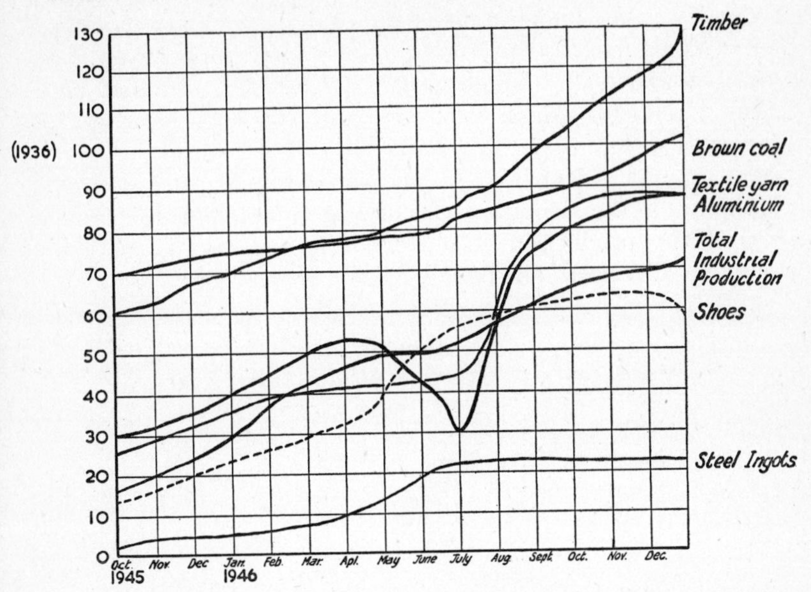

FIG. 2. *Graph of Industrial Production in Soviet Zone, 1945–6 as per cent of 1936*

(i) The changes during 1946 are greatest in secondary and tertiary products. The period of greatest fluctuation was the second and third quarter of 1946, when the organization of the Central Administrations and the provincial ministries was completed. Intensive reparation planning made a considerable inroad on hidden and official stocks of raw materials, and some of the production increase which became noticeable in the West after June 1948 had its counterpart in the Soviet zone two years earlier. The increase was also due to the stabilization of inter-zonal trade. Imports from abroad were only slightly larger than in 1945, and were insufficient to be a dynamic factor as far as industrial production was concerned.

(ii) The curve for timber and potash[1] illustrates the 'staple' policy of the SMA, chiefly for reparations and exports.[2] The ex-

[1] The detailed figures are not available, but the curve has been drawn from the available information, based on pre-war ratios, and is approximately correct for position and shape. As far as timber is concerned I have been unable to obtain accurate 'zonal' figures for 1936, and have had to collate figures for individual areas.

[2] See below, Chaps. IX and X.

pansion of timber felling and potash production required little marginal cost and could be undertaken at short notice. Any increase in the production of brown coal above pre-war level was more limited, since the marginal costs of any substantial increase were very great, and the necessary capital goods not available. Reparation removals of primary production facilities of these three staples were small, though processing facilities suffered more heavily, a factor which would not, of course, appear in the diagram.

(iii) The sharp drop in the production of primary and secondary aluminium in the second quarter of 1946 corresponds to a similar drop in the production of other non-ferrous metals, with the exception of copper. The figures, in metric tons, are:

TABLE X

Production of Non-ferrous Metals, Soviet Zone

	Zinc	*Lead*	*Copper*
1st Quarter 1946	1490	1140	3370
2nd ,, 1946	5016	2097	4518
3rd ,, 1946	4436	1852	5163
4th ,, 1946	3148	1477	5473
TOTAL 1946	14090	6566	18524

Similar fluctuations, on an even more violent scale, can be seen in the corresponding figures for the British zone. The main reason seems to have been the irregular exploitation of ore stocks, and the almost complete dearth of ore imports. In addition the fact that the new level-of-industry plans were to restrict the production of non-ferrous metals to well below the 1936 level perhaps made the SMA unwilling at first to give this production a high priority in its 1946 plans. Both smelting and electrolytic processes, consuming much coal or coal equivalent, would be heavily restricted during a coal shortage.

(iv) The very uneven production of shoes was due entirely to leather or canvas shortages. Inter-zonal imports from the French zone, the chief leather-processing area of Germany, were very small during 1946. Similar shortages existed in leather substitute material, though increasing Buna (artificial rubber) production accounted for much of the rise in footwear production during 1946. The decline in December marks the beginning of a long and steady downward trend all through 1947 owing to a shortage of raw materials.

(v) The figures relating to steel production are very important.

The Soviet zone had always been dependent on West German steel. In 1936 the zone only accounted for about 5 per cent of the 19 million tons of crude steel produced in the whole of Germany, or about 6 per cent of the 1936 total for the area now corresponding to Potsdam Germany.[1] At the end of 1946 production was less than a quarter of that of 1936.[2] If the supply of Western steel should be cut off at any time, clearly all the industries depending on steel, as well as the steel-processing industry itself, whose capacity was about 10–12 per cent of the total of Potsdam Germany,[3] would be in danger of complete standstill. Just as in the case of coal, the marginal costs of any new steel-refining project would be very great and the requirements of scarce materials considerable. It was not until the middle of 1948, when the prospects for inter-zonal trade began to worsen, that plans for new steel-rolling plant, new presses, and an extension of existing furnace capacity were put into execution.

The all-round improvement in industrial production in 1946 as compared to 1945, and the rise during 1946, are themselves no cause for surprise. But the extent of the recovery can be better appreciated by a comparison with other zones. The following are figures for selected items in the British zone:[4]

TABLE XI

Production of Selected Items, 1936 *and* 1946, *British Zone*

Hard Coal (1,000 m.t.)[5]		*Aluminium (m.t.)*	
1938 ..	138,300	1936 ..	59,800
1946 ..	53,957 or 39% (45% of *1936*)	1946 ..	19,225 or 32%

Textile yarns (1,000 m.t.)		*Footwear (millions of)*	
1936 ..	120	1936 ..	35.2
1946 ..	45.8 or 38%	1946 ..	9.5 or 27%

Total gross value of industrial production in 1946
7,150.5 million Rm or 31% of 1936

It is difficult to make a satisfactory comparison with the U.S. zone, since its industrial geography is very different and its problems and achievements of a different order. On the whole its

[1] Constructed from the German statistical survey of 1936. See also ECE report, *Economic Bulletin for Europe*, 3rd Quarter 1949, Vol. I, No. 3, p. 25.

[2] *Statistical Handbook*, p. 40.

[3] My own estimate.

[4] *Handbook*, p. 18, *passim*.

[5] The British zone is the biggest producer of hard coal by roughly the same ratio as the Soviet zone with regard to brown coal. There is no point in comparing the production of brown coal, in the two zones. The 1938 figure has been slightly amended, in view of the 1938 German Survey transport statistics, which make a slightly higher production total probable.

recovery would seem to have been slightly less than that of the Russian zone, and rather greater than that of its northern neighbour, although a comparison based on 1936 shows a recovery in comparable figures about equal to that of the Soviet zone.[1] The U.S. zone did, however, suffer rather less than any other zone from direct war damage.

Planning for the industry of the Soviet zone was still embryonic in 1946. The SMA, with the assistance of the Central Administration for Industry fixed the detailed quotas for each industry and area. The provincial ministries also made their own plans, and by July 1946 three separate yearly, quarterly, and monthly plans existed in each industry, that of the SMA, that of the Administration, and that of the provincial government. It need hardly be added that the SMA plan was the master plan. Quotas were fixed on a capacity/raw material supply basis, since there could be no fear of excess production. In other words, planning was based on existing output and potential increase rather than on demand,[2] and the distribution, allocation, retail, and export quotas were superimposed on production quotas in basic industries; plans for machinery production depended on those of steel instead of steel output being governed by the probable demand. It was not until the two-year plan in 1948 that the demand factor enters into planning, although we can see it creep in here and there during 1947. The earlier plans were frequently off the mark; in 1946, plan and result show a deficiency of about 10 per cent in textiles, 22 per cent in shoes, 5 per cent in brown coal, and an average of 15 per cent in the ferrous and non-ferrous metals. On the other hand potash showed a surplus, as did sugar and ceramics.

There is little doubt that the disorganization of economic processes in the Soviet zone made rigid planning essential. If planning had been less strict in the Soviet zone there might have been the same development as in the West, a recession of the productive investment in heavy industry in favour of certain consumer goods, chiefly luxuries. But it is also interesting to note the psychological effect of a comprehensive and, on the whole, rigidly enforced planning system on statistical tendencies and method. Gradually current industrial production ceased to be compared to pre-war figures and was compared more frequently to current plans. The basis of comparison was the planned present instead of the real

[1] This is also the opinion in the *Handbook*, p. 15.

[2] Except for reparation planning, which was based on demand overriding all considerations of production and its problems.

past. As the detailed assumptions of the plans are often unknown to any but their sponsors, this fact, coupled with a passion for percentages instead of real figures, has made the life of economists dealing with East German, and indeed all Russian, statistics a nightmare.

Finally, a word must be said about the economic effects of socialization during 1945–6.[1] Up to the end of 1946 some 7,000 firms had been taken over from their previous owners and distributed as follows: to the provincial governments about 3,000; to the Trades Unions, Co-operatives, and other semi-public bodies about 2,000; and to 'democratically suitable' persons (as the official phrase goes) about 2,000. Corresponding figures for the productive value of these firms greatly alter the effect of this redistribution. Of the total productive value of sequestrated firms remaining in German hands[2] 65 per cent went with the nationalized firms to the provincial governments, some 20 per cent to semi-public bodies and only 15 per cent to new private owners. Eventual destination was clearly determined by value and/or size of the firm. The rate and extent of socialization varied from land to land. We find it most rapid and intensive in Saxony and Saxony-Anhalt, slowest as well as most mild in Thuringia and Brandenburg, the latter largely agricultural, the former enjoying at that time a predominantly SPD and LDP cabinet.

At the end of 1946 the purely German production (i.e. excluding Soviet corporations) was divided into 40 per cent nationalized firms, public and semi-public, and 60 per cent private sector. In terms of value this proportion must be inverted, 60 per cent national firms and 40 per cent private sector. The percentages of the total sequestration, including firms handed to other private owners but excluding those taken over by the Russians, to the zonal totals of German production are: in the number of firms about 15 per cent, in quantity of production about 43 per cent, and in the value of production about 65 per cent. To argue purely on the basis of the number of firms is misleading, and the real extent of socialization was much larger than Schaffer would have us believe.[3] As we shall see, the process was by no means completed at the end of 1946.

[1] For this, see also above, p. 151, and Chap. V.

[2] This does not take into account Cat. C firms temporarily administered by the Russians, and Soviet Corporations, for which see below, p. 219 *passim*.

[3] *op. cit.* He follows the authorities of the Soviet zone in taking into official account only the number of firms. My figures are partly based on the article, quoted above, in the *Wirtschaftsarchiv* of December 1947.

(D) *Agriculture*

Agricultural policy was dominated from the first by the proposed Land reform. No one has claimed for this measure the purely utilitarian object of increasing agricultural production, and the reasons for it must be treated under a political heading.[1] Nevertheless the measure had far-reaching economic results; and its success or failure from this point of view has been the subject of three years' ever-fruitful argument within and without Germany.[2]

A lengthy discussion on the self-sufficiency potential of the Soviet zone is beyond the scope of this book, since it must take into account the exchange value of surplus agricultural products at an estimated post-war rate.[3] The fact that the Soviet zone produced and consumed in 1937 3,111 million Rm. worth of food, as a German survey estimated,[4] does not alone make it self-supporting. Germany as a whole had not been self-sufficient since 1870, although the gradient of population increase was much sharper than the decrease in self-sufficiency.

The Soviet zone, excluding Berlin, was not self-sufficient before the war. It produced a surplus of seed potatoes and potatoes for consumption, 41 per cent of the 1936 total of the area of Potsdam Germany and 35 per cent of the total consumed in the 1936 area of the whole Reich. The zone produced sufficient sugar for its own needs and for supplying other parts of Germany, enabling Germany as a whole to export this commodity in modest quantities. In wheat and rye, i.e. food grain, the Soviet zone was before the war more than self-sufficient, 'exporting' some 26 per cent of its production, or 1 million tons out of 3.8, to other parts of Germany.[5] A breakdown of these figures into its two component commodities would show that the surplus was largely rye, which was, and is, consumed in far greater proportion to wheat in Germany than in England or the United States. The zone was further almost self-sufficient in pork, but produced less beef and mutton than it

[1] See above, p. 85.

[2] Although the particular measure undertaken in the Soviet zone was planned and carried through unilaterally, the principle of a land reform, with similar political objects in view, was accepted for the whole of Germany by the four foreign ministers on 23 April 1947, at a time when the execution of the measure in the Soviet zone was almost complete. Since agreement on the details could not be reached by the Länder of the Western zones, no complete reform has yet taken place anywhere but in the Soviet zone.

[3] The figures in this section except where otherwise stated are taken from *Die Bodenreform in Deutschland* (Berlin, 1947), published by the official press of the Farmers' Co-operative.

[4] *R.S.L.*, Vol. III, p. 37.

[5] Compare the figures given in *United Nations Economic Bulletin for Europe*, 3rd Quarter 1949, Vol. I, No. 3.

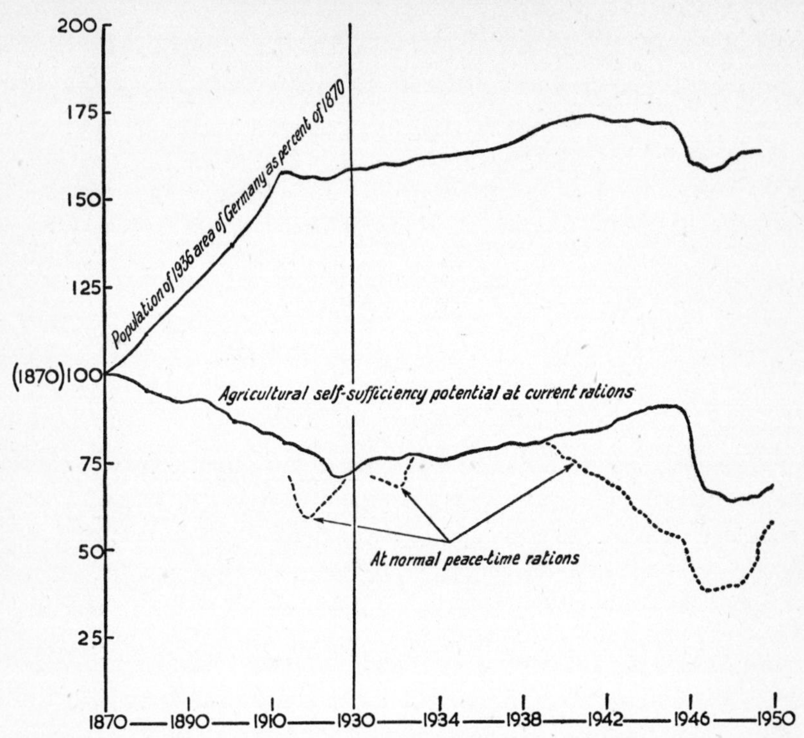

FIG. 3. [1] *German population and agricultural self-sufficiency, 1870–1950*

consumed. Its staple imports are those of Germany as a whole: fruits, legumes, fish, eggs. The milk, butter, and cheese consumption of the zone was considerably greater than its production, since German dairy farming was strongest in Schleswig-Holstein and Western Mecklenburg, now in the British zone. Finally, such commodities as tobacco, coffee, tea, cocoa, margarine, nuts, and cooking oil, which were almost entirely imported before the war, would be the first to become unobtainable in every zone once imports were cut off. On the other hand the demands of German war economy had brought into existence a considerable production of substitutes and a small amount of poor quality local produce of some of these commodities.

The pre-war task of German agriculture was the achievement of maximum production irrespective of cost to make Germany as self-sufficient as possible. Germany was not considered as an 'agricultural' country, and the protective measures of the Re-

[1] The adjustment of the self-sufficiency potential, by taking into account the loss of the Eastern territories, has not been made in this graph.

publican Government until 1933 show a self-conscious effort to keep agriculture on its feet rather than government investment in a national and exportable production of staple goods.

The table below shows the distribution of agricultural land in farms and agricultural undertakings of various sizes for all Germany and for the Soviet zone in 1939, and indicates the mixture of economic and social influences in pre-war German agriculture.

TABLE XII[1]

Distribution of Farms and Land-holdings by Size in 1939

GERMANY

Size of farm or Unit	*No. of Units*	%	*Total land holdings (acres)*	%	*Agric. land (acres)*	%
1–12 acres ..	1.505.198	56.4	7.739.000	9.7	7.018.000	13.9
12–50 ,, ..	878.580	32.9	22.112.500	27.7	19.050.750	37.7
50–250 ,, ..	262.021	9.9	23.428.750	29.3	17.588.000	34.4
Over 250 acres ..	23.678	0.9	26.619.250	33.3	7.074.250	14.0
Of these latter over 2,500 ..	2.028	0.1	12.816.500	16.0	819.250	1.6
TOTAL	2.669.477	100	79.899.500	100	50.731.000	100

SOVIET ZONE

Size of farm or Unit	*No. of Units*	%	*Total land holdings (acres)*	%	*Agric. land (acres)*	%
(*a*) 1– 12 acres ..	320.927	54	1.437.750	5.8	1.296.000	8.1
(*b*) 12–50 ,, ..	190.044	32	5.186.750	21.3	4.531.500	28.4
(*c*) 50–250 ,, ..	74.463	12.5	6.700.000	27.5	5.378.750	33.7
(*d*) Over 250 acres ..	9.024	1.5	11.055.250	45.4	4.738.250	29.8
Of these latter:						
250– 500 acres ..	3.889	0.7	1.338.500	5.5	969.000	6.1
500–1250 ,, ..	3.030	0.5	2.425.000	9.9	1.716.250	10.8
1250–2500 ,, ..	1.339	0.2	2.299.750	9.4	1.459.500	9.2
Over 2500 ,, ..	766	0.1	4.992.000	20.6	593.500	3.7
TOTAL (*a–d*) ..	594.458	100	24.379.750	100	15.944.500	100

Certain general proportions became evident. In the first place, the greater the size of land-holding, the smaller the proportion of agricultural land. The greatest quantity of agricultural land in the whole of Germany was held in units of between 12 and 50 acres, but within the Soviet zone the greatest quantity fell to holdings of 50 to 250 acres. This is primarily due to the nature of the agricultural products in the Soviet zone, with the predominance of arable land and root products over dairy farming. But the

[1] *Die Bodenreform*, pp. 11, 12, corrected from hectares to acres.

11:24 ratio of total land held in units of over 250 acres to the overall total as compared to a similar ratio of 27:80 for the whole of Germany, or 46 per cent to 34 per cent perhaps shows a tendency towards *Junkertum*, for the definition of that term after the middle of the nineteenth century was not so much tied to the exploitation of the soil as to the owning of it. This is further borne out by the fact that no less than 20.5 per cent of the total land of the Soviet zone was held in units of over 2,500 acres. If the land reform had as its object the breaking-up of large estates, it was most fitting that this operation should start in the Soviet zone.

The structure of German agriculture and the demands of the war economy on it had raised productivity per acre to a level apparently unequalled in any other European country just before the war.[1] There was little unused land and most agricultural soil was exploited to its full capacity. As in industry, but to an even greater extent, we must look to the disruption of a closely interlocking and complicated machine for an explanation of the fall of agricultural production in 1945 and of its low level ever since. The lack of farm machinery,[2] the shortage of artificial fertilizer (about 65 per cent production in 1946 as compared to 1939)[3] and the dislocation of transport explain far more than direct physical destruction.

The physical destruction of agricultural wealth falls chiefly under the heading of buildings and, more important, of cattle and farm animals generally.

TABLE XIII[4]

Animal Population—Soviet Zone and Potsdam Germany, 1946 as percentage of 1939

	Cattle	*Cows*	*Horses*	*Pigs*	*Sheep*	*Chicken*
Soviet zone ..	57	50	68	32	50	50
Potsdam Germany	83	72	80	36	93	48

[1] On some of the best English soils productivity was higher than in Germany, but taking into account the large-scale German use of marginal land at this time, while such land was uncultivated in England, productivity according to quality of soil was higher in Germany.

[2] The Soviet zone produced in 1936 about 20–25 per cent of the farm machinery and implements made in the whole of Germany. As with all steel production, particularly vehicles, post-war production has lagged.

[3] Detailed figures in *Handbook*, p. 23. While nitrogen and potash, though at first in short supply, later became more easily available, particularly in the Soviet zone, phosphoric acid was the greatest difficulty, since the import of phosphorus was and is heavily restricted. The only substitute is the phosphorus available as a by-product of a certain kind of steel (Thomas steel).

[4] Amended with private figures from *R.S.L.*, Vol. III, p. 47.

Compared to the rest of Germany, the animal population of the Soviet zone thus suffered relatively more from the effects of the war. The Russians also took quantities of livestock for reparation, in addition to the considerable depredations of the occupying army, which together account for the heavy losses of the zone.

This loss is to some extent balanced by the advantageous position of the Soviet zone in the ratio of agricultural land to population, as the following table shows:

TABLE XIV[1]

Land available per 100 people, 1946

Zone	*Total Agricultural land*	*Arable land*
Russian	85 acres	67 acres
American	80 ,,	47 ,,
British	62 ,,	37 ,,
French	95 ,,	50 ,,
German average	77 ,,	50 ,,

On the basis of these facts and figures it is now necessary to discuss first the details of the land reform itself and then its effects on agriculture production. The redistribution of land was not preceded by a formal nationalization of all land. No compensation was paid to the owners whose land was taken away. There was no universal deprivation, followed by a partial reallocation of small holdings to their former owner, but a direct transfer of certain lands to new owners. The ambiguity of this position allows two possible interpretations: either the measure was a utilitarian transfer of 'excessive' holdings to new landless or 'under-enfeoffed' peasants[2] or workers—as represented officially—or all land was in fact nationalized, but much of it handed back to the former small-owners. This latter interpretation would no doubt become official if a precedent for a further reform was ever required. For the moment such suspicions are heretical and even treasonable.

A study of the redistribution of land shows that about a third of the total land area of the Soviet zone was redistributed, but only about a quarter of the agricultural land, excluding forest. The greater part was left untouched by the reform. Of all the land apportioned to private owners (i.e. excluding grants to institutions or to the Farmers' Co-operative), 32 per cent of farm properties, and 18 per cent of the total land, went to persons already owning

[1] *R.S.L.*, Vol. III, p. 45. These figures appear to be on the large side in relation to other evidence, such as the article in *Die Neue Stadt*, 1948, Vol. II, No. 1, p. 37.

[2] The official German term is *Landarme Bauern*. See above, Chap. IV.

land. No less than 67.5 per cent of the total land involved in the reform went to private individuals. Clearly it is impossible to deny that the land reform in the Soviet zone resembles far more closely in effect if not in method, extent, and intention, the transfer of land in France during the decade of revolution 1789–99[1] than the collectivization of the early thirties in Soviet Russia.

The following table gives the figures in detail for the distribution of land under the reform as on 1 July 1947:

TABLE XV

Distribution of Land under Land Reform, Soviet Zone, 1947

Recipients	*No. of Units*	*Total land distributed (Acres)*	%	*Agric. land (Acres)*	%
I. As addition to personal property of farmers and persons already owning land:					
(*a*) Smallholders	49.138	135.250	1.8	95.000	2.0
(*b*) Under-enfeoffed peasants	113.324	800.750	10.5	633.250	9.2
II. As personal property to those not already owning land:					
(*a*) Agricultural labourers and landless population ..	119.650	2.202.250	29.0	1.833.250	38.9
(*b*) Refugees and resettlers ..	83.802	1.738.000	22.0	1.439.000	30.5
(*c*) Non-agricultural labourers and employees	130.881	251.000	3.3	181.750	3.9
III. To agricultural bodies as communal property:					
(*a*) Rural communities or parishes	33.681	423.500	5.6	82.000	1.7
(*b*) VDGB	4.122	81.500	1.0	49.500	1.1
IV. To non-agricultural bodies as communal property:					
(*a*) City corporations, hospitals and schools, SED party organisations	770	74.250	0.7	17.000	0.4
(*b*) Research stations, State agric. coll., SED schools and holiday resorts ..	1.849	1.633.750	21.5	458.000	9.7
V. Appropriated land remaining for disposal	—	283.250	3.7	122.500	2.6

The agricultural labourers' group is thus the greatest beneficiary. The greatest number of actual units was given to industrial workers, but these, as the acreage shows, received mostly small

[1] See, e.g., G. Lefebvre, 'Questions agraires au temps de la Terreür' in *Collection de Documents inédits sur l'histoire économique de la révolution française*; Strasbourg, 1932, for the view that this 'land reform' was almost accidentally part of a financial liquidation of church and empire lands.

properties and market gardens, and it seems an exaggeration to speak of making landed proprietors of this class, as some commentators on both sides have done. The average sizes of units of land given to various classes is as follows:

TABLE XVI

Average Receipt of Land by Individuals of Different Classes

	Total land	*Agricultural land*
Smallholders	2.75 acres	2.0 acres
Under-enfeoffed peasants	7.0 ,,	3.75 ,,
Agricultural labourers, etc.	18.5 ,,	15.25 ,,
Refugees	20.75 ,,	17.25 ,,
Non-agricultural labourers	2.0 ,,	1.5 ,,
Communes	12.5 ,,	2.5 ,,
VDGB	19.75 ,,	12.0 ,
Corporations, etc.	70.5 ,,	22.0 ,,
Research stations, etc.	883.5 ,,	247.75 ,,

The only owners of estates larger than 100 hectares (250 acres), the legal limit for private individuals, are municipal, political, and provincial bodies. Since Germany was not ill-provided with agricultural model farms and research stations, it is difficult to resist the tempting belief that a considerable quantity of land under the last heading went to swell the reserves of the SED[1] and its subsidiary organizations, and perhaps those of the occupation authorities.

The terms on which land affected by the reform was allocated varied considerably according to the nature of the recipient. Officially beneficiaries had to pay a sum equivalent to the value of one year's grain harvest, the figure being settled on the basis of their planned production instead of the result of the first year's experience. This agricultural equivalent of clerical first-fruits could be paid in instalments lasting up to ten or twenty years, 10 per cent being due at the end of the first year. For forest land only half the original cost price was due on similar terms.

Land was transferred free of debt or outstanding fiscal burdens, and the provincial government 'charter' for each recipient, which went with the land, replaced the old 'manorial records' which were officially destroyed in some parts. The whole operation has a curiously medieval flavour which would have delighted the heart of a Wat Tyler or a Rainborowe.

These terms were not usually carried out to the letter. Some of

[1] There was overwhelming evidence that estates were held in considerable numbers by the party and indirectly by some of its more prominent members. Conferences frequently took place in former *châteaux*, as did youth meetings of the Free German Youth, Trade Unions, etc.

the newly allocated lands were not taken up, but were used as building land without any attempt at cultivation. Often lack of machinery, seeds, and animals made the planned return impossible, and with it the expected payment. In many cases payment was dispensed with by order of the provincial government. Altogether only some 60–75 per cent of the money due was paid,[1] and occasionally certain units of land changed hands several times before a satisfactory purchaser could be found. The tendency was for the established farmers to buy out their speculative or improvident neighbours, and this process, although officially frowned upon, was accepted by the authorities as inevitable, at any rate at the beginning. Although agricultural rents underwent the inevitable inflationary rise of all prices in the immediate post-war period, this rise was partly balanced by the fall due to the land reform. Unlike the 'black' rents for houses, which jumped to some 1,200–1,500 per cent of 1936, 'black' agricultural rents rose to a mere 300–400 per cent. The new independent farmer was faced with rigid provincial control over his planned delivery, and a system of detailed supervision over the quality and quantity of his output, and of instructions as to his system of management prevailed. If it is true that independence was the historic aim of the peasant, he lost almost as much in this case as he had gained.

In fact, Table XV above, which is the work of an official German organization in the Russian zone, should be adjusted for 1946–7 in the direction of more large units to take into account the considerable underground transfer of land resulting from the impact of economic facts on the political motives of the land reform.[2]

The social effects of the land reform were considerable. The largest part of the agricultural land in the Soviet zone was now held in units of 12–50 acres (10,220,750 acres in 354,800 units), almost twice as much land in six-and-a-half as many units as was held in units of 50–250 acres. Whereas the present majority group worked some 28 per cent of the agricultural land in the zone in 1939, in 1950 it worked some 48.5 per cent. The category of units

[1] Official statement by the Central Administration for Agriculture, Dec. 1946.

[2] For many instances of the political chicanery against farmers who failed to fulfil their production quotas during the time of greatest shortage in 1947, see Löwenthal, *op. cit.* It is, however, misleading to suggest, as he does, that this was due to a general policy aimed at intimidating the peasants. As is shown below, p. 179, the demand of the plan figures was relatively mild for the peasants. It is suggested that the political and judicial measures against the peasantry were due to the frequent trafficking in new holdings, and to the attempt of many farmers, as in the Western zone, to profit from the food shortage. This would therefore be one of the few cases where the perpetual accusation of economic sabotage is partially justified.

over 250 acres, which used to work some 29.8 per cent of the agricultural land, in 1950 worked only 11.1 per cent. Nothing can show the change better than the actual increase of total farm units as a result of the land reform. According to official statistics, some 12,355 units were actually affected by the reform, of which 6,986 were over 250 acres in size, 3,280 belonged to alleged war criminals, and 2,089 had been national, provincial, or Nazi party property. Yet the number of new units allocated was 537,217, only some 57,000 less than the 1939 total of units in the whole Soviet zone. The geographical structure must have altered considerably since a considerable proportion of the total of 750,100 units separately owned in 1947 must have been simply bits of land arbitrarily cut out of the previous agricultural pattern of the land. The real 'independence' of many of the new units, and the security of their owners, thus seems somewhat chimerical.

But the main factors limiting the independence of farmers were the planning system of production and the communal ownership of implements. The former is closely tied up with, and the result of, the system of agricultural administration evolved in the Soviet zone. This can best be shown by a diagram (1946) FIG 4. The detailed plan figures for production were at first evolved by the SMA, which issued them annually, in certain cases, biannually. General instructions about times and methods of sowing, reaping and distribution were issued as commands by the Military Governor. During the latter part of 1946 the detail work for plans was taken over by the Administration for Agriculture, though not issued by the SMA until early 1947. The sowing and delivery plans

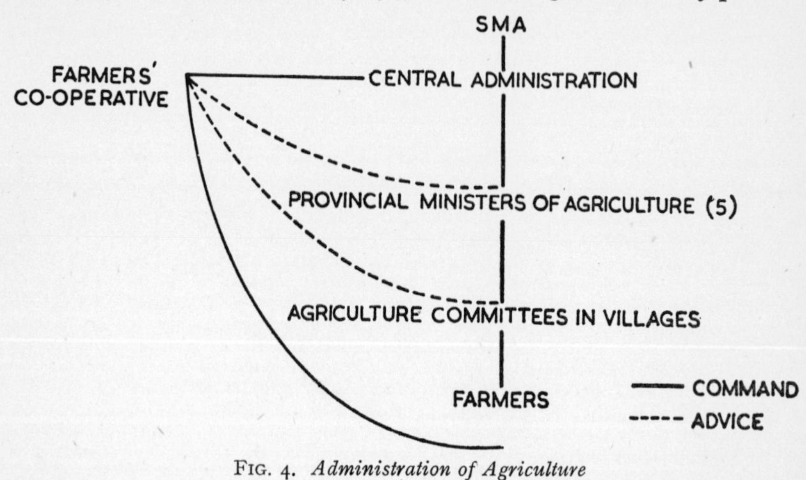

FIG. 4. *Administration of Agriculture*

were always in considerable detail; the provincial authorities allocated the share of the Land plan to individual units, but could not alter the total of the various items due. This agricultural planning resembled the Russian system under NEP.[1] The guiding principles were, first, a double market, controlled and free, the former covered by the plan figures, the latter consisting of any surplus to be sold at free prices to stimulate production; secondly, the self-provisioning of agricultural undertakings, with the additional factor that units of less than 1¼ acres, and bigger units owned by men over sixty or women over fifty-five, had no delivery quotas and were considered sufficient unto themselves. Those consistently or inexcusably failing to fulfil the plan were liable to expropriation, and such action has been taken quite frequently. As a general comment on the agricultural production plans, distinct from those of industry, it must be said that they reflect a reasonable level of production for the type of land with which they deal. As we shall see, they were frequently exceeded.

The other factor, the communal ownership of implements, was made possible by large-scale appropriation on the part of the Farmers' Co-operative Organization. Implements and machinery were hired out for use at very cheap rates, but were in short supply. This monopoly gives the Farmers' Co-operative a great share in the control and management of individual farms, and economic power to strangle political recalcitrants.

Some figures can be given:

TABLE XVII[2]

Distribution of Farm Machinery after Land Reform Soviet Zone

	To new farms		*Additions to old farms*		*Farmers' Co-operative*	*Total*
	Total	*per 100 farms*	*Total*	*per 100 farms*		
Motor tractors ..	—	—	—	—	6,004	6,004
Locomotive tractors ..	—	—	—	—	1,187	1,187
Electric motors ..	—	—	—	—	12,281	12,281
Lorries	—	—	—	—	450	450
Threshing machines ..	—	—	—	—	5,546	5,546
Ploughs	49,812	25	2,866	2	10,884	63,562
Rakes	39,637	20	2,135	1	1,803	43,562
Sowing machines ..	3,743	2	353	0.2	3,820	7,916
Harvesters and combines	13,234	7	1,067	1.0	18,622	32,923
Horse rakes	6,483	3	322	0.2	2,501	9,306
Potato and beet gathering machines ..	7,099	4	482	0.3	5,510	13,091
Cutters, sorters, etc. ..	5,491	3	425	0.3	5,817	11,733
Miscellaneous ..	3,861	2	353	0.2	22,787	27,001

[1] New Economic Policy, the more 'liberal' reaction after the failure of the 'War Communism' in Russia after 1922.

[2] *Die Bodenreform*, p. 24.

Finally, what was the effect on production, and what was the state of production itself? The various indirect effects of war, the lack of fertilizer, the shortage of machinery, and the intensive production of the immediate pre-war period caused a surprisingly large difference between 1938 and 1946. A comparison of production for various commodities per standard unit of land shows the following figures for the Soviet zone:

TABLE XVIII[1]

Production of Agricultural Commodities, Soviet Zone, 1938 and 1946

(In Cwt/Acre)

	Bread Grain	*Fodder Grain*	*Potatoes*	*Sugar Beet*
1938	16.7 cwt.	18.8 cwt.	144 cwt.	284 cwt.
1946	10.3 cwt.	11.3 cwt.	95.2 cwt.	174.2 cwt.
Fall in percentage	38%	40%	34%	30%

In view of the extent of the actual fighting in the Soviet zone and the fact that agriculture played such an important part in Eastern Germany, we should not be surprised to find that the percentage reduction is larger than in other zones. But the extent of the difference is such that it is necessary to find other causes as well. The percentage fall per acre compared with 1938 in the other zones is as follows:

TABLE XIX

Reduction per acre of Agricultural Production as Percentage of 1938, Western Zones

	Bread Grain	*Fodder Grain*	*Potatoes*	*Sugar Beet*
	%	%	%	%
British zone ..	26	30	31	31
U.S. zone ..	18	25	22	20
French zone ..	21	25	35	19
AVERAGE about	22	27	28	24

Clearly the reduction in yield per acre compared to 1938 is greater in grain than in root plants. Since the marginal difference in yield due to organizational changes and technique is much larger for grain than for roots, it is not unreasonable to assume that the discrepancy in this case may be due to the organizational and technical changes resulting from the break-up of large agricultural units under the land reform.

In spite of the fall in yield these figures are generally higher

[1] Converted from *R.S.L.*, Vol. III, p. 48.

than the plan or the delivery quota. The quotas for corn were as follows:

TABLE XX[1]

Corn Delivery Quotas, Soviet Zone, 1946 and 1947
(*In cwt per acre*)

	1946	1947
Units up to 12 acres	4.7 cwt.	4.1 cwt.
,, ,, ,, 25 ,, ...	5.9 ,,	5.0 ,,
,, ,, ,, 50 ,, ...	7.2 ,,	6.5 ,,
,, ,, ,, 125 ,, ...	8.4 ,,	7.8 ,,
Units above 125 acres	10.0 ,,	9.0 ,,

Both in 1946 and in 1947 a considerable amount of grain was distributed in the 'free' market as legal surplus.[2] Still greater relative quantities of sugar, potatoes and vegetables were sold in the free market. Most of this surplus, represented by the usual Marxist connotation of overfulfilment of plans by so much per cent, was due, however, to the low plan figures for 1947. Since they did not even take into account the floods of the Oderbruch near Frankfurt in July 1947, they can only have been intended as a concession to the peasants. The zonal figures of the 1946 harvest are as follows:

TABLE XXI[3]

Total Agricultural Production, Soviet Zone
(*in million metric tons*)

	Grain	Potatoes	Sugar Beet
1938 ..	6.8	14.5	6.41
1946 ..	3.8	9.4	4.2
1947 ..	3.35	8.8	4.1

Once again it is clear that the greatest fall in relation to 1938 was in that agricultural sector most affected by the land reform.

Finally, a survey of food production plans for the Soviet zone in the first quarter of 1947 is given below. The expectation of this plan appears to correspond to reality. Note the high figure for distilled alcohol, and its inevitable effects on the supply of food. Value is official production costs only.

[1] *Wirtschaftsprobleme der Besatzungszonen*, p. 191. The figures have been converted from Doppelzentner per hectar.

[2] *Freie Spitzen* in official terminology.

[3] From the data in *R.S.L.*, Vol. II, Part VI, and official figures in percentages. In view of the difficulty of calculating free market transactions these figures should be treated as minima.

TABLE XXII[1]

Production Plan of the Food-Processing Industry
(First quarter 1947)

Items	*Quantity*	*Total value 1947 prices*
	Tons	*Rm.*
Flour	70,000	19,040,000
Prepared foodstuffs	6,200	2,480,000
Noodles	1,000	600,000
Meat	4,255	5,957,000
Tinned meat	250	500,000
Animal fat	550	732,000
Vegetable Oils	1,000	1,500,000
Margarine	1,000	1,700,000
Butter	3,134	9,919,000
Cheese and cream cheese	3,600	2,700,000
Fish	30	—
Tinned fish	29	32,000
White sugar	75,000	32,250,000
Starch and syrup	4,000	1,800,000
Potato flour	4,750	2,328,000
	Hectolitres[2]	
Raw spirits	105,000	10,500,000
Distilled spirit	20,000	3,000,000
Liqueur and *Schnapps*	27,000	9,450,000
Wines	1,500	525,000
Beer	210,000	7,770,000
Non-alcoholic drink	50,000	1,000,000
	Tons	
Sweets and Chocolates	650	975,000
Coffee substitute	1,200	480,000
Marmalade	9,475	9,475,000
Salt	—	—
Tobacco	30	36,000
	Pieces	
Cigarettes	60,000,000	1,560,000
Cigars	5,000,000	600,000
Perfume	—	5,605,000
	Tons	
Washing powder	11,550	12,705,000
Soap, 40 per cent	1,100	1,870,000
Soap for SAG	360	1,052,000
Malt	4,500	4,500,000
Yeast	750	600,000
Vinegar, essences	—	900,000
Flavours	—	153,089
SAG contributions for German Consumption	—	1,052,000
		Rm.154,141,000

In summing up the agricultural situation of the zone in 1946 it is clear that in this field, as in every other, the war and the nature of its conduct and conclusion had considerable adverse

[1] This is the official plan of the DZV for Agriculture.
[2] 1 *hectolitre* = 22.2 gallons.

effects. Although the actual yield figures seem to belie the statement that German agriculture suffered less severely than other branches of the economy, their low post-war level was to a considerable extent a hangover from that temporary disintegration of modern political and economic society which we noted earlier,[1] and to which agriculture, particularly when it aims at self-sufficiency, is most prone. The step from organized national production and distribution in agriculture to mere family or regional self-sufficiency is small. An organized black market is usually the first to appear in food, placing the agricultural producer in a dominating position. Industry, on the other hand, is either highly organized or dies. The disintegration was artificially prolonged by the small-holders' land reform, which reduced units to often uneconomic sizes by legislative enactment. In addition it created a considerable structural gulf between East and West Germany. This can clearly be seen from the anxious communist hopes of land reform in the West, and the fury of disappointment at Western obstinacy in clinging to the *status quo*.

The effects of the land reform on the consumer are relatively small. The greatest shortages are in dairy products and meat, shortages not much affected by the land reform, and unlikely to be overcome in the near future. The increase of livestock was one of the main worries of the DZV for Agriculture. An attempt was made to extend fishing facilities, and in this field the results seem to have been satisfactory. As fish became a substitute for meat to a previously unprecedented extent, a comparison with pre-war fishery figures is not altogether satisfactory. The disproportion of the agricultural yield of the Soviet zone is reflected not only in agricultural production figures, but in the ration scale of the consumer, though here distribution problems inevitably play an important part.[2] Both in 1946 and 1947 serious distribution breakdowns occurred, which directly affected the consumer's ration, while the same on an even more catastrophic scale repeatedly occurred in the West. But in any comparison of production and consumption between East and West, the Russian zone—mostly in spite, but partly because, of the land reform—must come out more favourably. During 1946 it was the best-fed zone in spite of its 'parasitic' occupation authority; an additional burden which neither the British nor the U.S. zone had to bear. In 1947 the

[1] See Chap. I.

[2] Serious distribution problems had appeared already during the war when a number of cases of hunger oedema occurred in the Ruhr.

Soviet zone was still as well fed as the U.S. zone, and considerably better than the British zone. A comparison of the population's food supply in the different zones is a matter of some difficulty. There are first the official statements of rations. In Germany almost all edible commodities were rationed at first. The table below gives samples of rations in the Soviet zone and the Anglo-American zones (Bizone) of occupation respectively at different periods:

TABLE XXIII[1]

Comparative Post-War Rations in Calories per day, Soviet and Western Zones

(Figures in brackets denote ration scale in large towns)

SOVIET ZONE

	Normal Consumer	*Heavy Worker*	*Miner*
March 1946 ..	1,100 (1 200)	1,903	3,023
November 1947 ..	1,325 (1,517)	2,053	3,911
March 1948 ..	1,336 (1,552)	2,369 (2,614)	3,991
December 1948 ..	1,526 (1,587)	2,525 (2,733)	3,990
June 1949	1,526 (1,587)	2,525 (2,733)	3,990
January 1950 ..	2,200	—	—

WESTERN ZONES

	Normal Consumer	*Heavy Worker*	*Miner*
March 1946 ..	1,025 (1,330)	2,230	2,495
November 1947 ..	1,100 (1,394)	2,302	3,100
March 1948 ..	1,190 (1,410)	2,335 (2,555)	2,910 (3,130)
December 1948 ..	1,549	2,162	3,653
June 1949	1,569	2,182	4,329
January 1950 ..	—	—	—

The normal consumer's average minimum food consumption per day in the rest of Europe is estimated at about 3,100 calories.

By itself this table is, of course, entirely misleading. The full ration scale was sometimes not available, and though the figures are supposed to represent issued rations as opposed to coupon value, they do not always do even that.[2] Secondly, no account is taken of food purchased outside the ration, either legally or illegally. Finally, as things improved, the ration comprised only a few items in short supply, and the calorific value of the 'ration' was accordingly reduced, though the consumer's intake was much greater.

[1] Ministry of Food Weekly Bulletin, Intelligence Division (Europe). Figures for 1946 and 1947 from *Tägliche Rundschau*, *Neue Zeitung*, *News Chronicle*. Bizonal figures are averages between the British and U.S. zones. For a general discussion, see Werner Klatt, *Food and Farming in Germany; Past, Present, and Future*. See also Friedmann, *op. cit.*, p. 193.

[2] Thus, official coupons in the Bizone represented over 1,500 calories for the normal consumer in March 1948. *U.S. Military Governor's Report*, April 1948, p. 16.

It is impossible, however, to make any accurate estimate of real comparative consumption during the period under examination. In 1945 the food shortage had not yet made itself greatly felt.[1] The 1946 harvest was good; we know that the agricultural production plans in the Soviet zone were exceeded, and that rations, except for meat and fats, were on the whole fully met, and some excess production was available. In the West, rations were frequently not met, particularly in the industrial areas. Shipments of food from abroad arrived only towards the middle of the year, just before the harvest. In 1947 the harvest was bad throughout Germany, but probably worse in the Soviet zone, owing to heavy flooding. Rations were still very low, and little was available 'on the side' except in the black market. In the West there were violent fluctuations owing to distribution troubles, imports were not enough to cover the deficit of home production, and control of agricultural deliveries less strict than in the East. It is probable that on the whole the Eastern zone was still better fed during 1947.[2] In 1948 imports into the Western zones had risen considerably, and the currency reform there altered the situation entirely, so that income and not allocation was soon the more satisfactory guide to food consumption. In the Soviet zone, however, though rations were now raised, they were only irregularly met and frequently by substitutes, such as fish for meat, noodles for fat, sugar for almost everything. While privileged classes were in an improved position, the non-privileged average consumer was worse off than in 1947, and much worse after July than his Western opposite number. During 1949 and 1950 the position in the East improved somewhat; the first imports of meat took place, and there was a reduction in the Soviet demands on the part of both army and reparation agencies. During 1949 certain commodities, such as certain kinds of fish and sugar as well as some vegetables and prepared foods (noodles, macaroni, etc.), were taken off the ration. More items, according to the Ministry of Trade and Supply, were scheduled to come off the ration in 1950, but meat and fats remained in very short supply. There was a marked improvement in supplies in the West in 1949–50, and food rationing there was exclusively by the purse.

[1] Some estimates in *R.S.L.*, Vol. III, p. 40.

[2] This is disputed by *R.S.L.*, Vol. III, also by the official British and American view.

(E) *Transport*

(i) *Railways.*[1] The German State Railways (DR) played a vital part in Germany's war economy, both in the Reich itself and as the directing organ for the railways of the occupied countries. The total extent of the railway system in the area of the Reich in 1936 was about 61,000 km., of which 19,000 were in the present Soviet zone and Berlin. The internal expansion of this system in Germany just before and during the war was not very considerable, though certainly bigger than the equivalent expansion in England or France, consisting of about 1,500 km. of new track, chiefly extensions of existing main-line facilities. Without doubt the railways were by far the outstanding means of transportation in Germany before and during the war, carrying 73 per cent of all transported goods in 1939, and 79 per cent in 1941, including internal army traffic. The German railways carried proportionately more goods than the railways of any other country.[2]

In spite of the heavy demands and losses during the war, the railways emerged, as far as transport capacity was concerned, in a remarkably sound position. Losses in rolling stock during the war had been considerable, and replacements for France and the East often came from German stock. Yet an intensive production and repair programme enabled Germany to emerge with almost as many locomotives as in 1938, and a not too greatly reduced quantity of waggons and coaches.

TABLE XXIV[3]

Pre-war and Post-war Locomotives and Rolling Stocks, Germany and Soviet Zone

	Locomotives (including Diesel units)	*Goods Waggons*
Germany in 1938	22,909	575,000
Germany in 1946	21,789	485,922
Russian zone 1938	7,100 + 750[4]	140,000
Russian zone 1946	6,800 + 650[4]	90,000

By themselves these figures are deceptive. If the percentage of locomotives and waggons always under repair in the Soviet zone is considered, locomotives 20 per cent in 1938, 45 per cent in 1946,

[1] The figures in this section, except where otherwise stated, are based on a detailed survey of Railway Transport conditions in pre-war and post-war Germany undertaken privately by a group of experts in Berlin.

[2] For this, see figures in *R.S.L.*, Vol. III, p. 100 *passim*.

[3] Official DR investigation, December 1946, corrected on the basis of private survey.

[4] Locomotive units of Berlin city railway.

goods waggons 5 per cent in 1938 and 25 per cent in 1946, figures of total stock take on a very different aspect. The effective operating capacity was far below that of the potential suggested by the gross total, and where before the war repair quotas in locomotives and waggons could be reckoned as a small constant factor, they now form the most variable and vital component in transport plans.

The dismantling of equipment and manufacturing capacity made a chronic and widening deficiency out of a post-war bottleneck. Dismantling of German locomotive and waggon plants and repair shops was heavy, and by the end of 1946 only some 35–40 per cent[1] of the original capacity remained. Any large-scale replacement of rolling stock, and an achievement of a better repair-to-running ratio was made impossible. The coincidence of heavy repair quotas and shortage of repair shops and manufacturing plant was a post-war phenomenon mostly due to Soviet reparation policy. To this was added the ever-present shortage of steel.

The other vital factor limiting the transport capacity of the railways was the dismantling of track and track installation. This began as early as the end of 1945, and by the end of 1946 some 5,500 km. of track had been dismantled, consisting of 1,800 km. of single or double track totally removed, and 3,700 km. of double to single track reduction.[2] This is 29 per cent of the total system, and includes some 9,000 switches, or 35 per cent of the total. As far as track installations are concerned, dismantling was not confined to removed track, but extended to most of the central German main lines, Berlin–Leipzig, Magdeburg–Berlin, Berlin–Frankfurt/Oder and Berlin–Stettin, etc. Signalling installations, safety devices, and telephone facilities were mainly affected. The losses in track installations necessitated a change in the organization of operational activities; running times and times of complete turn-round were increased, archaic signalling and safety devices had to be resorted to, and, since modern single-track main lines are particularly dependent on a complicated and efficient system of signalling and communication, the general speed of railway transport was greatly hampered until a new system could be devised and perfected.

From the beginning of 1946 very strenuous plan figures for turn-round times were issued. An attempt was made to maximize

[1] Some estimates put it as low as 10 per cent. *R.S.L.*, Vol. III, Chap. 8, p. 101.

[2] The figure of 10,000 km. by the end of 1948 has a surprising vogue, e.g., *R.S.L.*, Vol. III, Chap. 8, p. 100. This would be 53 per cent of the total system and is patently exaggerated.

the daily utilization capacity of goods waggons. In 1938 the turn-round average had been 3.98 days for the Soviet zone, while the daily availability of goods-waggon capacity had been 45,756 waggons per working day. In 1946 these figures were 5.2 days and 11,700 waggons per working day. In spite of prodigious efforts achievement fell short of the 1946 plan, which demanded a 5-days' turn-round and 15,000 waggons daily. It is in these figures that the effects of the repair quota, the dismantling, the shortage and unsuitability of the fuel, can be seen. Lack of hard coal led to increasing use of brown coal substitute. The wastage arising from the use of this fuel was stressed in the official statement of the vice-president of the Central Administration for Transport, Kühne: that 'where a heavy goods locomotive would use 19 metric tons hard coal per 1,000 km. in 1936, present operational difficulties, depreciation, etc., have increased this to 23 tons hard coal or 46–60 tons of brown coal'.[1] The influence of these facts can also be seen in a calculation of annual goods weight transported altogether and per waggon.

The organization of transport has already been briefly mentioned.[2] The war-time connection between the old Ministry of Transport and the Central Directorate of Railways was tightened up by the complete subordination of the railway administration to the new Administration for Transport in July 1945, and the process was completed when the DR directorate, together with the directorates of motor transport and inland shipping, were brought together under one roof, the headquarters of the Administration. The old *Reichsbahn* officials, who had been surprisingly immune from direct Nazi influence,[3] resented this post-war subordination and were generally not spared the current anti-Nazi investigations and removals. Consequently the railways suffered from the general dismissal of 'expert' functionaries with rather less justification than the other branches of the administration. By the end of 1946 the railway directorate had become only the executive organ of the Central Administration, which was entirely responsible for planning and supervision, tasks which, except for co-ordination at government level, had previously been within the sphere of the railway administration. The relationship and internal organization of the railways can best be shown by the following diagram:

[1] Preamble to the Transport plan for 1947 issued internally by the Administration for Transport, December 1946.

[2] See above, p. 115.

[3] Even Dorpmüller, the head of the DR during most of the Nazi period, was not a member of the Party.

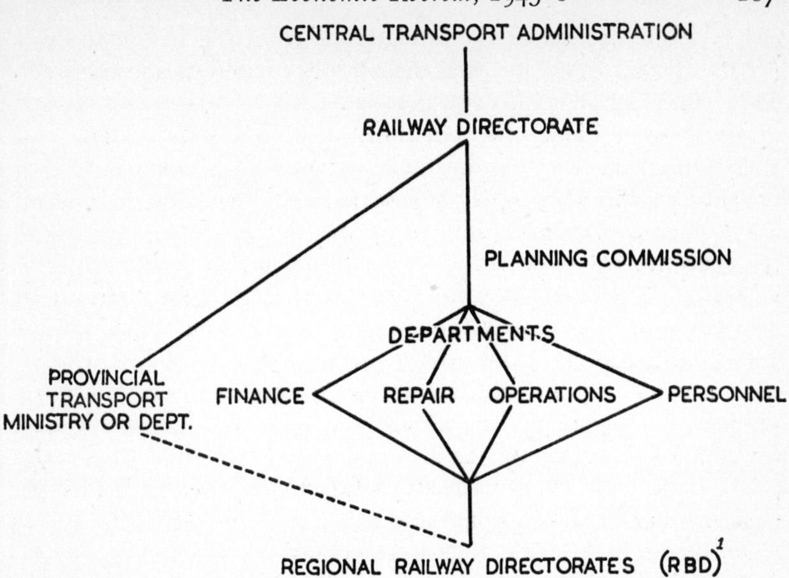

FIG. 5. *Administrative Organization of the Railways, Soviet Zone 1946.*

In spite of the draconian measures to step up the transport performance of the railways in 1947, it proved impossible to do more than increase the total amount of goods and passengers carried by a fraction. The Russians let loose a new wave of dismantling in August, and their demands for transport of reparations increased considerably during the year.[2] The plans, according to the Central Administration, were only about 90 per cent fulfilled, and even this claim is almost certainly exaggerated.

(ii) *Internal and coastal shipping.*[3] The general department for waterways of the Transport Administration dealt with the control of inland shipping and the upkeep of canals. At the beginning it also had a department for the scientific study of drainage, waterfall, and navigation, though this was transferred in 1947 to the Administration for Agriculture. The relationship between the general department for inland waterways and shipping and the Administration was very similar to that of the railway directorate, but the former did not possess the same long-standing tradition of independence and, being born in subordination, gave no trouble to the controlling body.

[1] At Magdeburg, Schwerin, Cottbus, Frankfurt, Halle, Erfurt, Dresden.

[2] See below, p. 206.

[3] The control of ocean shipping did not arise in the Soviet zone, partly on account of its geographical situation but mostly because all ocean-going vessels were either destroyed or placed on the reparations list in accordance with the Potsdam plan.

The canal system of the Soviet zone consisted before the war (1939) of some 1,300 km. and did not alter much during the war[1]. The system divides into two general categories, that of the Elbe and that of the Mark (Brandenburg area). There are in addition the connections with the system of the Oder, now under Polish administration, and with the northern and central systems of West Germany, which would add some 300–400 km. to the 1,300 given above. The effects of war were mostly destruction of bridges, locks, etc., rather than extensive damage to the canal system itself. By the end of 1946 the entire system was once again navigable, with the exception of the waterways in and just around Berlin, where repairs on a greater scale were required. However, the heavy flooding of the Oder plains in the late spring and summer of 1947 showed that it was extremely difficult for the administration to deal with an emergency of this kind without extraordinary organizational and material efforts.

As far as barges and tugs were concerned, the German Fleet lost more through reparations, both requisition for work *in situ* and removals to the East, than through war damage. From a pre-war (1939) total of 17,740 tugs and barges with a total carrying capacity of 6,475,000 tons, some 3,240 tugs and barges with a capacity of about 1,184,500 fell to the 1950 area of the Soviet zone. Of this, some 700 tugs and barges were taken as reparations by the Russians, some of them on behalf of the Poles, whose reparation demands the U.S.S.R. had undertaken to satisfy out of her own share.[2] Without taking into account the tonnage operating on Soviet orders and for Russian cargoes, this left 78 per cent of the pre-war tonnage. It should be borne in mind, however, that the German inland fleet was more old fashioned than that, for instance, of Belgium or Holland, a far higher percentage being steam driven instead of motorized, and consisting of a higher proportion of barges as opposed to self-propelled vessels. In view of the predominance of railway traffic, modernization of the inland shipping facilities had been belated and limited. Also half the tugs in 1939 were 30–50 years old, while two-thirds of the barges had been built 20–50 years before.[3]

The post-war cut in railway transport enhanced the importance of waterways transport. The raising of barges which had been sunk during the war was successfully undertaken as an early priority,

[1] The figures in this section are based on a private report prepared by officials in the Transport Administration for the SMA. See also *R.S.L.*, Vol. III, p. 105, *passim*. [2] See *Protocol* of Berlin Conference, III, para. 2.

[3] *R.S.L.*, Vol. III, p. 107, for comparative figures.

and by the end of 1946 some 200,000 tons had been salvaged. The plan for 1946 envisaged the transport of some 4.5 million tons of goods, and was successfully carried out. For 1947 the plan was 5 million tons and was carried out by 108.5 per cent according to official German figures; in other words, some 5,425,000 tons were transported. For 1948 the plan was ambitiously increased by 20 per cent to 6 million tons, and in the first six months of 1948 some 3.9 million tons were in fact transported, a figure which, as far as the second half of the year is concerned, would naturally be reduced by winter conditions.[1] All these figures include transports on Russian account, under red licence, as they are called, the purely German transports carrying a green licence. The subject of internal waterways is one of the few bright spots in the Soviet zone economy after 1946.

(iii) *Motor Transport*. The principal administrative achievement of the authorities in the Soviet zone with regard to motor transport was the permanent organization of the General Transport Pools,[2] a number of joint transport undertakings to which all private haulage contractors had to belong, and which were controlled by the provincial authorities. The pooling of transport facilities had been a wartime measure in Germany as in England, and was now made permanent as an alternative to nationalization. Membership of any Transport Pool was the only means of obtaining licences and petrol. The provincial governments also operated transport pools of their own, consisting of the former property of the Reich Ministry of Transport and of Nazi or monopoly-capitalist firms, lumped together as war criminals. In view of the great shortage of operational transport some joint organization was anyhow inevitable. The control obtained by the ministries was considered sufficient to prevent nationalization for three years after the end of the war. In fact transport was nationalized in Britain earlier than in the Soviet zone, where the typically Nazi system of State control through federation of private owners was continued until some time in 1948.

Current depreciation of vehicles plays a very important part in the motor transport system, which is particularly dependent on adequate replacement and repair services, or, in other words, on material supply. In addition to the heavy demands of the Armed Services and the large-scale losses during the war, motor transport

[1] Official transport figures of annual plan and its achievement, issued December 1946, 1947. The 3.9 million tons for 1948 are a semi-official estimate.

[2] *Allgemeine Transport Gesellschaften*, not to be confused with the well-known German forwarding firm of the same name.

capacity suffered above all from the desperate shortage of spare parts and new vehicles. The same observation as with inland water transport must be made: the German motor transport service was far less highly developed than that of Britain, Belgium, or Holland, and only half as extensive in relation to size of population as that of France.[1] Although in the 1930s the same marginal competition between road and rail transport became noticeable as in other countries, the railways were in a far firmer position in Germany than elsewhere. The total figures for lorries in the Germany of 1938 (excluding Austria) was 365,700, having risen from 143,950 in 1929.[2] In the same two years there were 5.3 lorries per 1,000 inhabitants, or 190 population per lorry (1938) as compared to 2.2 lorries per 100 inhabitants or 450 population per lorry in 1929. Comparative European figures of population per lorry in 1939 were: Czechoslovakia, 615; Russia, 390; Switzerland, 205; Holland, 165; Belgium, 101; Great Britain, 99; Denmark, 96; France, 90.[3]

Of these totals some 30 per cent[4] belong to the Soviet zone, or about 73,000 lorries, and some 162,000 tons net transport capacity. In 1946 the figures for the zone were about 33,000 lorries and 69,000 tons net transport capacity, a reduction of over 50 per cent. Of these a considerable percentage (exact figures are impossible to obtain) were immobilized by shortage of tyres and awaiting repair.[5] The following road transport figures are for Land Saxony-Anhalt only:

TABLE XXV[6]

Road Transport Vehicles and Carrying Capacity, Land Saxony-Anhalt, 1946 and 1938

(*End of 1946*)

9,440 lorries with a net capacity of 14,225 tons.
7,789 trailers with a gross net capacity of 26,348 tons.
9,120 motor-cars. 14,900 motor cycles.

The equivalent figures for 1938 are:[7]

16,400 lorries (800 trailers) with a net capacity of 26,000 tons (27,000 tons).
65,000 motor-cars. 88,000 motor cycles.

[1] *R.S.L.*, Vol. III, p. 110 *passim*, for comparative figures.

[2] These figures are partly from *R.S.L.*, *loc. cit.*, partly from a private survey.

[3] *R.S.L.*, *loc. cit.* (slightly amended against official figures of these countries, given in their various statistical surveys before the war).

[4] i.e. 20 per cent of the 1938 German total, including East Prussia, Pomerania, Silesia, Saar, etc.

[5] See *Tagliche Rundschau*, 10 Aug. 1947 for the statement that on 30 June 1947 8,000 lorries and vans and 7,500 trailers were out of action for lack of tyres.

[6] Private survey based on official Transport Administration figures.

[7] For districts of Magdeburg, Merseburg, and Land Anhalt, roughly equal to the present Land Saxony-Anhalt.

A similar reduction was noticeable in the actual loads carried, although the demands on the motor transport services in relation to the railways were proportionately greater. Local haulage space from and to railheads was being increasingly used for long-distance work. Nevertheless in 1946 some 27.5 million tons were carried by road in the Soviet zone as compared to some 42 million tons in 1938. The plan stipulated a figure of 25 million tons. For 1947 some 30 million tons were carried, 5 million more than the yearly plan demanded. Road transport plans were very low and were surpassed as a result of a considerable purchase of tyres from the British zone. For example, the plan figure of 1948 was only 28 million tons, but the inter-zonal blockade, which prevented Western German supply of tyres and spare parts—particularly from the firms of Ford, Borgward, and Büssing in the British zone—from entering the Soviet zone, made even this figure difficult to reach.

Finally, a word about the production of new vehicles. These were particularly important in view of the bad conditions of all but the most important roads, and the material and labour difficulties in keeping the roads repaired. Almost the entire stock of lorries, cars, and motor cycles was of pre-war manufacture, and the annual rate of depreciation is normally at its highest after eight years. A very great part of lorry and motor-car building plant was dismantled by the Russians, including the Auto-Union works in Saxony and the large Opel lorry factory in Brandenburg. As far as motor-cars are concerned, only the BMW works at Eisenach were producing during 1946 and 1947, and their output went almost entirely to the Russians for use or re-export, leaving only a small allocation for official German organizations. In 1938 there were about 318,000 motor-cars in the Soviet zone; at the end of 1946, according to the *Handelsblatt* of 13 February 1947, this number was reduced to 74,000 and to 62,000 in 1947. The corresponding figure for motor cycles is 378,250 for 1938, 107,000 in 1946, and 94,000 in 1947. Even the reduced figures for 1946 declined in 1947, owing to the restricted repair facilities and the almost complete lack of new vehicles. The motor transport outlook for the future was one of the gloomiest features of the Soviet zone.

(F) *Employment, Labour Supply, and Distribution*

The question of employment has already been raised in the introductory remarks to this chapter. The conditions described in the foregoing sections at first glance suggest considerable unemployment, particularly in those industries whose output suffered the greatest reductions. Such an expectation is based on the experience of the 1932 slump, when both unemployment and under-capacity production were present. But the comparison is not exact. In 1932 the slump was world-wide, restriction of credit and of consumption being followed by a sharp decline of industrial production and unemployment. In 1945 the level of industrial production was physically restricted and a considerable part of the economy was directly pole-axed. Under-exploitation of capacity was certainly present, but not as a result of restricted demand. Moreover, orders to produce—the Soviet equivalent of effective demand—were at a maximum. The greatest influence off-setting potential unemployment was the reduction in productivity. Other factors being equal, and cost no object, a reduction of individual productivity by, say, a half will necessitate almost twice the original labour force. In other words, at a constant output productivity and the size of the labour force are in inverse proportion.

Let us now examine the employment figures in the Soviet zone as far as they are available.

TABLE XXVI[1]

Employment of Workers and Salaried Employees

	Soviet zone	*Potsdam Germany*
2nd Quarter 1939 ..	5,757	21,222
2nd ,, 1946 ..	5,431	17,821
4th ,, 1946 ..	5,769	19,559
2nd ,, 1947 ..	5,900	20,532
4th ,, 1947 ..	5,932	20,799

Thus, not only did employment rise steadily in the Soviet zone, largely absorbing the influx of population, but the level of employment was higher than that in the rest of Germany, where the total figure at the end of 1947 was still below that of 1939, whereas the figure in the Soviet zone was greater by some 180,000. The German Institute of Economic Research expresses this graphically as follows:

[1] *Wirtschaftsprobleme der Besatzungszonen*, p. 38.

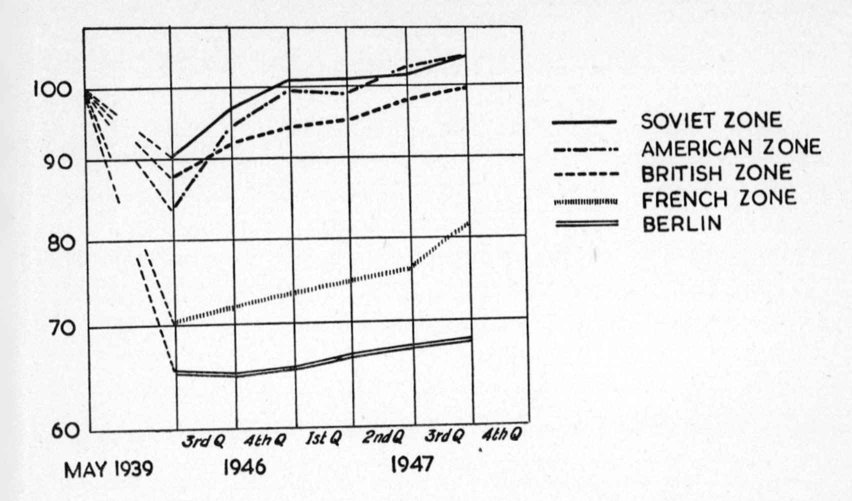

FIG. 6.[1] *Comparative Levels of Employment, Potsdam Germany* (1939 = 100)

The above categories, workers and salaried employees, represent some 33 per cent of the total population in 1947 as compared to 38 per cent in 1939.[2] Except for Berlin itself, the Soviet zone had and has the greatest percentage of wage and salary earners in relation to the total population. The reduction in the proportion of wage-earners is due to the particularly heavy restriction of industrial production everywhere.

Even so, the result appears satisfactory. But bearing in mind various qualifications, fall in productivity, uneconomic employment, etc., the total employment figures need further investigation. Accurate zonal distribution figures for the various branches of employment before the war are unfortunately not available, but certain inferences can be drawn in any comparison between 1946 and 1936, the last year before the intensive rearmament plan. The table on p. 194 gives the distribution for 1946 and 1947 in the Soviet zone. The plus or minus sign in brackets after the 1946 figures shows the increase or decrease as compared with 1936.

[1] *Wirtschaftsprobleme der Besatzungszonen*, p. 37.
[2] The figures given in this section are mostly from the article quoted above and from *Statistical Handbook*.

TABLE XXVII[1]

Distribution and Changes of Employment, Soviet Zone

Employment	*No. employed Dec. 1946*	*No. employed Dec. 1947*	*1946–7 Increase/ Decrease*	*Percentage*
TOTAL	5,771,740 (+)	5,994,139	+ 222,399	+
Mining	156,894 (+)	213,079	+ 56,185	+ 35.8
Administration	305,266 (+)	348,618	+ 43,352	+ 14.2
Building and Associated industries (rubble clearing)	386,861 (+)	426,561	+ 39,700	+ 10.3
Wood and Carpentry industries	196,403 (–)	228,480	+ 32,077	+ 16.3
Machine, Steel and Vehicle industry	278,125 (–)	307,067	+ 28,942	+ 10.4
Commerce, Banking, Insurance	369,699 (–)	398,140	+ 28,441	+ 7.7
Chemical industry ..	162,093 (–)	184,384	+ 22,291	+ 13.8
Education, Church, Law, Science, etc.	97,223 (–)	116,485	+ 19.262	+ 19.8
Railways, Autobahnen ..	207,835 (+)	224,134	+ 16,299	+ 7.8
Transport (except above and Postal)	75,338 (+)	85,905	+ 10,567	+ 14.0
Textile industry ..	365,793 (–)	375,917	+ 10,124	+ 2.8
Iron and Metal industry ..	25,342 (–)	34,540	+ 9,198	+ 36.3
Food and Food Processing Industry and Trade ..	229,849 (–)	238,091	+ 88,242	+ 3.6
Ceramic and Glass industry	56,659 (–)	64,566	+ 7,907	+ 14.0
Electrical industry ..	80,261 (+)	88,159	+ 7,898	+ 9.8
Postal services	62,622 (+)	70,174	+ 7,552	+ 12.1
Health and Hygienic Services	187,016 (+)	194,298	+ 7,282	+ 3.9
Agriculture	1,067,968 (+)	960,552	– 107,416	– 10.1
Military Government employees	174,333 (+)	110,959	– 63,274	– 36.3
Domestic services ..	247,933 (+)	239,790	– 8,143	– 3.3
Precision Tools and Optics	49,063 (–)	45,219	– 3,844	– 2.1

The changes in employment distribution between 1936 and 1946 seem to show no very clear pattern. This is partly due to the widely varying tendencies between 1938 and 1944 on the one hand, and after 1945 on the other; between 1938 and 1944 the figures for general employment fell considerably owing to the demands of the armed forces, etc., and the partial replacement of Germans by foreign labour. Such items as commerce, transport, postal, and domestic services lost relatively more labour than industry, particularly basic industries. On the other hand, these same employments which had been depleted most by the demands of war received most labour immediately after the war. With the prevailing state of affairs in 1945–6 the railways, postal services, com-

[1] *Ibid.*, p. 44.

merce, and domestic services could absorb more labour than might have been expected in pre-war circumstances, not because the need was greater, but partly because more labour was needed to fulfil the same tasks as before the war. In view of the difficulties of industrial production, these jobs offered a better prospect of an immediate, if slender, income. With the exception of mining, which had been considerably expanded in 1936–9, and the electrical industry, which had also been expanded and was one of the first industries to restart production on an increasing scale after May 1945, industry as a whole employed less labour in 1946 than in 1936. Transport and other services absorbed most of the new labour, while military government provided an altogether novel means of employment. The land reform absorbed some labour previously in industry. There was a general if temporary preference for working on the land even before the land reform.

The period 1946–7 partly rectified this undesirable state of affairs. The greatest percentage increases of employed labour were in mining and iron and steel processing. Of the increase in mining almost 80 per cent was due to the demands of the uranium mines in Germany, accounting in 1946 for about 40,000 of the total 56,000 new workers. The increase in the ferrous metal industries was a sign of attempts to increase production. Wood-processing and carpentry increased their labour force by 10 per cent, chemical industries by 13 per cent, ceramics and glass by 14 per cent, machines and steel-processing by 10 per cent, and the building and associated industries by 10 per cent. Employment in administration also increased by 14 per cent, commerce and banking by 7 per cent, education, etc., by 20 per cent, postal services and railways by 12 per cent and 8 per cent respectively. Most of the latter increases were counter movements to the great wartime comb-out, though demands for labour based on pre-war 'productivity' expectation would not have warranted such increases. These figures are minima and do not take into account the post-war phenomenon of considerable casual labour. The decreases in employment arise from the reaction in agriculture against some of the less economical results of the land reform, from the selling out by the least competent and poorest beneficiaries, and from the reduction in temporary farm labour once industry began to recover. The Soviet authorities, unlike the British and American, succeeded in cutting down the considerable German staff working for the military authorities. In the Soviet zone some 110,959 persons were in December 1947 employed in this way while the equivalent figure in the British zone was 435,314.[1] Finally, the reduction of labour in precision tool and optical industries was due almost entirely to dismantling, chiefly at Zeiss. Compared to the British and U.S. zones these figures as a whole show a greater trend towards distributional normality and a sound state of affairs. The distinct preponderance in the increase of labour in basic industries in the Soviet zone as compared to consumer-goods industries is evidence of this.

It must be remembered that an increase in the total of those employed in 1946 and 1947, as compared to 1936, by no means implies a decrease in unemployment figures. The amount of employed female labour increased sharply during the war, and the post-war situation produced some competition between the sexes in certain employments, particularly salaried and official positions. While some 14 per cent of all employed persons were salaried employees in offices, the corresponding figure of unemployed in this category was 18 per cent. This compared with 26 per cent unemployed and 20 per cent employed office workers out of the respective labour totals in the British zone. The total unemployment figures for the Soviet zone are 3.2 per cent, or 2 per cent male and 5.2 per cent female. This total is higher than the corresponding figures for Saxony, and lower than that for Mecklenburg and Brandenburg, and does not include Berlin. The total takes into account temporary unemployment of a seasonal and frictional character. Unemployment percentages are thus only slightly higher than the minima of 2–3 per cent taken as normal in an almost full-employment economy.

As has been stated, the low level of individual productivity partly accounts for the high employment level in industry, transport, postal services, commerce, and professions and administration. In industry the level of individual productivity was governed by the actual working-capacity of the operative, and by the shortening of the working week, often to three or four days. The average level of industrial productivity in the Soviet zone compared to 1936 seems to have been about 75 per cent in 1946, and to have been reduced to 50–60 per cent in 1947 and slightly further in 1948.[2] This figure takes into account not only the physical reduction in productive effort on the part of individuals, but also the shortage of modern equipment, particularly in mining, and of suitable raw materials in consumers-goods industries. For

[1] *Wirtschaftsprobleme der Besatzungszonen*, pp. 42, 44.
[2] My own estimate.

instance, the poor quality of nails and screws in the handtool industry of the *Werkzeug-Union* of Thuringia necessitated frequent rejects, and thus extra sorters and more labour. The time spent filling in allocation forms for every kind of raw material and accessory, and the effort expended on 'scrounging' suitable substitute raw materials, further reduced production per factory. In the *Sachsische Emaillier-und Stanzwerke*, a Saxon factory making cooking materials, pots and pans, etc., the workers were allowed a day off per week to dig peat for fuel. The same factory had to carry out a constant search for raw material in the Soviet zone and the West, although engaged fully on reparation work. Consequently 60 per cent labour excess was employed so that a full week's output could be achieved. When raw material stocks ran out, the whole labour force might be idle for anything up to a fortnight. Yet on the official returns the whole 160 per cent of the 1936 labour force would be shown as gainfully employed. Such instances were the rule rather than the exception in the whole of Germany. Clearly, official employment figures are most misleading.

The official labour policy in the Soviet zone was very stringent. Free movement of labour was prohibited, registration made compulsory, complete control given to the local labour offices, and compulsory direction of labour sanctioned by order of the SMA, all some two months before these powers were made universal in Germany by Control Council decision.[1] Any infraction was punishable by withdrawal of ration cards. In the Soviet zone the amount of compulsorily directed labour in 1946 was almost 14 per cent of the total number of new employment registrations.[2] Complete control of labour gave the authorities great power over industry generally, particularly the private sector, and enabled the Russians to use the German labour machinery for their own purpose.[3] All this was in full accord with the best Communist principles, and labour was almost the first branch of the economy to be fully organized on Russian lines.

As long as there was a considerable pool of unemployed or partially unemployed labour on which to draw, satisfactory distribution of labour by the use of the vast powers of the Central Administration was simple. By the end of 1946 the problem of shifting labour from one employment to another had already become acute, particularly since some employments, such as

[1] *C.C. Order* No. 3 of 17 January 1946.
[2] *Wirtschaftsprobleme der Besatzungszonen*, p. 62.
[3] See above, Chap. V, p. 122.

uranium mining, offered conditions which would attract no one. Between November 1946 and July 1948, compulsory labour directions for these mines could invariably be measured by the corresponding increase of refugees coming into the Western zones.[1] The labour shortage in these mines, or rather the deficit of supply in relation to the increasing Russian demands, was such that convicts were sent to work there from the prisons of Saxony. In other fields of the economy, the stringency of labour direction was somewhat softened in October 1947 by command of the SMA,[2] which warned against indiscriminate and excessive use of compulsory direction. In 1948 the proportion of compulsory registrations or changes therein, was about 8.5 per cent of all registrations.

However, the same SMA order, headed 'Measures for increasing the productivity of labour and the further improvement in the material welfare of workers and employees in industry and the transport services', introduced the beginning of a Russian-type Stakhanov system. The chief, perhaps the only, industry in which this would work effectively was coal-mining, since raw material shortages had no effect on production in this case. It was appropriate that Hennecke, who gave his name to the German edition of the system, was, like his Russian opposite, a coalminer. A considerable fuss was made in 1947 and 1948 about increases in the output of single shifts as a result of the operation of the system, but its total effect on output is unlikely to have had the effect claimed by the German authorities. The actual level of brown coal production in the zone was lower in 1947 than in 1946, and prospects for 1948 were only for a slight improvement on 1946. Considering the influx of new labour into the mines, as shown by the table above,[3] the productivity of labour does not seem to have improved greatly. However, Stakhanovitism was henceforward as much a part of the Communist industrial equipment as were detailed plan figures.

[1] 146,000 between January 1947 and April 1948, according to OMGUS press statement, 26 April 1948. Some other figures are also given by Löwenthal, *op. cit.*, pp. 200–3: 189,000 to the British zone, Jan. to Oct. 1947, quoting Mr. Bevin.

[2] SMA Order 234. Löwenthal, *op. cit.*, p. 301, denies that the order was intended to be, or was put into effect as a genuine means of improving labour conditions. The figures of compulsory direction, at any rate, are against him.

[3] See p. 194.

CHAPTER VII

SOVIET REPARATIONS POLICY

So far we have dealt with the economic development of the Soviet zone from 1945 to 1947. Reparations had been an important factor since July 1945, but it was only in the autumn of 1946 that the German public and the Western powers became aware of the real purpose and extent of the Russian plans. From that time onwards, until the end of 1948, reparations in one form or another became the dominating factor in the economic field, indeed in every field. We must now turn our attention to this question in some detail.[1] First, in the narrowest sense: i.e. reparations from capital goods, from current production, and from labour —the three items mentioned in the Yalta and Potsdam agreements.[2] Then we must discuss the Soviet organization of industrial and other property in Germany, the export of German production on Russian account, and the Soviet-operated black market in certain scarce commodities.

Very few of the detailed reparation figures have been published, and the unofficial material that has appeared in the Press is unreliable. It is no exaggeration to say that outside a handful of Russians in Germany and perhaps one or two Germans, no one was in a position to survey the field entirely. Nor is this obscurity the incidental result of a complex system; all economic statistics, with the exception of a few niggardly percentages, were treated as secret by the Russians in the Soviet Union as well as in Germany, and reparations statistics were top secret. Indeed, the desire for secrecy directly explains some of the complications of the system. On the Russian side there was no single agency dealing with all forms of reparation. Some of the agencies were directly controlled by the office of the Four Year Plan, others by the Ministry of Foreign Trade, others by the Ministries of the Interior and of the Armed Services. The SMA had no control over reparation policy.[3] Such division of responsibility had an adverse effect on efficiency; competition between different offices in procurement and export

[1] For a valuation of reparations in figures, see Appendix C to this chapter.

[2] See above, Chapter II.

[3] Löwenthal fails to make the distinction between SMA exports on German account and exports by the Soviet corporations and trading companies on Russian account. The difference, as will be seen, is very important.

of reparation goods was frequent. It is extremely difficult to obtain a satisfactory idea of either the method or the extent of reparations.

The question can be treated under the following heads, distinct both in the method of procurement and in the time during which they were chiefly in vogue.

(A) *Reparations from capital goods*

It was under this head that the conference at Potsdam envisaged the greater part of reparations to be taken. The restriction and proscription of certain industries served not only as a means of preventing German economic rearmament, but at the same time provided the basis for reparations. Such was the dual purpose of the Control Council list of restricted and prohibited industries issued in March 1946, and the 'Revised Level of Industry' of July 1947 for the Bizone.[1] But an analysis of reparations in the Soviet zone on the basis of this plan is wasted effort, since resemblances are purely accidental. It is clear that the Soviet authorities were working on a separate plan, prepared before the long-drawn-out discussions in the Allied Control Council had even begun. The plan was in operation at a time when the Western Reparations Agency[2] had only begun to register the individual claims of the participating powers and was tentatively having particular works earmarked for dismantling.

The Soviet dismantling teams arrived in the Soviet zone almost with the second echelon of the occupying armies. It was made clear to the SMA and to the army commanders, to whom these teams were attached, that they had no power over them. Wide discretionary powers of selection and removal were given, and the assistance both of the SMA and of the Red Army could be called upon. Certain major factories, such as Zeiss, seem to have been earmarked long before for dismantling, but in addition the teams could take what in their view was worth dismantling and removing. Certainly they availed themselves of these powers to the full.

Much of the early dismantling was haphazard and hasty. Apart from factories, such installations as telephone exchanges, post office depots, railway workshops, line equipment, and haulage equipment were affected. Even University laboratories, such as

[1] For a short discussion of these plans see Chapter II above.

[2] Inter-Allied Reparations Agency (IARA) in Brussels. For a very brief discussion of the work of this organization see David Bolster, 'The end of Reparations', *Contemporary Review*, No. 1020, December 1950, p. 337.

the one at Rostock, were dismantled.[1] The work was at first handled exclusively by untrained Red Army personnel and the damage to reparation value was considerable. Transport difficulties, which arose from the sudden flow of goods to be transported, and which greatly exceeded the available capacity of the railways, caused quantities of material to be abandoned in or near sidings. The same waste was increased by the failure to provide adequate packing material, or skilled labour to handle the highly complicated machinery. Trails of abandoned reparation materials could be seen littering the countryside around the works recently favoured by a visit from the Russians, to the double fury of the wastefully deprived Germans. The difference between the value of capital reparations taken from the Germans and their value to the Russian economy must be considerable, and would be interesting to investigate.[2]

A short note needs to be made on the valuation of reparations. It is the subtraction from the total value of a factory or installation that must be counted, rather than the net value of equipment taken. The difference may be considerable, even with the most scientific dismantling. To take one example, if the entire electrical installation from an aluminium electrolysis plant was removed, the loss was much greater than the value of the actual installation as long as replacement was impossible. In certain cases, such as telephone exchanges or railway lines, where the loss was partially replaceable from stock, and where reorganization could distribute the additional load satisfactorily, the replacement cost only has been reckoned. As all other general calculations of value are in 1936 prices, replacement costs are reckoned on the same terms. Finally, supplementary costs, transport, German labour when and if used, and the actual costs of dismantling are not reckoned either. Although these items were charged to the Germany economy, they will be dealt with separately as occupation costs paid out of the Länder budgets.

The following table gives a general survey of dismantled capacity as a percentage of 1946 capacity in selected industries. In addition to my own estimate, I have included the estimates of the *Manchester Guardian Weekly* of 20 March 1947,[3] and those given in *Reparationen, Sozialprodukt, Lebensstandard,* Vol. IV, p. 52. These two estimates give in addition a compound figure for each industry

[1] Löwenthal, *op. cit.*, p. 168.

[2] The value of Reparations to the victor nations, as opposed to the Germans, after 1945 would make an interesting study in applied international economics.

[3] The figures are allegedly those of the German Administration for Industry.

consisting of reductions through dismantling plus war damage, but with the latter item we are not here concerned.

TABLE XXVIII

Reduction of capacity by industries through dismantling in percentages of 1936 at end of 1946, Soviet zone

Branch of Industry	*My Estimate*	*German Estimate*	*Manchester Guardian Estimate*
Heavy Machinery	60	55–63	55
Iron Forges and Smelting ..	40	50–55	80
Vehicles	65	55–63	55
Electrical	60	55–63	60
Electrical Generating Plant ..	45–50	50–55	—
Precision Tool and Optical ..	70	55–63	60
Cement	40	—	40
Plaster and Building Material ..	—	—	35
Glass and Ceramics	40	40–45	35
Plywood	80	100	100
Cellulose and Paper	40	40–50	45
Other industries working and processing wood	15	30–35	15
Rubber Goods..	70–80	—	80
Sulphur Processing ($S.So_2H_3So_4$)	60	50–55	60
Sodium Processing (Na.NaOH) ..	45	50–55	80
Hydrogen Producing and Processing	65–70	50–55	60
Synthetic Fibre and Fabric ..	30	50–55	35
Synthetic Fibre (stocks) ..	–[1]	30–35	–
Textile	10–12	20–30	15
Leather Goods	–[1]	20–30	25
Shoes	15–20[1]	30–35	15

My own estimates are based mainly on two considerations: firms known to have been wholly or partially dismantled,[2] and the actual output in the various industries during 1946 and 1947 in relation to 1936. Clearly the percentage of dismantled capacity on a 1936 index figure of 100 cannot exceed the equivalent percentages of actual production loss in any particular industry; the fact that the capacity may have greatly increased between 1936 and 1944 is irrelevant. Thus if post-war production in any industry was 60 per cent of 1936, its capacity must have been greater than 60 per cent of 1936. On the other hand, the difference between post-war and 1936 production cannot be explained exclusively in terms of a restriction of capacity, be it through war damage or dismantling. Thus post-war production percentages of 1936 were in the nature of a maximum ceiling for the equivalent proportion

[1] Although both the other estimates mentioned include stocks, I have omitted this item here as it is strictly speaking reparations from finished goods and will therefore be treated under the heading: 'Reparations from current production'.

[2] See Appendix A to this chapter.

of dismantling, always provided that no new capital investment in the industry concerned took place since the dismantling. Post-war instances of this were rare, and it is safe to rely on the official figures of capital investment as maxima. There were no important instances at all, except for coal mines and railway repair shops, until the end of 1947.

This invalidates some of the extreme figures of dismantling given by the two other surveys. The other main reason for differences between the figures of the two surveys cited above and my own arise out of the technical details of dismantling. There has been a tendency in German calculations to write off dismantled works altogether. This may be justified when sufficient machinery, generating plant, fittings, etc., were removed from the works to make the remaining equipment useless. The latter situation could be envisaged in the case of precision instruments or briquette-making works by the removal of certain standard cutters or ovens respectively. But in many cases dismantling was only partial, certain items could be immediately replaced out of stock, in which case only the spare stock-value is reckonable. For instance, in the iron forges and smelting works, a considerable amount of machinery was often left behind which could either be transferred to other works or used when the removed items were replaced. Textile factories, chiefly weaving mills, sometimes lost only their automatic looms and continued to function with old-fashioned power looms. On the other hand, heavy machine or precision tool works were often blighted by the removal of key machines, which served to bring output to a temporary standstill. If both the nature of the industry and the extent of dismantling in different industries are fully taken into account, the figures of both the German survey and the *Manchester Guardian* may have to be altered in the direction that I have indicated.[1]

Finally, I have attempted in my estimate to eliminate certain duplications. Some partially dismantled works were afterwards made over to the Russians, or, while under the control of the provinces, had to devote their entire production to reparation orders. In this case the dismantling extent has frequently been reckoned as a loss to the Germany economy, while the entire production value of the same factory on a 1936 basis was later counted as reparations out of current production or as property of the

[1] Thus *R.S.L.*, Vol. III, p. 87, for the statement that in the Soviet zone dismantling of works was generally complete. The evidence against this statement is incontrovertible.

Soviet Corporations. Also the removal of stocks of raw material has been counted as 'dismantled' reparations, while the gross value of their later manufacture into finished articles by SAG or by a 'provincial' factory working on reparation orders has been written off as reparations out of current production, thus counting the raw-material value twice. It will be found that in the industries where I differ most from the other two surveys, my estimate of the relative amount of reparations extracted from current production will perhaps be somewhat higher than their figure would have been. This is true of the chemical industries, textile industries, synthetic fibre industry, paper industry, certain kinds of wood, and of the iron industry as far as by-product scrap is concerned.

A certain pattern of dismantling emerged from the distribution by industries.[1] The first consideration governing direct dismantling was the need of the Soviet Union. This seems to have accounted for the removal of transport and postal equipment, and for much of the dismantling in the heavy industries, particularly the machinery, ferrous metal, and vehicle industries. These were the first industries affected. Another major objective was the plywood industry, and the hydrogen processing plants, both of which suffered considerable and early dismantling to satisfy the internal requirements of the Soviet Union. The hydrogen plants (Bayrische Stickstoff Werke, Piesteritz; Nicholaus & Co., and others) possessed modern equipment and used up-to-date processes.

The second factor might be called the utility of dismantling. It would appear that the original Soviet intention was to take away the maximum amount of capital goods and to subordinate other kinds of reparation to this principle. The idea was current during the early part of 1946, but gave way slowly to the increasing extraction of reparations from current production and their re-export on Russian account. At first a considerable quantity of consumer-goods industries were dismantled, particularly those which had reached a high level of technical development, such as the textile industry, the shoe industry, and particularly the rubber goods industry. A large proportion of the cement industry, glass and ceramics industry, plaster and binding material industry, and the packing industry, was also affected.

In another group of industries re-consideration of the position led to the early abandonment of dismantling and, in one or two cases, to the restoration of partially dismantled equipment. This was the case in coal mining and to some extent in briquette mak-

[1] See Appendix A to this chapter.

ing, in sugar refining and other food processing plants, and in the case of the Leuna chemical works, where dismantling orders were several times given and then withdrawn. These industries were closely tied to their locality, and afterwards formed the nucleus of the SAG. It is significant that of certain works removed in October 1946 from the dismantling list for the first quarter of 1947, all but one were in the above categories. In a very few cases there is some evidence that German intercession saved all or part of the factory from dismantling; for instance at Rudolf Sack, Leipzig, a factory making agricultural implements, one shed was left in the hands of the management complete with machinery, though the power generators were removed.[1]

We have so far dealt only with capacity. If we re-examine the dismantling process in the Soviet zone on the basis of value rather different results are obtained. Absolute figures are unobtainable, and even those we have lose much of their accuracy when expressed in terms of currency, as there are no standard methods of valuation.

The table below makes an attempt to estimate the reduction in value through dismantling of the total existing 'value' (i.e cost price) of certain industries, and also the reduction in value of the 1946 output as compared to 1936 (both in percentages).

TABLE XXIX

Reduction by industries through dismantling in value of capital and output, 1946, as percentage of 1936

Branch of Industry	*Reduction in total value*	*Reduction in output value 1936 = 100*
Coalmining	10–15	—
Iron	45	50–60
Electrical	55–60	50–55
Chemical	55–60	45–50
Textile	10–15	5–10
Leather Goods	25	25–30
Rubber Goods	75	65–70
Metal Goods	35–40	35–40
Building	35–40	50
Machinery	50	65–75
Food Processing	15–20	20–25

[1] See Schaffer, *op. cit.*, p. 30. The figure given there of the capacity retained, 35 per cent, is rather large; 20 per cent would seem nearer the real amount. Löwenthal, *op. cit.*, p. 207, states that the re-assembling of factories in Russia was a failure. Also Bedell Smith, *Moscow Mission, 1946–1949* (London, 1950), p. 210. Against this is the fact that the Soviet Government has great experience of removing and re-assembling complete factories. Much was done during the war, but the principle goes back to Tsarist days. There is a special word in Russian for the large-scale removal of population and industry.

Generally speaking, the loss in value was greater than the loss in capacity, compared to the figures of 1936, particularly since some of the industries had a greater capacity in 1946, e.g. coal-mining, chemicals, and rubber goods. Where the post-war capacity exceeded that of 1936, the reduction in total value may have been larger than the reduction in relative output. The same was true in those cases where a process of manufacture was simplified or improved after 1936, as in the chemical industry. But, generally speaking, the fact that the best plant was usually taken and that partial dismantling was uneven, that the same machines would sometimes be taken from all similar factories instead of a certain part of the whole equipment,[1] made a greater comparative inroad into the value, both of the actual factory and of its relative production per year, than into its capacity.

Though we have dealt primarily with 1946, dismantling continued on a considerable scale all through 1947 and spasmodically in 1948 in spite of definite Russian assurance to the contrary. The last works, which are known to have been dismantled as late as July 1948, were the Buna works at Schkopau, of which some 65–70 per cent of capacity was removed. During 1947 railway locomotive works, certain railway repair shops which had resumed operations, and a further quantity of railway track to the extent of some 5,600 km. were dismantled. Compared to previous removals, the extent of this wave of dismantling was small, but to the German economy, painfully striving for a new equilibrium, the blow was heavy and out of proportion to the actual quantity.

The psychological influence of perpetual insecurity was considerable. From August 1947 to August 1948 dismantlings were mostly confined to SAG which were considered to serve a more useful purpose in Russia or whose capacity was excessive for present German and European needs. Thus the SAG at Siemens Gera (condensors), Siemens-Arnstadt (electrical goods), and Hescho-Kahla (china and wireless equipment) were partially dismantled. Further, two smaller SAG, S. Koch at Steinbach and Telefunken at Thalheim (valves), were affected. There is something to be said for the view that the SAG Buna works mentioned above were partly dismantled owing to a temporary glut of synthetic rubber in Eastern Germany, which had lost much of its Buna processing capacity. The large bulk purchases of Malayan rubber by Soviet Russia may also have had a share in the decision. The arrest

[1] For instance, the Russians gave a special priority for dismantling new worsted yarn doubling machines, and took these even from mills otherwise left untouched.

of the management of a large weaving mill at Leipzig in July 1948 was promptly followed by partial dismantling, though this firm was previously in private hands. As far as is known, no dismantling of property not already Russian had taken place up to the middle of 1950 since the issue of the two-year plan for the Soviet zone, and the fact that a relatively long-term plan had been issued publicly for the first time seemed to indicate that as far as capital goods were concerned, the *status quo* might be maintained.

Finally, it is tempting to make an estimate of the actual value of capital goods reparation taken by the Russians from the Soviet zone.[1] Of course, no official figures exist. Certain figures were mentioned on both sides of the conference table at Moscow and London in April and November 1947 in the course of the embittered recriminations. But it may be doubted whether either the Soviet or the Anglo-American estimates were based on a detailed analysis of the situation. They resemble a general figure intended to refute the claims of the opposition. The most detailed Western analysis at the time of the blockade put the total value at about 4 milliard Rm. (1936 prices). The estimate in *R.S.L.* is 4.8[2] milliard Rm. The estimate of the German Economic Institute, which is concerned with reduction through dismantlings of actual production rather than capacity, has been converted by *R.S.L.* into a capacity reduction of 45 per cent of 1936, again 4.8 milliard Rm. Since in my view a direct par conversion from output value reduction to capacity value reduction errs in favour of the former, the amount of reparations under this head may be nearer 4–4.5 milliard Rm. Taking into account the dismantling which took place after the time these estimates were made, that is, after the end of October 1947, my own estimate is somewhere in the region of 4.1–4.3 milliards, excluding dismantling of SAG since 1948 and the removal of industrial raw material and of finished stock, though including direct reparations of unprocessed wood, which alone amounts to some 1,700,000 Rm. in value. My total at 1936 prices would be worth between £342,000,000 ($1.368 million) and £358,000,000 ($1.432 million). Compared to current British production or national income figures the extent of this loss to the German economy can be appreciated.[3]

[1] A discussion of the quantity obtained by the Russians from the Western zones under the Potsdam agreement is, of course, outside the scope of this work.

[2] Vol. IV, p. 51.

[3] My estimates are based on semi-official estimates made by functionaries in the Soviet zone, and on private analyses.

(B) *Reparations out of current production*

The legality of this form of reparations was in dispute between the Russians and the Western powers between 1945 and 1950. Whatever the legal position, such reparations were clearly part of the Russian plan over and above the removal of industrial plant by dismantling. The choice of one alternative in preference to another was governed partly by the situation of the industry itself, by the urgency of the Russian need for the finished product, and lastly by the desire to give employment to workers and factories in the zone. It may well be doubted whether the last of those reasons did in fact play the most important part, but it was repeatedly stressed by the Soviet authorities as an alternative to dismantling beneficial to the German economy. The Soviet Commander-in-Chief called it the main *raison d'être* for this kind of reparations.[1]

However this may be, it is clear that the measure, undertaken ostensibly for the benefit of the Germans, proved of great value to the Russians. Their demands, as any visitor to the Leipzig Fair well knows, extended to every sphere of production. The reparation goods had two alternative destinations, either the home market of the Soviet Union and of certain satellites, or the Soviet export market. As far as the Germans carrying out particular reparation orders were concerned, the eventual destination was a mystery. A Saxon firm making cooking utensils firmly believed, as stated by the SED works council, that their entire production was making good the war losses for the Soviet consumer, until they received a letter from a pre-war customer in South America congratulating them on the fact that their goods were once more competing in South American markets! Occasionally snap orders of goods to particular specifications and in limited quantities gave evidence of foreign orders, but this refinement was of fairly late origin.

Any German firm was liable for part-time or whole-time reparation orders at short notice, whether privately owned, provincially run, or one of the zonal undertakings formed in 1948. It appeared to be usual, however, for small orders to be given to private firms, while long-term and permanent contracts existed with the larger firms, which are therefore provincially or zonally owned. Payment was strictly in 1936 prices with certain very limited increases in exceptional cases. Generally prices paid by the Russians for

[1] For instance, Marshal Sokolovsky's press statement of 11 January 1947. See *Tägliche Rundschau* of that date.

reparation goods were 5–10 per cent lower than official German prices. In cases where raw material was provided by the Russians, manufacturing costs based on 1936, i.e. labour costs plus price of subsidiary materials used during processing plus a 5–10 per cent *ad valorem* manufacturing bonus, were paid; where the raw materials were furnished by the German firm this was paid for—again at 1936 prices. The same applies to reparation orders for primary products such as coal, potash, etc. Either flat 1936 prices were paid by the Russians, or sometimes a cost estimate was submitted by the firm to the Russians, and either approved or altered, in which case the Russian decision stood. It need hardly be pointed out that in cases where raw material was not officially supplied, the German firm was incapable of balancing its budget and invariably became dependent on subsidies, since any unofficially obtained raw materials were much more expensive than those allocated. Financial and raw-materials loans were sometimes made by the Russians to a provincial government, to be distributed as the government desired. In return, specific orders had to be completed by the province concerned. These were known as 'credit amortization deliveries', but since the terms usually worked out at an equivalent of the 1936 price, they were in effect reparation deliveries, and were counted as such by the Germans.

The cost of all reparations was finally borne by the German economy. Compulsory transfers of provincial income, labelled 'transfer to Central Administration for finance' in the Länder budgets, were in fact destined to cover occupation costs and were collected in a certain bank account at Potsdam. From this payments to factories working on reparation orders were made. Here were financed all 'open' reparations out of German production or capacity (when dismantling charges arose through the employment of German technicians) though any receipts from the export of reparations were handled by the State Bank of the Soviet Union.

The extent and value of reparations from current production in the period under review are, like everything else in Eastern Germany, impossible to ascertain exactly. We know some of the main firms permanently engaged on reparation orders since 1946. We also know some of the goods exported by the Russians and the nature and location of their origin. Finally some railway figures for the transport of reparations have emerged. From this information it is possible to form a fairly clear picture. Another method has sometimes been used, for instance by *R.S.L.*,[1] that of calcula-

[1] Vol. IV, p. 54.

ting the value of reparations from the financial exactions of the Russians out of the provincial budgets, the proceeds of which, as we have seen, were used for paying reparation orders. But two difficulties arise here: firstly, that these amounts were used for a variety of other purposes as well; secondly, that the amount paid by the Russians for reparation goods is only a limited guide to the value of these reparations in terms of loss to the German economy. The budget estimate for 1945–March 1948 in *R.S.L.* is given below.

TABLE XXX

Official transfer of income from provincial budgets to Russian agencies

1945–1948	*20.7 Mrd. Rm. of which*
Occupation costs	5.5 Mrd. Rm.
Subsidies to Central Administrations, Trades Unions, etc.	0.8 ,, ,,
Costs of Reparations from current production ..	4.4 ,, ,,
In hand	1.0 ,, ,,
At disposal for further reparations	9.0 Mrd. Rm.

We shall later have cause to undertake a detailed criticism of these estimates.[1] For the moment we are concerned only with the reparation costs item of 4.4 milliard Rm. This is based on an American estimate[2] of 4 milliard Rm., to which a 'corresponding' amount for the three relevant quarters of 1945 has been added. Now it is difficult to accept such an addition for 1945, since the organization of large-scale reparations out of current production was still in a very incomplete stage during 1945. The figure of 4 milliards as such is almost certainly a mere guess, as it purports to be the sum set aside by the Russians for their payment for current production reparations out of their total receipts from the provinces, and is thus an arbitrary assumption of their internal budget. The figures for each item in the table above should be rearranged; it will be seen that the items 'occupation costs' and 'subsidies to Central Administrations' (not to be confused with transfers to the Russians via the Finance Administration) were considerably lower, while the sum of 9 milliards, given under 'disposal', seems a grossly inflated guess.

Using our method of calculation, we reach the following estimate for reparations out of current German production, excluding production of SAG and reparations in foodstuffs.

[1] Below, p. 238.
[2] *Economic Data on Potsdam Germany*, Report of Military Governor, 1948 p. 81.

TABLE XXXI

Estimate of reparations out of current production in 1936 prices (million Rm.)

Branch of Industry	*1945 & 1946*	*1947*	*First half 1948*
Primary raw material production[1] ..	220	160	70
Investment Goods[2]	720	780	340
Consumer Goods	640	810	400
Stocks of raw material and finished goods	210	35	—
TOTALS	1,790	1,785 (40%)	810 (38%)

OVERALL TOTAL: 4,385 mill. Rm. (35 per cent of total zone production).

Now this 4,385 million Rm. is the 1936 price of certain goods whose quantity is calculated from real figures, such as transport logs, production statistics of individual firms, and sales of goods by the Soviet Trading Corporations in Berlin. Consequently the relation between this figure and the 4.4 milliards given in *R.S.L.* is by no means one in which the same figure is reached by two different means. Since the price paid for reparation goods is often up to 10 per cent lower than official German prices, and since much of the actual cost of production is very much bigger than 1936 costs, a figure of 4.4 milliards evolved from payments by the Russians is really a very low minimum in relation to a post-war price index based on a mean between official and black market prices. In other words, the 1936 basis is almost irrelevant in any post-war discussion of production value. We know that this 4.4 is supposed to be a real figure of payments made, and consequently we must turn our own figure of 4.385 milliards 1936 value into an equally real post-war figure, so that a basis of comparison between the two estimates is created. The value of these reparations to the Russians can be measured by an adjustment of our figure in terms of Russian prices and/or world market prices. For the Germans, however, the value of the loss can best be reckoned by adjustment to a current price index of industrial products. Such an index it is impossible to construct accurately. If, however, we add the subventions received by reparation firms from the provincial governments, we shall have included most of the post-war increases in production costs in our final valuation. The subsidies amounted to about 1.8 milliard Rm.[3] for the period under review.

[1] Including coal, potash, and wood.

[2] Heavy machinery, chemicals, and secondary stages of raw-material processing.

[3] This figure includes cost of subsidies from the provinces to SAG. An unknown part of this figure ought therefore to be added to the value of the loss to the German economy from SAG production and subtracted from the value of reparations from current production, making this figure rather lower. The total value of solid reparations, calculated in Appendix C, remains the same, however.

The minimum value of reparations out of current production therefore is 4,385 + 1,800 = 6,185 million Rm. It is this figure which should be compared with the 4.4 milliard Rm. of the German survey.

In order to illustrate this considerable diversion of German production, we will examine some detailed figures of reparations in Saxony-Anhalt. These figures are accurate and official, and go up to 30 September 1946, when the balance sheet was made. Value is counted in terms of production cost estimates, not necessarily by the amount paid by the Russians.

TABLE XXXII

Industrial Reparation deliveries up to September 1946, Saxony-Anhalt

Category of goods	*Reparation orders received 30.9.46* Units	*Reparation orders received 30.9.46* Value (1,000 Rm.)	*Extent to which completed 30.9.46* Units	*Extent to which completed 30.9.46* Value (1,000 Rm.)
Railway waggons and tenders	2,083	16,623.8	75	1,698.5
Metal working machines	293	2,545.1	98	1,004.6
Various hard tools	—	54.0	—	42.0
Electrical and power equipment				
(a) Steam boilers	5	1,643.9	—	—
(b) Electric tractors and engines	—	6.047.2	—	1,287.1
(c) Small furnaces	553	625.4	344	308.9
(d) Diesel motors	416	1,733.2	7	49.8
(e) Electric motors[1]	—	—	—	—
(f) Electric installations	—	193.8	—	—
(g) Power station equipment	—	19.1	—	—
Installations for briquette works	—	5,639.1	—	—
Installations for coalmines				
(a) Coalface equipment	—	26,241.0	—	393.1
(b) Compressor, pumps, etc.	—	216.0	—	48.9
Ropetwisting machines	—	1,587.4	—	57.2
Installations for presses[1] and forges	—	—	—	—
Installations for lifting and transport				
(a) Various cranes	20	1,807.1	5	88.4
(b) Transporters	315	926.2	135	369.6
Installations for building material factories				
(a) Complete cement works	24	155,828.8	—	—
(b) Spare equipment for cement works	—	416.6	—	156.7
(c) Various building installations	—	2,736.6	—	73.6

[1] No estimate of costs included. As the Russians often made their arrangements direct with individual firms, the provincial government was sometimes unable to book the precise amount for as long as twelve months.

Category of goods	Reparation orders received 30.9.46 Units	Value (1,000 Rm.)	Extent to which completed 30.9.46 Units	Value (1,000 Rm.)
Installations for food processing industry				
(a) Various refrigerating equipment	—	—	—	—
(b) Vacuum pumps and other vacuum equipment ..	—	7,165.9	—	516.1
(c) Various general installations	—	57,523.9	—	2,580.2
Printing equipment	—	—	—	—
Installations for chemical industry				
(a) Enamelled equipment ..	—	794.2	—	217.8
(b) Various equipment ..	—	10,639.3	—	664.4
Complete unit welding installations	—	1,265.0	—	818.5
Milling equipment (grain)				
(a) Elevator installations ..	—	—	—	—
(b) Various mill installations ..	—	504.2	—	185.2
Drumfilters	—	1,558.2	—	225.2
Fittings for marine craft				
(a) Various fittings, 31 ships ..	—	13,950.2	—	—
(b) Pumps and compressors ..	1,551	680.7	260	282.6
(c) Steam armatures	—	452.1	—	428.5
Steel and cast-iron armatures ..	—	2,795.1	—	2,214.4
Bicycles	30,250	2,914.5	1,187	111.7
Road construction equipment ..	—	—	—	—
Self-regulators, measurement and optical equipment	—	5,269.8	—	1,921.9
Weighing machines, scales, etc.	—	709.7	—	36.2
Agricultural machinery ..	—	3,142.6	—	105.9
Alloys and N.F. metals—raw material and primary products	*1,000 tons*		*1,000 tons*	
(a) Copper	37,800.0	27,793.8	28,819.0	21,166.7
(b) Zinc	14,040.4	3,700.3	11,143.8	2,973.5
(c) Lead	700.0	154.0	500.0	110.0
(d) Secondary aluminium ..	15,040.0	16,431.8	1,941.2	2,149.2
(e) Other N.F. metals ..	—	6,589.9	—	5,695.8
(f) Copper tubes	675.0	910.8	256.2	370.9
(g) Copper wire	2,621.2	3,332.9	1,450.5	1,598.5
(h) Copper plate	—	—	—	—
(i) Aluminium strips ..	300.0	594.0	61.7	159.9
(j) Brass strips	31.8	46.7	31.0	46.5
(k) Various rolled brass products	8,122.0	10,036.0	3,607.1	5,082.9
Various ferrous metals and finished goods				
a) Steel tresses	1,400.0	1,183.0	—	—
(b) Various chain material ..	—	—	—	—
(c) Wiring material	—	692.3	—	—
(d) Building nails	1,100.0	257.6	33.3	9.6
(e) Corrugated iron roofing ..	1,200.0	339.8	700.0	198.2
(f) Ship's anchors	—	1,616.6	—	123.2
Potash salts ..	180,022.5	8,465.9	172,029.3	5,257.8
Lubricating grease	4,000.0	2,000.0	3,119.0	1,559.5
Synthetic rubber (Buna) ..	16,000.0	36,910.0	10,938.0	25,037.3
Rubber goods	—	495.9	—	201.9
Paints and lacquers	691.5	1,957.0	—	846.2

Category of goods	Reparation orders received 30.9.46 Units	Value (1,000 Rm.)	Extent to which completed 30.9.46 Units	Value (1,000 Rm.)
Medical gypsum	2,800.0	107.8	2,732.8	90.4
Chemical products	—	27,081.2	—	25,582.2
Industrial consumer goods, rations				
(*a*) Finished textile pieces	—	2,173.5	—	1,604.1
(*b*) Footwear	193,902 prs.	5,768.4	460,741 prs.	2,683.5
(*c*) Various gloves	232,549 ,,	2,555.9	145,500 ,,	1,339.0
(*d*) Musical instruments	90 pcs.	88.2	67 pcs.	65.7
(*e*) Cartridges	7,300 ,,	1,378.0	3,802 ,,	730.2
(*f*) Household crockery	—	1,759.7	—	809.8
(*g*) Other consumer goods	—	6,952.2	—	3,256.5
Cement	152,000 tons	4,159.0	102,438 tons	3,363.2
Health service equipment	—	865.0	—	509.7
Paper	—	1,837.7	—	761.8
Various goods by arrangement with Soviet Reparations administration	—	6,725.1	—	3,365.8
TOTAL		507,240.4		133,127.4
In addition, certain orders were fulfilled against a money and goods loan from the Russians (Credit amortization deliveries):				
TOTAL		24,276.8		25,937.8[1]
OVERALL TOTAL		531,517.2 Rm.		159,065.2 Rm.

Thus by 30 September 1946 reparation orders worth 532 million Rm. had been received by the provincial government of Saxony-Anhalt alone and some 159 million Rm. worth of goods had been delivered. The equivalent figures for Saxony itself are 1,093 million Rm. and 598 million Rm., though the date of the survey is 30 October 1946. The heavy preponderance of investment goods over consumer goods in the early period of reparation orders should be noted. It was during this period that dismantling reached its highest level. By 1947 the proportion was reversed and consumer goods, chiefly for re-export, were most in demand.

Two other items must be added to the list, items which have not yet been discussed. Food deliveries were not specifically forbidden at Potsdam, but since Germany was an importer of food, and particularly in view of the food shortage in Germany, it was improbable that reparation demands of any size were seriously contemplated in this sphere—by any but the Russians. Below are the food reparation orders for Saxony-Anhalt up to 13 November 1946. This list is the counterpart of the industrial list given above.[2]

[1] The slight excess of delivery over order is due to films where the respective figures are: 7,507,700 Rm. of orders and 18,407,400 Rm. delivered.

[2] Three agricultural items are also included in the industrial list: sugar, starch, and spirits. Although the industrial list closed at an earlier date, the figures for these items are larger than in the agricultural list below. I have taken only the lower figure from the second list. Such discrepancies are typical of Soviet zone statistics.

TABLE XXXIII

Agricultural reparation deliveries, Saxony-Anhalt

Item	*Firm*	*Units*	*Quantity*	*Delivered to date*
Sugar	Aderstedt	tons	4,500	4,500
,,	Artern	,,	4,500	3,000
,,	Gentin (refinery)	,,	2,000	677
,,	Gemmern	,,	1,000	666
,,	Elsnigk	,,	2,500	1,846
,,	Halle (commercial organization)	,,	7,000	6,846
,,	Zeitch	,,	2,700	2,000
,,	Artern	,,	2,000	1,451
,,	,, ...	,,	3,000	—
,,	,, ...	,,	3,000	—
,,	Gentin (refinery)	,,	2,000	—
,,	,, ,, ...	,,	3,000	—
,,	,, ,, ...	,,	2,000	—
,,	Groningen	,,	500	—
,,	Halle (comm. org.) ..	,,	4,000	—
,,	,, ,, ,, ..	,,	6,000	—
,,	,, ,, ,, ..	,,	5,000	—
,,	Oschersleben	,,	2,000	—
,,	,, ...	,,	2,000	—
,,	,, ...	,,	3,000	—
,,	Zeitz	,,	6,500	1,615
,,	,, ...	,,	7,000	—
,,	,, ...	,,	6,500	—
TOTAL SUGAR			80,700 tons	22,601
Plus previously completed orders ..				184,192
Spirits (raw)	Sugar refinery, Dessau ..	HL[1]	12,000	9,510
,, ,,	,, ,, ...	,,	8,000	—
TOTAL SPIRITS (RAW)			20,000 HL	9,510 HL
Plus previously completed orders: ..				74,349 HL
Starch	Mitteldeutsches Maiswerk Zerbet	tons	300	—
,,	,, ,, ...	,,	600	—
,,	,, ,, ...	,,	600	—
,,	Kartoffelverwertungsgenossenschaft G.M.B.H. Gross-Apenburg	,,	200	—
,,	,, ,, ..	,,	400	—
,,	,, ,, ..	,,	400	—
TOTAL STARCH			2,500 tons	—
Plus previously completed orders (various starches and glucose) ..				4,100 tons
Salt (rough lumps)	Deutscher Salzverband, Berlin	Tons	38,670	38,617
Salt (pickling)	,, ...	,,	4,000	28,476
,, ,,	,, ...	,,	13,000	—
,, ,,	,, ...	,,	13,000	—
,, (rock)	,, ...	,,	46,383	—
TOTAL SALT			115,053 tons	122,902 tons
Plus previously completed orders (table salt) ..				1,968 ,,

[1] HL = *hectolitre* = 22.2 gallons.

Thus the total orders given to date (13 November 1946) in Saxony-Anhalt are:

TABLE XXXIV

Sugar	264,892 tons
Spirits	94,349 *hectolitres* or 2,096.640 galls.
Starch	6,600 tons
Salt	117,011 tons, or 124,870 tons actually delivered

The amount paid by the Russians for these items is as follows:

TABLE XXXV

Sugar	168,471,300 Rm.
Spirits	10,984,000 Rm.
Starch	3,312,100 Rm.
Salt	998,960 Rm.
TOTAL	183,766,360 Rm.

To this must be added considerable removals of cattle, corn, poultry, eggs, pigs, sheep, horses, and feeding stuffs. Since no accurate figures of livestock removals from the different provinces are available, an estimate of the probable minimum figure for the whole zone will be made. The total figure for food reparations from the zone in the commodities given above for Saxony-Anhalt is about 970 million Rm. for the period May 1945 to July 1948. Our estimate for the commodities not included in the official figures for the same period is about 80 million Rm., which is again the minimum.[1] We must add another 1.15 milliards to our figure for current production reparations, making the total 7.335 milliards. It seems hardly necessary to point out that this estimate of the purely financial value of reparations in foodstuffs would be greatly exceeded by any calculation in terms of loss to the German economy through reduced labour output, the necessity for using export proceeds for food imports, and the hundred and one evils of an underfed population.

One final item must also be included in any estimate of the extent of reparations from current production. The Russian demands of the German transport system greatly exceeded the routine demands of an occupation army. While the British and Americans took over some 7 per cent of all the locomotives for their exclusive or partial use in the West, the Russians took some 1,000 locomotives alone for their exclusive use in Germany out

[1] A standard proportion of the difference between 1936 and 1947 livestock figures in the Soviet zone has been converted into value at 1936 prices, and taken as removals.

of a total of 7,000 existing engines, and out of a maximum of only 3,000 locomotives in perfect running order. This equals 14 per cent and 33 per cent respectively. The locomotives running for the occupation authorities, known officially as 'Brigade' locomotives, consisted of 900 of the best and newest goods and passenger engines, taken over in summer 1947, and about 100 shunting engines. This figure is quite separate from the locomotives permanently removed to Russia out of reserves.[1]

Goods waggons, unlike locomotives, were not permanently allocated to the occupation authorities, but had to be provided on demand for specific tasks and periods, and were diverted from current DR operations. During May 1946, 125,000 goods waggons were put at the disposal of the occupation authorities at different times out of a total of 343,000 for the whole zonal transport service, and in May 1947 the total was reduced to 92,000 out of 365,000. The difference is partly due to the different nature of most of the reparation items in the latter years as compared to 1946. The proportion of services demanded by the Russians can also be seen from the fact that in December 1947 the 'Brigade' locomotives travelled a total of 703,000 km.—674,000 for long-distance trains and 29,000 local trains—out of a DR total for the Soviet zone of 2,836,000 km., or 1,196,000 km. long-distance and 1,640,000 km. local. In January 1948 the distance travelled by the ('Brigade') locomotives increased to 1,659,000 km. In addition some 1,057,000 km. were completed outside the Soviet zone during these two months, chiefly through Poland to Brest-Litovsk and occasionally into the Soviet Union proper.

In order to achieve these services, which obtain an absolute priority over normal railway traffic, the organization of the railways was considerably strained. A railway system with so many deficiences and difficulties found it impossible to render the extra service in addition to its normal schedules. Soviet demands were often at short notice, and were made regardless of existing commitments. Consequently it has been calculated that the German railway transport services were reduced by between $\frac{3}{2}$ and $\frac{7}{4}$ times the carrying capacity actually provided for the Russians. The demands of reparation transport greatly exceeded the demands of the occupation army. Although there is no satisfactory way of converting the total figures of Russian transport demands into a monetary cost equivalent, the charges, which must certainly run into millions of Rm., should be borne in mind.

[1] The railway figures are taken from accurate Reichsbahn statistics.

(C) *Labour*

A brief word must be said about reparations of labour, though this subject has already been partially dealt with. On the whole, it was the form of reparations least damaging to the German economy, for it provided the means of keeping the level of employment higher than that of the other zones, higher even than the 1936 level.[1] This applied chiefly to unskilled and semi-skilled labour. On the other hand, the deportation of specialists must have deprived German economy and science of valuable labour. None the less, shortage of experts did not noticeably make itself felt in the Soviet zone; where special technicians were required for work of which the Russians approved, they could apparently always be found.

Apart from the uranium projects and a number of temporary tasks such as the extension of the military facilities of the Baltic harbours in 1948, most of the labour conscripted by the Russians has gone to the Soviet Union. Occasionally unskilled labour was conscripted in large numbers, as in operation *Ossawakim*,[2] but most often individual specialists were affected. Their whereabouts and qualifications were easily discoverable as a result of the complete registration early undertaken in the Eastern zone.[3] It is impossible to estimate their number.

The labour conscripted for use in Germany and the Soviet Union was twofold; officially registered labour and inmates of concentration camps. The former was conscripted through the German labour exchanges, and was officially paid at normal rates. As the evidence of refugees from the uranium mines and other Soviet projects shows, conditions were generally bad, and rates of pay well below the official minima. The demands on the workers were very heavy, and each failure to reach the stipulated norm resulted in considerable deductions from pay.[4] Of conditions of labour transferred to Russia we know nothing, but they may correspond to those described by Nikolayevsky and Dallin.[5] The labour obtained by the employment or removal of concentration camp inmates was considerable. The railway logs at the frontier towns showed that up to the end of 1948 a total of over 40,000 'prisoners' were

[1] See above, p. 193. For the previous discussion of Soviet labour reparations, see above, p. 140.

[2] See above, p. 141.

[3] SMA Order 42, 25 August 1945.

[4] For details of the misery of the uranium mines, see Löwenthal, *op. cit.*, pp. 186–200.

[5] D. Dallin and B. Nicolayevsky, *Forced Labour in Soviet Russia* (London, 1948)

transported eastwards, though this total may include some non-prisoner labour.[1] A certain amount of labour appears to have been carried out within the camps themselves, but this only began late in 1947; the primary purpose of concentration camps does not appear to have been the supply of cheap labour for the Russians any more than it originally was for the Nazis. Like the latter, however, the Russians came to look on internees increasingly as a source of labour. Conditions for such labour were reported to be horrible.[2]

It is almost impossible to sum up the amount of reparation labour exacted by the Russians, or the resultant loss to the German economy. Technically, prisoner-of-war labour, which was used extensively by the Russians in the U.S.S.R., though far more rarely in Eastern Germany than in the Western zones by the British and American occupation forces,[3] is a legitimate exaction in the period between armistice and peace treaty. The enticement of individuals by contracts, perhaps with the use of moral or other pressure, which was certainly done by the Americans, is not strictly labour conscription for reparations. We are thus left with the wholesale conscription of labour for use in and beyond Germany, and here the loss to the German economy was offset by the dangers of potential unemployment. Thus labour seems to be the sole form of reparations valuable to the U.S.S.R. without at the same time doing great damage to the German economy, unless the long-term effect on the health and labour power of the unfortunate conscripts is taken into consideration. Curiously enough, this form of reparation was at the same time the only one which the Russians, on the evidence available, failed to exploit in the same well planned and methodical way apparent in the rest of their reparations policy after 1945.

(D) *Russian real property acquisitions in Germany*[4]

This category of reparations divides into two somewhat unequal items: industrial property and land. Of these the former, the Soviet Corporations or SAG, were by far the most important. The Soviet Corporations consisted of some of the biggest and most

[1] Non-prisoner labour is shown in the logs as *Arbeiter*, whereas the category *Häftlinge* probably refers to deported internees. The Germans may not have observed the distinction all the time.

[2] For individual details, see Löwenthal, *op. cit.*

[3] Judging by visible signs of PW labour. This fact was not exploited by Soviet propaganda, beyond the sustained attacks on the PW labour battalions (*Dienstgruppen*) in the West as 'secret re-militarization'.

[4] See Appendix B.

important works in the zone, transferred entirely to Soviet ownership and management as a result of the Military Governor's Orders Nos. 124 and 126, dated December 1945. These listed a number of categories of undertakings *sui generis* to be transferred from existing ownership, and included the property of the German State, of the Nazi Party and other illegal organizations, and property belonging to Germany's wartime allies. The necessary investigations into this property were carried out by the local Commissions for Sequestration. In theory most of these plants were originally to be dismantled, but were saved 'in order to provide employment and part of the output for the German economy'.[1] This legal fiction did away with the need for any compensation. The same statement gave the following figures: 200 works as a total, out of which 74 were eventually to be returned to German ownership. These numbers are approximately correct; by the end of 1947 some 134 SAG firms were in existence, though some of those returned had been partially or wholly dismantled and 23 more were handed back to the Germans two years later.

The organization of the SAG was relatively simple. The works are registered in Germany as public companies of limited liability owned by the Soviet Union, and are presumably also registered in Russia. At first each factory was held as a separate unit: certain individuals, usually the Russian manager and chief engineer, as well as certain unknown individuals domiciled in the Soviet Union, being cited as principal shareholders.[2] The German headquarters was a 'Head office for all SAG' in Berlin. In 1947 the organization was changed into group combines according to the type of industry, with the central office in Berlin listed as the controlling company. The majority of the shares were transferred to the external property department of the Soviet Ministry for Foreign Trade, while some were acquired by the Soviet trading companies. This development brought the SAG more into line with the industrial trust system flourishing in the Soviet Union.

It is not clear whether the SAG were subordinated to the Russian trusts under the ministries, whether for instance the chemical SAG group in Germany was a copy of, or part of, the chemical industrial combine in the Soviet Union.[3]

The operation of these firms was entirely out of German control.

[1] Marshal Sokolovsky's Press statement, 11 January 1947.

[2] According to Löwenthal, *op, cit.*, p. 293, even the meagre information given by the entries in the German commercial registers about the SAG provoked Moscow's strong disapproval.

[3] For further details of the organization, see Appendix C.

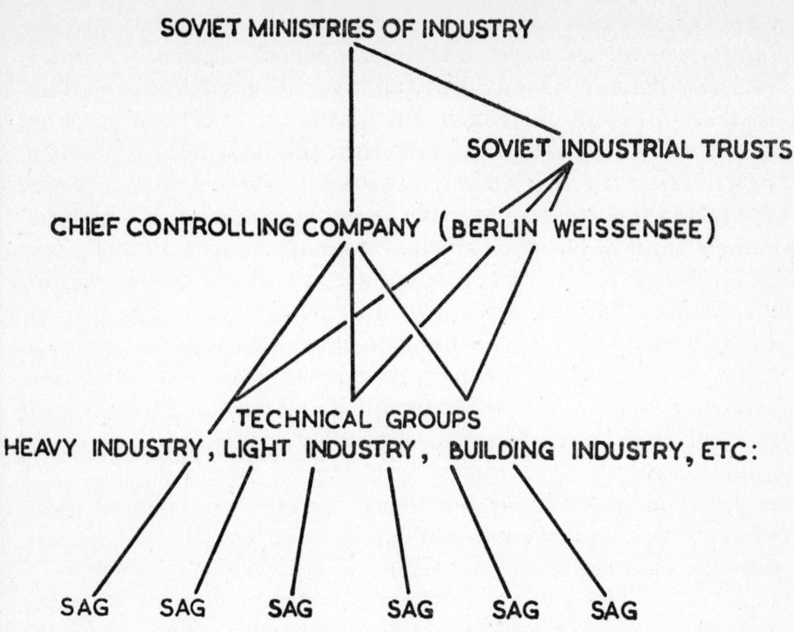

FIG. 7. *Organization of Soviet Corporation 1947.*

No German could hold a position in the organization higher than the sub-directorial function known in Germany as *Prokurist.* Round the SAG grew a whole series of ancillary Russian organizations with all the functions associated with an industrial economy; a Russian monopoly transport firm (*Derutra*),[2] a Russian bank (*Garantie-und Kreditbank*) and finally the Soviet export-import caucus. Thus, inside the Russian controlled economy of the Soviet zone there existed an exclusively Russian economy, an *imperium in imperio.* The influence of the SAG on the German economy was considerable. By far the greater part of their raw-material supplies were taken from German sources, and a certain part of their production was sold to German consumers. Both raw-material supply and allocation of production were arranged by the SAG combine with the corresponding ministry of the province. In no sense had the latter a right to SAG production.

The value of the SAG must be reckoned as follows: the yearly value of production must be taken into account as far as German-produced or German-imported raw materials are involved; where raw materials were provided by the Russians on their own account we must add only the value added by manufacture. From the

[2] Short for *Deutsch-Russische Transport Gesellschaft.*

total of these items must be subtracted the value of the SAG products made available to the German economy.[1] It will be seen that this balance sheet is really an inverted foreign trade account. Instead of listing German raw material 'exports' to the SAG on the credit side and 'imports' from their production as a debit item, we are assuming that all the raw materials sold at 1936 prices to the SAG would preferably have been distributed to German consumers, and were thus involuntary exports at nominal prices; while the purchases of SAG products, when and where possible, are imports unhampered by currency restrictions, again at nominal prices. This somewhat unusual method seems to represent the actual situation as accurately as possible.

The 1936 value of the industry making up the SAG would be somewhere in the region of 2 milliard Rm. or slightly higher. This figure is given by the German Economic Institute, and is accepted as being fairly accurate.[2] Any 1936 price figure is, of course, purely nominal under post-war conditions. The SAG share of 1937 gross zonal production in percentages should be compared to their capacity as a percentage of the whole remaining capacity in the zone. Both are given below. The greater proportion of SAG pro-

TABLE XXXVI[3]

Share of Soviet Corporations in industrial capacity and production of Soviet Zone, 1947

Industry	*SAG percentage of total production 1947*	*SAG percentage of total capacity 1947*
Coalmining	15–20	15–20
Potash mining	40	40
Liquid Fuels	80	70
Chemicals	55	40
Vehicles	70	60
Machines	40	30
Rubber and Asbestos	70	55
Electrical	50	35
Metal Goods	40	20
Metal Ore mining and refining	40	30
Building Materials	18	8
Synthetic Fibres (rayon, etc.), and Paper	30	15
Textiles	5	2–3
Ceramics	8	5
TOTAL INDUSTRY[4]	25	15–17

[1] As long as these works remain in Germany, their actual value cannot be counted as reparations; some estimates have so counted it, thus duplicating the loss to the German economy. If and when the SAG are dismantled, their value, allowing for depreciation, can be counted as reparations from capital goods, but not before.

[2] *Wirtschaftsprobleme der Besatzungszonen*, p. 228.

[3] My own estimate based on private surveys and information.

[4] Taking into account the 74 temporarily Russian operated works handed back in 1947. 25 per cent is also the official U.S. estimate.

duction compared to capacity arises from their priority in raw material, labour, and fuel supply.

We may take it that the overall figure of 25 per cent applied also to 1946, though individual industries would show somewhat different results. A general average of $\frac{1}{4}$ of total production from the beginning of 1946 to the end of June 1948 is equivalent to about

$$\frac{7.25\ (1946)\ +7.15\ (1947)\ +4\ \text{mrd. Rm.}\ (6\ \text{months}\ 1948)}{4}$$

= 4,600 million Rm. From this total of gross manufacturing value must be subtracted the value of raw materials whose origin was not German. For SAG producing primary raw materials the value strictly added by manufacture was very small, for such items as liquid fuel production and synthetic fibres it was relatively small, while the real duplication which a net valuation is supposed to avoid comes only in consumer goods industries, investment goods industries and certain chemical and metal processes. The net value of SAG production during these two and a half years would appear to have been about 2.2 mrd. Rm.; the low ratio of net to gross value, 22 : 46 as compared to the pre-war general ratio in all German industry of 34 : 60, being due to the nature of the industries making up the SAG.

We are thus left with a raw material consumption by the SAG of 2.4 mrd. Rm. Of this about 40 per cent was obtained from the German economy, directly through purchase or allocation, and indirectly through purchases abroad out of German export credit balances. This 40 per cent proportion gives a figure of 960 million Rm., and the remaining 60 per cent or 1,440 million Rm., originating from Russian or SAG sources, must therefore be subtracted from the gross manufacturing value of the SAG, leaving a figure of 3,160 million Rm. Some SAG devoted almost their entire output to the use of the German economy, such as the Buna works at Schkopau; others, such as Hesho-Kahla and both chemical works at Wolfen, almost none. A general estimate would give no more than between 25–30 per cent as an overall average for the period. If we subtract a quarter of the total production value as returned to the German economy, this would be 1,150 million Rm.[1] Thus the oss caused by the SAG to the German economy can be shown as gross production value 1946–June 1948 minus duplicate counting of raw materials from Russian or SAG sources minus the value of SAG

[1] Since the value of raw materials has already been taken into account in the valuation of SAG production, the gross value of production returned to the German economy must be taken here.

production made available to the German economy. This gives us a figure of value for goods lost to the German economy in 1936 prices, a figure of 4.6 milliard Rm. minus 1.44 milliard Rm. minus 1.15 milliard Rm. = 2,010,000.000 Rm. Neither the real value of the SAG, nor the financial burden of their operation on the German economy have been taken into account.[1]

The vital position of the industries comprised in the Soviet complex is such that it is hardly possible to represent their real value in terms of money. Had the SAG been in fact dismantled, the long term effects on the German economy would have been truly catastrophic. As it was, in spite of repeated Soviet and SED promises to the contrary, the dismantling of certain SAG was undertaken in June 1948, but was apparently an isolated instance. The exact significance of this step is impossible to estimate, but the Soviet proposal of general withdrawal of armed forces from Germany, made in October 1948 and since repeated, might well, if accepted, be preceded by large-scale dismantling of SAG. It would be unsafe to regard the SAG arrangement in Germany as permanent; indeed, in May 1950, 23 works of the SAG trusts were reported to have been handed back to the German government, including part of the Meissen porcelain works.[2]

The other real property acquisitions in Germany need only be mentioned in passing. There is some evidence of Soviet acquisition of land, estates, housing sites and houses through the agency of German middlemen. This was separate from the requisitions of the occupation authorities, and the methods employed point more to individual acquisitions by Soviet functionaries and official bodies for their private use than to any large-scale real property investment. The full black market price has often been paid by the purchaser's agent, and on the face of it the property has merely been transferred from one private owner to another. The whole thing is chiefly worth mentioning for the fact that had an inventory of real estate been made after 1948, particularly in the Western sectors of Berlin, the amount of property acquired by the Russians might well have caused surprise. In the Eastern sector

[1] The 1936 value of the SAG has already been discussed. A discussion of the financial burden must include the profit and loss balance sheet of the SAG, taking into account the fact that disposal of SAG production to the German economy is done at a profit at the expense if necessary of the price limit, quite apart from the allocation of German raw materials to the SAG, which bear no relation to such disposal. The wage bill paid by the SAG to its German workers and staff must also be included in this case. SAG, showing a current trading loss, are subsidized by contributions from the German provinces. See also Appendix D to this chapter.

[2] For some further statistical data see Appendix B to this chapter.

of Berlin it has been privately estimated that as much as 3 per cent of the total house property was acquired in this way.

(E) *Soviet Trade, official and unofficial*

The final proof, if such were needed, of the Russian intention to exploit their zone of Germany to the greatest possible extent, was provided by the establishment of the Soviet Trading Companies. These monopoly concerns were branches of parent firms in Russia, and with a few exceptions have been present in the name of the Soviet Union wherever business with that country was conducted. In Germany, as elsewhere, they had the scope which specific missions, interested in particular sales or purchases, could not hope to obtain, and in addition they acted as the general economic feelers of the Soviet Ministry of Foreign Trade, indeed of all the economic ministries, in foreign countries. Their multifarious, complicated, and often subterranean activities found their *juste milieu* in Germany.

The following is a list of the major companies with their respective sphere of interest, to which they are, however, by no means rigidly confined.

TABLE XXXVII

List of Soviet Trading Companies operating in the Soviet Zone

Company	Sphere of interest
Rasno-Export GMBH[1]	General import and export
Techno-Export GMBH[1]	Machinery
Promexport GMBH[1]	Coal, chemicals
Rasno-Import GMBH[1]	General import and export
Exportlion GMBH[1]	Textiles
Technoprom-Export	Potash, industrial chemicals, cameras
Promsyrio-Import	Export and import of industrial waste and by-products (steel scrap, etc.)
Sojusbushnina	Furs, skins, etc.
Voyentorg	Food, luxury goods
Ossobtorg[1]	Jewels, personal effects, cameras, etc.
Derunapht[2]	Petrol, oil, pumps, and retail service
Intourist[1]	Hotels, restaurants

There were other Soviet organizations of a purely technical nature, who occasionally engaged in commercial activities. Thus Sovexportfilm is known to have been engaged in the purchase of cameras and in giving reparations orders for film material, though its main task was the technical side of all film production and distribution for Soviet films in the U.S.S.R. and in Germany.

[1] These firms are known to operate in other countries also.

[2] This firm was originally founded in the 1920s as an import company, and later became purely German. It is now solely Russian. It has a basic capital of 20 million Rm. and gradually obtained a monopoly even in the retail trade.

The first appearance of the commercial caucus seems to have been in the early months of 1946, and Rasno was probably the first firm to operate. At the 1946 Autum Fair in Leipzig, just five and a half years after their last exhibition there, they were present in force. Many of their directors had studied in Germany between 1939 and 1941, the time of Russo-German economic co-operation. Experience has shown that the men who ran these firms in Germany were among the most able Soviet commercial experts, and the results they achieved were impressive.

The organization of the caucus was simple. German headquarters for all firms were in Berlin. The larger firms had branches in the major towns of the zone, particularly Rasno and the other firms dealing in consumer goods, which were represented in at least six towns. Their staff was as considerable as their activities were various. The chief task was the organization of export of reparation and SAG goods. The companies had authority over the disposal of goods produced by SAG or German firms working on reparations, provided these goods had not previously been allocated for specific purposes in the Soviet Union. Thus the jet motor works in Eastern Berlin (Köpenick) belonged to the Soviet Ministry of the Armed Forces and their production was devoted entirely to the defence needs of the U.S.S.R. During 1947 and 1948 the increasing emphasis on consumer-goods production for reparations was mainly due to increased export efforts of those companies at the expense of the Soviet home market. In many cases reparations orders were placed by a Trading firm against a definite export order or for stock. The large orders for sugar are included in this category.[1] It seems that by 1948 the control of reparation production had gradually passed from the reparations agency to the Trading caucus, the former being reduced to the rôle of an administrative organ. The production of the SAG was increasingly at the disposal of the Trading firms in so far as it was not tied to the internal five year plan of the U.S.S.R., and it was the Trading company, in conjunction with the SAG directorate at Weissensee, which decided the amount of SAG production to be delivered to the German market. In addition to its rôle of export agency for reparations the commercial caucus acted as a normal competitor for export orders in the ordinary German market, if necessary purchasing goods on its own account for export abroad. Much of

[1] As can be seen from the table on p. 215, orders and deliveries do not necessarily coincide. An order for 500 tons of sugar might be given to a firm, yet far more might be taken if supplies seemed plentiful.

the steel scrap exported by Promsyrio-Import was obtained by competitive purchase from German firms as well as by reparation orders. Few German State works would turn down an offer from a Russian Trading firm, even if the product concerned had already been allocated elsewhere in the production or distribution plan of the zone.

On the import side their task was not the supply of raw materials for the SAG, which was done by demand on the German import agency, but the procurement of scarce raw materials and goods for the Soviet Union itself. This covered a very large range, from strategic war materials to precision instruments, bicycles, metals, etc. Their method of operating made the Trading firms particularly suitable instruments for purchases of special lots, or scarce commodities, though there were many exceptions to this. On the whole, while the quantities exported by the Soviet Trading firms were large, the quantities imported were generally small. There is less evidence of imports against currency than of export, which took place chiefly against dollars. The chief import methods were compensation deals and barter transactions—import into the U.S.S.R. against export from Germany. In many cases, particularly for purchases or barter of goods in short supply from the Western zones, German middlemen were used, individuals with good contacts in the West, or transport firms with interzonal facilities. Occasionally special supplies for SAG, otherwise unobtainable, were handled by the Trading firms. A certain number of long-term manufacturing projects were started by the commercial caucus in Germany, such as the production of cigarettes in the zone for export to all European countries, and a small amount of commission work, chiefly in textile spinning and weaving, was undertaken. In both cases the capacity of non-SAG firms was made available for Russian account by arrangements with the SMA, and in the former case Rasno invested some capital in the German economy.

The power and flexibility of these firms has enabled them to turn the German economic situation of the moment to great advantage. The Rasno cigarettes were more than a normal commercial venture. They were used to procure scarce materials for the Russians ranging from scientific instruments from Hamburg to antiques and jewellery in Berlin. At the time of the great cigarette shortage in Germany during 1947 and 1948 these Soviet cigarettes acted like a magnet for those who had material of interest to the Russians. The substitution of cigarettes for currency was thus actively encouraged by the Russians at the same time as stricter enforcement of the anti-black market laws was being demanded by the SMA and the Unity Party. During the blockade these cigarettes were peddled in Berlin on a large scale on behalf of the Soviet economic caucus in order to obtain a supply of D mark, and in order to shake the stability of the new currency. At the same time individuals living in the Soviet sector who were discovered in possession of the foreign currency were liable to long sentences of imprisonment for 'economic sabotage'. In addition to these tactical moves the cigarette shortage was exploited by the Russians in Eastern and Western Germany for the more normal purpose of making a financial profit, and an estimate made by German officials in the Eastern zone puts the trading profit of the Rasno cigarette venture during 1948 at no less than 8½ million Rm.

During the economic counter blockade of the Eastern zone in the last six months of 1948, the Soviet Trading firms were in the forefront of the attempt to beat the watchfulness of the Western powers, and obtain essential goods from the Western zones and Western Europe. So long as goods destined officially for Eastern Europe could still leave the Western zones, all that was required was a false label of destination. When this was discovered—and stopped—after a few weeks, complicated purchases through Switzerland, Liechtenstein, and Austria had to be arranged, under cover of middlemen. But at no time did inter-zonal trade cease altogether. D mark receipts in Berlin were smuggled to cover firms in the West. Towards the end of the year the Ministry of Economic Affairs in North-Rhine / Westphalia in the British zone announced the discovery of illegal currency and goods transactions involving almost 5 million Dm. This was an isolated example—not indeed of the blockade-running, but of German official vigilance and disapproval.

The discovery of this series of deals had an interesting and typical aftermath. Part of the goods involved in the transaction from East to West had been finished textiles, which had been made available by a Soviet firm in return for specified goods from the West. As the matter was dragged further into the light, the names of the participants became known, and some of those resident in the East were promptly indicted for economic sabotage, heavily sentenced and deprived of their property under the pressure of 'popular fury at the misappropriation of the people's goods'. Thus the official organ of the SED in Saxony. The Russians, of course, did not appear in the open at any stage, nor did the fact that the

German authorities were encouraging such transactions in the East under their own auspices.

The commercial methods of the Soviet firms were not above the use of intimidation and trickery. The system of retail petrol and oil distribution was apparently acquired by the Derunapht company from the provincial governments (which in turn had acquired them through expropriation) by first playing off one provincial government against another, and, when this failed, by threats of Soviet displeasure.[1] Incidentally, this was one of the Russian measures which provoked vociferous protests from official German authorities as late as 1947. Another instance was the expropriation of German hotels and restaurants by Intourist. Once taken over by the Soviet travel agency, these establishments were well supplied by the German authorities on Russian orders, and supplies, though paid for at controlled prices, were sold at fancy prices, particularly to hard-currency customers. Some of the Intourist establishments were closed to Germans. Visitors to the Leipzig Fair in 1947 will recall the transformation of the once-famous *Auerbach-Keller* into a black-market restaurant where payment could only be made in dollars, Swiss francs, and Swedish kroner.

There was thus a vantage point of Soviet commerce in Berlin, where not only the export of German produced goods took place, but where the peculiar position of Berlin was exploited to the full for the import needs and export potentialities of the U.S.S.R. All the small subterranean transactions which the Soviet government would have been chary of conducting with the inevitable influx of foreigners on Soviet soil could be handled in Berlin without becoming apparent to the outside world. The Soviet export-import caucus, with its German subsidiaries, cover firms, puppets, holding firms, and the whole bag of disguised trade tricks, were expert fishermen in troubled economic waters.

It is quite impossible to estimate the value of goods bought and sold in Germany by these firms. The chief detriment they caused the German economy, in addition to their participation in reparations production, is the difference between the 1936 price they paid to the German supplier and the world market price in hard currency which they obtained from foreign customers. There was no question of 'dumping' any of these goods;[2] until 1949 the Russians

[1] Löwenthal, *op. cit.*, p. 298.

[2] Löwenthal, *op. cit.*, p. 296 *passim*, states that dumping was frequent. The available evidence, of which he cites none, leads exactly to the opposite conclusion. He mentions scrap. One of the biggest single scrap export contracts from Eastern Germany was signed on 23 September 1947 between Promsyrio-Export.

were not always competitive, since they sometimes asked prices far above the current world market, particularly for items generally in demand such as steel scrap or brown coal. Instead they resorted to offers of fat personal commissions to foreign negotiators to get the orders booked. The exports of the caucus have directly competed with the export efforts of the zone itself, though organized and fostered by the SMA. Ironically, the same goods were being offered in Berlin by two different Soviet agencies, the Russian export firms and the SMA in conjunction with the former Administration, now Ministry, of Foreign Trade. Frequently the goods of one producer were offered by both agencies. The priority of reparation orders over German demands assured that the exports on Soviet account would be more competitive in quality and delivery time, even if not in price. Visitors to the Leipzig Fair noticed this duality —or rather, trinity, since some of the purchases from seemingly German firms like *Texta*,[1] or *Süd-Ost*,[2] were in effect purchases from the Soviet export caucus. Clearly the detriment to the German export trade was considerable.

A word must be said about the two main auxiliary agencies to the Soviet industrial and commercial caucus in Eastern Germany. The *Garantie- and Kreditbank* was created in 1946 as the means of financing internally all Soviet owned and controlled firms. Its declared foundation share capital was 150 million Rm., but it was increased considerably afterwards, and was in the region of 210 million Rm. at the end of 1947.[3] The capital of the SAG is separately held at this bank. The original assets were taken from *Reichsbank* capital, from the proceeds of the liquidation of the big banks, and from diverted tax receipts of the provincial governments. Its capital turnover in 1946 was 900 million Rm., in 1947 2.1 milliard Rm., and was estimated at 2.25 milliards for 1948.[4] These figures serve to show the scale of activity of Soviet controlled industry and commerce in Eastern Germany, particularly since the funds of this bank were not the only financial means

and the *Comptoir Industriel* of Liège, Belgium. The amount was 100,000 tons, followed by 200,000 more. The price was 23 U.S. dollars per metric ton. The then British import price was £3 5*s*. 0*d*. per ton, or \$13.00, and £3 8*s*. 9*d*. or \$13·72 in 1947. (Yearly average for steel and iron scrap from totals in *British Iron and Steel Federation Statistical Year Book*, 1949. These averages are therefore a little on the low side.)

[1] On the face of it a German competitor of Exportlion; in reality an alternative Soviet-controlled textile firm.

[2] An allegedly Balkan firm exporting in fact German medical appliances on Russian account.

[3] Private figures. The 1947 figure is an estimate only.

[4] *Wirtschaftsprobleme der Besatzungszonen*, p. 264.

available to the SAG and the Trading companies. Branches of the bank were established in the main centres of industry, at Leipzig, Dresden, Chemnitz, Erfurt, Halle, Magdeburg, Potsdam, Schwerin, and Frankfurt, as well as in Berlin. The activities of the bank were purely those of a large industrial and commercial bank, it did not discount nor did it handle the foreign exchange obtained by the export of the caucus. This, as indeed all foreign exchange in the Soviet zone, was handled exclusively by the State bank of the U.S.S.R.[1]

The other auxiliary organization is the Russo-German transport company, or *Derutra*. The name 'German' is a geographical euphemism, since this was a purely Russian organization, in which Germans were only employed in a junior executive and, in two cases, in an advisory capacity. Its chief task was to serve as a general forwarding agency for SAG production, and reparation deliveries, both for export and for the Soviet Union. For this purpose it had priority on German Railway movements and on the haulage capacity of the provincial motor transport pools. From 1947 onward *Derutra* made spasmodic appearances as a competitive haulage contractor and agent throughout Germany and the Eastern countries of Europe. Further, the company controlled the Baltic harbours of Wismar, Rostock, Warnemunde, and Stralsund, which were repaired and greatly extended during 1947 and 1948. A large part of the existing dock space and warehouse capacity was exclusively reserved for its use; some reliable estimates give a figure of 70 per cent. The company's working capital is not known exactly, but was believed to have been about 20 million Rm. in 1948. Like the other Soviet firms, it frequently operated through German subsidiaries and middlemen.

Clearly this Soviet economic empire was very nearly watertight and independent. Its only contact with the German economy was through the supply of labour and industrial user material. If we see in all this economic activity, direct and indirect, the fundamental reason not only for the Soviet occupation itself but for much of the German policy of the Soviet Union, we may have discovered the plan of an otherwise incomprehensible series of mazes.

[1] An exception was made with the Westmark (D Mark), which was handled by the bank direct as well as by licensed German financial institutions, such as the Foreign Exchange Equalization Office.

APPENDIX A

TABLE XXXVIII

R.S.L. list of dismantled works to June 1948 (total or partial dismantling)[1]

Breakdown by regions

Region	
Berlin, Soviet Sector	143
Land Brandenburg	50
Land Saxony	414
Land Saxony-Anhalt	118[2]
Land Thuringia	335
Land Mecklenburg	312
TOTAL	1,372

Breakdown by industries

Industry	
Stones and earth	64
Machines, steel and iron products	854[2]
Mining and briquette making	17
Iron and steel refining	41
Electrical	42
Chemical	49[2]
Textile	23
Food processing	34
Precision tool and optical	16
Power stations	9
Wood processing	129
Printing installations	35
Building	11
Various	48
TOTAL	1,372

TABLE XXXIX

List of dismantled works given by the Social Democratic Party (SPD) Berlin to end of 1946[3]

	Thuringia	*Saxony*	*Saxony-Anhalt*	*Mecklenburg*	*Brandenburg*
Metallurgy	4			21	
Metal Processing, Electric Machine industries, etc.	236			80	
Chemical industry	8			7	
Building materials	9	No complete figures	No complete figures	54	No figures
Building industry	—			2	
Wood Processing	28			141	
Textile industry	6			3	
Paper industry	—			2	
Printing industry	7			18	
Other light industries	20			2	
Food Processing	—			22	
TOTALS	318	189[4]	122[2]	353	

[1] Vol. I, pp. 113, *passim*. I have made a few alterations on the basis of more recent information.

[2] Incomplete figure.

[3] See a pamphlet entitled *Ostdemontage*, published by the SPD secretariat, Berlin, January 1948. The list given above is my compilation of their details. Owing to its privileged position the SPD information may be treated as fairly accurate; on the other hand the pamphlet is purely propagandist in purpose.

[4] Incomplete totals.

TABLE XL

List of Reparation Transports (including Current Production) from 15 December 1945 to 31 August 1947[1]

1945	34,954	goods waggons	
1946	391,313	,, ,,	
1947	79,031	,, ,,	
TOTAL	505,298	,, ,,	= 12,632 trains

APPENDIX B

TABLE XLI

R.S.L. List of SAG—Breakdown by Industries and Regions[2]
No. of Works

Industry	*Berlin*	*Saxony*	*Saxony-Anhalt*	*Thuringia*	*Brandenburg*	*Total*
Coalmining and Fuel production ..	—	9	10	—	—	19
Ore mining ..	—	1	—	3	—	4
Potash mining ..	—	—	2	5	—	7
Electric Power Plants ..	—	2[3]	1[3]	—	—	3
Metals	—	3	8	3	—	14
Machinery ..	1	9	7	9	—	27
Vehicles	—	1	5	3	—	9
Electrical ..	5	4	—	7	2	18
Precision Tools and Optics ..	—	2	1	2	1	6
Chemicals ..	—	1	12	—	—	13
Cement	—	—	2	1	—	3
Miscellaneous ..	—	1	2	4	—	7
TOTALS	6	33	50	37	3	129

[1] *Ostdemontage*, p. 27.
[2] Vol. I, p. 125 *passim*. Constructed from details of individual firms.
[3] These include several individual power stations in one combine.

TABLE XLII

German Economic Institute List of SAG by Industries and Regions[1]

Industry	*Berlin*	*Saxony-Anhalt*	*Saxony*	*Thuringia*	*Brandenburg*	*Total*
Coalmining and Fuel	—	10	8	—	2	20
Ore mining ..	—	—	1	3	—	4
Potash mining ..	—	2	—	5	—	7
Electric Power Plant	—	1	2	—	—	3
Metals	—	8	3	3	—	14
Machinery ..	—	8	9	6	—	23
Vehicles	1	5	1	3	—	10
Electrical ..	5	—	5	6	—	16
Precision Tools and Optics ..	—	1	2	2	—	5
Chemicals ..	—	12	1	—	—	13
Cement	—	2	—	1	—	3
Miscellaneous ..	—	2	1	4	—	7
TOTALS	6	51	33	33	2	125

The slight discrepency between Tables XLI and XLII may be due to partial dismantling of SAG in summer 1948.[2]

Thuringia was not only the second most dismantled province, but also suffers from the largest Soviet industrial cancer, although its industrial capacity is lower than that of Saxony and Saxony-Anhalt. The SPD gives the following table:

TABLE XLIII

Distribution of Thuringian Industry between Russian and German Firms at end of 1947[3]

	No. of firms		*Total of labour*		*1946 gross production value in 1,000 Rm.*	
Industry	*German*	*Russian*	*German*	*Russian*	*German*	*Russian*
Metals ..	61	5	2,385	3,916	1,338	2,464
Machinery	793	21	37,797	16,007	10,623	8,145
Electrical ..	185	7	10,485	2,684	4,795	1,386
Pharmaceutical ..	—	8	—	11,369	—	4,670
Rubber	16	4	1,009	1,404	727	1,560
Building	256	4	8,111	1,000	8,380	1,079
Glass and Ceramics ..	539	4	18,786	1,146	6,945	357
Precision instruments ..	16	4	3,302	5,279	143	535
TOTAL	1,866	50	81,848	42,805	32,951	20,196

[1] *Wirtschaftsprobleme der Besatzungszonen*, p. 231.
[2] See above, p. 206.
[3] *Ostdemontage*, p. 29.

APPENDIX C

ORGANIZATION OF SAG[1]

I. *Early Organization*

The formation of SAG took place after the first lists of expropriated works had been submitted to the SMA by the Commission for Sequestration. The relevant SMA order is No. 167 of June 1946, which quotes as its authority (quite unjustifiably) Section 4, para. 1 of the Potsdam Agreement. At first the SAG were organized centrally according to technical groups by industry, as follows:

Fuel	Electrical industry
Ore mining	Chemical ,,
Iron processing	Fertilizer ,,
Metallurgy	Rubber ,,
Machine industry	Potash ,,
Transport machine industry	Cement ,,

II. *Later Organization*

During 1947 this system of technical branches was further developed by a more detailed breakdown, under Russian group names:

Briket:	Coalmining, Generation of electricity
Topliwo:	Coalmining, Generation of electricity, Fuel production
Burii-Ugol:	Coalmining
Karjer:	Coalmining
Smola:	Coalmining, Fuel production
Rasres:	Coalmining
Bagger:	Coalmining
Gasolin:	Fuel production
Synthes:	Fuel productjon
Maslo:	Coalmining
Mineralnye Udobrenya:	Fertilizer
Kali:	Fertilizer
Kainit:	Fertilizer
Silvinit:	Fertilizer
Marten:	Iron and steel industry
Medj:	Soft metal industry
Wismut:	Uranium mining

[1] The tables and figures given in this section are taken partly from pp. 218–32 of *Wirtschaftsprobleme, op. cit.*, and from an article in *Europa Archiv*, June–July 1948, p. 1,428. The list of SAG works is my own.

Amo:	Machine industry
Podjemnik:	Machine industry
Totshmash:	Machine industry
Auto Velo:	Vehicle industry
Pribor:	Precision instruments
Transmash:	Vehicle industry
Kabel:	Electrical industry
Isolator:	Electrical industry
Linsa:	Film production
Photoplenka:	Photochemical industry
Kaustik:	Electro-Chemical industry
Plastik:	Chemical industry
Zelluloid:	Chemical industry
Kraska:	Paints and dyes
Kautschuk:	Synthetic rubber production
Resino Technika:	Rubber processing
Zement:	Building materials

At the end of 1947 these groups and sub-groups were divided into intermediary combines of one or more works and individual factories.

The geographical and individual distribution of the coalmining and fuel production of the SAG was as follows (end of 1948; no accurate reports since):

TABLE XLIV

Breakdown of SAG Organization in Solid and Liquid Fuel Industries

SAG Group	*Combine*	*Individual Works*	*Province*	*Production in 1000 m. tons.*	
				1943	*1946*
(1) Briket ..	Espenhain	Espenhain (2 works)	Saxony	3,972	3,624
(2) Topliwo ..	Böhlen	Böhlen (4 works)	Saxony	7,911	5,009
(3) Burii-Ugol	Borna	Borna		2,468	3,218
	Deutzen	Deutzen (power)			
		Kraft Thräna			
		Kraft I	Saxony	2,148	2,014
		Neuk. Wyhra			
	Salzdethfurt	Neukirchen (3 works)		—	—
(4) Karjer ..	Nachterstedt	Concordia (4 works)	Saxony-Anhalt	3,463	4,079
(5) Smola ..	Deuben	Bosch		3,022	1,977
		Scharf		—	2,590
		Deuben (3 works)	Saxony-Anhalt	—	—
		Marie		—	—
		V. Voss		—	—

SAG Group	*Combine*	*Individual Works*	*Province*	*Production in 1000 m. tons.* 1943	1946
(6) RASRES ..	Pfännerhall	Pfännerhall (4 works)		1,878	1,582
	Gölzau	Gölzau (4 works)	Saxony-Anhalt	532	360
	Friedlander	Friedlander Lauchammer (2 briquette works)		4,497	4,022
(7) BAGGER ..	Golpa	Golpa	Saxony-Anhalt	6,481	2,117
(8) GASOLIN ..	Tröglitz	Brabag Granschutz Kopsen Rositz (2 works)	Saxony-Anhalt	—	—
(9) SYNTHES ..	Schwarzheide	Brabag (2 works)	Brandenburg	—	—
(10) MASLO ..	Profen	Wehlitz (2 works) Profen (3 works) Hedwig	Saxony-Anhalt	552	2,594

The system of organization was thus closely modelled on that of the trusts in the U.S.S.R. The groups were of varying size, and usually consisted of one combine, or a number of adjacent combines, related either vertically or horizontally. Such combinations of works in one combine or SAG group seem to have been created without regard to size or rigid system, though the object was clearly centralization of control. The names for the groups are partly symbols, partly the Russian term for the industry concerned. The total share capital of the SAG is estimated at 3 milliard roubles before the 1949 Russian currency reform and 2½ milliard Rm. fixed capital at 1936 value. The total labour force was about 300,000–320,000 (1949).

APPENDIX D

TABLE XLV

Estimate of Total Value of Soviet Reparation Demands in the Soviet zone only (*1945–8* (*July*))

I. *Value of solid reparations, excluding services*

	Rm. 1936 value
(*a*) Dismantling of capital goods (replacement value) ..	4,100,000,000
(*b*) Reparations from current production and stocks ..	4,390,000,000
(*c*) Food	970,000,000
(*d*) Value of SAG production	2,010,000,000
TOTAL	11,470,000,000

TABLE XLVI

II. *Financial balance sheet 1945–8 (July)*

II. *Financial balance sheet 1945–8 (July)*

Soviet receipts		*Soviet investments and payments*	
From German public bodies through liquidation	13,200,000,000	Payment under Cat. I (*a*), (*b*), (*c*)	10,000,000,000
From German public bodies through diversion of current receipts	13,200,000,000	Occupation costs, including individual Soviet investment and expenditure in German economy ..	4,300,000,000
Land subsidies to German firms engaged on I (*b*) and to SAG ..	1,800,000,000	Subsidies to official German organizations: (DZV, FDGB, SED, etc.)	900,000,000
		Investment in Russian controlled enterprises	6,000,000,000
		Reserves	7,000,000,000
TOTAL	28,200,000,000	TOTAL	28,200,000,000
Less re-investment in German economy ..	15,200,000,000		
Soviet Investments and Reserves ..	13,000,000,000		

CHAPTER VIII

THE PLANNED ECONOMY (1948–50)

Though the economic situation in the Soviet zone was much improved by the summer of 1947, at least from the point of view of production, the position of the German consumer was probably no better than during the war. The best part of East Germany's production potential and actual output went to the Russians. No overall estimate of the Russian share in the consumption of the physical zonal product is possible. The German Institute of Economics gives the following figures in the financial year 1946–7, for certain financial exactions and physical contributions converted into money value[1] (in milliard Rm.). The value of the Rm. is here taken as 3 : 2 for the years 1936 : 1946.

TABLE XLVII

Zonal Incomes and Consumption by the Occupying Powers
1946

Zonal Income 1946	*Zonal Income 1936*	*Russian consumption*	*In % of Z.I.*
16.5	16.8	4.3	26.1

This can be compared to the following figures for the British and U.S. zones with consumption by the respective occupation authority.

B. zone ..	17.3	22.8	2.2	12.7
U.S. zone ..	13.2	13.8	2.1	15.9

It should be borne in mind that the Soviet figure is made up only of reparations from current production, secret purchases under the aegis of German cover firms, and occupation costs. When Soviet financial exactions out of the provincial budgets are taken into account, the total for the Soviet zone was 7.6 milliard Rm. compared to 2.775 milliard Rm. for the British, and 2.1 milliard for the U.S. zone, the proportion of the Soviet zone having jumped to over three times that of the other zones instead of double.[2] No account is taken of Soviet production (SAG), or of dismantling.

In 1947–8 the situation was somewhat different: inflation was

[1] *Wirtschaftsprobleme der Besatzungszonen*, p. 135.
[2] *ibid.*, p. 126. In calculating national income the smaller figures given here must be taken, as the totals include duplications.

cantering, whereas in 1946 it had been trotting. Direct provincial payments to the Russians in lump sums decreased, but payments to individual Soviet agencies and works increased considerably. In addition, Soviet expenditure was increased by the utilization of the reserves accumulated the previous year. On the other hand, the reparation demands from current production appear to have been moderated. In view of these changes and the further depreciation of currency followed by the reform, no figures for zonal income are available, but the proportion of Soviet consumption to the total is probably similar to that of the year before. In 1948–9 the same development was continued, official Soviet exactions from the zonal budget fed by provincial contributions were considerably reduced, while subventions to cover the increasing individual deficits of Soviet undertakings and German works producing for reparations were doubled. The physical quantity of reparations was in fact reduced to some extent, though their cost to the German economy had clearly increased. Soviet expenditure still further exceeded apparent receipts compared to the year before, as financial reserves, whose amount is unknown, were again brought into play.

The rate of overall Soviet reparation demands, and of Russian consumption of German national income, had little relation to production trends. In 1946 both reparation demands and zonal production had risen sharply. In 1947 Soviet reparation demands largely changed their form, but reached unprecedented heights. Yet the production suffered a slight but significant recess. The winter of 1946–7 was very severe, the summer produced heavy floods. Coal production was reduced by 10 per cent compared to 1946 and this drop was reflected throughout industry. Owing to the demands of the railways and Russian reparation exports, briquette production, which was to have been greatly extended, also fell slightly. There were slight improvements in the production of iron and metal goods, the chemical industry, and certain consumer goods. The comparison of real production with the zonal plans looked particularly unfortunate, since the latter had been drawn with the confident expectation of a corresponding improvement in 1947 to that which had taken place during 1946. No amount of 'rounding-off' could disguise the fact that the industry of the Soviet zone could not withstand any serious, even though only temporary, hardening of conditions.[1] In spite of steady

[1] The same fact was made clear in Britain by the 1946-7 winter 'freeze-up', though the effects were not as severe.

improvements during the summer, and new production maxima in the last quarter, the heavy drop in production during the first three months could not be made good in the figures for the whole year.

By the end of 1947 difficulties of a secondary nature were making themselves felt. The major reconstitution of industrial organization effected during the previous two years was taking its toll. The productivity of labour had been heavily affected by the hard winter of 1946–7 and by the efforts before and after it. There were, in addition, serious problems of distribution. The railways were in a parlous state. The priority of Soviet demands and undertakings made the planning of German production almost impossible, at any rate such planning as had any bearing on reality. In addition the hand-to-mouth existence of inter-zonal and foreign trade was reflected by frequent stoppages in production, and called for a new basis for zonal planning, including increased capital development to foster increased domestic production of commodities previously imported almost entirely. Thus, in addition to the sharp recess at the beginning of 1947, the zonal production curve shows a more permanent tendency to flatten at the turn of the years 1947–8, and to remain at a constant level in spite of all efforts to make it rise further. Neither the Eastern currency reform, nor the two year plan proved capable of driving it significantly upwards, and the rise during the course of 1949 was due to the abatement of Soviet reparation demands. The curve rises by almost exactly the amount by which the Russians abated their demands, and by the increase in the amount of SAG production

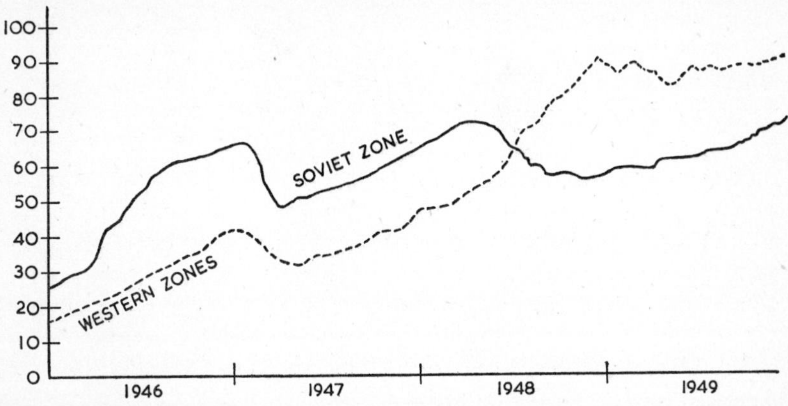

FIG. 8. *Quantity of industrial production 1946–9, as percentage of 1936, of Western Germany and Soviet zone (including reparations from primary products and SAG)*

made available to the German economy. Graphically this might be shown on p. 241, in comparison to the Bizone.

But the most important as well as the most imponderable factor governing the economic situation in the Eastern zone after 1946 was inflation. As planning became less and less flexible, through its increasing ramification, the position of the currency, and of prices governed by it, gave way almost completely. This field of the economy, it must be admitted, was the most difficult to control, as well as the most awkward to arrange neatly with the help of plans.

The inflationary pressure of the currency was higher than at any time since the war. The Russians had injected several doses of credit inflation in the form of new flotations of SAG, and in addition the scale of subsidies to official bodies such as the Trades Unions, the Farmers' Co-operative and the SED had risen continuously. Strict adherence to the controlled-price system in the distribution of the production of the national industries necessitated the payment of ever-increasing subsidies, sometimes as much as 30 per cent of the total value of industrial production of the provincial and zonal works in Saxony.[1] Even the support of the shrinking controlled-price consumer market became an increasingly costly operation of subventions. This was reflected by a rise in black-market prices during 1947, but even more by the increasing contraction of the official price sector. Even rationed goods tended to disappear or to be sold at premia. It was during the latter part of 1947 that the food and clothing rations failed to be met regularly, though the goods were often obtainable in the black market. Nevertheless, savings deposits showed a steady increase during 1947 and 1948. Official policy still discouraged loans to any but national industry. Thus in spite of the high cost of living and the considerable Russian demands on both the fiscal income of the provinces and the holdings of the Credit institutions,[2] the liquid assets of the banks in the Soviet zone showed a considerable increase. During 1947 the savings in the zonal credit institutions rose from 2.8 milliard Rm. to 3.3 milliard Rm. The balances, mostly cash holdings, of the Land central banks in the Soviet zone rose by 514 million Rm. in December 1947, by 1,391 million Rm. in January 1948, and by 1,811 million Rm. in February. The Land credit banks showed a

[1] Official report to the SMA on the financial position of the provincial and zonal industries, May 1948.

[2] The Russians only began this 'silent finance' during 1947, and then on a relatively small scale, preferring direct cash transfers from the provincial governments, as the latter seemed to have a less obvious inflationary aspect.

similar accumulation of cash in their balances, which rose from 13,560 million Rm. in December 1947 to 14,400 million Rm. in January 1948. Of this increase a considerable proportion was due to personal savings; the deposit accounts in the five Land credit banks increased by 59 million Rm. in January 1948 and by 29 million Rm. in February, making a total of 601 million Rm. Similarly the accounts in the Post Office Banking accounts (*Post-checkkonten*) rose to 1,028 million Rm. Yet credits to the economy from the zonal credit institutions during 1947 rose by only 300 millions compared to 1946, from 1.6 milliard Rm. to 1.9 milliard Rm., this being 12 per cent of their total cash and security assets.

TABLE XLVIII[1]

Provision of Credit, Soviet Zone, 1947

1,550	million Rm. came from the Land Credit Banks;
160	,, ,, ,, ,, ,, agricultural co-operatives;
87.8	,, ,, ,, ,, ,, industrial and commercial banks;
91	,, ,, ,, ,, ,, savings banks.
TOTAL 1,888.8	million Rm.

Thus the contraction of the official price market and the corresponding extension of the black market brought about the unusual situation of a rate of saving higher than the rate of increase in the cost of living, though the latter was dominated by ever-spreading inflation. This was due, not to the success of the price stabilization measures of the authorities, but to the practical non-availability of goods, which drove money from all but the highest incomes into savings and out of circulation, and thus left a clear field to official and reparation consumption.

Against this inflationary pressure the social services made little headway, though they should not be ignored. Both the new farmers and the refugees could obtain credits on fairly easy terms, the latter far more favourably than their colleagues in misfortune in the West. The zonal health services provided medical attention cheaply and worked with considerable success. The comprehensive insurance service paid out 1,504,800,000 Rm. during 1947 for medical services, hospital charges, pensions, and cash assistance or doles according to official figures.[2] But no monetary aid could

[1] These figures variously from the *Neue Zeitung*, 6 April 1948 and 13 April 1948 *Telegraf*, 4 April 1948, *et al.*

[2] *Tägliche Rundschau*, 27 April 1948.

counterbalance the over-riding shortage of the necessaries of life which was felt by rich and poor alike.

The fiscal policy of the provinces had to make certain of raising sufficient revenue to meet their considerable commitments, in addition to using taxation as a means to combat inflation. For this purpose even the large burden of taxation had proved inadequate, as had the orthodox Communist expedients of strict planning and control of production and distribution. But the revenue raised by this means was generally sufficient to cover provincial commitments.

These fell into the following groups:

(*a*) The demands of the Soviet authorities, payable via the Finance Administration.
(*b*) Price stabilization and subsidies.
(*c*) Social services and relief costs.
(*d*) Planned capital projects.
(*e*) Costs of administration, wages of civil servants, etc.

The receipts were derived chiefly from the old Reich taxes, though their distribution and relative yield had changed greatly. In the Soviet zone, where the occupation demands on provincial finance were the heaviest in Germany, the level of taxation was very high, and in view of the frequently unregulated income sources and low level of official wages, the greatest yield came from taxes on consumption. Of these the chief were the taxes on spirits and tobacco. In addition there were taxes on almost all non-essential consumer goods and services, the definition of 'essential' covering only food and certain articles of clothing. Of the old Reich taxes on monetary income the turnover tax and direct income tax showed the greatest yield. As well as the previously national (later provincial and zonal) taxes, the former local taxes, rates, house and property tax, still existed, and part of their proceeds was often diverted to the provincial government, as for example in Saxony. Railway and postal receipts were not within the sphere of the provincial governments.

Some examples from actual budgets are given on facing page.

TABLE XLIX

Planned Budget for the year April 1948–9 for Land Saxony-Anhalt[1]

Receipts		*Expenditure*	
Income tax ..	.. 236 mill. Rm.	Transfer to DZV ..	975 mill. Rm.
Turnover tax	.. 152 ,, ,,	Subsidies, price stabilization ..	.. 333 ,, ,,
Tobacco tax	.. 80 ,, ,,	Social services	.. 348 ,, ,,
Spirits tax ..	.. 550 ,, ,,	Administration costs	140 ,, ,,
Other sources	.. 974 ,, ,,	Capital projects and other items	.. 196 ,, ,,
TOTAL ..	1,992 ,, ,,	TOTAL ..	1,992 ,, ,,

For the whole Soviet zone the consolidated budget figures work out as follows (in million Rm.):[2]

TABLE L

Consolidated Budget, Soviet Zone, 1947–9

Province	*Cons. receipt and exp. 1947–8 mill. Rm.*	*To DZV mill. Rm.*	%	*Cons. figure 1948–9 mill. Rm.*	*DZV mill. Rm.*	%
Saxony ..	2,515	1,690	68	2,667	1,365	52
Saxony-Anhalt ..	1,989	1,170	60	1,992	920	46
Thuringia ..	1,583	933	64	1,551	753	48
Brandenburg[3] ..	1,529	880	58	1,494	730	49
Mecklenburg ..	869	390	45	953	315	33
TOTAL SOVIET Z.	8,485	5,083	60	8,657	4,083	47

The proportion of reparation payments, and its uneven incidence in different provinces, will be appreciated. The gross increase in taxation of only 172 million Rm. during 1948, with its suggestion of limited genuine economic expansion, is also noticeable, the incidence of individual taxes remaining the same. The 1948–9 budget figures were announced before the blockade and the currency reform, and consequently the estimated figures would not have been correct, and it is therefore impossible to compare the final figures directly with those of the year before. But the original proposals before the events of July 1948 had a value of their own as reflecting the official view of the future. In 1949–50 the planned receipts remained at almost the same level, though actual receipts decreased slightly. Provincial payments to the Russians were

[1] *Tägliche Rundschau*, 4 April 1948, and other sources.
[2] *Wirtschafts Zeitung*, Stuttgart, 30 April 1948, and other sources.
[3] The relatively high figures for this province include large receipts from Berlin.

reduced to 3,144 million Rm. compared to the consolidated provincial and zonal tax receipts of 7,900 million Rm.

The average individual burden of taxation also differed from province to province. In 1947 Brandenburg headed the list with an individual tax liability of 630 Rm. per head,[1] then Thuringia with 561 Rm. per head, Saxony-Anhalt with 505 Rm., and Saxony with 480 Rm. per head, but since most of the yield came from the spirits tax, of which Brandenburg collected some 890 million Rm. in 1947, it is clear that by far the greater part was paid not out of the pockets of the Brandenburgers, but out of those of the Berliners. Brandenburg's position would thus come behind Saxony with some 469 Rm. These figures should be compared with the 1936 all-German average of 229 Rm., the figure of 275 Rm. in 1937, and that of 314 Rm. in 1938. They are also much higher than the corresponding figures for the Bizone.

It is impossible to discover the true tax burden on different groups of incomes, since less than half the yield was taken from incomes at source. This preponderance of consumer-tax yield over other taxes is peculiar to the Soviet zone. In the Bizone, for instance, only 20 per cent of the annual tax yield in 1947 came from the spirit monopoly, as opposed to 43 per cent in the Soviet zone.[2] But certain it is that as the greater part of the tax yield came from purchase taxes on consumer goods, official money incomes are no accurate guide to individual tax burdens.

The process of socialization was carried much further during 1947 and 1948. At the time of the currency reform in June 1948 over 65 per cent of the total industrial capacity in the zone had been taken over either by the Economic Commission or by the provinces.[3] In one or two isolated instances in 1948 compensation was actually paid—at least officially—to those who could not be squeezed into the category of Nazi or monopolist. Thus on 10 December 1948 the Saxon diet expropriated cinema owners on this basis, and the other provinces followed suit. In terms of value the nationalized sector produced 85–90 per cent of the annual production in 1948. In coal-mining and power production the entire zonal capacity was in the hands of the State, in heavy industry over 80 per cent, and in the light industries about 50 per cent. Almost

[1] For this paragraph see *Telegraf* of 4 May 1948.

[2] For the average tax burden figures see *Wirtschaftsprobleme*, p. 120 *passim*.

[3] cp. the official 1948 figures for the U.S.S.R.: 87 per cent of total industrial production from national undertakings, 12½ per cent from industrial co-operatives (*Artels*) and ½ per cent from one-man private undertakings. The German industrial co-operatives are, by nature and tradition, much more powerful than the Soviet *artels*.

700,000 workers were employed in the zonal (VEB) and provincial (LEB) works, and the national trading corporations, between 35–40 per cent of the total labour force in the zone. Taking into account the SAG, this leaves only 30–35 per cent of labour in private industry or commerce.

On 29 June 1948 the man who was generally considered the most influential German Communist in Eastern Germany, Walter Ulbricht, the Deputy-Chairman of the SED, announced the plan for 1948, and the two year plan 1949–50, to the central party executive. This was the first time that either the annual economic plan had been announced in public, or that a long-term plan had been announced at all. Due importance may therefore be given to this *motu proprio* of the German Communists. The administrative departments were known to have co-operated closely in preparing the plan, and the Soviet authorities must have approved it. Much of Ulbricht's speech was political bombast.[1] Some of it was economic misrepresentation.[2] The figure of 111 per cent industrial production in 1947 over 1946 was given without classification of value or quantity, indeed without any classification at all.[3] Industrial production in 1947 was quoted as 59 per cent of 1936. A 10 per cent increase in 1948 of total industrial output over 1947 was aimed at. This, said the plan, 'will require great efforts'. But such an increase, as the speech failed to mention, would only bring a return to the level towards the end of 1946. The speech of the deputy-chairman envisaged great improvements in the allocation of clothing for the population. The comparative figures are given below:

TABLE LI

Allocation of Textiles under the Two Year Plan

	Second half 1947	*Second half 1948*
Knitted underwear	1,468,000 pieces	5,900,000 pieces
Knitted overwear (pullovers, etc.)	505,000 ,,	1,050,000 ,,
Stockings	5,599,000 pairs	21,000,000 pairs
Leather shoes	366,800 ,,	1,170,000 ,,
Other shoes	3,616,000 ,,	5,400,000 ,,

It was, however, in these particular industries that the shortage of raw material brought about the widespread practice of commission

[1] e.g., the mention of the 'development of a national popular movement against the colonization of Western Germany'. *The German Two Year Plan*, official edition, Berlin 1948, p. 13.

[2] For a detailed criticism of the plan see *The Economist*, 9 August 1948, and below.

[3] *Two Year Plan*, p. 17.

work for foreign customers, while for reparations most of the raw material had to be provided by the Soviet authorities. Much of the Soviet bulk purchase of raw wool in Australia and New Zealand was processed in Germany.

The influence of raw material shortages, and the recession in 1947 as compared to 1946, when stocks were being used up, can be seen from the following table. It includes production for the German market and for reparations.

TABLE LII

Estimate of textile production in the Soviet zone, 1936, 1946, 1947, in major works only[1]
(*In 1,000 Rm.*)

	1936	*1946*	*1947*
Artificial silk and rayon	105,800	73,333	55,167
Processing for spinning	29,125	—	—
Spinning	628,000	271,178	255,863
Weaving	1,008,000	397,463	377,881
Knitting industry	509,600	204,840	194,683
Cloth processing, dyeing, etc. ..	164,500	(Included in spinning and weaving)	
GROSS PRODUCTION VALUE ..	2,445,025	946,814	883,594

Yet 75–80 per cent of the 1947 production is estimated to have been destined for reparations or for foreign countries as commission work.

The two year plan forecast an improvement in distribution as a result of 'the statement of the SMA that in 1948 not a single meter of this quantity [the estimated 138 million metres of various materials to be produced in Eastern Germany] will be taken as reparations'.[2] As it was very unlikely that such quantities would be delivered by the Russians for German consumption, it is difficult to imagine the provenance of the necessary raw materials. The total delivery of textile raw material by the U.S.S.R. for German consumption up to July 1948 was given by official Soviet zone sources as 23 thousand tons of cotton and 7 thousand tons of wool.[3] This amount, sufficient to occupy two large woollen plants per year, was far below the zone's requirements. In fact, some of the imported material consisted of unsorted Russian camel hair, which became the nightmare of the textile industries of all Eastern Europe after the war. But—this exaggerated figure apart—probable raw material imports were obviously inadequate to account

[1] *Europa Archiv*, June–July 1948, p. 1,434.
[2] *Two Year Plan*, p. 22. [3] *ibid.*, p. 22.

for such planned increases in home consumption during 1948, even if only the coarsest materials were made. The same promise about cessation of reparations was made by Marshal Sokolovsky on 11 January 1947, and its repetition eighteen months later alone shows that it was not kept.

The two year plan 1949–50 started off with four major propositions:

(*a*) Production (presumably quantity) in 1950 was to be 81 per cent of 1936 and 135 per cent of 1947.
(*b*) Productivity of labour in 1950 was to be 30 per cent higher than in 1947.
(*c*) The overall wage total in 1950 was to be 15 per cent higher than in 1948.[1]
(*d*) The internal production costs in national undertakings were to be reduced by 7 per cent at least. In other words, the annual deficit of these works, for which the provinces were responsible, was to be reduced by an amount equivalent to 7 per cent of present production costs.

Of these four major points (*b*) and (*a*) can be partly connected as cause and effect. But not even the most convinced Stakhanovite in Germany would have claimed that productivity was more than part of the problem. Unless other factors reacted simultaneously, an increase in productivity without corresponding increase elsewhere, were such a thing possible, would probably have led to unemployment by reducing the semi-employment of large numbers in certain industries. After the stoppage of trade between Eastern and Western Germany in 1948, the programme could only be carried out if imports of raw materials and basic capital goods could be assured, or local production built up. With the question of imports and their future prospects we shall be concerned in the next chapter. As far as the internal investment programme is concerned, the plan noted its urgency, though as a surprisingly low priority. Steel production was to be increased to 875,000 tons in 1950, and to that end new plants were envisaged at Riesa and Hennigsdorf, while the existing plant *Maximilianshütte* at Unter-

[1] The fact that the planned rate of increase in productivity should be twice that of the increase in the wage total within a given time is a practical application of the Soviet 'Rule of Socialist development' evolved by Koslov and Turetzky. Briefly, if money wages rise more slowly than productivity, cheaper goods will raise real wages and will eventually tend to bring level the value of labour's product and its reward. This is, of course, based on a pure labour theory of value. In fact, both in Germany and in Russia, the difference between labour's product and its reward carries the whole enormous cost burden of rearmament and government.

wellenborn was to be extended and re-equipped. But even if these works were producing at full capacity by the end of 1950, only some 800,000 tons would be available from their full output, while the other small works of the zone could not produce more than 20–30 thousand tons in 1948. Yet the minimum needs for the 35 per cent increase in gross industrial output would call for at least 1,800,000 tons of crude steel per year.[1] On the question of coal the prevalent shortage of hard coal could only very partially and expensively be filled by brown coal substitution. The ambitious briquette-making programme was endangered by the ever-present difficulty that so much of the actual brown coal was swallowed up by direct consumption. To fulfil it required, in the absence of hard coal imports, such a quantity of brown coal for briquette-making, as well as a briquette-making capacity, as did not in 1948 exist, and has since been only slightly increased. The total planned increase in chemical production is deceptive, since no distinction was made between increases in production of chemicals out of imported raw materials such as sulphur or phosphorus, and such indigenous production as potash. The yield of one can be improved by productivity methods, the other only by hard cash in foreign exchange.

Apart from the matter of allocated textiles, little was heard of increases in consumer-goods supplies for the population. These do not normally play a great part in the 'production' plans of Communist countries, but since the SED specialized in specious promises of welfare to the electorate, this omission from the speech to the political executive of the party had considerable significance. It is indeed difficult to imagine that even the, in the Marxist sense, most 'free' proletarian can get more than a temporary elation out of the fact that his country's production of steel ingots has improved by x per cent, if this result of class-conscious effort does not improve the availability of scarce consumer-goods, much less his capacity to obtain them. However this may be, the plan did not foresee any considerable amelioration of the shortage of essential consumer-goods. Hastened by increased depreciation during the war, personal stocks of clothes, household goods, furniture, etc., were dwindling fast. The question of productivity was, of course, closely tied up with all this, and even more with food. Provided that food reparations ceased, as promised by the

[1] The Soviet zone used far more than this quantity annually during the years of expansion, 1936–9, and the 1948 need for industrial re-equipment called for at least as much steel. Imports from Western Germany during 1947 were about 500,000 tons.

Russians,[1] there was a reasonable prospect that some of the shortages could be filled by barter from the staple surplus. Agricultural production in the zone was likely to remain constant or to increase slightly; a real intensification of production was very unlikely in the near future. If a series of bad harvests should ensue, it was still possible, in spite of present assertions to the contrary, that *vox populi* would demand a further reform in the direction of collectivization. The figures of planned increases in agriculture for 1950, 23 per cent over 1947 in corn and legumes, 38 per cent in potatoes and 73 per cent in vegetable-oil extraction, were but modest hopes for the future, and perhaps an incidental reflection on the detrimental effects of the land reform. A minimum consumption figure of 2,000 calories daily on the ration was aimed at, which would have meant about 2,400 calories including free surpluses. Although the constitution of these calories would continue to be arbitrary and abnormal, there was at least a possibility that some such figure would indeed be reached, and by the beginning of 1950 it was reached. It is also worth mentioning that, unlike industrial production, agricultural production was not in the plan thought capable of being improved by better arrangements in distribution. The distributional side of agriculture was as inefficient in the Soviet zone as in the West, and its improvement seemed an essential prerequisite of increased rations. By this is meant the improvement of the distributional machinery as well as the abolition of deliberately unequal distribution according to political status. Equal rations are as important in misery as in prosperity.

Any examination of the possibilities of implementing the planned increase in the overall sum of wages must be based on the fact that an increase in the wage bill without corresponding increase in the volume of goods available would either increase the inflationary pressure in the black market, or at best swell the total of savings. It is interesting that this, the only point of the four main items of the plan to deal with matters of immediate interest to the wage-earner, should have promised neither greater availability of rationed goods at controlled prices, nor an increase in real wages, nor even, in accordance with Marxist theory, a redistribution of national income in favour of the lower industries income groups. What was proposed was a net lump sum extra in the overall wage bill, not a specified increase in wages. It was unlikely that this extra amount would be distributed evenly. It

[1] *Two Year Plan*, p. 29.

was promised that a 'stern battle will be waged against [the doctrine of] levelling [wages and bonuses]'; 'workers and engineers must be made to develop initiative and [capacity for] hard work'.[1] Therefore it may well be that the extra 15 per cent were intended to find their way into the pockets of budding Stakhanovites, both industrial and political.

This proposal thus seems, at first sight, an inflationary measure in violation of all attempts to reduce pressure on prices outside the narrow circle of strictly rationed goods. This can be illustrated by a simple formula. Assuming a wage of x Rm., this wage would, after a 15 per cent increase, be $\frac{23x}{20}$. If the wage x was previously divided into half spent in goods at official prices (1936) and half at black-market prices on an average 10 times as high as 1936, the real wage of x compared to 1936 would be $\frac{x}{2} + \frac{x}{20} = \frac{11x}{20}$ Rm. If the availability of goods at controlled prices does not increase for the recipient of the increased money wage, the new real wage, providing it is all spent, will be $\frac{x}{2} + \frac{13x}{20 \times 10} = \frac{113x}{200}$, only 1.5 per cent more than the previous real wage. If, however, the two year plan enabled wage earners to continue to spend half their new income on goods controlled in price, by increasing the supply of such goods, the new real wage would be $\frac{23x}{20 \times 2} + \frac{23x}{20 \times 2 \times 10} = \frac{253x}{400}$ or $\frac{126.5x}{200}$ or 8.25 per cent more than the previous real wage and 6.75 per cent more than the new real wage without increase of controlled-price goods. Thus, unless the proportion of income spent on goods at controlled and uncontrolled prices was kept the same for new as for old incomes, or unless the proportion of the former was increased, the increase of money wages would have been of little value to the consumer, and would either have had inflationary effects,[2] or would have had to be put aside as savings. Should the purchasing power of money here be increased later, it was unlikely that these savings would be allowed to emerge at full value—there was the danger of another currency reform.

[1] *Two Year Plan*, p. 26.

[2] One interesting result of this small increase in real purchasing power of any increase in money holding was the unwillingness, during the latter part of 1947 and 1948, to take up loans on the part of the only class of consumers able to obtain them on easy, indeed, on any, terms. Thus the SMA authorized a credit extension of 38 million Rm. to new farmers (*Neubauern*) during the second half of 1947, of which only 10 million Rm. were taken up. (*Telegraf*, 30 April 1948.) Similarly, credits for refugees only rose by 200,000 marks during this period (*Tribüne*, 13 May 1948). This unwillingness perhaps explains the generally low level of credit to industry at this time as much as the official anti-inflationary policy of grudging accommodation except for the normal short-term advances to nationalized industries, and also the sudden propensity to save. See also above, pp. 242–43.

The so-called currency reform which took place in the Soviet zone a few days after that carried out in the West was primarily aimed not at the currency volume as a whole, but at the financial resources available at that moment to the individual as a consumer, and thus, instead of completing what was begun in 1945, as did the Western currency reform, merely repeated the performance in a different way without greatly affecting the volume of currency in circulation. By converting his money at ratios varying from 3 : 1 to 10 : 1, while converting the official money belonging to State works, provincial governments, official parties, Trades Unions, etc., at par, a situation was supposed to be created in which money would be available for production but not for individual consumption. The effect resembled a partial confiscation of private savings and investments, and a gift of the proceeds to selected political associations and economic production groups. In view of the highly inflationary situation the measure had only a temporary effect; within a fortnight black market prices had returned to their previous level. The 'class' object of the measure had a more permanent effect. Not only did the few remaining large private firms, whose financial resources were converted at an average of about 6 : 1, mostly pass into the direct control of the provincial government by immediately becoming illiquid, but, as in all currency reforms, those incapable of increasing the speed of their income and expenditure circulation were the greatest sufferers. Among these were the farmers. Where the hoarder of stocks profited in the West, the hoarder of money gained in the East. While the entrepreneurial class turned the currency reform in the West to its own profit at the expense of the wage-earner, the Eastern reform was planned to benefit the State and all organizations under its control, as well as the various Soviet authorities and organizations. It made little difference to the majority of the wage-earners, and 'liquidated' a number of individuals and groups. This social effect was desirable for the Russians. If the Western currency reform had not taken place, an excuse for the measure, instead of being ready to hand, might have had to be invented.

There is some evidence that the original scheme, planned by the then Vice-President of the Central Administration for Finance some time before the Western currency reform took place,[1]

[1] Apparently some time in May. There was nothing spontaneous about reform either in the West or in the East. The two-year plan, based on an accomplished currency reform, must have been prepared for much more than a week befo r its publication.

envisaged more stringent conversion all round and a real reduction of inflationary pressure. Apparently the SED, with Russian support, weakened this proposal into a measure purely of wealth redistribution. Certainly the Vice-President was later attacked for the fact that the reform, to which his name was tied, was economically a failure. It may be that, under the original scheme, the 15 per cent increase in the wage total was planned as a consolation for a more strict conversion, and that this was retained after the change in the intended currency reform itself. As the provincial governments and the Economic Commission paid the wages of two-thirds of German labour in the zone, they would, by authorizing the individual wage increases making up the 15 per cent, only return some of the extra money they received at the time of the currency reform.

The last of the four points, the lowering of the running costs of the provincial and national works, needs little discussion. Since the price of the products could only be increased slightly, and wages could not be reduced, the question became one of internal organization, or 'rationalization', so beloved of Marxist economists. A report made to the SMA during the spring of 1948 showed that subsidies in many of these undertakings were as high as 30 per cent of costs per year. When it is borne in mind that part of the foundation capital of many of these works was put up by the provincial central banks and that subsidies continued to be an important item in provincial budget planning, it is clear that though a reduction was possible, the principle of subsidizing production was regarded as inevitable. When such a principle is once accepted as normal, the extent of its application can rarely be reduced.

To what extent was this plan carried out? If it was based partly on the expected imports from the West under the Minden and Berlin agreements, the Western embargo on exports to the Soviet zone during much of 1948 made the plan almost impossible to fulfil. Modest as it was, the 1948 plan was not quite fulfilled as far as industrial production is concerned, chiefly because of the Berlin blockade and its concomitant results. The chief shortage was in steel and iron, and the processing industries lagged behind the comparative averages, reaching only a level lower than that of 1947. We do not know if the distribution of textiles was in fact as had been promised, but from available reports it appears most unlikely. Russian imports of wool and cotton increased but lightly compared to the year before. During 1949 a general improvement took place; in the last quarter production was about 72 per cent of 1936, and prospects for 1950 appeared bright. If, as is probable, the plan foresaw the achievement of a level of production by the end of 1950 equivalent to 81 per cent of 1936, instead of a production value for the year of 81 per cent of the value of 1936 production, it seemed that this part of the plan would be fulfilled. Indeed, it was announced by the East German government in January 1950 that the plan would be completed in eighteen months instead of twenty-four. Though there was an improvement in output in most sectors except coalmining, the increased production figures were largely due to the reduction in Soviet reparation demands, which, according to the Soviet papers of February 1950, were by then a mere 7 per cent of current production value. Unofficial estimates, however, put them at about 16–18 per cent. In addition, 23 SAG works were handed back to the German economy on 19 May. Given this proportion as a constant, the zone should eventually be capable of reaching and sustaining a level of production in the region of 7.0 milliard Rm. (net value), or 85 per cent of 1936. On 16 May 1950, however, Tass, the Soviet News agency, announced that Stalin had written to Grotewohl to the effect that total Soviet reparation demands had been reduced from $10.000 million, demanded at Yalta, to $6.829 million, but that only $3.658 million would have been paid altogether by the end of 1951. Thus $3.171 million would still have to be paid by 1965.

Thus the quantity of goods for reparations from current production may even go up again, but will probably not decrease, and even the most optimistic forecast could promise little immediate increase in overall production beyond 1950. Until a good deal of renovation and new investment had taken place, it would be difficult to surpass the 1950 level, whatever the next long-term plan might provide. In the meantime the position of industry in the Soviet zone was such that any unexpected difficulties would have an effect on production quite out of proportion to that in a well-balanced economy with normal reserves.

One of the most important effects of the two year plan was to inaugurate a considerable change in the economic structure of the Soviet zone. The preponderance of investment and consumer goods production was to be replaced by a new emphasis on capital goods and raw materials. Strenuous efforts were immediately made to increase the proportion of brown coal made into briquettes, while industry and services using raw brown coal, such as the railways, were heavily restricted where no distribution of imported hard coal was possible. Similarly, the investment programme in steel, iron and soft metals had top priority. The Russians increasingly confined their reparation demands to finished consumer-goods and specialized machines,[1] making almost the entire raw material production available to the Germans. This reorganization was largely at the expense of consumer goods and, since the Russians were still interested, the German consumer continued to suffer even more. In fact, during 1949 the availability of many consumer goods was as low as in 1946. The distribution of leather shoes during the first six months of 1949 was 400,000 pairs, compared to 497,000 during the second half of 1948[2]. The plan, it may be recalled, provided for 1,170,000 in the second half of 1948. Leather was in any case very scarce, but much that had been intended for shoe production went elsewhere. This situation was likely to develop still further in the future; if the plans for the next period called for further steps in this direction the comparison of the value of zonal production between 1936 and 1950 would become meaningless, since the rate of labour value in total zonal production must eventually decrease as the proportion of basic industry increases. A general expansion in all directions comparable to 1936 was not likely under the conditions of the Soviet zone for a decade. A reorganization of the banking system took place during 1948–9 to facilitate the direction of credit to industry. On 20 July 1948 as an aftermath of the currency reform, the *Emissions-und Giro Banken* of the five provinces were incorporated into the *Deutsche Notenbank*, a new central bank carrying out the policy first of the Economic Commission and later of the East German Government. On 13 October 1948 another new bank, the *Deutsche Investitions Bank*, was incorporated to finance the 'People's Works' owned and managed zonally and to provide credit for all nationalized industry. The Land banks for investment and savings, however, continued to function.

The agricultural plans were more modest. Since the dislocating effects of the Land reform had partially worn off, production did increase in 1948, and again slightly in 1949.

TABLE LIII

Estimate of harvest yields, Soviet zone, 1948 and 1949

(*in million tons*)

	Bread grain	*Fodder grain*	*Total grains*	*Potatoes*	*Sugar beet*
1948 ..	2.2	1.7	3.9	10.0	4.65
1949 ..	2.35	1.9	4.25	10.2	4.9

[1] *Two Year Plan*. Speech of Fritz Selbmann, p. 51.
[2] Private report from Trades Union sources.

No figures are available as to whether the planned increase in vegetable-oil extraction has in fact taken place. However, as regards agriculture, the planned improvements over 1947, a particularly bad year, were achieved, or at any rate nearly achieved. As in industry, the possibilities of increased production were limited by certain long-term factors; the irrational parcelling-up of estates and frequent changes of ownership, the shortage of fertilizer (since ameliorated somewhat) and of agricultural machinery, and above all the ever-present danger of distribution difficulties such as the frequent breakdown of local transport and supply services.

The position of the Eastern zone with regard to dairy farming and livestock was less promising. Judging from the cautious references by speakers at the SED party congress on 29 June 1948 to 'administrative-mechanical mistakes' as well as to natural causes,[1] the improvements expected from the land reform had not taken place. The official plan had nothing beyond a reference to the effect that more livestock meant more food for the population![2] Figures for 1949 show that the improvement in the livestock position since the war was very slight.

TABLE LIV

Livestock Population, Soviet Zone[3]
(*in millions*)

	Cows	*Horses*	*Pigs*	*Sheep*	*Chicken*
1939 ..	1.8	.87	6.5	1.7	19.2
1946 ..	.99	.41	2.18	.75	10.4
1948 ..	1.1	.49	2.15	.9	10.9
1949 ..	1.2	.54	2.17	1.0	11.4

In consequence of this the milk ration became but little higher than it was, while the meat and fat ration remained almost constant from the end of the war until the middle of 1949, when increases were promised for 1950.

The employment position in the Soviet zone was somewhat obscure in 1949. The Soviet demands for labour decreased considerably in every field, and some 380,000–400,000 men were estimated to be fully and directly employed by all Soviet agencies at the end of 1949, including indirect labour employed through German authorities, as on the Baltic defences and harbours. Official German figures of employment showed little change com-

[1] *Two Year Plan*. Speech of Edwin Hörnle, p. 68. [2] *ibid.*, p. 29.
[3] 1939 figures from *R.S.L.*, Vol. III, p. 47; later figures from private reports and *Der Bauer*, published by the Farmers' Co-operative.

pared to 1947, but these were unreliable. Similarly we do not know how far the productivity campaign was successful, since Stakhanovite records are no guide at all. In the long run the absence of consumer incentives and food made any general improvement in productivity improbable; indeed, the evidence of arrivals in the Western zones early in 1950 gave the impression that productivity was once more on the decline. It was possible, however, that the slightly improved position during 1949 would be sustained. The political organs of control carried out a sustained campaign to keep up the performance of individual production units, and in order to publicize and dragoon noticeable failures to comply with official norms.

Finally wages. During 1948 a series of collective revisions of wage schedules were undertaken by the provincial governments and by the Department for Labour. On 13 May 1948 300,000 workers in the clothing industry were allowed up to 23 per cent higher wages,[1] and other industries, heavy machinery, precision instruments, and railway repair shops, followed suit. The policy of wage increases was intended to counteract the failure to make allocation and rationing satisfactory incentives to work. This system had worked for party functionaries, but could not be extended to embrace the whole labour force. Therefore during 1948 a more orthodox system of money-wage differentiation was adopted, and by the summer of 1949 a system of carefully graded wage-scales had been put into operation. At the same time, in line with recent developments in the U.S.S.R., the system of preferential allocations was restricted to a narrower circle of beneficiaries. The level of real wages did not move up with money wages; as has been suggested, the average increase of money wages by 12 per cent in 1949 over 1947 corresponded to a real wage increase of only 2 per cent. As the level of savings decreased slightly during 1949, the general effect was to make the value of money depreciate further still. This fact can be corroborated by the increasing disproportion of the rate of exchange between D mark and Eastmark, which, according to available figures, was 1 : 7 in March 1950. For the time being the position was likely to remain static, as German expansion was to some extent offset by Russian contraction, but the Soviet statement on reparations in May 1950 made the rate of reduction of reparation demands likely to be a temporary factor.

[1] *Tagesspiegel*, 14 May 1948.

CHAPTER IX

THE SOVIET ZONE AND WESTERN GERMANY

THE division of the Reich into zones of occupation was intended to combine the prestige demands of the four major powers with the most effective machinery possible to ensure four-power control of Germany. Yet Germany was to continue as a single national entity, and for this purpose the Control Council was given sovereign status, collectively responsible only to the joint decisions of four-power conferences at governmental level. But the dual function of the Control Council and of its constituent delegations could only be combined into a harmonious whole as long as there was fundamental agreement between the four powers. The conception of Potsdam was of a Germany undivided in principle, but administered in four parts.

In the event, the unity of Germany proved far more precarious. By 1946 the country was divided in principle, though united for certain purposes, and the Control Council had become a permanent four-power conference instead of a governmental unit. But great as the differences were between one zone and another, they can be, and have been exaggerated. The greatest difference at the beginning was that between the Anglo-American zones and the French zone.[1] It has become the practice to blame most of Germany's post-war difficulties on the division between East and West, so much so that almost any effect, if blamed on this cause, has been taken for granted.[1] The economic position of post-war Germany has often been put down to the system of occupation by zones, and it is now currently held in Germany that had the zones not been created, the German economy would have recovered much more quickly. An examination of the facts may, however, show that the split between East and West Germany was not an inevitable consequence of the system of occupation, and that even the fundamental political differences do not inevitably lead to economic isolation.

[1] Until the end of 1945, the French were at loggerheads with the other three powers in the Control Council. For a discussion of French obstruction of the implementation of Potsdam, see Basil Davidson, *op. cit.*, Chap. V. Also Lucius D. Clay, *Decision in Germany*. At the end of 1945 Clay told an American correspondent: 'I have voted with the Russians more often than with any other delegation.' Russell Hill, *Struggle for Germany* (London, 1947).

No one has yet attempted to show the real influence of the zonal barriers on post-war German political and economic development without at the same time pleading a special case.[1] Such an impartial inquiry will be our primary object here. Let us take the political aspect first.

The original purpose of the zones was to mark off the areas of occupation of the four occupying powers. Zonal frontiers were not intended primarily as frontiers for the Germans, but between the different Allies. Once the worst chaos was over after the cease fire, zonal frontiers soon came to be regarded in this, their correct, light. In the immediate post-war period, lasting until August 1945, travel for Germans into the Russian zone was admittedly a risky venture and usually took the form of an exploratory expedition for property and family rather than a civilized journey. This was not due to anyone's policy, but to the nature of conditions immediately following cessation of hostilities. From August 1945 onwards, passage across the East-West frontier was in fact far easier for the Germans than for the occupying troops. No official pass had yet been agreed upon, but transit took place with any kind of spurious authority, generally with no authority at all. The short walk from one railhead to another presented no difficulties, and was undertaken by many thousands each month. While a document of identity was usually accepted for German travellers, travel between zones was very difficult for Allied soldiers, and the arrest of unauthorized Allied personnel in other zones was already occurring in 1945 with some frequency on both sides. It was clearly implied to whom the zonal frontiers were intended to represent real barriers.

The similarity of political activity in East and West from August 1945 to April 1946 made political contact natural. The major parties were interzonal from the beginning and political contact between East and West was frequent and unhampered. Party congresses took place in either area, and Berlin provided a useful compromise solution where any question of interzonal difficulty arose. There was a tendency for private political discussions, which might have raised objections from any one of the occupying powers, to take place in the neutral city, but official party congresses continued to be held in either Eastern or Western zones as late as summer 1947.[2] The fact that political activity was in a

[1] The only exception is the study in *U.N. Economic Bulletin for Europe.* 3rd quarter 1949. Vol. I, No. 3, p. 25.

[2] The last interzonal congress to take place in the Russian zone was apparently that of the LDP in the summer of 1947.

very infant stage made the potential difference arising from zonal frontiers even smaller. The importance of local affairs pushed questions of national import into the background. It is indeed surprising that interzonal affiliation of political parties took place as early as September 1945, and that may be ascribed to the pressure of the Allies in creating parties out of the void rather than to the rapid growth and integration of spontaneous political activity. Certainly the facilities for interzonal contact seem to have been adequate for the political and social needs of Germany during the period August 1945 to October 1946. There were also a considerable number of non-political organizations with complete interzonal freedom. The churches and their social organizations took little notice of zones; indeed, the Lutheran Church even in 1950 maintained its relations almost intact, notwithstanding the iron curtain. Moreover, the Trades Unions and the organizations of Nazi victims were interzonal from the start, and remained so long after their political tinge had become obvious. Only in 1948 did the dissident non-communist Unions obtain full Western recognition in Berlin.

April 1946 is as significant a date in the relations between Eastern and Western Germany as for the internal development of the Soviet zone. The SPD had ceased to exist in the East and the SED and the socialists of the West became firm enemies, especially after the October election in Berlin. The two bourgeois parties were soon effectually split into different organizations in the East, where they became increasingly confined to a negative rôle, and the West, where they gained rather than lost strength. Though interzonal contact was still maintained up to 1948, there was no common policy. Those leaders in the East who advocated close relations with party headquarters in the West were eliminated by the Russians. The only party whose interzonal connections increased after 1946 was the KPD, which from that time onwards undisguisedly took its orders from the SED headquarters in Berlin,[1] though it was announced at the end of 1948 that the Communists in Western Germany would adopt different policies to deal with different problems from those of the SED in the East.

[1] Contact between the Western Communists and the SED is very clearly established. A number of prominent Communists resigned their posts after October 1946 and were soon found in leading trade union posts in the Western zones. There is further evidence of financial support by the SED for the Western Communists both before and after the currency reform in the West. Thus the value of such documents as the infamous 'M' Plan of 1947 is not of immediate importance in proving the already known connection between the SED and the Communists in the West.

The difficulties of zonal intercourse can be traced in direct relation to the increasing Communist control of Eastern Germany. Personal as well as political intercourse between the Russian zone and the rest of Germany became more and more undesirable for the Russians, and more fraught with danger for the opponents of the SED. But it must be emphasized that there is no evidence of any official increase in the tightness of the zonal frontiers on the part of the Russians until the end of 1947. Even unauthorized travellers remained generally unmolested until the summer of that year, and the official interzonal passes continued to be issued on much the same terms as before.[1] It was the fear of arrest in the Soviet zone, and the general psychosis about conditions there which influenced potential German visitors, rather than an actual tightening of the formalities on crossing the border. The transit from East to West certainly continued without much Russian interference. The reason appeared to be that, important as was the achievement of a watertight political area for the unhampered development of Russian plans, the momentary advantage of contact with the West, particularly economic contact, was still greater. In order to strike the desirable mean between complete suspension of contact and unrestricted intercourse the frontiers were left as open as they were before, but the danger for West Germans of being molested inside the Soviet zone increased. It was hoped to give the impression that only politically well-disposed persons were welcome, and in effect the attempt succeeded. This distinction explains the frequent and otherwise inexplicable divergence of travellers' tales about the Soviet zone; that of the journalist who was given every facility, and his colleague who was flung into jail on a charge of spying.

It was during the summer of 1947 that unauthorized entry to and exit from the Soviet zone first became a really hazardous undertaking without official Russian permission. The frontier control of the Russian side was greatly strengthened with both troops and German police, and those caught crossing in either direction without permission were frequently sent to work in the uranium mines of Saxony or interned in one of the camps. This was about the time that four-power agreement showed real signs of deliberate disruption rather than mere filibustering activities. The official rupture between East and West can be dated accu-

[1] See Löwenthal, *op. cit.*, p. 262, for evidence that the Russians sometimes recommended people to go over the frontier illegally in the absence of valid passes.

rately from the abortive Munich Conference of provincial delegates from all over Germany in July 1947. The much publicized report of the meeting and the commentary on its failure given by Dr. Fischer, the Saxon Minister for Internal Affairs, in the Land diet formally opened the intense press campaign in the Soviet zone against Western Germany. Individual attacks against particular men and events now changed to an organized and sustained campaign of defamation. It was made clear to Eastern zonal officials that meetings with Western functionaries, except on direct Russian orders, were considered undesirable and could be dangerous. Consequently such meetings as still took place officially could with justice be suspected of ulterior Russian motives. One of these was the hope of acquiring confidential information about Western German affairs. The blockade of Berlin in 1948 and its political results only threw into sharp relief the existing and almost complete political isolation between East and West.

The nadir of bad relations between East and West was thus reached in 1948. It was the deliberate policy of the Russians to eliminate all political contact with the Western zones except such as had their official approval. For this purpose the zonal division was turned into a frontier between two foreign, and none too friendly, countries. Yet their success was not complete. Frontier crossing continued on a reduced but still considerable scale. Moreover, contact went on unmolested in Berlin. The exchange of information about conditions similarly could not be stopped. Common language, identical currency, and a single tradition all helped to overcome the artificial administrative barrier. Even during the blockade relations were never altogether broken off. The SED never subscribed to any doctrine of separation, but accused the Western powers of pursuing a policy of splitting Germany. Indeed, it was held that the blockade of Berlin was a necessary step in the direction of German unity. All this made it clear to the Russians that the tradition and desire for German unity was a vital factor among Germans of all political shades. Their task now was to harness this feeling to their own policy instead of combating it.

With the end of 1948 a new relationship emerged between East and West. Instead of pursuing a policy aimed at separation, the Russians now began a campaign for unity—on their own terms. This did not mean that the separation of Eastern Germany was to give way to free intercourse between it and the West. No relaxation was made in the efforts to confine contact to channels controlled by the SED and the administration. But within that framework contact was to be re-established and extended, with the object of obtaining popular support in all Germany for unity under the administration of what was soon to be the new East German government.

The methods adopted were various. The National Democratic party became active in Western Germany as the self-appointed mouthpiece of militant nationalism. A number of individuals and groups appeared on the political and cultural horizon to advocate the benefits which might accrue to a united Germany looking to the Soviet Union as its protector and friend. Similarly the activities of such men as Nadolny, former German ambassador in Moscow, and of Professor Noack in the West, were reciprocated in the Eastern zone by large rallies for German unity, to which all those likely to support the campaign, whether Communists or not, were invited. Concurrently with this campaign, the economic experts of the SED foresaw a grave crisis of unemployment and deflation in the West. Not content with mere prediction, the Communist party in the West was instructed to help to bring it about. Propaganda was intensified, comparing employment and wage-scales in the two parts of Germany. The continued dismantling in the British zone was exploited to the full, and Communist agitators found themselves in the unusual rôle of martyrs for the cause of German industrial *status quo*. The verdict in the Manstein trial was used as a means of demonstrating the implacable hostility of the English Labour government to the youthful German democracy, while the speeches of accused's counsel were ready-made ammunition in the effort to brand the Western powers as the disguised friends of Hitler. In fact, the previous Communist attempt to separate East and West Germany now became an all-out effort to unite Germany against the Western powers, and to shift the cause of disunity from political creeds to national incompatibility. One of the lines of propaganda most insistently urged was concerned with showing the Germans in the West that they were being treated by their occupation powers as a colony. The slogan 'Marshall plan means enslavement' sums up this theory, launched officially in March 1947 by Professor E. Tarlé, of the Soviet Academy of Sciences, under the name 'industrial feudalism'. It was based on a complicated evaluation of the connexion between foreign loans to Germany and interest as well as reparations payments to the Western powers. Like many of the heaviest shafts from the Soviet armoury, it was merely a rehash of a theory evolved in 1920 by Professor Varga, writing under the name Pavlovsky, to give National Bolshevism some theoretical respectability.[1]

The foundation of the East German government gave this campaign an exclusively German flavour. Instead of being dependent on differences between the allies, German could now talk to German directly through elected governments. The zonal frontiers, originally castigated as instruments of division, were now represented as a means of achieving unity, by making possible the establishment of at least one truly democratic government. The official policy of the East German government was to devote itself to the cause of German unity.[2] By the end of 1949 the position was such that Western Germany was less interested in the establishment of a united Germany than the East German republic. The period of separation had coincided with the revival of West German prosperity and the beginnings of independence. People had become adjusted to the lack of political and social contact. Even Berlin was regarded more as an outpost of Western Germany than as a former or future capital. To this extent, therefore, Communist propaganda fell on deaf ears. In the East, however, the achievement of a single German republic continued to be advocated; to some as the crowning achievement of Communist policy, to others as its sole consolation. But while the political influence of the campaign was limited, its economic counterpart had more appeal.

It has always been held as an axiom that political frontiers drawn through the middle of a single economic structure must produce fatal results on the life of that economy. This view was held as strongly after the first world war as it is now. The present arguments about the economic consequences of frontiers were foreshadowed almost *verbatim* by Keynes, writing in 1919 about the political division of the tightly-knit economic complexes of Upper Silesia and the Saar.[3] Presumably frontiers between foreign powers should have a still more prohibitive effect than administrative boundaries drawn for the convenience of the occupying powers in Germany. Yet even the sovereign frontiers between victor and vanquished after 1918, separated by all the national prejudices resulting from four years of major war, failed to fulfil Mr. Keynes's expectations. In Upper Silesia 'the living web of

[1] See Ruth Fischer, *op. cit.*, pp. 197–8.

[2] Speeches of Grotewohl and Pieck, August–September 1949. See also their respective collected speeches, *Reden und Aufsätze* (Dietz, Berlin, 1948).

[3] See Keynes, *The Economic Consequences of the Peace* (London, 1919), p. 240 and *passim*, and *A Revision of the Treaty* (London, 1922), pp. 5–12 and 45 *passim*.

modern industry had been cut apart, and yet lived. None of the disasters so freely prophesied had come to pass.'[1] The plea of destruction by division was deafeningly amplified by German propaganda, especially after 1933, and by those who echoed it in this country.[2] Similarly, the modern version was taken up by the Germans in respect of the zonal frontiers, and again found a strong echo in the British and American press. It may therefore be necessary to show that it is no more justified to-day than M. Mantoux showed it to be after the first world war.[3]

No one would attempt to deny the national interdependence of German industry before and during the war. In 1936 the Soviet zone 'exported' 0.9 milliard Rm. worth of food and feeding stuffs to the rest of Germany, and 3.3 milliard Rm. of other commodities. It imported from the rest of Germany 0.5 milliard Rm. of food, etc., and 3.6 milliard Rm. of other commodities. Its total inter-zonal exports were thus 4.2 milliard Rm. against imports of 4.1 milliard Rm., a balanced position with a total turnover of 8.3 milliard Rm. Of this amount 2.7 milliards was confined to the trade between the Soviet zone and the area of the Bizone. Foreign trade by comparison was only 1.8 milliard Rm. Thus interzonal trade represented before the war between 40–45 per cent of gross zonal production value, whereas in the Western zones a proportion of only 20 per cent went into interzonal trade.[4] On the basis of these figures the Soviet zone was more dependent than Western Germany on interzonal economic relations. A more detailed breakdown is given in the table below.[5]

TABLE LV

Interzonal and Foreign Trade, Soviet Zone, 1936
as percentage of total values

	To rest of Germany	*Abroad*	
Soviet zone 'exports'	31%	3%	of value of agricultural production (in 1936)
,, ,, ,, ..	49%	15%	of value of industrial production (in 1936)
,, ,, ,, ..	43%	11%	of total output

[1] Dr. Wambaugh, *Plebiscites Since the World War*, quoted by E. Mantoux, *The Carthaginian Peace*, p. 80.

[2] Lt.-Col. G. S. Hutchison, *Silesia Revisited* (London, 1929).

[3] Mantoux, *The Carthaginian Peace*, does more than provide a refutation of Keynes's book; it explodes the entire German economic case for the revision of the Versailles Treaty. One could wish that its perusal had been compulsory for all Anglo-American administrators in Germany.

[4] *U.N. Bulletin*, 1949, p. 26. [5] *ibid.*, p. 29.

	From rest of Germany	*Abroad*	
Soviet zone 'imports'	19%	11%	of value of consumption of agricultural products
,, ,, ,, ..	55%	6%	of value of consumption of industrial products
,, ,, ,, ..	45%	8%	of value of total consumption

The monthly total turnover of trade between the present Soviet zonal area and that of the Bizone in 1938 appears to be somewhere in the region of 300 to 350 million Rm., or 3½ times that of foreign trade.[1] But the very complexity of German industry makes the isolated calculation of 'pre-war interzonal trade' for any one zone doubly difficult. Without disputing the size of this enormous movement of wealth between one area and another, it must, however, be emphasized that it is erroneous to consider this in the same way as one would consider a volume of trade between two foreign countries. The latter automatically implies a considerable degree of rationalization. Before a manufacturing process is undertaken in another country for goods produced at home there must be strong reasons, such as lack of processing means at home or the great difference in the price or quality of the process between one country and another. This would not have been the case as far as pre-war 'interzonal' relations in Germany were concerned, where factors of relatively small importance might have been sufficient to cause the movement of goods. This is clearly noticeable when the movement of such standard products as wheat and flour is considered. In 1937 the Soviet zone seems to have supplied some 650 thousand tons of wheat and flour to the British zone, while the latter supplied 250 thousand tons to the Soviet zone. At the same time the British zone imported from abroad some 960 thousand tons. There could be no question of the British zone importing wheat and flour from the Soviet zone as a standard commodity, but the movement of these commodities should rather be viewed in the light of the location of flour mills and the facilities of transport.[2]

With the reservation that pre-war movement of commodities between the present zonal areas cannot be viewed in terms of foreign trade, it is possible to produce a list of commodities in which the Soviet zone was then, and still would be at the end of

[1] *Wirtschaftsprobleme*, p. 90; *U.N. Bulletin*, p. 27.

[2] *Wirtschaftsprobleme der Besatzungszonen*, p. 82. While these figures may not be altogether correct, it should be borne in mind that they appear as part of a survey designed to show the size of pre-war interzonal trade as compared to the present dearth and are therefore likely to err on the large rather than the small side.

the war, generally deficient, and which it had obtained, and would obtain, from the Western zones.[1]

TABLE LVI

Commodities normally imported and exported by Soviet Zone

Particular commodities 'exported' by the Soviet zone	*Particular commodities 'imported' by the Soviet zone from the West*
Brown coal	Mechanical rubber products (cushions, etc.)
Grain	Iron and Steel
Artificial rubber (Buna)	Metal
Alcohol	Heavy machinery and spare parts
Sugar	Dye stuffs
Molasses	Vehicles (lorries)
Seeds	Chemicals (chiefly medical)
Optical glass	Tyres and tubes
Starch	Bearings
Potatoes	Livestock, dairy products, meat
Pulp wood	
Potash	
Newsprint	
Tyre cord	
Machinery (textile, printing, etc.)	

If we accept the postulate that the post-war development of economic conditions in the zone was governed as much by the destruction of an economic organization as by the destruction of the actual means of production and sources of raw materials, the question we must now answer is: How much of the development and difficulties of the post-war economy in the Soviet zone were due to effects of the division of Germany into zones for economic organization?

A whole year was needed to organize the distribution of raw materials and the retailing of essential commodities inside the Soviet zone, although the quantities involved were small. The difficulties of a central agency for allocation and distribution would have been correspondingly greater. The system of barter deals flourished internally both in the Eastern and Western zones; if Allied control by zones was unable to prevent such transactions, it is reasonable to assume that the far remoter supervision of one economic directorate in Berlin would have succeeded even less.

In 1945 the disturbed conditions in Germany, the dislocation of Ruhr coal distribution in the British zone, the failure to produce sufficient clothing even for local needs in Saxony, and the general shortage of rolling stock and destruction of permanent way on the railways, show that distribution problems were acute even inside the zones. There was no one to allocate the steel output of the

[1] *Statistical Handbook*, p. 42.

Ruhr, such as it was, in the summer of 1945, yet even the local Ruhr industries, which were among the leading consumers of the local steel production, failed to obtain more than a small percentage of the amount they required. If it was impossible to obtain hard coal in Hamburg, it was not surprising that it was impossible in Saxony. If the leather manufacturers of the French zone received no supplies from the local tanneries, the shoe factories of Schleswig-Holstein or Chemnitz were even less likely to receive supplies. In 1945 no one was in a position to re-establish contact with other parts of Germany; firms with raw material stocks and unimpaired productive capacity continued to produce, those unable to do so closed their factories.

For 1946 it was already possible to illustrate the argument with figures. In 1937 the British zone produced 80 million tons of clean hard coal,[1] of which 34 million tons were exported, 15 million tons went to other zones of Germany, and 31 million tons were consumed in the area of the present British zone. In percentages, 19 per cent was sent to other parts of Germany, and 39 per cent was used by the 'zonal area' itself. In 1946, out of a total production of 38 million tons, 12 million were used for export to countries outside the Eastern bloc, 9 million tons for transfer to other zones, including 6 million to the Soviet zone, and 17 million for British zonal consumption. In percentages this is 32 per cent for export, 24 per cent to other zones, including 16 per cent to the Soviet zone, and 44 per cent for internal consumption. In tabular form the figures are as follows:[2]

TABLE LVII

Production and Export of Coal, British Zone, 1937 and 1946
(in million tons)

	Total production	*Export*	%	*Inter-zonal*	%	*Home consumption*	%
1937	80	34	42	15	19	31	39
1946	38	12	32	9 (6)	24 (16)	17	44

The equivalent table for brown coal briquettes in which the Soviet zone is the main producer:[3]

[1] Excluding consumption by mines as well as residual by-products or coal for coke and briquette production.

[2] These figures from *Wirtschaftsprobleme der Bestazungszonen*, p. 70 *passim*.

[3] Although the actual brown coal production figures for 1946 are roughly the same as those for 1936, the destruction and dismantling of briquette works was heavy and accounts for the drop in brickette production. Export and interzonal trade was frequently in raw brown coal, but has been converted into briquette equivalent for convenience.

TABLE LVIII

Production and Export of Brown coal Briquettes, Soviet Zone, 1937 and 1946 (in million tons)

	Total production Soviet zone	Export	%	Inter-zonal	%	Home con-sumption	%	Repara-tions	%
1937 ..	28	—	—	3	11	25	89	—	—
1946 ..	19	1	5	2	11	9	47	7	37

It is unfortunately very difficult to make similar tables for consumer goods, as comparative tables for pre-war figures are impossible to construct. But without reading too much into the two tables quoted, it becomes clear that in the case of hard coal and brown coal the percentage of interzonal trade increased in one case and remained level in the other. While Soviet zonal consumption of brown coal fell from 89 per cent to 47 per cent of total zonal production, the interzonal trade percentage quoted remained the same. It is no doubt true that the total interzonal trade in consumer goods represented only a fraction of the pre-war movement in these commodities; but, quite apart from the much heavier fall in comparative production, the disappearance of consumer goods into the black market at every stage of production and disposal must be borne in mind, though it is impossible to calculate. It may therefore be assumed that the reduction of production due to reparations, war damage, disorganization, dismantling, and lack of raw materials from abroad played an infinitely greater part than did the effects of zonal barriers. Yet the first semi-official German survey since the war, which used some of the figures quoted above, stated in its summing-up: 'The above explanation of the interdependence of pre-war German economy clearly shows that the division of Germany into a number of economically independent zones must have led to incalculable economic difficulties. If these did not appear in full force for the moment, this was only due to their being fundamentally obscured by the results of the collapse at the end of the war.'[1] At the time of writing, this qualifying phrase about war destruction, anaemic as it is, presumably still needed to be inserted. In a few years' time 'the collapse at the end of the war' will be forgotten and the 'incalculable economic difficulties' arising out of the arbitrary Allied 'division of Germany' will be the cause assigned for Germany's post-war miseries.

[1] *Wirtschaftsprobleme der Besatzungszonen*, p. 89.

The official Russian figures for the interzonal trade of the Soviet zone in 1946 are as follows:

TABLE LIX

Commodity	*Imports*	*Exports*
	(*in 1,000 Rm.*)	
Ores and Minerals	nil	174.3
Metals	20,484.1	166.5
Metal Goods	197.4	427.2
Industrial Equipment and Spare Parts	1,779.4	1,343.1
Small and Consumer Machinery	1,006.8	1,413.9
Vehicles and Spare Parts	1,203.1	89.3
Electrical Equipment	1,439.1	569.1
Fine Mechanical and Optical Equipment	220.8	684.3
Building Materials	360.0	427.8
Glass and Ceramics	93.6	6,029.8
Timber	22.6	1,079.9
Chemicals	10,734.2	5,087.1
Rubber and Asbestos Products	5,421.1	5,083.7
Pulp and Paper	121.7	1,472.5
Textiles	1,738.8	3,381.1
Leather and Leather Products	1,130.8	631.5
Solid and Liquid Fuel	28,288.9	34.75
Fat and Food Products	2,132.0	9,288.6
Agricultural Produce	9,844.2	18,865.3
	85,718.6	90,971.1[1]

The total trade turnover in 1946 between the Soviet zone and the rest of Germany was only about $\frac{1}{15}$ of that existing pre-war (1936). This proportion to pre-war figures might usefully be compared to the reduction in the same year of total production remaining for German use in the Eastern zone to between $\frac{1}{4}$ and $\frac{1}{3}$ of 1936, or $\frac{1}{5}$ of 1938, the reduction of railway rolling-stock throughout Germany to $\frac{1}{2}$–$\frac{2}{3}$ of 1938, of road transport to $\frac{1}{4}$. This trade ratio was in fact altered by the enormous growth of the black market, of 'unregistered' interzonal barter deals, and finally by the depreciated value of the currency, which often made local distribution of products more profitable than participation in a zonal clearing arrangement. Moreover, the disproportion of post-war and pre-war interzonal value of trade was enhanced by the relative reduction since the war in the movement of high-cost finished articles in favour of primary products and semi-processed materials. Taking into account these influences the interzonal figures of almost 86 million Rm. for imports and of 91 million Rm. for exports were relatively high, and were both in fact increased by as much as 50 per cent when private and illegal barter deals are included.

[1] The detailed figures should be treated with reserve.

As we have seen, 1946 was a year of real progress for the Soviet zone. In 1947 the comparative tables of the two commodities, hard coal and brown coal, are as follows:[1]

TABLE LX

British and Soviet Zone Coal Production and Export, 1947
(*in million*)

Total Hard Coal production British Zone	*Export to Soviet Zone*	%	*Export abroad*	%	*Home consumption*	%
48	7	15	11	23	30	62

Total Briquette production Soviet zone	*Export to Bizone*	%	*Export*	%	*Home consumption*	%	*Reparations*	%
17	2	12	3	18	8½[2]	0	3½	20[3]

In 1947, when a very hard winter and the increase of capital reparations deliveries caused a reduction of about 5–10 per cent in the gross value of production in the zone compared to 1946, the interzonal export of briquettes and its equivalent in raw brown coal remained level in quantity and increased slightly in proportion to total output. The improvement of commercial distribution and amelioration of the immediate 'results of the collapse' caused a rise in the volume of interzonal trade, though overall production fell slightly. These increased figures of interzonal trade in 1947 should be viewed against a background of increasing political tension between East and West. Clearly the fall in production could not be due to the influence of zonal frontiers.

The various figures for the total interzonal trade between the East and the Bizone vary considerably according to their German, Anglo-American, or Russian origin. The value of such trade evidently achieved its maximum prior to the blockade during the last months of 1947, and appears then to have reached an average monthly turnover of about 42 million Rms.[4] My own assumption of the total figure for 1947 is in the region of 400 million Rms. Allowing a considerable margin for error the substantial increase over 1946 is still evident. The increase in production in the Bizone during 1947 offset the fall in the East, and German production

[1] Figures from *Wirtschaftsprobleme*, Control Commission Bulletins 1947, and private reports.
[2] Including the SAG.
[3] There is some doubt about the German or Russian sponsorship of much of the quantity exported by the Soviet zone, e.g. to Switzerland, so the reparation figure may be on the large side.
[4] Own estimate.

may be taken as roughly of the same total value in 1946 and in 1947. The almost complete breakdown of transportation in Germany during the first two months of 1947 must be taken into account as an adverse factor. Once more the 'zonal isolation' is not to blame for the failure to increase production in Germany as a whole.

Nevertheless, a significant change in the method of trade inside Germany since the war can be attributed to the zonal system. The rationalization and bulk buying necessitated by zonal division resulted in changes of trade organization. Much of the post-war economic intercourse between East and West took place within the framework of large centrally negotiated transactions or clearing agreements based on monetary ceilings. The latter were usually fixed by production capacity on the one hand, and capacity for absorption of 'import' commodities on the other. Such arrangements were concluded either by the German commercial authorities of the zones, or, particularly between 1946 and 1948, by the Allied economic authorities in Berlin. As political contact between the zones became more remote, and authorized personal travel more difficult, the monopolistic tendency in interzonal commerce increased, to the exclusion of individual firms negotiating directly with their customers or suppliers in the other zone. By spring 1947 interzonal trade was already concentrated in the hands of one single competent authority in the Soviet zone, a department of the Administration for Commerce. From July 1947 onwards this department, together with that for foreign trade, obtained the status of a separate central administration, the Central Administration for Foreign and Interzonal Trade.[1] Permission of the SMA for interzonal transactions was still required. But though this system undoubtedly caused inconvenience and delay to individual firms, particularly in the West, where a corresponding nationalization of factories had not taken place, the volume of interzonal trade was not affected. The main result was that commercial relations between the West and the East increasingly resembled trade between one foreign country and another. Thus the first large-scale trade agreement was negotiated at the end of 1947 to regulate trade in 1948 between Eastern Germany and the Bizone. It was known as the Berlin Agreement, and was negotiated by German authorities under the auspices of the Allied commercial officials. The following exchanges were provided for:

[1] See above, p. 141.

TABLE LXI

Proposed Interzonal Trade under Berlin Agreement for 1948[1]

Commodity	*West to East* (*in million Rm. at 1947 value*)		*East to West*
Agricultural Products	1.7		30.7
Mining Products (except coal)	—		2.6
Lubricants	0.8		0.7
Iron and Steel	42.3		—
Machinery	34.1		14.3
Iron and Steel Construction	0.5		—
Electrical Machinery	3.0		1.5
Optical and Precision Instruments	1.2		1.2
Chemicals	14.7		17.4
Rubber Goods	12.8		4.3
Stones and Earths	1.1		1.1
Glass Goods	0.9		5.0
Forestry Products	—		28.8
Cellulose and Paper	1.3		7.5
Textiles	42.5		41.7
	156.9	+	156.8 = 6% of 1936 turnover

During the first half of 1948 the comparative position of production, foreign trade, and interzonal trade in proportion to 1936 was as follows:

TABLE LXII

Production, Foreign and Interzonal Trade, First Six Months of 1948 (expressed as figures for a year) for Soviet zone and Bizone as percentages of 1936.[2] (*In 1936 value*)

	Agricultural Commodities		*Industrial Commodities*		*All commodities*	
	Bizone	*Soviet zone*	*Bizone*	*Soviet zone*	*Bizone*	*Soviet zone*
Production	67	60	49	63	53	62
Foreign Imports	96	16	40	30	60	22
Foreign Exports	43	68	20	15	20	15
Interzonal Imports	4	14	6	6	6	7
Interzonal Exports	14	4	6	6	7	6

It seems that, while the interzonal trade agreement was being fulfilled, interzonal trade was out of all proportion below foreign trade and production compared to the 1936 level. Some of this was no doubt due to the low levels fixed in the Berlin Agreement, which were supplemented by unofficial barter deals between individuals, but it must again be emphasized that a direct comparison is fallacious since trade between two separately governed

[1] *U.N. Bulletin*, 1949, p. 26.
[2] *U.N. Bulletin*, 1949, p. 43.

areas, even under the most favourable circumstances, will be well below the figure of 'trade' which would have taken place had the two areas been part of a single integrated economy. In spite of this system of interzonal commerce organized on the basis of foreign trade, the factor governing such trade, the relation between two different currencies, did not arise until after the Western currency reform of June 1948. The excess of the value of circulating currency over the value of total production and available goods in Germany before that date prevented the normal financial consequences of an adverse balance of trade between one zone and another. In the glorified barter system of interzonal trade, currency only appeared as a quantitative unit of definition rather than as a means of balancing payments. After the blockade, however, the difference in the currencies circulating in East and West, and the varying rate of exchange, made formal trade agreements as between one country and another the only possible vehicle for large-scale trade.

It may be argued that the mutual economic blockade itself and the events leading up to it, could not have taken place if the zonal arrangement for the occupation of Germany had never been instituted. The only alternative, however, would have been a series of four-power committees in each sphere of government and in each region or town of Germany. Presumably the existing veto arrangement on the quadripartite level in Berlin would have been reproduced on every four-power Committee at every level. Failure to reach agreement would have meant the reference of every problem to the next higher authority. The present difficulties at the top level would have been present at every level all the time. Instead of being divided into four zones Germany would have been split into innumerable independent towns and *Kreise*, a prospect which does not bear contemplation.

When regarded in this light, the evil of zones turns into a qualified blessing. An important part of Germany has, it is true, been delivered into the hands of the Russians. To have foreseen in May 1945 the extent to which the latter would exploit their zone politically and economically would have needed prescience or bad faith on the part of the Western allies. The fact that the present arrangement was agreed upon is a clear refutation of the present Russian accusation that the United States and Great Britain never considered Nazi Germany as the real enemy, but only as a sideshow in the fundamental struggle against Russia and Communism.

Yet the same zonal border which permitted Russian exploitation of their zone prevented similar depredations in the West. It was the reluctant realization of Russia's real intentions which brought the economic closing of the frontier between East and West—by the West. 'In developing the bizonal plan [for a revised level of industry] the over-riding requirement has been to . . . make the area self-supporting',[1] or, as the British spokesman at the Foreign Ministers' conference in London put it in 1947: 'It is intolerable that the millions spent annually on Germany by the United Kingdom should in fact finance . . . Russian reparations.' The first stage in the reaction against Russian policy was the cessation of reparation deliveries from the U.S. zone to Russia in spring 1946; the logical conclusion was the 'blockade' of the Eastern zone in response to the Russian blockade of Berlin. The proof that our counter-blockade of the Soviet zone was not primarily a measure of retaliation is the fact that trade between the Soviet zone and the United Kingdom itself did not cease after 20 July 1948, when the blockade was announced, and from the general refusal of the Western powers to take even the most elementary retaliation for the Berlin blockade in the city itself. The creation of economic zonal barriers was the last resort of the Western powers in response to Russian political and economic policy. They were not the 'natural outcome of a number of economically independent zones.[2]'

While interzonal trade was thus almost at a standstill[3] and all Eastern zone trade with as well as through Western Germany was officially declared at a standstill for lack of transit facilities, both sides computed the others' dependence on interzonal trade, and calculated their probable economic collapse. On the facts the Eastern zone suffered rather more than the West. Here the currency reform and the economic revolution kept attention concentrated on home affairs. The chief items imported from the East, agricultural produce and processed wood, became less vital for the West as Marshall Aid began to take effect and Western Germany began to import from abroad. On the other hand, the need of the markets in the Eastern zone in order to maintain the level of employment did not make itself felt during

[1] *Revised plan for level of industry in the U.K./U.S. zones of Germany*, Berlin, August 1947, p. 1, paragraph (*c*).

[2] *Wirtschaftsprobleme der Besatzungszonen*, p. 90.

[3] It never ceased altogether. In summer 1948 a certain amount of barter deals were concluded in Berlin, and carried out under the nose of the Western authorities by the use of false labels and roundabout routes through Austria and Czechoslovakia. See above, p. 228.

the boom period. In the East, however, there was neither Marshall Aid nor effective currency reform. When imports of iron, steel, and machinery suddenly ceased almost altogether, the production of the Soviet zone was badly hit. In November 1948 the Economic Commission, in an official letter to the Soviet Military Governor, represented that while there was a good chance of obtaining a proportion of the zone's requirements of hard coal from Poland and Czechoslovakia, 'the plan [for 1948] was only capable of fulfilment when steel and iron imports from the West become available. We cannot count on planned capital projects for another twelve to eighteen months at least.'[1] It was very much in the interest of the Soviet zone that the economic embargo from the West should be lifted.

The dependence of the Soviet zone at this time can well be illustrated by the following figures.[2] The zone imported 890,000 tons of hard coal from the West in the first half of 1948, and about 600,000 tons from Poland, against a pre-war half-yearly import (average for the years 1936–1939) of 2,600,000 tons almost entirely from the Western zones and Upper Silesia. These 1948 imports were separate from the Berlin agreement. With regard to steel ingots, however, the zone imported during the first six months of 1948 about 190,000 tons, or about 43 million Rm. worth. This was considerably in excess of the plan for the entire year. But it should be compared with a local production during the whole of 1948 of 215,000 tons, making together 405,000 tons, while the zonal consumption during 1936 was 2,400,000 tons.

The resumption of interzonal trade during 1949 was proclaimed by the signature in late summer 1949 at Frankfurt of the most extensive interzonal trade agreement made since the war. The period to be covered was from October 1949 to June 1950, a total of nine months. Unlike the Berlin agreement, this proposal included West Berlin in the figures for the West German Republic. The items are as follows:[3]

[1] I have seen an alleged transcript of this letter, from which the above quotation is taken. Its accuracy cannot, however, be vouched for.

[2] *U.N. Bulletin*, p. 49.

[3] *U.N. Bulletin*, p. 45. Figures in brackets have been converted, the others are given in the agreement.

TABLE LXIII

Proposed Interzonal Trade under Frankfurt Agreement from October 1949 to June 1950

Commodity	*West to East*	*East to West*
	(*in million D. Mark*)	
Agricultural Products	(7.2)	(61.2)
Mining Products (excluding Coal)	1.5	(7.1)
Liquid Fuels and Lubricants	.6	22.5
Iron and Steel	(76.4)	—
N.F. Metals	10.0	—
Steel and Metal Goods	3.0	2.0
Machinery, Vehicles, Iron and Steel Construction	75.0	29.0
Ships	1.2	—
Electrical Machinery and Appliances	24.0	5.0
Optical and Precision Instruments	2.5	4.5
Chemicals	30.0	21.0
Rubber Goods	16.5	1.5
Stones and Earths	4.0	6.5
Glass, Glass Goods, Ceramics	1.0	10.0
Forestry Products	—	(26.5)
Paper and Pulp	2.0	(5.5)
Textiles	20.0	80.0
	(280.3)	(282.3)

This plan thus provided for more than twice the annual volume of trade envisaged in the Berlin agreement, or 10–11 per cent of 1936, a figure which is perhaps nearly half of the optimum amount of trade between the two republics under separate administrations and with different currencies. Nor was the trade between the two republics confined to the agreement; both coal and potash deliveries were handled outside of it. Even before the operation of the agreement, in August 1949, interzonal trade was reputed to have been 25 per cent higher than during an average month in the first half of 1948.[1] Thus it is clear that the political hostility between East and West, the constant vituperation of the SED against Western Germany, and the open and the underhand campaigns for German unity at the expense of the Bonn government, did not prevent the achievement of a level of trade between the two republics higher than at any time since 1945. The political frontier marking the iron curtain cannot be blamed indiscriminately for the previous small volume of trade and its effects in both areas, and we must look to the more local causes, such as dismantling, disorganization, and reparations, for part of the reason for the slowness of East German economic recovery.

[1] U.N. Bulletin, p. 50.

With this return to organized trading, there was a tendency in 1950 for the Soviet zone to change the pattern of its trade in the direction of that existing before the war. Thus the staple export products of the immediate post-war period, wood, grains, sugar, and potash, were now being exported in a smaller proportion to manufactured articles. The abnormal deforestation, both for reparations and export, was slowly decreasing, and a larger proportion of the other raw materials remained for home consumption. On the other hand, exports of textiles at the beginning of 1950 were reputedly ten times as large as during the corresponding period of 1948. The link between the Western combing and spinning capacity and the weaving capacity of the East seems to have been re-established, though the semi-processed textiles are woven and finished largely on commission instead of being purchased outright as before the war. Thus, on the one hand, trade for the Eastern zone was once more beginning to follow its normal pattern, and to fulfil its function of maximizing real national income instead of providing a frequently uneconomic means of just keeping alive.

Moreover, by 1950 the relationship of one zone to another had also tended to change. Much as the Eastern republic needed to import certain commodities from the West, the latter increasingly needed to export to the East as a means of keeping up profits and employment. The financial policy of the Bonn government made Western Germany very dependent on exports as a means of preventing even greater unemployment; the effective demand of the domestic market, in view of the deflationary policy of the Western government, was bound to decrease sharply. Hence the conflict between the High Commission and the representatives of West German industry over the question of suspending deliveries to the East German republic under the Frankfurt agreement until the latter had caught up with their obligations. The Eastern zone, in spite of claims by its government that it would fulfil the two year plan in eighteen months, found it difficult to deliver punctually. Western Germany, however, required to export against currency more urgently than it needed to import from the East. The allied demand, that the balance of payments in kind should be evened out before the resumption of deliveries to the East, thus affected German manufacturers adversely. There was strong pressure on the West German government to resume trade, if necessary on terms easy for the Eastern zone.

This situation leads to the suspicion that the East German

republic's failure to fulfil its obligation on time may have been due to policy as much as inability. The suspension of trade, though affecting the economy of Eastern Germany to a considerable extent, appeared as an obvious means of bringing nearer the Marxist prediction of economic crisis in the West. Judging from the outcry there, and the American statement that ERP aid to Germany had been rapidly frittered away, this crisis must have appeared to be just round the corner, and the chance of helping it along may have seemed very tempting. The suspicion of Communist motives was increased by their declared intention to wreck Marshall Aid everywhere, and by the tempting bait held out from Berlin of the possibilities of increased trade which would result from the unity campaign. This propaganda was not unsuccessful. In fact, the economic arguments, reinforced by American rebukes and threats of reduced aid, may have played a more important part than the political arguments advanced in favour of a strong and united Germany, particularly as the former were more tangible. Thus it is possible to interpret the economic policy of the East German government in 1950 as one of full support for the unity campaign, even at the expense of the Soviet zone's economy and particularly of the consumer. Such a policy was likely to be all the more successful if some of the vital imports from the West could be replaced from the East European countries, and if the East German republic, whose economic crisis was over, could safely wait for the crisis in the West, which was yet to come.

But the effect of the zonal system, followed by the division between West and East, if it did not cause the economic effects often assigned to it, did certainly make for a significant change in the industrial pattern of Germany. In the first place there was a considerable flight of capital from East to West. Some of this was in the shape of goods and machinery smuggled across between 1946 and 1948. But the greatest part was indirect; the Soviet measures of expropriation caused a constant flow to the West of patented designs, plans, and technical skill.[1] To some extent, therefore, the East was in 1950 less well equipped in the race for expansion of industrial production.

In the second place, political exigencies produced a tendency towards increased regional self-sufficiency. Post-war capital development was directed towards the replacement, through domestic production, of essential goods previously obtained from other parts of Germany. This was particularly true of Western

[1] See Löwenthal, *op. cit.*; also *U. N. Bulletin*.

Germany,[1] but the two year plan in the East foreshadowed similar patterns, particularly as regards steel. Up to 1950 capital expansion in the East was fairly small, and the progress towards autonomy limited. In any case, the accident of natural deposits of hard coal and iron ore could not be overcome by planned development. Nevertheless a beginning was made with textiles, steel production' and shipbuilding. This tendency added additional momentum to the division of Germany: 'it is easier to break up an economic union than to create one',[2] and new, expensively nurtured interests, particularly when they are governmental projects as in the East, may become vested interests in need of protection. Finally, according to the theory of international trade, such a development is the direct opposite of the policy which seeks to maximize national income by maximizing trade. All this, however, was the result of the political encroachment on economic possibilities of maximum interzonal trade, which were not *a priori* impaired by the mere existence of zones or regions.

[1] For instance, the expansion of the electrical industry in 1948–9, though this was largely at the expense of Berlin, and the development of printing.
[2] *U.N. Bulletin*, p. 52.

CHAPTER X

THE SOVIET ZONE AND THE EASTERN BLOC

RUSSIAN policy with regard to Western Germany can be summarized as an attempt to reconcile political hostility with economic intercourse, and to obtain the advantages of political warfare and economic exploitation at the same time. Was it the ultimate object of Russian policy to bring Eastern Germany into a new political and economic orbit, that of Communist controlled Eastern Europe, after prising it loose from its old political ties? Before discussing this problem two general observations must be made. First, if this was the ultimate object of Russian policy, it did not necessarily conflict with the Communist interpretation of German unity. If unity were achieved on Russian terms, the remarks we are about to make, instead of applying only to the Soviet zone, would apply to all parts of Germany under Communist control. The relations of the Soviet zone with Eastern Europe would become the relations of the whole of Germany with Eastern Europe. Secondly, integration into the Eastern bloc and direct exploitation by Russia for her own purposes were not the same thing. In the long run all the countries in the Russian controlled bloc of Eastern Europe, including Eastern Germany, may well be considered as pawns in the Soviet game of power politics. But while the other Eastern European countries were by 1950 no more than individual political and economic entities of similar construction fulfilling their alloted rôles in the Soviet plan, the Eastern zone had been until recently conquered territory and exploited as such by the victor. A comparison with occupied and unoccupied France in 1941 illustrates the point. Direct exploitation of occupied France made it more difficult for Germany to evolve a constructive policy towards France as a whole. The greater the direct exploitation, the smaller the value of a single France as an economic and political power. In the same way the large-scale exploitation of the Soviet zone proportionately reduced its value as a unit of the Eastern bloc, though both were organized to further Soviet interests. Just as the German military occupation of part of France tended to strain relations between Vichy and Paris, so the relations between the German Communists in Berlin and the governments of Warsaw, Prague, and Budapest never achieved more than the appearance of concord, in spite of the common Communist denominator. The importance of direct Soviet interests in Eastern Germany must be borne in mind as a factor militating against any policy attempting to integrate the Russian zone with the Eastern bloc.

Immediately after the war the social, political, and economic barriers between Germany and her Eastern neighbours were impassable. In the countries of Eastern Europe the predominant feeling at the end of the war was hatred of Germany and all things German. The transfer of German minority populations was a high priority for the governments and the concrete expression of the violent feelings of the population. The universal hatred of Germany had been a Communist mainstay. The beat of the anti-German drum provided the keynote of post-war Communist policy in Eastern Germany, and it is significant that in spite of the gradual Russian attempt to substitute Nazi for German no such distinction was made in any of the Eastern countries. German Jews and even Communists were treated not very differently from their Nazi fellow-nationals by Czechs and Poles.

This anti-German campaign in Eastern Europe was the corollary of the Communist anti-Nazi campaign in Germany itself, and the fact that one policy contradicted the other deterred neither the Communists of Germany nor those of Eastern Europe from pursuing them. The countries of Eastern Europe showed little inclination to accept post-war Germany as a friend, whatever its political complexion. This mattered little enough at first, since the political and economic life of Germany in the first twelve months after the war was still so chaotic that the necessity for an arrangement with her neighbours did not arise. The Russians were quite content to carry out their early policy in Germany without doing anything to counter the continuous anti-German propaganda in Eastern Europe. It was at that time worth far more to enlist Polish good will by a guarantee of her new Western frontier than to appease the wounded feelings of the defeated Germans. It is very doubtful whether anything could have stopped the spontaneous popular expression of hatred against the German aggressor in Eastern Europe, and anyone bold enough to try would have been swept aside. Common sense demanded that the Communist resistance leaders adopt Ledru-Rollin's dictum: 'I am their leader, I have to follow them.'

Economic relations between the Eastern zone and Eastern Europe did not exist until the middle of 1946, and what previous contact there was cannot be expressed in terms of figures. The one-sided movement of industrial wealth in the shape of reparations cannot be counted as a factor in economic relations, since the amount was fixed arbitrarily by the victor nations. Apart from reparations, economic contact immediately after the war was confined to the activities of a few individual pioneers carrying out small-scale transactions. The fact that economically valuable Germans were frequently retained in Eastern Europe, while their less valuable compatriots were expelled with all haste and ignominy, should be mentioned here. These Germans varied from high-ranking Nazi economists like Neubacher, former city governor of Vienna, who is believed to have been retained by the government of Yugoslavia,[1] to insignificant weavers and technicians in Czech textile works, running the factories as shadows for the new 'national trustees'. The total of this retained labour may be small, but its existence illustrates the attitude of Eastern Europe towards Germany: contemptuous isolation coupled with the desire to exploit the value of the Germans *gratis*. Nor was this attitude confined to the Eastern powers.

The military missions of such of the Eastern countries as had not been Germany's allies during the war played a peculiar rôle in the first three years after the war. One of their functions was to assist the Russians in their exploitation of Germany. Since these missions were attached to the Allied Control Authority, and thus had rights of access into all four zones, or at least to representatives in each zone, the Russians used them for tasks which they were unable to carry out themselves. These tasks ranged from the location of wanted individuals to the negotiation of black-market deals. The evidence available, which is naturally limited, shows the Yugoslavs to have been the most active. But these activities were not confined to aiding the Russians. The search for individuals wanted by particular countries, either war criminals or particular scientists and technicians, was carried out by all these missions. In addition they negotiated official deals with German firms, and supplemented them with unofficial deals in materials not normally available for export. In the long run such activities could not prove a satisfactory means of re-establishing political and trade relations between Eastern Europe and Germany, and in 1948, as regular trade increased and political relations first became stabilized, these missions were gradually dissolved.

The production of German industry as a whole was essential

[1] In the same capacity of adviser on Balkan economic affairs; he was pronounced dead when his presence was demanded by the IMT, but there is good evidence to believe that he was alive and working in Belgrade.

for Eastern Europe, however much the latter's official attitude seemed to deny it. Once it was clear that even reparation demands must be limited, and that the fulfilment of Russian claims would not bring economic advantage to her satellites, trade agreements with Germany were the only alternative. Before Germany could become a satisfactory trading partner, investment in German industrial production on a vast scale, and on a long-term basis, was needed. For the moment Germany was incapable of fulfilling her traditional rôle of industrial supplier to the predominantly agrarian countries of Eastern and South Eastern Europe. The hoped-for era of living free on Germany's wealth proved a pipe-dream, and her utter poverty and long-term reparation obligations prevented the countries of Eastern Europe from obtaining their own terms almost as effectually as had German economic predominance before the war. For one country to achieve mutually favourable economic relations with another, the latter must be neither too strong nor too weak, neither too rich nor too poor, for in the case of either extreme considerations of advantage may become one-sided. The credit basis which would have been the only possibility for establishing long-term economic relations with the Germany of 1946 was not a programme which the governments of Eastern Europe would or could follow eighteen months after the end of the war. Even if they had succeeded in overcoming national public opinion, they would soon have discovered, together with the Western powers, that their credits to Germany were largely financing Soviet reparations.

Until 1947 the governments of Eastern Europe had one policy towards Germany, and made no distinction between one zone and another. The influence of Russian reparation exactions was felt throughout Germany and made all four zones proportionately less valuable partners for bilateral trade agreements. The Germans needed the goods of the rest of Europe but were generally unable to supply the demands, irrespective of their Communist, bourgeois, or reactionary politics. The only creature more disliked in Eastern Europe than a German was a German who had nothing to offer but much to ask.

With the foundation of the SED as the dominating instrument of Russian political policy the relations of Germany with the Eastern bloc underwent significant changes. The emergence of a Communist Eastern zone was bound to necessitate a distinction between it and the rest of Germany as far as her Eastern neighbours were concerned. No one could doubt Soviet influence behind the recent events, and henceforth any expression of doubt regarding the democratic or peaceful nature of Germany's future development would have to be confined to those parts not under Russian domination. The solution was obvious, and the Soviet occupation authorities gave the Russian satellites in the East a clear lead. It became the task of the Communist controlled governments to direct the anti-German feelings of their populations against Western Germany, and to accept developments in the Soviet zone as a genuine democratic evolution. The *volte-face* required was considerable, and it is a significant comment on the strength of the hatred against Germany in the Eastern European countries that it did not succeed altogether.

A typical example of what was required was provided by Molotov at the peace conferences in Moscow, Paris, and London. The most loyal support was obtained from the Poles, who occasionally acted on behalf of the Russians in sending a series of regular protests to London and Washington against alleged rearmament of Western Germany. The Russian answer to the three-power conferences on Western Germany took place on Polish soil in the Warsaw conference and resolutions of June 1948. The series of defence pacts between the countries of the Eastern bloc against a renewal of German aggression was not the mere flummery which it seemed at the time, but fitted into the pattern as the means of bringing all the countries concerned into line with the new policy of differentiation between Western and Eastern Germany. Such a pact would have been unthinkable at a time when the Russians still appeared to have a stake in the four-power administration of Germany. Finally, the bogey of Western German aggression backed by America and England played an important part in the justification at home of the Communist coup in Czechoslovakia in March 1948.

The joint Eastern policy towards Germany which emerged at this time is one more proof that during the early part of 1947 the Soviet government made a vital decision with regard to their own future conduct, not only in Germany, but throughout the world. The formation of the SED a year earlier had been the curtain-raiser in Germany. Anti-German propaganda in the Polish and Czechoslovakian press tended to focus on up-to-date events in the Western zones, instead of reminiscences of German brutalities during the war. The French Communist press began to denounce the Western policy towards Germany and to warn against French acquiescence in a settlement on the terms desired by the Anglo-

American authorities. But while there was little difficulty in carrying public opinion in any campaign against Germany, it was far more difficult to establish the nice distinction between the Eastern and Western zones. As a result, the ironic contradiction of the Russian Foreign Minister preaching German unity in Paris, while the French Communist leaders were advocating the economic disintegration of Germany, was thrown into sharp relief. The fact that Molotov and Thorez were offering the world the two alternatives arising out of a single policy was hidden by the blatant paradox.

What were the political and economic results arising from this new relationship between the Soviet zone and its Eastern neighbours? The feelings of popular opinion in Eastern Europe towards the new policy have little practical importance for us, since popular opinion found difficulty in expressing dissatisfaction with the policy of its governments. Evidence of popular sympathy with a complete reversal of policy could be manufactured.[1] Even so, it is doubtful whether a political rapprochement to Eastern Germany was really the object of the Eastern European governments. During 1947 there was a patchy sequence of good will missions, lecture tours, and exchange visits between politicians and a few men of letters—but little evidence of genuine political friendship. The real object seems to have been economic. Since Germany had so little to offer, self-interest was not enough to persuade Czechs and Poles to enter into close economic relations with the Soviet zone. The attraction of the zone was declining as Soviet reparation demands increased. In Czechoslovakia, where a democratic government still existed, political reasons were added to economic reservations with regard to co-operation with Germany. As yet the Russians were not prepared to order such economic intercourse against the will of the satellite governments, or to provide the machinery of supervising its execution in the teeth of hostile governments and population. They contented themselves with the expectation that the new policy of giving political support to German Communists in public would bring in its train increasing economic collaboration between Soviet Germany and the Soviet satellites.

[1] The most blatant example of pretence is the evidence for Slovak joy at the Czech-Hungarian treaty of 1948, which, it was claimed, removed outstanding differences and past grievances. Dr. Clementis, the Slovak foreign minister of Czechoslovakia, who signed and eulogized the treaty, had frequently gone out of his way to express the fury of himself and his countrymen at Hungarian treatment of Czechoslovakia in 1939 and during the war.

There were three main channels of trade, trade agreements, competitive export, and individual barter deals. From the beginning of 1947 a series of trade agreements was concluded between the Soviet zone and the countries of Eastern Europe.[1] Very little is known of the details, and even their total monetary value was not made public. The principles were simple enough. Much of the German contribution was labour or manufacturing value only, the customer supplying raw materials and receiving the manufactured article after completion. Payment for the work was made either in currency or preferably in a proportion of the commission material. In yarn as much as 45 per cent of the total value of the yarn to be turned into cloth is known to have been paid. Machinery and textiles were the chief items of this trade. The excess spinning and weaving capacity of Saxony was thus employed in making cloth from imported tops and noils. Since the Czechs and Poles themselves have a considerable textile industry, this particular arrangement, as far as they were concerned was not likely to be a long-term factor. Instead, attempts were made to arrange such commission work with Western countries such as England or Switzerland. Commission work on a large scale is unsatisfactory for an economy such as that of Eastern Germany. The shortage of basic raw materials such as hard coal, steel, pig and sheet iron, chemicals, etc., was acute in all the Eastern countries as well as Germany, and for the processing of other materials such as wool, cotton, and leather some of the Eastern countries possess native industries capable of consuming all the supply of raw material available, which their foreign exchange holdings enable them to purchase. Russian bulk imports for herself and her satellites left only very insignificant quantities for manufacturing or export on German account, once the SAG and reparation firms had been supplied. The integration of the Soviet zone into the Eastern bloc had certainly not gone far enough for her to obtain a share in the yield from the occasionally transferable sterling or dollar holdings of the Eastern countries. Great efforts were made to increase the production of three staples for export to the Eastern countries. These were wood, sugar, and potash, of which the two former had only become bulk exports since the war. Wood particularly was not a desirable export commodity for Germany, whose re-afforestation had been neglected. Before the war pit-props were exported to

[1] Agreements had previously been concluded with Austria, Belgium, Holland, and Switzerland in 1947, and with Sweden in 1948. Temporary arrangements existed with Italy and Norway. But these are not strictly relevant to the subject here.

Poland and to a lesser extent to Czechoslovakia and Yugoslavia. Now pulp wood and hard wood for consumer goods were included in the export programme, which, while satisfying the demands of Eastern Europe unable to purchase from hard currency countries like Sweden, left the Eastern zone itself heavily depleted. The Soviet zone was relatively well provided with sugar, containing Germany's second biggest sugar beet area round Magdeburg, as well as a considerable processing industry. But export of this commodity meant privation at home, for sugar had been issued since 1946 to meet current shortages of fats and meat on the ration, and had become one of the mainstays of the population's food. Moreover, both Poland and Czechoslovakia were nearly self-supporting in sugar before the war, and the new areas of Western Poland made the self-sufficiency complete. Potash was an important factor in trade with Eastern Europe, but the zone's European predominance made potash a vital earner of hard currency in the trade agreements with Switzerland and Sweden, and almost 70 per cent of the total post-war export from the Soviet zone went either to Western Germany or to other countries outside Eastern Europe.

There were naturally other commodities which figured in the trade of Eastern zone with Eastern Europe. Buna (artificial rubber) production was greatly increased by the German government during the war, and the surplus, now that war requirements no longer existed, was available for export to Poland and South Eastern Europe. Since the beginning of 1948, this demand for Buna has declined, chiefly owing to Russian bulk buying of natural rubber in Malaya. As a result, the main Buna works, the SAG at Schkopau, have been partially dismantled. Brown coal also figured increasingly on the export list since the beginning of 1947. Switzerland and Sweden received most of the coal exported by the Soviet zone. The quantities involved during 1947 seemed relatively small compared to the total output, even after dismantling and reparations were accounted for. But the substitution of brown coal for almost all normal hard coal consumption inside the zone made the zonal production insufficient even for essential home demands. Scrap metal, in so far as it was not sold on Russian account, was used for hard currency export rather than for supply to the countries of Eastern Europe. Finally, pre-war and wartime stocks of manufactured goods were a preferred hard currency export to Western Europe.

The evidence of the Leipzig Fair, which restarted its bi-annual existence in September 1946, bore out these general principles.

The lack of a proper schedule of export prices, and the indefinite delivery terms for offered lots, the preponderance of goods for display over those for sale, showed the difficulties of the Eastern zone in the competitive export market. There were very few buyers from Eastern Europe at the fair, while most of the purchases were destined for hard currency countries in Western Europe. In fact the representatives of the Eastern European countries used the Leipzig Fair not to buy, but to sell their own export commodities. In 1947 Baťa and Škoda were both represented, and the Czech and Polish Information Bureaux at the Fair existed to give information of their own products rather than to help potential customers for German goods. Some products of Eastern European origin were actually sold by firms pretending to be German. There remained individual barter deals in particular commodities. These were almost invariably arrangements of momentary convenience and often brought strange commodities into one transaction. Nails from Czechoslovakia were obtained by a German tool-making firm in exchange for tool casings, bicycles by a municipal corporation in Saxony in exchange for stockings. The need to rely to an increasing extent on such deals inevitably made the process more complicated; up to twelve firms have been known to be associated in a chain of barter transactions before the two original parties could obtain the commodities required. The principle of chain-barter deals has also appeared in official trade agreements. Hungary, Czechoslovakia, and the zone have concluded at least two such three-cornered agreements.[1] Although such deals were forbidden between German and German, economic necessity made them legal with other countries, and public companies as well as the Import-Export Agency engaged in them. In the absence of economic flexibility the barter principle supplied the missing lubricant and helped to fulfil the rigid production plans. A temporary surplus of precision cutters was exchanged by the Thuringian Tool Production Union (*Werkzeugunion Schmalkalden*) for a delivery of hand pliers from Czechoslovakia, and thus the firm's plus and minus balance in relation to the production plan was evened out. The flow of commodities in the Soviet zone accounted for trade as well as for movements of capital in a normal economy.

A study of all these economic activities leaves an impression of improvization, of makeshift contact instead of permanent ties.

[1] The Russians on their own account have also traded in this way. Not infrequently they have insisted on payment for reparation goods by instructing the customer-country to purchase specified commodities from a specified third party, occasionally even at specified prices.

The Communist answer was that co-operation between the new democracies was bound to be slow after overcoming inbred nationalist suspicions and the evil legacy of capitalist systems. Up to the middle of 1948, Eastern Germany had not attained the status of a partner in any Eastern European co-operative block, if there is such a thing. The Soviet zone was treated partly as an underling, partly as a poor relation. This attitude was not expressed openly by the governments of Eastern Europe. But the reception given to Pieck and Grotewohl on their begging tour in Warsaw, Prague, and Budapest in the summer of 1948 was sufficiently chilly to cause not only very pointed comments in the Press of Western Germany, but an unusually apologetic tone in that of the SED. The expected announcement of the triumphant readmission of the 'democratic' half of Germany into the civilized part of Europe, degenerated into carefully-guarded phrases about closer economic ties. As one of the Vice-Chairmen of the Economic Commission put it: 'We hope now [as the result of the trip] to receive from Poland almost half the hard coal necessary to guarantee a reasonable ration to private consumers during the winter of 1949–50. We have already received 25 per cent of this amount.' In view of the low priority of private-consumer needs, and the extraordinary vagueness of the statement itself, no one was really much the wiser about the actual import of coal from Poland. A statement of success would have sounded very different. On the German side and on that of the SMA, it was realized that any trade which would go some way to restoring the productive capacity and the standard of life of the zone must primarily be with hard currency countries and with Western Germany.

The period of trade preference with the West necessarily came to an end at the time of the blockade. In spite of the relative failure of Pieck and Grotewohl's journey, strenuous efforts were made to renew trade with Eastern Europe. The trade agreements with Poland and Yugoslavia were extended, while imports of Czech metal products and coal were somewhat increased. No exact figures are available, but it appears that some of these agreements were on a credit basis against return deliveries during 1949. Some of the quantities involved were commission work, though the chief items were machinery production from supplied metal instead of textiles. It appears that for a time trade with Yugoslavia showed the biggest turnover of all. To what extent the Russo-Yugoslav conflict cut down trade relations between the latter country and the Soviet zone is not clear, but there is no evidence to show that commercial relations were broken off altogether. To this extent the zone may have profited from the fact that it was not a fully-fledged member of the Cominform. From the Yugoslav side the trade was certainly encouraged. Nevertheless, as has been indicated earlier, a revival of the zonal production from its depressed level depended on the resumption of trade with the West.

Thus, from the available evidence, it seems that there was no question of an economic alignment exclusively towards the East. All Eastern European countries profess their desire for trade relations with Western Europe and the United States, but their economies are closely linked to the Eastern bloc; they are dependent on Russian assistance in the form of gold loans and loans of raw materials.[1] The Germans, however, received only small quantities of raw material and certainly no gold. Instead, they have supplied reparations to Russia compared to which the Soviet exactions from other countries, even Finland,[2] are insignificant. Consequently Eastern Germany's trade relations were largely with non-Communist Europe; quite apart from the traditional Western connection, Eastern Europe at first found little advantage in trading with the Soviet zone, and the Soviet zone could only obtain its essential supplies and its hard currencies from the West. The SMA did little to force integration in Eastern Europe; instead they encouraged trade with the West. It may well be that if Germany as a whole were to come under Communist control this situation would change, as Germany would then be in a position to fill the gaps in the economy of Eastern Europe. Since the Eastern zone, even in 1950, had to import most of the raw materials of which she could export the finished product to Eastern European countries, she only filled the rôle of a middleman. It was therefore apparently the policy of the Russians to defer integration of the German and Eastern European economies until Germany could supply the coal, steel, iron, and machinery directly. For a long time the Eastern zone alone would be unable to do this.

Politically, relations had by 1950 improved. Indeed, some of the trade between Eastern Germany and its neighbours took on a purely political character. The People's Police in Germany was supplied with a large proportion of Czech small-arms and some from Manfred Weiss in Hungary. Some of the printing of Com-

[1] The Czechs seem to have been the chief beneficiaries, particularly with regard to gold.

[2] For some details of Finnish reparations, see *Quarterly Review of Trade Conditions in Finland*, No. 3, August 1948, pp. 63–70.

munist literature in Eastern Europe was done in Germany. Even the frontier control was relaxed in special cases. For instance, by the end of 1948 the Soviet uranium project, instead of being divided into two parts on either side of the Czech-German border, was controlled by a single headquarters in Czechoslovakia, and for this purpose frontier regulations were relaxed, so that German labour frequently worked inside Czechoslovakia. The formation of the East German republic gave Germany a status comparable to that of the people's democracies. The establishment of direct quasi-diplomatic relations between the East German republic and the countries of Eastern Europe enabled the German government to be at any rate consulted in formulation of Cominform policy, and in decisions affecting Eastern Europe as a whole. For the first nine months after its formulation the East German government signed only trade agreements. In the spring of 1950, the moderates of the SED, whose spokesman was Grotewohl, advocated consolidation—perhaps of 'Socialism in one country'—by the conclusion of a peace treaty between the U.S.S.R. and Eastern Germany. This demand was overruled by Ulbricht and the militants, who demanded all-out priority for the National Front and the campaign against the West German republic. Traces of the dispute could be seen in the official press and in public speeches. In July 1950 the East German republic formally emerged from the diplomatic dog-house and signed its first political treaties with Poland, Czechoslovakia, and Hungary. The permanent renunciation on the part of Germany of the Polish-occupied areas and the Sudetenland was confirmed in return for increased political co-operation against the Western occupation of Germany and for increased trade—meaning greater approximation to equality of status for Eastern Germany. As they stood, the treaties, except for the economic provisions, were of little practical importance. Eastern European support for the struggle of the German national front was anyhow assured, and as regards the territorial renunciation, this was sharply repudiated by the Bonn government. Therefore the treaties were more a declaration of policy for the future when all Germany would be under Russian control, a policy ensuring Germany's place among Soviet satellites. Only acceptance of the territorial *status quo* could do that, and only the Grotewohl-Ulbricht government has accepted it. In doing so the Unity party made a *volte-face* from the days when it was still expected to obtain independent political support in the Eastern zone. On 14 September 1946 *Neues Deutschland*, the official organ of the party, had said: 'On the Eastern frontier question the SED . . . will oppose any loss of German territory. The . . . frontier is provisional and can be fixed only at the Peace Conference with the help of all the victorious Powers.'

Personal relations between Eastern Europe and Eastern Germany also improved after October 1949. Germans appeared as observers at meetings of the Cominform, and kept a permanent representative at Cominform headquarters. A few tame German Communists attended the Wroclaw Congress of Intellectuals in 1948. Reciprocally, privileged visitors from Eastern Europe visited the Soviet Zone. Communist meetings were attended by foreign delegations and the SED frequently entertained political visitors, lecturers, and advisers from other Communist countries. The first big international meeting in Germany of Communist youth took place over Whitsun 1950 in Berlin, and though it proved a damp squib this example of German rehabilitation was to be marked by mass demonstrations against the Western powers in Berlin. Though still more directly controlled by Russia than the people's democracies of Eastern Europe, the Soviet zone government had won its spurs as a Communist state; regarded by its Eastern neighbours as a junior partner rather than a recently defeated enemy, and treated in July 1950 as a slightly more senior partner than was its Western brother in the competitor's firm.

CHAPTER XI

CONCLUSIONS

I

THEORY AND PRACTICE

BEFORE the nineteenth century it was an accepted maxim in England that it was not the task of government to propose legislation until such time as the facts of the situation or the demands of public opinion clearly made it necessary. While the speech from the throne at the opening of a parliamentary session announced the broad policy of government, no detailed legislative plans were ever prepared beforehand. In the stormy constitutional period of the sixeenth and seventeenth centuries, it had sometimes been the practice to prepare legislation before, and this occasionally determined the choice of the King's Ministers. But even in those days, and particularly after the Hanoverian succession in 1714, the English genius for improvized and *ad hoc* legislation to meet a given situation, or to supplement custom and common law by statute, had repudiated any attempt to put a speculative political theory, however sound it seemed, into practice. English political thought, from Hooker and Hobbes to Green and J. S. Mill, was always empirical, and rarely found its way into the programme of legislators and politicians except as a vague background. Such legislation as the Constitution of the U.S., or that of the Constituent Assembly in the France of 1789, or the Frankfurt parliament of 1848, are unknown in England.

In the last seventy-five years this aversion to long-prepared legislation has partly disappeared, and political parties now fight elections on a detailed programme, but the British dislike and distrust of governmental theory still remains. With it goes an even stronger distrust of the theorists in question: those who would subordinate facts and men to a theory which they believe to be the final panacea of all the political ills of mankind. Political theory is little studied outside the universities and small groups of earnest seekers. For these reasons the greater part of public opinion in England disliked and ridiculed National Socialism, and now dislikes and ridicules Communism.

Since the disintegration of the Western spiritual Empire of the

Catholic church, no theory of government has claimed such universality, such unfailing obedience from its followers, and such infallibility for its dogma, as Communism. It purports to be entirely self-sufficient. Since 1917 Communist governments have used only their theory to justify their action, and have confined their action to the demands of their theory. At any rate until 1945.

The post-war outlook for Communism was bright. In the democracies of Western Europe there was bound to come a period of economic distress which could be used as an illustration of the Communist thesis that capitalism in those highly developed political and economic societies was approaching a collapse. The Communist parties in those countries were in a strong position as champions of the fight against National Socialism and, in the countries occupied by Germany, as the chief martyrs of the occupation. In Eastern Europe the most important factor was the presence of the Russians themselves, a fact which gave incalculable support to the Communist parties there. Their size was more than offset by the moral and physical support of the Soviet armies. In the countries bordering on Russian-occupied Eastern Europe the proximity of the Russians was almost as effective a weapon as their actual presence; the Communists in Czechoslovakia and Finland could point to the need of placating the great and powerful neighbour by giving them a considerable share in the control of the State. The Communist aim in Europe was twofold: to obtain popular support for their programme, and to come within the Russian orbit. The method of gaining popular support within the framework of a democratic constitution was used in the Western democracies where direct Russian interference was impossible, and, if necessary, included strikes and armed *coups-de-main*. In Eastern Europe, on the other hand, the Russian occupation or the threat of it imposed Communism from above by placing in power Communist parties small in number. There the effort to obtain popular support could wait until the Communists had firm control of all governmental posts.

Differences of strategy produced differences in the application of Marxist theory. In the East where the Communists could do what they liked, they could enforce their interpretation of Marx arbitrarily. Anti-Fascism was useful but not essential. In Rumania and Bulgaria, for instance, the 'elimination of Fascist elements' was soon dropped in favour of the institution of undisguised Communism. In the West, the need for obtaining popular support necessitated the use of time-honoured methods to gain the votes of the electorate. Local political factors, prejudices, and desires were exploited. The anti-German factor was used with great effect; while the exploitation of the antipathy of part of the Italian and French population to Catholic 'clericalism' may be mentioned.

In Germany the situation called for the use of both methods. Russian occupation was an established fact; an occupation, moreover, sanctioned by international agreement and undisguised. Nowhere outside Soviet Russia, except for the Soviet zone of Korea, had the Russians such vast legal powers as in the Eastern zone of Germany. The theoretical possibilities were also highly favourable for Communism. The collapse of Nazi Germany provided an almost perfect example of the collapse of capitalist society in its final monopolistic form from sheer inability to cope with its task. This, according to Marx, was an historic inevitability, and provided the necessary situation for the institution of Socialism. Though Marx did not envisage an external war between capitalist and socialist powers, the Stalinist principle of Socialism in one country implies that the death blow to capitalism in one state may be given by Socialism in another. Lenin, Trotsky, and finally Stalin, had brought Marxism up to date by assigning to Communist Russia the rôle of armed ally to any Communist party engaged, Samson-like, in shaking the foundations of their particular capitalist state. This was the overt reasoning of those Bolsheviks who supported the Polish campaign of 1920.[1]

The picture of Nazi Germany as the embodiment of the last stages of capitalism left something to be desired. The war economy of the Third Reich did indeed put supreme and monopolistic power into the hands of a relatively small body of men, but not in quite the way that Marx had foreseen. Not only did the workers resign their powers of association with alacrity in 1933, but they were content to accept the wartime 'apogee of capitalism' in the cause of the most imperialistic of wars. The idealized Nazi *Betriebsgemeinschaft*[2] replaced the Trades Unions in spirit and in practice. Finally, Soviet Russia was neither the first nor the natural enemy of Nazi Germany; for two years capitalist Britain fought capitalist Germany with whom Socialist Russia had a

[1] See Stalin, *Problems of Leninism* (11th edition, Moscow, 1945), where it is however claimed that such a war could only arise after the inevitable attack of the capitalist states on the Soviet Union. Also the first use of force by the decaying monopoly-capitalists against the progressive forces within a state is one of the main postulates of genuine Marxism, as expounded for instance by Rosa Luxemburg.

[2] See Chapter I for the use of these organizations as a means of circumventing he class war.

non-aggression pact. Even the man Kautsky called 'that vile opportunist Bernstein' might have baulked at such co-operation.

But in spite of these contradictions the Communists could with some justice claim that the collapse of Nazi Germany was inevitable as a terrible example of the misuse of economic power in the hands of the very few, and that 'Fascist Imperialism', as the Nazis themselves were fond of pointing out, was a natural and logical development of capitalist society one stage further. The other highly capitalist economies of the world, U.S.A. and Great Britain, had undoubtedly supported Germany economically almost up to the outbreak of war.[1] Now Germany was clearly ripe for a new philosophy to replace National Socialism. Instead of having to compete with established rival philosophies for living space, the Communists had the advantage of being the first political rush of air into a vacuum. Above all, Germany was a far better economic illustration of a state ready for Socialism than Russia had ever been.

As we have seen, the Communists took full advantage of their position. They were the first to reorganize local action committees in the Soviet zone, in order to keep essential services going. By the time the Russians started to reorganize a system of administration they already found the Communists and Socialists installed in positions of responsibility. From the very beginning, however, two main problems had to be decided by the Russians in Germany.

On what grounds should the measures long prepared in Moscow be put into effect? With the exception of the land reform, they were all in accordance with the basic principles of Marxist theory. The programme included nationalization of the means of production, except land, of commercial undertakings of any size, of banks, transport, insurance, and medical services. It called for State control of education, law, labour, and the arts, a centralized police force, a predominant Communist party, a centralized civil administration, and the ruthless destruction of potential as well as real opponents. In Russia these measures had been carried out early under Communist rule. The process had been complete, and, in spite of backward conditions, rapid. Under the favourable conditions in Germany the process could have been even more rapid. But haste and thoroughness cut out explanations, proposals, and compromises, the normal apparatus of democracy. The only

[1] The fact that this support is now regarded by the majority in these countries as a mistake will not placate the Communists, whose dialectic awareness, it is claimed, makes mistakes of such magnitude impossible in Russia, and their occurrence in other countries a hypocritical disguise of machiavellian intentions.

moral support for complete and rapid action in Germany along the lines of early Soviet Russia was the same now as then, the conviction of absolute right, based on the theories of Marx. The coffin of capitalist Germany could only be fastened rapidly with the naked tools of Communism.

There could be no question of Russian inability to carry out this task. Their power in the Soviet zone was undisputed and complete. Fear of disrupting the Allied Control Council with unilateral measures was at best only a partial deterrent. To make four-power government in Germany a reality would have meant that only important measures which had previously been agreed by the four powers could be brought into effect in any zone. This proviso was very soon broken; Russian reparations, the most important reason for their presence in Germany, destroyed quadripartite unanimity as soon as the first reparations train left the Eastern zone for the Soviet Union. Within six months measures had been taken in all four zones which were plainly unilateral. It is improbable that Russian respect for the importance of four-power government was a strong reason for not adopting a wholehearted Communist policy in the East.

In the event, most of the measures, particularly before summer 1947, were put through with an almost comic effort to avoid any breath of suspicion that they might be promoted by the exigencies of Communist theory. The land reform, it was claimed, was destined chiefly to break the power of the Junkers, and secondly to provide land, and with it a means of existence, for the two million or so German refugees from other countries. Not even the most radical member of the KPD was allowed to see in the reform the beginnings of a Communist system. The utilitarian purpose of the measure was enhanced by the public announcement that, while co-operatives would be encouraged, the property of the new farmers was sacred and that collectivization was not intended. One KPD functionary who stated that 'collectivization would follow automatically' was sharply and openly rebuked. The socialization of factories was painstakingly carried through piecemeal. The identification of the owners as Nazis or militarists was formally carried out even if the relevant evidence available was negligible. As prominent members of the SED did not fail to point out to visiting journalists: 'the basic factor for determining the economic development of the Soviet zone was the conviction and penalties falling on the war criminals and war profiteers . . . whose undertakings were taken over as the result of a plebiscite of June

1946 [in Saxony] with a majority of nearly 80 per cent.'[1] This would mean that all nationalized industries were seized from Nazis or war criminals and only nationalized after a period of trusteeship, during which their eventual disposal was an open question. In fact no 'nationalization' took place at all, but certain factories had to be taken out of the hands of Nazis and war criminals, and after due consideration it was felt that they would be best preserved in the hands of the State!

The advantages of disguising Communist intentions as long as there was no Communist supremacy have been mentioned. Their moderation enabled the Russians to obtain the services of men who might never have agreed to serve under a purely Communist régime; it provided a measure of popular support for the SED in the early days; and it helped to convince a considerable number of people both inside and outside Germany of the good intentions of the Russians. On the other hand it ran counter to the most sacred principles of Communism and to the established practice of the Soviet government during its twenty-eight years of existence. The question of co-operation with bourgeois parties in office before the conquest of supreme power had constituted an insurmountable obstacle to the unity of the Second International as early as 1903; the majority, the *bolsheviki*, taking the view that even in the circumstances of the time such co-operation in forming a government was inexcusable, that historically the time for it had passed. Yet after 1945 a bloc policy of co-operation with bourgeois parties was an accepted principle of government in the Soviet zone, indeed throughout Eastern Europe.

We see a Soviet occupation, run by Russian Communists, instituting measures which seem Communist in tendency, but which these same Russians, and the Germans under them, were at great pains to prove to have been inspired only by the immediate needs of the situation. Marx and Engels envisaged, as part of the inevitable development of the Socialist situation, that the bourgeoisie in its last stages might take action which would unconsciously accelerate their own downfall. But the founders of historical materialism in its modern sense would have been astounded to find a Communist government *in plena potestate* adopting the reactionary expedient of explaining its actions in terms of bourgeois necessity. The dialectic, after years of struggle against its blind opponents, was discarded at the moment of vindication in favour of the tattered shreds of empirical legisla-

[1] Schaffer, *op. cit.*, p. 47.

tion! What explanation can be given for this fundamental contradiction between theory and practice?

The possibility of Russia's abandoning her fundamental aims of introducing a Communist government in Germany must be ruled out. Political and economic developments since 1946 have made this all too clear. The use of empirical-looking legislation and the disclaimer of Communist intentions was a means rather than an end; strategy, not principle. Were the means used by the Russians more effective in gaining the ultimate ends of a Communist system than would have been an open avowal of Communist intentions from the first day of occupation? If they were, we have a possible explanation for Soviet actions.

The basis conditions for Communism were, as we have seen, highly favourable in May 1945. The very fact that Russia had been victorious gave Russian actions a certain *de facto* justification. Popular resistance in 1945 to even a radical Communist programme in Eastern Germany would have been impossible. The Western Allies were favourably disposed to Russia, and even if the governments of Britain and the United States had protested against a vigorous Communist policy in Germany from the start, public opinion in these countries would have taken a considerable time to turn against Russia. It was not wholly anti-Russian even in 1950. If fundamental discord over Germany was inevitable, the advantage to be gained by rushing things in 1945 was greater than that of attempting to make the change to an openly Communist policy two years later, by which time world events would in any case have stiffened the attitude of the Western Allies. Communist policy in Eastern Germany would have had to be much the same as that adopted by the Communist governments in Rumania, Bulgaria, and Hungary, a policy of taking the public by surprise and crushing opposition before it could be organized effectively. Such a policy in Germany would probably have achieved considerable success. Clearly this cannot be the explanation of the course of Soviet action.

In many recent discussions of Russian post-war policy the conflict between Communist theory and Russian interests has been stressed to underline contradictory and puzzling Soviet actions.[1] In Germany this conflict is particularly marked. Once its underlying causes are understood it is possible to explain the contradiction between theory and practice whose existence we have tried to establish.

[1] For instance, in *The Economist*, 9 October 1948: 'One Year of Cominform'. That organization exists chiefly to resolve and by-pass this potential conflict.

Communist theory takes it for granted that the final dialectic will result in an improvement of conditions 'in the operation of the means of production, after the breakdown of bourgeois society' as Marx himself put it. If a nation undergoing the last social struggle is fortunate enough to have the presence of a Socialist power at hand, it would be the rôle of the latter to smooth the path for its neighbour and to help to make the period of transition as easy and rapid as possible. Such certainly was the view of Lenin, Radek and all those Russians who supported the Rapallo policy, as well as of Lauffenberg, the 'inventor' of National Bolshevism, in 1920; no new Communist state could be held responsible for the misdeeds of its bourgeois predecessor. The same principle had been tentatively expressed by the Soviet government during the last war. Strict adherence to theory demanded that Communism in Germany should be assisted into power by the Russians, and that the war guilt slate would then be wiped clean, reparations waived, punishment confined to bourgeois inperialists, and both moral and physical assistance given to the Germans. Inside the Soviet Union the hatred of Germany inevitably fostered by the invasion and the resultant atrocities would have to be combated by means of an acrobatic somersault of propaganda.

But this was not and could not be the case. It is doubtful whether even the Soviet propaganda machine could carry such a campaign in the teeth of a population whose national fervour had been roused. It is easy to exaggerate national feelings, and difficult to estimate their influence, but a perusal of *Pravda* or *Izvestia* during the war shows that the Soviet government at any rate was consciously playing on the patriotism of its citizens, and such feelings, once aroused, are difficult to quench at will. Reparations were, as we have seen, one of the three main reasons why the Soviet government considered the occupation of Germany to be essential. Enormous damage had to be made good, and both necessity and prestige demanded the exploitation of Germany for the benefit of Russia. The Yalta agreement shows that the demand for reparations then already formed one of the chief bases of Russian policy. As soon as Germany was occupied the detailed reparations programme was put into operation with speed and efficiency, directly supervised from Moscow.

Thus the rôle of 'benevolent Socialist neighbour' went unperformed. While the Germans were inevitably prepared to see a considerable part of their industrial potential, their labour, and even their current production, go to Russia as reparations, they resented the fact that what had seemed and had been made to seem a genuine revival in the East was ultimately designed only to further reparations in different guises. The German administration laboured under difficult conditions to fulfil the SMA plans for rehabilitation, only to find their work exploited and diverted by another, superior, Soviet agency. There was a chronic uncertainty in Soviet reparation demands which interfered with all planning. Moreover, the reparations scheme was arbitrary in the extreme; the SMA and control administration often received notice of dismantlings only when the German 'Pilgrimage of Grace' arrived to bemoan the disappearance of a factory. The great Russian object was to keep the Germans ignorant of the state of reparations and dismantlings, and the Germans resented it.

Even more opposed to a friendly relationship between post-war Germany and Russia were the Soviet-owned Trusts within the German economy; the SAG. While the principle of reparation was admitted, if reluctantly, by nearly every German, even though the degree was considered excessive, this Russian interference in German domestic property-holding could only be the action of a victorious power over an enemy to be exploited at will. The purchase of real estate, the officially operated black market in scarce goods, and the use of German reparations for Russian re-export, all facts of which the Germans were mistily aware, increased the tension.[1] It is notable that even the most ardent Communist, who was prepared to explain every action of the Russians in terms of genuine Soviet interest in the rebuilding of a progressive Germany, found it impossible to digest the question of reparations altogether. The explanation that Russia had after all been victorious, and that the damage done by Germany gave the Russians moral *carte blanche* to take what they liked (which became the official SED thesis when the question could no longer be ignored in public) was utterly irreconcilable with the usual picture presented by the SED of the benevolence of the Soviet Union towards Germany. The same was true of Soviet support for the permanence of Germany's Eastern frontier.

The Russians were fully aware that their reparation policy, which they intended to carry out at all costs, involved permanent disagreement with the Western Allies, and would tend to nullify all their other actions in Germany capable of presentation in a favourable light. It is partly for this reason that the question of reparations was kept so completely out of German hands, and

[1] See above, Chapter VII.

entirely separate from their general administrative policy in Germany. The separation existed even in the philosophical sphere. An openly Communist policy in Eastern Germany would have been in such glaring contrast to the facts of reparation payments, and would have so discredited Communist policy, that it was considered best, since a choice between the two had to be made, to drop the pursuit of Communism rather than the pursuit of reparations. In the initial period of May 1945 to May 1946 it was hoped that the Germans would come to accept a picture of Russia taking her reparations on the one hand, and on the other attempting to ameliorate the lot of the population by a series of progressive measures which were not intended to culminate in a purely Communist régime. A measure of political liberty was offered in return for economic exploitation. But the relative prosperity of the Soviet zone at this time, and the efforts of the political parties to obtain popular support, were strengthening parties which, once they had obtained sufficient popular strength, were likely to attack Russian reparation policy, in much the same way as the political parties in the West already attacked the far smaller demands of the Western Allies. This was an intrusion on the policy in which the Soviet Union was above all interested in Eastern Germany, and it had to be prevented at all costs, even if the Communist government, now to be instituted by force, suffered the odium of being a Russian tool undemocratically elected and supported only by force.

The new system of government after April 1946 was above all intended to ensure the safety of the Occupation while unhampered reparations continued to flow eastward. There was no real government, but only an administration. A Germany copy of the Supreme Soviet was dispensed with, but the Politburo and the executive departments of the U.S.S.R. were faithfully reproduced. Wherever possible, the shreds of the anti-Nazi system were retained, but they were never allowed to interfered in any way with the unhampered activities of the Russian reparation agencies and the Russian-owned industrial combines and trading companies. This was the middle period, characterized by maximum reparations and a system of administration designed to facilitate them.

By the summer of 1947 it was clear that Communism in Germany must be based on Russian power and could never have the strength of popular support sufficient to enable it to stand on its own democratic feet. Spasmodic attempts were still made by the political department of the SMA and by the SED to obtain popular support for specific measures, and to recruit members for the SED, but no great success was expected from these half-hearted gestures, and little was achieved. By the end of 1947 the continued flow of reparations to the east as well as the political power of the SED were seen by the Germans to be entirely dependent on the armed presence of the Russians. Both would disappear at the moment when the Russians left. The institution of Communism on a firm basis had become an impossibility. Even in the most extreme Leninist interpretation of Communism, with the 'cadre-party' reduced to an absolute minimum in relation to the size of the population, it is still necessary that this party should, whether by popular support or by its own hold on government, be enabled to stand on its own feet. This the SED was never, and seems unlikely ever, to be able to do. The very fact that Communism was not introduced in its entirety in the early days of the Occupation means that a Communist party backed by Russian bayonets is even now running a predominantly bourgeois society. On the other hand it was impossible to institute Communism completely as long as large parts of the prerogative of the dictatorship of the German proletariat continued to be reserved and used by the Russians themselves for their own immediate purposes. The Communist apparatus was there, but it was built on sand, and supported by foreign props. Its existence did not serve German political development, but Russian economic expansion.

The difference between Eastern Germany and the Communist states of Eastern Europe is clear. In the latter countries Soviet demands for goods and services, though often irksome, were never the main object of Russian presence or control. In all these countries the strength of the local Communist governments arose out of their control of an armed movement fighting the Germans during the war. The step from there to control of the State was easy in the confused situation following the expulsion of the Germans. In Germany, however, reparations formed the basis of Russian occupation and all other measures were subordinate; the German Communists were treated as members of a defeated nation and their power came not from their own efforts but by command of the occupying power. Had the Russians been willing, the power of the German Communists in Germany could have been as great as that of their comrades in the Eastern countries, but as long as reparations were the chief object of Russian policy the Communists in Eastern Germany were merely a means for their easy extraction.

In 1948 the initiative passed to Western Germany. The absence of a dynamic policy in the East, the absorption in economic destruction instead of political fortification, enabled the Western powers, once they had cut themselves loose from the inhibitions of an out-of-date Potsdam Agreement, to embark on a constructive policy undisturbed by the resultant breakdown of the last political ties binding East and West Germany. The risks involved in this forward movement were greatly reduced by the fact that there was no constructive policy in the Soviet zone. Instead of being able to rely on the political momentum of Communism in Germany to counteract the Western currency reform and the concomitant reduction of Allied control, the Russians were forced to intervene directly, and mount a military blockade of Berlin. Even this failed dismally to arrest the Western movement towards independence from restraint by the Russians, and in 1950 the Russians had to resort to an *ultima ratio*, a direct threat of military action against a resuscitated Western Germany. Thus it became clear that the reparations policy had involved the sacrifice of the most elementary political weapon of Communism, its initiative of political action. Instead of being able to call its own tune, the SED now found itself in the rôle normally assigned to its opponents; it had to adapt itself to a series of *faits accomplis* and to show cause why it had failed to achieve similar success in the East.

This situation was peculiar to Germany. The people's democracies of the East had been sufficiently sealed off by this time to enable the ruling Communist party to operate in a politically uncompetitive atmosphere. Moreover, Soviet exploitation had not been on a sufficient scale to attract the attention of the entire population. Communism in these countries was in power and could behave with the insouciance of unchallengeable supremacy. In Germany the Communist party, though technically in almost complete control, had the uphill task of defending Soviet measures against a hostile population encouraged by the recovery of more than half their fellow countrymen. If the Russians had been prepared to extract their reparations and then abandon, for all constructive political purposes, the shell of Eastern Germany, this situation would not have mattered greatly. It was frequently believed in the West at this time that Russian plans were along these lines, and that an impoverished Eastern Germany would be left as an added burden for the struggling economy of Western Germany. But it was apparently decided otherwise. Possibly because the Russians were unwilling to abandon any territory once under their control; perhaps, encouraged by their successes since the war and the predictions of economic collapse in the West, they prepared for an experiment in a unique situation. Reparations were to be reduced to a level compatible with a measure of economic recovery in Eastern Germany. With the exception of the export of special consumer-goods on reparations account, the reparations potential of the zone had been reduced to a stark alternative of considerable reduction in removals or speedy economic collapse. An utterly bankrupt Eastern Germany could do nothing to further Russian plans of consolidation in Eastern Europe or for a political and economic attack against the West. If the economy of Eastern Europe could, by a series of long-term plans, be made to recover sufficiently, the division of Germany could still be used to serve Russian ends. From behind the East-West frontier of Germany, the initiative might be wrested from the West and the SED might become the means of bringing about the unification of Germany under Russian control.

Soviet diplomacy had always been, and was still, prepared to help with all the means at its disposal. As long as reparations hampered the Soviet representative at the Council of Foreign Ministers, his tactics were, in spite of all efforts, unlikely to succeed.[1] But now that the demand for a United Germany could be put at the forefront of the German political scene, the Soviet diplomats and the Communist puppets of Eastern Germany were, for the first time since the war, talking the same language for the same ends. The demand for a share in the control of the Ruhr, based on the return to Potsdam, and the East German threat to the independence of the Bonn Republic, became part and parcel of the same objective, the extension of Soviet control to Western Germany—even though the Russians might be thinking of extending their reparations policy to Western Germany as well as the blessings of Communist domination.

The task of running the Unity campaign produced an unprecedented rôle for a Communist party in power, that of hiding behind a bourgeois-nationalist façade. In undisputed control of Eastern Germany, the SED had on the one hand to control a partly Communist-type economy, on the other to adopt the opportunist tactics of the Communist parties in bourgeois countries. This led to all sorts of crass ideological paradoxes. In Western Germany workers were

[1] Bedell Smith, *Moscow Mission 1946–1949* (London, 1950), p. 208, quotes one outstanding example: During the Moscow Conference, Molotov made it clear that he would back the French proposal for economic integration of the Saar into France only on condition that Bidault backed the Russian demand for a share in the control of the Ruhr.

encouraged to strike against dismantling, and the SED press in Berlin carried such slogans as: 'Workers strike in protest against British monopolistic dismantling.' In the East the Party press announced that 'deliberate failure to fulfil production norms can only be treated as economic sabotage'. On the question of re-armament, *Neues Deutschland* said in a single issue that 'German rearmament can only lead to the resurgence of Fascist aggressiveness under the direction of American monopoly capitalism', and on another page that 'the well-equipped People's Police is a solid bulwark against reaction . . . seeking to interfere with the legitimate demands of all Germans for a single strong and united Fatherland'. The SED leadership journal, in defining the party's attitude to reparations, prescribed that 'Germany must, for a long time, pay towards the restitution of the enormous damage wantonly inflicted on the U.S.S.R.' The official newspapers, on the other hand, stated that the export efforts of Western Germany had shown British business that only the continued dismantling of German industry could prevent the replacement of British goods by goods made in Germany. The best example of all is probably the mildness, almost conciliatory benevolence, with which the East German government dealt with the accusations of intolerance and repression which both Catholic and Protestant bishops suddenly unleashed in May 1950. Grotewohl promised freedom to the church as guaranteed under the constitution, did not answer with menaces—as did his colleagues in Czechoslovakia and Hungary—indeed did not answer the more violent protests at all, and apparently took no measures of personal reprisal against the clergy. No doubt his restraint was due to care not to offend his imagined bourgeois sympathizers, like Noack, in the West. Yet the SED press was full of orthodox fulminations against political priests, (an attitude as acceptable to the Communists of Eastern Europe as to the bourgeois 'priest-eaters' of the Third Republic.[1]) Thus, instead of being able to profit from its supremacy in Eastern Germany by coming out openly as a Communist party, the SED had to run two simultaneous and contradictory lines of policy and perform unheard-of masterpieces of illogicality.

At first sight the SED unity campaign resembles the so-called doctrine of National Bolshevism, linked with the name of Radek, the one-time envoy of the Comintern in Germany.[2] He had been

[1] For the attitude of the church, see Pastoral Letter of Bishop Dibelius, 23 April 1950, and letter of Cardinal Preysing in *Der Tag*, 30 April 1950 (Berlin).

[2] See above, p. 75. Also Ruth Fischer, *op. cit.*, Part II, p. 189–291; Max Beloff, *The Foreign Policy of Soviet Russia*, Vol. I (London, 1947), p. 58.

acutely conscious of the need for the Communist party to rally the German proletariat behind it, and believed that this could be achieved by an appeal to nationalist feelings.[1] In both cases it was necessary to wrest a valuable means of popular appeal from the bourgeois parties, and in both cases the basis of the appeal was the same. But in one case the Communist party was following the Leninist tradition of flexibility in order to gain power by obtaining overwhelming working-class support, while in the present case a Communist party in power, having carried out a large part of the 'orthodox' Communist programme, was appealing to the bourgeois classes of Germany. Between 1921 and 1933 the Communists, and particularly the German Communists, envisaged a mass proletarian movement. In 1950 the SED relied on a police army whose leadership was composed mostly of non-proletarians co-operating with nationalistic elements in the West to achieve its aims. Until the expected economic crisis in the West produced the necessary unemployment, an appeal to the workers there had been shown to be in vain, partly because the Communists were in a minority among them, but chiefly because the iron curtain in Germany was sufficiently transparent for all to see precisely what they could expect from the Russians. In fact the SED unity campaign went to unprecedented lengths in discarding the most elementary tenets of Communism.

The philosophy of Communism, however, remained unchanged in Eastern Germany, as elsewhere. The teachings of the Marxist authorities were not, and could not be, adjusted to the existing situation. What happened was that the last restraints imposed by theory on practice disappeared. In this respect the SED was in advance of other Communist parties. Irrespective of their tactics before taking over the government completely, the Communists of Eastern Europe, once in power, followed a pattern of policy which held good in every case except one, where differences arose over subordination to Russia. In Eastern Germany tactical adjustments to policy continued long after the advent of the party to power, and exceeded the limits imposed by class division. The cause may be found in the artificial division of Germany, which the Communists helped to complete in order to further the national interests of Russia, and in the absence of responsibility under Russian occupation, of which the SED unconsciously availed itself. Without the need to build up its own strength for its own permanent protection, the Party could devote itself to the task

[1] *ibid.*, p. 67.

of furthering Russian aims throughout Germany. It is perhaps fitting that the depth of political irresponsibility and dishonesty should again have been reached in Germany.

Ultimately the responsibility lay with the Russians. If a country is occupied by us, they seemed to argue, an independent local Communist party has no useful functions to fulfil, for its normal function, that of ruling, is taken over by ourselves. While we continue to rule, it must attempt to make everything we do palatable to the population, and, since we are disciples of Marx, Lenin, and Stalin, they must be disciples too. Therefore even this task can only be carried out by a Communist-dominated party. If in time the Party succeeds in establishing itself firmly in the political and administrative power we allow to it, it will gradually be permitted to take over an increasing share in the government of the occupied area. It will not be allowed, however, to sit back and consolidate this power, for we control only part of the country, and once the first flow of reparations has been taken, we may concentrate on taking control of the rest of the country. This has become a more difficult and urgent task as the portion of the country outside our control has cut itself loose from the restrictive agreement previously negotiated with the Western powers, and since its recovery is undermining the safety of our strategic frontier. Moreover, the attempt to separate the two parts of the country has failed. Therefore it is now the task of our local Communists to devote themselves to the destruction of the government created on the other side of the frontier by every means at their disposal, and, since Germans are not Koreans, this may involve an appeal to bourgeois nationalist sentiment. In return, if the object is achieved, we will take our share in economic value, and the SED will obtain the measure of independent control over the whole of Germany which Communist governments have in Eastern Europe, subject to the demands of Soviet policy.

An examination of Russian policy in Eastern Germany cannot therefore be made at all in terms of Marxist, Leninist, or Stalinist theory. For those who follow its beliefs and translate its theories into actions, Marxism is the prime reason for their political existence. The moment Communist theory is subordinated to other interests it ceases by its very nature to be Communist. We are forced to come to the conclusion that the government in Eastern Germany was not a Communist government at all, but a makeshift arrangement designed to fulfil certain immediate Russian needs, and therefore liable to be changed as the demands made on it changed. Those who measure Eastern Germany by Marxist standards apply a yard measure to a metric scale, whether they are observers outside Germany or Soviet zone Communists. If the latter believed in their own Marxist orthodoxy, they were the biggest dupes of Russian policy.

Many of the institutions and measures in the Soviet zone undoubtedly originated in Communist theory, and while the method of government bore strong traces of Communist technique, these things were incidental and of secondary importance. They were mostly due to the routine of Soviet methods which imposed a pattern of their own on all actions and institutions under Russian control. The resemblances of Eastern Germany to a state methodically organized on deliberate Communist lines in order to achieve, as quickly as possible, a Communist society, was purely accidental. The completion of such a state and society, including nationalization of the land, local government by Soviets, and sensational spy trials of those with contacts in the West, would have made the success of the political unity campaign impossible.

2

CONCLUSION

The fascination of studying the Soviet zone is in the interplay of Russia and Germany. The Russians, apart from their deliberate policy, did and ordered many things in their zone out of sheer force of habit, ranging from the ridiculous instance of the confiscation of all law books bearing the signature of the Nazi Ministers of the Interior and of Justice, on the ground that no criminal's name may appear in public,[1] to the prevailing secrecy of the most routine economic facts. Thus, studying the Soviet zone inevitably helps us to understand the Soviet Union. On the other hand these five years were an integral part of German history. At the worst, five years of Soviet Communist domination could not eradicate the essentially German way of life and the national character of many institutions. Communism is no enemy of many local traditions, provided these are not of a religious nature, and cannot be labelled 'reactionary'. Moreover, as we have seen, the process of change went less far in Germany, and was less severely enforced, than in other Communist countries. The obstinate

[1] Löwenthal, *op. cit.*, p. 133; also for what happened when the cashier of the National Bank of the U.S.S.R., whose signature was on all the notes, was tried and hanged for sabotage in 1937.

middle-class nature of German society survived surprisingly well. Underneath an economic and political crust of Communist domination, Eastern Germany was in 1950 still a predominantly bourgeois country. There should be no mistake about that.

More than anything else, this made it impossible to break the contact between East and West Germany. And therefore it was possible to write a reasonably accurate study of part of the world behind the official iron curtain in spite of all efforts to prevent the facts leaking out. Even a regular perusal of the non-Communist press in Berlin and Western Germany gave a picture of life as it was in the Soviet zone, albeit with gaps and occasional unfounded rumours. I do not believe the same is possible for other Eastern European countries, certainly not for the Soviet Union itself.

It would be idle to speculate on the outcome of the present struggle in Germany. Short of the exigencies of military warfare, however, only a series of major political blunders on the part of the West German government and the Western powers can bring about Communist control in Western Germany. The initiative, the balance of power, and the feelings of the population were by 1948 against the Russians and their German allies. But we may profitably examine the ultimate effect on Germany of the five years under review. Far-reaching changes in the social structure of the Eastern zone took place. The economic power of the bourgeoisie and the landed aristocracy were replaced by an all-powerful state, the direction of which was out of the hands of the so-called electorate. But the professional classes, many officials, the majority of small traders, and almost all technicians, scientists, and men of learning, were in 1950 still much as they had been in 1945. Their way of life, in spite of great privations, was essentially similar. The cafés and bars of Eastern Germany were not filled exclusively, as they were in Czechoslovakia, by workers and political functionaries. Above all, their influence on the SED itself was not negligible. Their sons swelled the ranks of the People's Police. They were not vociferous, but they were there. Similarly, the peasants were conservative. They may not have wanted the return of the former owners (though in some cases they did), but they hated and feared the idea of collective farming. Like all farmers, they were *kulaks* at heart. And there was a section of the SED which supported the agricultural experts against the control of the quota commissions from the cities.[1]

[1] *Two Year Plan*. Speech of Walter Biering, p. 100.

Who were the genuine supporters of the régime? First, the Communists and ex-Social Democrats who had become committed to the policy of the SED, and thus to the policy of the Russians. Secondly, the opportunists who made a career in the Eastern zone by subscribing to the politics of those in power. Finally, those who received real personal advantages, the ex-workers now promoted to managerial posts in the nationalized industries, refugees from Eastern Europe who received land and property for their support, a small number of landless agricultural labourers who became small farmers and liked it. But the most important class is missing from this list. As both Trotsky and Stalin's latest biographers have shown us, the chief political props of the Soviet régime in Russia during the thirties, and Stalin's particular supporters, were the new cadres of managers and officials. Their power was cumulative, for each appointment gave someone a new stake in the régime, and the means to drive it in. Yet there was no Communist cadre of officials in Germany except at the top, though almost all officials were members of the SED. Such cadres can only be forged from political struggles within or without the Party and the State. The puppet functions of the SED avoided any test of its internal and external strength, and its members were able to hide behind verbal professions of adherence. They were, therefore, not finally committed and could prefer, should circumstances change, to retain their freedom and their jobs rather than their political allegiance. Like the Nazis, the SED was on the other hand desperately anxious to commit as many people as possible to its policy by assuming responsibility for almost all Russian orders and by continuing the pretence of the democratic bloc. Thus, while Party headquarters ordered, explained, and took action over its own signature, German officials cautiously quoted superior orders before doing anything of importance.

There was something curiously ephemeral about the structure of society in Eastern Germany. The only other Eastern European country where one was struck by a similar unreality was Hungary, but there the national way of life contrasted sharply with Marxist exigencies. Hence the attempt of the country's Communist rulers to force people to take life more seriously by a series of frightening political trials and condemnations, which seemed quite different from the barren brutality of Bulgaria and Rumania. Though there was nothing *légère* about the attitude of the Germans, the result was similar, a partial refusal to accept the ultimate consequences of Communism. But the Germans set about their resistance in a stolid rather than in an offhand way. Every time a business meeting took place between East and West Germans, there was an automatic return to a pre-Communist era. It was as though there were contact between *émigrés* and those who remained behind; both parties spoke the same language and often thought the same way (unless one was a convinced Communist) even if the discussion was purely factual.

No clearer proof of Russian awareness of these distinctive features in their zone of Germany can be given than the events of January and February 1951. The struggle for German unity on Soviet terms, with the secondary objective of disrupting Western German's independent progress, had clearly failed. Hence the Russians resorted to the penultimate means of achieving policy—the direct threat of war, uttered by the Soviet Foreign Ministry and by Otto Grotewohl on their behalf. At the same time the restraints imposed by the unity campaign on Communist policy in Eastern Germany began to be lifted; support, even of a passive nature, of Western politicians became, under the label 'warmongering', punishable by law with life imprisonment or death. Finally the SED began to be reorganized as a Stalinist cadre party, and the first large party purge was reported in February 1951 to be scheduled for the Spring of that year. Thus with the threat of war all need of subterfuge disappeared, and Communism could come increasingly into its own. How far this development would go remained to be seen.

Unless the *status quo* could last for at least another generation, however, Eastern Germany would shed its Communist superstructure without much difficulty once the direct military control of the Russians was removed to a safe distance. Since Communism had been brought in by Russian bayonets, and served exclusively Russian purposes, it was entirely dependent on their continued presence, until sufficient German bayonets could be found to take their place.

INDEX